Public Finance and Public Employment

Finances Publiques et Emploi Public

PUBLIC FINANCE AND PUBLIC EMPLOYMENT

FINANCES PUBLIQUES ET EMPLOI PUBLIC

Proceedings of the 36th Congress
of the International Institute of Public Finance
Jerusalem, 1980

Edited by Robert H. Haveman

Wayne State University Press, Detroit, 1982

Library of Congress Cataloging in Publication Data
Main entry under title:

Public finance and public employment-Finances
  publiques et emploi public.

  English and French.
  1. Finance, Public—Congresses. 2. Public
service employment—Congresses. I. Haveman,
Robert H. II. International Institute of Public
Finance. III. Title: Finances publiques et emploi
public.
HJ236.P8   331.12'042   82-1844
ISBN 0-8143-1712-X   AACR2

Produced in the United States of America.

Officers of the board of management 1981
Membres du comité de direction 1981

Président/President
> Horst Claus Recktentwald, République Fédérale d'Allemagne/Federal Republic of Germany

Futur Président/President elect
> Jean-Claude Dischamps, France

Vice-Présidents/Vice-Presidents
> André van Buggenhout, Belgique/Belgium
> Jean-Claude Dischamps, France
> Francesco Forte, Italie/Italy
> Victor Halberstadt, Pays-Bas/Netherlands
> Karl W. Roskamp, Etats-Unis/USA
> Nikolai Sichev, URSS/USSR

Vice-Présidents Exécutifs/Executive Vice-Presidents
> André van Buggenhout, Belgique/Belgium
> Victor Halberstadt, Pays-Bas/Netherlands
> Karl W. Roskamp, Etats-Unis/USA

Membres du Comité/Board Members
> Narciso Amorós Rica, Espagne/Spain
> Richard Bird, Canada
> Kenan Bulutoglu, Turquie/Turkey
> Natalia Gajl, Pologne/Poland
> Elias Gannagé, Liban/Lebanon
> Motokazu Kimura, Japon/Japan
> Erhart Knauthe, RDA/GDR
> André Middelhoek, Pays-Bas/Netherlands
> Helga Pollak, République Fédérale d'Allemagne/Federal Republic of Germany
> Alan Prest, Royaume-Uni/United Kingdom
> Franco Reviglio, Italie/Italy
> Miklós Riesz, Hongrie/Hungary
> Elisabeth Vessilier, France

Censeurs/Auditors
> Maurice Heimann, Suisse/Switzerland
> Marcel Zimmer, Belgique/Belgium

Secrétaire Administrative/Executive Secretary
> Mrs. Birgit Schneider, République Fédérale d'Allemagne/Federal Republic of Germany

International Institute of Public Finance

A Brief Survey of Historical and Current Matters

The International Institute of Public Finance was founded in Paris in 1937. It held two conferences before the Second World War, and members have since met at least once a year from 1947 until the present. The Institute now has over 800 members from some 50 countries, and annual conferences are normally attended also by some non-members with a special interest in the particular topic.

The aims of the Institute are scientific. Its objectives include in particular: the study of Public Finance and Public Economics, the research and publications in both of these areas, the establishment of scientific contacts and exchange of knowledge and experience between persons of all nationalities. The Institute is exclusively and directly concerned with the furthering of public interest. The activities of the Institute have been recognized on an international level by the Economic and Social Council of the United Nations, which conferred upon it the Statut Consultatif B.

The Institute provides a forum for those concerned with problems of public economics, broadly defined. It has over the years aspired to sustain high academic standards. In the selection of topics and their investigation, it has directed itself towards matters of practical importance and towards issues of implementation, as well as of principle. The membership embraces both academic economists whose prime interests are in teaching and research, and public officials who face the problems "on the ground": the unifying characteristic is acceptance of a proper standard of intellectual rigor.

Membership is essentially individual though corporate subscriptions are welcome. The Institute is proud of the involvement in its activities of members from countries of all kinds of political persuasion and all levels of economic development.

The Institute is governed by a Board of Management whose decisions require approval by the general assembly of members, with a President and Vice-Presidents elected for a period of three years. The Institute is administered by an Executive Committee (present membership, Professor Jean-Claude Dischamps, President, Paris; Professor André van Buggenhout, Brussels; Professor Victor Halberstadt, Leyden; Professor Karl W. Roskamp, Detroit).

All questions concerning the Institute should be directed to:

Mrs. B. Schneider, Executive Secretary
International Institute of Public Finance
Université de la Sarre
D-6600 Saarbrücken 11
WEST GERMANY

Institut International de Finances Publiques

Un aperçu de son passé et de ses activités actuelles.

L'Institut International de Finances Publiques fut fondé à PARIS, en 1937. Il tint deux congrès avant la dernière guerre mondiale. En 1947, il put réunir à nouveau ses membres et, depuis, ceux-ci se sont rencontrés au moins une fois par an aux quatre coins du globe. L'Institut compte, aujourd'hui, 800 membres appartenant à 50 pays et ses congrès annuels sont régulièrement suivis non seulement par ceux-ci mais également par des non-membres intéressés par tel ou tel sujet.

Les buts poursuivis par l'Institut sont purement scientifiques. Ses objectifs incluent en particulier: l'étude des finances publiques et de l'économie publique, la mise en oeuvre de recherches et la publication de travaux dans ces domaines ainsi que l'établissement de contacts scientifiques et l'échange de connaissances et d'expériences entre des personnes de toute nationalité. L'Institut est guidé exclusivement et directement par le souci de l'intérêt général. L'Institut a vu sa mission reconnue, sur le plan international, par le Conseil économique et social des Nations-Unies, qui lui a conféré le statut consultatif B.

L'Institut offre un terrain de rencontre pour les spécialistes intéressés par les problèmes d'économie publique, au sens large du terme. Le maintien d'un niveau scientifique très élevé est pour ses responsables une préoccupation permanente. Dans le choix des sujets et la manière de les traiter, il s'attache aussi bien aux problèmes théoriques qu'aux problèmes pratiques et à leurs solutions. Ses membres sont des spécialistes universitaires et de la recherche scientifique, et des hauts fonctionnaires qui assument d'importantes responsabilités. Tous sont d'un niveau intellectuel notoirement reconnu.

L'Institut est composé essentiellement de membres individuels et il réunit dans ses activités des personnalités de pays relevant de tous les systèmes d'organisation politique et de tous les niveaux de développement économique.

La direction de l'Institut est assurée par un Comité de Direction conformément aux orientations définies par l'Assemblée Générale des membres. Son administration incombe à un Comité Exécutif actuellement composé de:

-Président, le Professeur Jean-Claude DISCHAMPS, PARIS.
-Vice-Présidents, les Professeurs André van BUGGENHOUT, BRUXELLES, Victor HALBERSTADT, LEYDEN, et Karl W. ROSKAMP, DETROIT.

Toute question relative à l'Institut est à adresser à:
Madame B. SCHNEIDER, Secrétaire Administrative,
Institut International de Finances Publiques
Université de la Sarre
D-6600 SAARBRÜCKEN 11
(R.F.A.)

Contributors

Professor Robert W. Bacon, *Fellow and Tutor in Economics, Lincoln College, University of Oxford, Oxford, OXL 3DR England, U.K.*

Professor Richard M. Bird, *Department of Political Economy, 100 St. George Street, University of Toronto, Toronto, Canada M5S 1A1*

Dr. John Bishop, *Institute for Research on Poverty, 3412 Social Science Building, University of Wisconsin, Madison, Wisconsin 53706 U.S.A.*

Professor José Cezar Castanhar, *Brazilian School of Public Administration of the Getúlio Vargas Foundation, Rio de Janeiro, Brazil*

Professor Sheldon Danziger, *Institute for Research on Poverty, 3412 Social Science Building, University of Wisconsin, Madison, Wisconsin 53706 U.S.A.*

Dr. Haim Factor, *Brookdale Institute, P.O.B. 13087, Jerusalem, J.D.C. Hill, Israel*

Professor David K. Foot, *Institute for Policy Analysis, University of Toronto, 150 St. George Street, Toronto, Canada M5S 1A1*

Professor Edward M. Gramlich, Director, *Institute of Public Policy Studies, 1516 Rackham Building, University of Michigan, Ann Arbor, Michigan 48109 U.S.A.*

Dr. Hans de Groot, *Social and Cultural Planning Office, J. C. van Markenlaan 3, Rijswijk (ZH), The Netherlands*

Dr. Jack Habib, *Brookdale Institute, P.O.B. 13087, Jerusalem, J.D.C. Hill, Israel*

Professor Victor Halberstadt, *Center for Research in Public Economics, Hugo de Grootstraat 32, University of Leiden, 2311 XK Leiden, The Netherlands*

Prof. Dr. Horst Hanusch, *Lehrstuhl für Volkswirtschaftslehre V, Universität Augsburg, Memminger Strasse 14, 8900 Augsburg, Federal Republic of Germany*

Professor Robert H. Haveman, *Department of Economics, 1180 Observatory Drive, University of Wisconsin, Madison, Wisconsin 53706 U.S.A.*

Mr. George Jakubson, *Department of Economics, 1180 Observatory Drive, University of Wisconsin, Madison, Wisconsin 53706 U.S.A.*

Professor George E. Johnson, *Department of Economics, University of Michigan, Ann Arbor, Michigan 48104 U.S.A.*

Professor P. R. G. Layard, *Centre for Labour Economics, London School of Economics and Political Science, Houghton Street, London WC2A 2AE, England, U.K.*

Professor Wassily Leontief, Director, *Institute for Economic Analysis, New York University, 269 Mercer Street, New York, New York 10003 U.S.A.*

Dr. John P. Martin, *Directorate for Social Affairs, Manpower and Education, Organisation for Economic Co-operation and Development (OECD), 2, rue André-Pascal, 75775 Paris Cedex 16, France*

Professor Richard A. Musgrave, *Department of Economics, Crown College, University of California-Santa Cruz, Santa Cruz, California 59064 U.S.A.*

Dr. Werner W. Pommerehne, *Institut für Empirische Wirtschaftsforschung der Universität Zürich, Forchstrasse 145, 8032 Zürich, Switzerland*

Professor Joseph F. Quinn, *Department of Economics, Boston College, Chestnut Hill, Massachusetts 02167 U.S.A.*

Mr. Erik de Regt, *Department of Economics, Erasmus Universiteit Rotterdam, Postbus 1738, 3000 DR Rotterdam, The Netherlands*

Professor Fernando Rezende, *Av. President Antonio Carlos, 51/15° andar, IPEA/INPES, 20 020 – Rio de Janeiro, RJ, Brazil*

Dr. Jozef M. M. Ritzen, *Social and Cultural Planning Office, J. C. van Markenlaan 3, Rijswijk (ZH), The Netherlands*

Prof. Dr. Günther Schmid, *Wissenschaftszentrum-Berlin, International Institute of Management, Platz der Luftbrücke 1-3, D-1000 Berlin 42, Federal Republic of Germany*

Dr. Friedrich Schneider, *Institut Für Empirische Wirtschaftsforschung Der Universität Zürich, Forchstrasse 145, 8032 Zürich, Switzerland*

Dr. Edward Scicluna, *Faculty of Management Studies, University of Malta, Msida, Malta*

Professor Eytan Sheshinski, *Department of Economics, Hebrew University, Jerusalem, Israel*

Dr. Wouter Siddré, *Department of Economics, Erasmus Universiteit Rotterdam, Postbus 1738, 3000 DR Rotterdam, The Netherlands*

Dr. Jiří Skolka, *Austrian Institute for Economic Research, P.O. Box 91, A-1103 Vienna, Austria*

Professor Burton A. Weisbrod, *Department of Economics, 1180 Observatory Drive, University of Wisconsin, Madison, Wisconsin 53706 U.S.A.*

Professor Niels Westergaard-Nielsen, *Institute of Economics, University of Copenhagen, Studiestraede 6, DK-1455 Copenhagen K, Denmark*

Preface

The 36th Congress of the International Institute of Public Finance was held in Jerusalem, Israel on August 25–29, 1980. The topic of that Congress was "Public Finance and Public Employment." The merging of these two quite disparate themes was unique, yet timely. In the decade of the 1970s, both industrialized and less developed countries experienced economic difficulties. Price inflation was high and unemployment as well. The public sector was increasingly relied on to provide work for groups in the labor force unable to find private employment. Direct job creation, industrial subsidies, and employment subsidies became important policy instruments during this period. And public employment as a percent of total employment grew as a result.

Aside from these stimuli to the growth of public sector employment, a variety of other factors were at work. Many of these were longer term trends relating to citizen demands for the outputs of services whose production is traditionally located in the public sector. Others related to the differences in the growth rate of productivity between the public and private sectors. If, as many believe, productivity growth in service sectors lags behind that in nonservice sectors, the implications for the growth in public employment are clear.

While the factors determining the growth in public sector employment are complex, the impacts of growing public employment on economic performance are equally so. For many, government is seen as a constraint on economic performance and low economic growth, high inflation, and lagging productivity are seen to be the inevitable result of growing public employment.

For all these reasons, then, public employment in the context of public finance is a topic filled with important economic relationships and policy issues. The Jerusalem conference explored a wide variety of these. The main questions posed were as follows:

— What is the nature of public employment growth and what are its determinants?
— What are the impacts of public employment growth on economic performance?
— What is the effect on efficiency in resource allocation and on the income distribution of direct public job creation?
— How does public employment compensation compare with that in the private sector, and what are the implications of public employee compensation growth?

— What is the record of productivity growth in the public sector relative to the private sector?

— Can public employees influence public sector choices through political power or voting behavior?

The organization of the volume follows these themes.

Numerous people were instrumental in organizing the Congress and in assisting in the timely publication of this volume. All of their contributions are greatly appreciated. The Hebrew University, the Ministry of Finance of the government of Israel, the Bank of Israel, the German Marshall Fund, and anonymous Dutch donors deserve special thanks for assistance in financing the Congress. Support for assistance in editing the volume was provided by the Institute for Research on Poverty of the University of Wisconsin-Madison. Professor Eugene Smolensky, the Director of the Institute, was helpful in securing this support. The actual editing was done with great competence by Judy Kirkwood and Elizabeth Evanson. And, Madame Bernadette Dischamps in Clermont-Ferrand, France translated the summaries into the French language.

The arduous task of organizing the Congress was assisted by several people. The assistance of Professor Victor Halberstadt of the University of Leiden in the Netherlands was crucial. He gave sound advice on behalf of the Executive Committee, made contacts, and in numerous other ways provided support and assistance. Professor Horst Claus Recktenwald, President of the IIPF, and the members of the Scientific Committee for the 36th Congress also provided support, advice, and assistance. The Organizing Committee in Jerusalem, comprised of Professor H. Barkai, Professor D. Ben-Natan, Mr. E. N. Flug, Dr. J. Gabai, Dr. A. Gafni, Dr. I. Nebenzahl, Professor E. Sheshinski, Mr. D. Wainshal, Professor A. Yoran, and Dr. B. A. Zuckerman, arranged a convenient and attractive facility, and secured well all of the other assistance required for a successful Congress. The Hebrew University in Jerusalem, under the Presidency of Dr. Avraham Harman, served well as host of the Congress. In Jerusalem, logistical assistance and secretarial functions were ably performed by Birgit Schneider, Saskia ten Asbroek, and Agnes Peter. Finally, the organization of the Congress, the logistical and secretarial arrangements in Jerusalem, and the nearly infinite set of tasks associated with preparing the papers for publication could not have been carried out without the able assistance of Virginia Martens. She receives special thanks for the care, patience, good humor, and stamina which accompanied all of her help.

Robert H. Haveman
University of Wisconsin-Madison, U.S.A.
Editor

President of International Institute of Public Finance – responsible for the 36th Congress: Professor Horst Claus Recktenwald, Federal Republic of Germany

Members of the Scientific Committee for the 36th Congress were:

Robert H. Haveman, Chairman
Victor Halberstadt, Executive Vice President
Norbert Andel
Fernando Rezende
Elisabeth Vessillier

Contents

NA

Public Finance and Public Employment: An Introduction

Robert H. Haveman*
Victor Halberstadt**

The theme of the Jerusalem IIPF Congress is not a common one in the public finance literature. The two foci—public finance and public employment—are seldom discussed in tandem and, on the surface at least, there is little which binds them together. The purpose of this overview is to place the diverse issues which lie at the intersection of public finance and public employment into some perspective, some organized framework. In presenting this overview, we will refer to a number of the papers included in this volume and presented at the Congress; to attempt to "shoehorn" all of them into the framework would be both artificial and tedious.

Although the topic of the Congress was chosen over two years before the Congress, the state of the world economy made it a uniquely appropriate one at the time of the Congress and today. "Stagflation" has strained public finances, and has pushed government into the role of direct creator of jobs on a scale not practiced seriously since the 1930s. Some of the papers presented at the Congress addressed this direct job creation strategy, and provided evaluations of its effectiveness in a number of countries.

There are several reasons why the topics of public finance and public employment do not make a neat fit. First, the public employment focus places stress on but a single input to the public sector—labor—and seeks to tie this input to the financing of the entire public sector—financing which covers capital expenditures and income transfers in addition to labor costs. Second, there is no obvious reason why one would focus on a single *input* to the public production process, rather than on the *output* of that process. This is so, of course, unless the input is simultaneously an output, which—as some of the papers suggest—may well be the case. Third, the concept of public employment is ill-defined. It ranges from standard employment by the government in carrying out its administrative, production and income

*Professor of Economics, University of Wisconsin-Madison, U.S.A.
**Professor of Economics, University of Leiden, The Netherlands

Public Finance and Public Employment. Proceedings of the 36th Congress of the International Institute of Public Finance. Jerusalem, 1980.

transfer responsibilities (as in the paper by John Martin) to this concept plus public service employment of low-skilled workers to these plus employment in enterprises owned by government or dependent on government controls to these plus employment in the not-for-profit sector. Quite different patterns emerge depending on the definition employed. Finally, the definitional problems are sufficiently serious as to prohibit many important types of cross-national comparison. Clearly, the extreme example of this problem is in comparing capitalist and socialist states; in the latter countries, some would consider all employment to be public.

Given, then, the absence of a clear definition of this theme, why study Public Finance and Public Employment? Several reasons can be identified, many of which are developed at more length in the papers in this volume. Here they will only be noted.

A *first* reason is fundamental. Citizens may simply have a preference for consuming goods and services produced by public sector employees as opposed to private enterprises. The basis of this citizen preference may well be rooted in ideology, but if it exists it must be reflected in the allocation of production between private and public sectors. Similarly, and perhaps more basic, are the preferences of workers themselves. If the conditions of employment in the public sector differ from those in the private sector, and if these conditions are relevant to the tastes of workers, welfare maximization decrees that such worker preferences must also be considered in public sector-private sector allocation decisions. In short, the level of public employment should be larger than otherwise if workers have a preference for it.

A *second* reason is more pragmatic. Public sector employment growth has been substantial in western economies in the post-war period. Whether this growth has reflected citizen preferences or not, the fact is that it is now a political issue. And, as such, assertions regarding the impact of this growth on tax burdens, labor supply, private capital formation, productivity, and economic growth abound. These assertions warrant scrutiny.

The *third* reason is related to the second. In the current macroeconomic context, the provision of jobs to those seeking work may be possible only through direct job creation measures—employment subsidies and public service employment. Such programs, increasingly prominent in Western economies, deserve evaluation of their efficiency and equity consequences. Moreover, their purpose as instruments to correct structural problems or to offset cyclical changes is also worthy of study.

A *fourth* reason is also tied to the effect of public employment on economic growth. As is well-known, the incentives for the performance of public employees are quite different from those affecting private employees. In the public sector, there is no clear link between reward and economic performance—as a result, there is some presumption that productivity differentials between the two sectors will exist and become larger over time. This presumption also deserves study.

The *fifth* reason for studying public employment and its public finance implications concerns the dynamic which such employment may create in a political economy context. Public employees can be expected to be self-interested maximizers. And, in a democratic political context, they will vote (or lobby or bargain) so as to achieve their own objectives—for example, higher wages or expansion of their numbers. When the magnitude of public employment is a politically determined variable, a dynamic may be at work which leads to public sector growth irrespective of citizen preferences. The efficiency and equity implications of this growth are significant. For example, if organized public employee groups can influence public sector wage policy, they are also able to directly influence both the distribution of income and the incentives for the allocation of workers of various tasks and abilities between the private and public sectors.

Finally, while concern with employment has become central in the macroeconomic literature, it has not found a significant niche in the literature of welfare economics or public finance. This imbalance deserves to be righted. The traditional public finance categories—allocation, distribution, and stabilization—should be expanded so as to include the public employment issue.

In the Jerusalem Congress and this volume, all of these issues are addressed. The volume is organized so as to aid in sorting out these issues. The first two papers were plenary addresses at the Congress. That by Richard Musgrave seeks to set the public employment concept in a public finance context and to provide a theoretical rationale for isolating this concept as a subject worthy of study. The paper by Wassily Leontief raises important questions about the role of public employment—indeed, employment in general—in a world of rapid technological change.

Section I focuses on one of the main themes of the Congress—What is the nature of public employment growth and what are its determinants? John Martin's paper documents this growth for all of the OECD countries, and explores the role of demographic, income, bureaucratic, and productivity factors in this growth. While the facts of this growth seem clear, allocating responsibility for this growth among its determinants is less clear. In his contribution, Niels Westergaard-Nielsen examines the nature and determinants of public employment growth in a single country—Denmark. The breadth of the analysis in the Martin paper is complemented by this in-depth case study, as many of the same causal factors are explored in both papers. The paper by Hans de Groot and Jozef Ritzen presents a novel model of the supply and demand for public sector manpower in which a collective welfare function determines the allocation of public services. In projecting future public employment growth, they find slower future growth in public employment than that of the 1970's. Burton Weisbrod's paper explores an expanded concept of "public employment"—one which includes that in the non-private, non-public sector—and explores the magnitude of employment in this sector in the U.S. and the determinants of its growth. Finally, the paper by Fernando Rezende and José Cezar Castanhar argues that employment intensive activities must be undertaken by the public sector, even in the face of available capital intensive, lower cost technologies, if the social problems associated with high unemployment levels in developing countries are to be avoided.

The papers in this section, then, provide some insight into the sources of the recent growth in public employment, and the prospects for future growth in this sector. A reasonable bottom-line would seem to run as follows: Among the large catalogue of potential determinants of this growth, demand factors—for example, the desire for increased education, health care, income security, reduced unemployment—would seem to play a significant though by no means overwhelming role. Supply factors—bureaucratic control, voting influence of public employees, distance of political authorities from individual voters—also play some non-trivial role. Some support for the Baumol differential productivity hypothesis was found, but no clear pattern supporting a simple Wagner's law explanation is in evidence.

Section II of the volume addresses a second, related theme of the Congress—What are the impacts of public employment growth on the performance of the economy? Because both the financing of this growth and the diversion of resources from the private sector which it implies are relevant to economic performance, both elements must be considered. The papers by Robert Bacon and Jiří Skolka are concerned with this issue, and both see adverse macro-economic effects from the expansion of public employment. The perspective in these papers is "supply side economics"—for Bacon, inflation is seen as a result of the growth of public employment, for Skolka *reduced* productivity growth.

Section III is the largest section of the volume and contains papers dealing with the evaluation of the allocative efficiency and equity effects of government efforts to create jobs directly—largely public service employment and employment subsidy programs. The paper by George Johnson and Richard Layard is a basic conceptual paper. In it, the authors outline the theoretical considerations relevant for determining the optimal level of public employment in economies with labor market distortions—for example, high minimum wages. They demonstrate that with such distortions government should employ low-skill workers beyond the level suggested by the minimum cost criterion. Even better, wage subsidies targetted on this group should be granted to both private and public sector employers.

The other papers in this section also focus on public job creation efforts, but are empirical or institutional in nature. The paper by Jack Habib and Haim Factor is a broad paper, reviewing the basic economic issues underlying the public employment policy discussion. The paper by John Bishop narrows this conceptual focus and discusses the experience of the United States in attempting to directly create jobs. Both the paper by Günther Schmid and that by Sheldon Danziger and George Jakubson are empirical studies, the former emphasizing the efficiency (or net job creation) impacts of the direct job creation strategy and the latter emphasizing equity effects.

Taken together, these papers suggest a rather favorable view of public employment and wage subsidy measures to achieve social objectives. To be sure, reservations to such measures are noted and discussed. These involve the administration and design of such programs, their relationship to manpower training programs, the need for effective targeting on high unemployment groups, and their integration with regional development policies. A reasonable bottom-line would seem to run as follows. A well-designed targeted public employment or wage subsidy policy can (1) induce employment increases at lower budget cost per job created than general macroeconomic policy increases, (2) induce employment increases with less inflationary pressure than general aggregate demand measures, (3) shift the structure of employment toward low skill workers, equalizing the income distribution, and (4) be just as effective in reducing poverty as additional equivalent cash transfers, while simultaneously inducing additional labor supply.

Overall evaluation of this strategy, however, must rest on several other factors. These include the conditions of unemployment in the economy, the relationship of public employment efforts to income transfer policy, and—as emphasized—the design characteristics of the programs being evaluated.

Section IV focuses on the issue of the compensation of public employees. As the paper by Eytan Sheshinski suggests, in a dynamic context wage policy towards public employees affects the allocation of members of the labor force between the public and private sectors. Given varying abilities and labor-leisure tastes, public sector wage policy may cause distinct patterns of worker self-selection into the public and private sectors. The resulting allocation has obvious implications for both public and private sector performance, and the rates of growth of output and productivity in both sectors. The paper by Joseph Quinn directly addresses the issue of public sector compensation. By a careful analysis of the U.S. data, he finds that both average earnings (holding human capital and demographic characteristics constant) and pension benefits for public sector employees are higher than for their private sector counterparts.

Again, a general conclusion is suggested by these papers: Existing real income advantages accruing to public employment will expand the demand for these jobs and the growth of public employment. Such advantages also have implications for the "adverse selection" of individuals into public employment.

The final section contains a series of papers on important topics not neatly categorized in the preceding sections. Two issues dominate this section. First, what is the record of public sector productivity and productivity growth relative to that in the private sector? The papers by Richard Bird, David Foot, and Edward Scicluna and by Horst Hanusch deal with this issue, employing quite different methodologies. The second issue is the political economy issue already alluded to: Under what conditions can public employees influence public sector decisions through their political power or voting behavior, and is there evidence that they have exercised this influence? The papers by Edward Gramlich, and by Werner Pommerehne and Friedrich Schneider deal with this question, again with quite different approaches and types of evidence. Finally, there is the paper on work sharing as an employment generating device, prepared by Wouter Siddré and Erik de Regt.

Altogether, then, the menu of issues discussed at the Jerusalem Congress is a rich one. Even so, some important issues in the public employment and public finance area are neglected. For example, no adequate theoretical framework has yet been developed to guide the study of public employment. What are the welfare implications of public employment, and from what attributes of this form of employment do they spring? Should public employment be considered simply as a by-product of public goods provision, or is its existence an "output" in its own right? Does public employment convey external benefits and/or costs which are not reflected in standard cost and output measures? While the paper by Richard Musgrave contains the seeds of such a framework, it is not a full blown treatment.

A second related issue is akin to what is currently referred to as "supply side" economics: Does growing public employment have macroeconomic implications which are external side effects of the use of this form of labor? Are economic growth, capital formation, and productivity inhibited by growing public employment, and are inflationary pressures exacerbated? These questions are of crucial importance, and while papers at the Congress suggested such negative impacts, the analyses of these relationships are not definitive.

To answer these questions, more attention must be paid to the design and administration of public employment programs. Public employment is not a homogeneous input. Used in some ways and activities, productivity may be enhanced; other uses may deter economic growth. In short, understanding the effects and economic implications of public employment requires a more disaggregated view of what it is public employees are doing, who they are, and what they would be doing if not employed in the public sector.

Finally, no full evaluation of public employment—especially targeted public service employment—can be made without simultaneously considering the relationship of income transfer programs and their growth to public job creation efforts. Is it efficient to stimulate the demand site of the low skill labor market (by means of, say, targeted employment subsidies) while incentives in growing public transfer programs simultaneously inhibit the supply of labor? Only in the roundtable discussion at the Jerusalem Conference was this issue discussed—no paper included in this volume directly addresses this potential conflict.

8226
32/2

Why Public Employment?

Richard A. Musgrave

This paper addresses the narrower issue of public finance and public employment, rather than the more usual one of fiscal effects on employment at large. This renders my task more difficult because public employment has not occupied a central place in the theory of public finance. Although public employment has been discussed as a means of employment creation, little attention has been paid to its role in a fully employed economy. Much of public employment occurs in the context of public enterprise but the economics of public enterprise, not being part of the budgetary process, have remained somewhat outside our discipline. Within the budgetary framework, emphasis has been on the kind of goods and services which are to be provided for and not on which employees (civil servants or private-sector workers) should produce them.

To begin with, we note that the share of public budgets in Western countries typically absorbs from 30 to 50 percent of GNP, while public employment (including employment in public enterprises which are not reflected in the budget) typically accounts for 15 to 20 percent of total employment only.[1] The gap arises because a large portion of public budgets is in transfers and because goods and service expenditures are divided between purchases from private industry and compensation to public employees. Nevertheless, employee compensation is an important budget item and the planners of this conference are to be congratulated for having chosen this neglected topic.

The analyst in search of a theory of public employment, similar in elegance to that of social goods, will be disappointed. Public employment may be needed for quite different reasons, calling for quite different explanations. Public employment may occur as a by-product of public production, and public production may be appropriate under various conditions. Or,

---

1. See Bird, 1979, p. 49.

Public Finance and Public Employment. Proceedings of the 36th Congress of the International Institute of Public Finance. Jerusalem, 1980.

public employment may be called for as a way of providing employment, and there may again be various reasons why this particular route of employment creation is needed.

I.   Public Employment as a By-product of Public Production

I begin with situations where public employment results because it is desirable that certain production activities be undertaken publicly. In its most general form, this poses the issue of socialist versus capitalist organization. In socialist economies, the bulk of production, and hence employment, is carried on by public enterprises. The question to be asked is what exceptional circumstances call for private production and employment. In capitalist economies most production and hence employment is private and the question to be asked is what special circumstances call for public undertaking. The issue of public versus private employment in this basic sense might thus be interpreted as that of public versus private ownership of the means of production, a problem which is too broad for consideration here. Nor am I well equipped to examine why, in the socialist case, some exceptions of private employment are called for. I shall therefore focus on the question of why, in the case of generally private enterprise or mixed economies, instances of public production (and with it public employment) are called for. This will be of interest also to a socialist setting where, I suspect, one might draw a parallel distinction between employment in state enterprises (more or less similar to the private sector) and employment in governmental agencies.

Public Provision versus Public Production

I begin by drawing a sharp distinction between the case for public provision and that for public production. The theory of public finance has dealt at great length with the former. This is the question of why certain goods and services should be provided for directly through the market, i.e. purchased and paid for by individual consumers, while others should be provided publicly, that is, paid for by the budget and made available free of direct charge to the users. Central to this discussion has been the feature of joint or non-rival consumption which renders exclusion inefficient, as well as the difficulty of excluding particular consumers. As a result, provision for such goods through the market mechanism is difficult or infeasible and budgetary *provision* is called for. This is an important conclusion but it tells us nothing about whether the government itself should undertake the *production* of such goods or whether it should purchase them from private firms.

Services which are paid for through the budget may be produced publicly or may involve public purchases from private firms. Thus military hardware may be produced publicly or be purchased from private firms. Similarly, services which are paid for directly by the user may be produced publicly or by private firms. Thus, airlines may be operated by public enterprises or by private firms, with costs met in each case by ticket sales to the consumer.

The rationale for public production, therefore, is not to be found in the non-rival consumption characteristics of social goods. Social-good theory, developed as a theory of social consumption (or, for that matter, capital) goods, is not relevant to our problem. What is needed is a theory of "public production goods."

As I see it, there is no unique or central feature around which such a theory can be constructed, comparable to non-rival use in the theory of social goods. Public production may be in order for a number of reasons. Among others, these include (1) production characteristics which, if left to private firms, would call for extensive regulation such that public ownership offers the simpler solution, and (2) innate characteristics, or an x coefficient in the production function, which call for public production.[2]

Public Production Due to Natural Monopoly

I begin with situations where production characteristics are such that private production based on profit-maximizing behavior will not yield efficient results, so that public policy is called for. This includes the textbook example of natural monopolies and decreasing cost industries such as public utilities with their widespread public ownership. It also includes industries which generate external benefits or, more important, external costs with resulting oversupply through the market mechanism. Much has been said about this in recent years in connection with rising concern about the environment.

In either case, profit-maximizing behavior of private firms leads to faulty results, but this leaves open the question of whether the remedy is to be found in the operation of public enterprises or in regulation of private firm behavior. In the case of natural monopolies, pricing policies of private firms may be subjected to regulation and, if the efficient output involves a loss,

---

2. This, of course, is not a complete list of instances of public production. Other occasions for public production may arise (1) in extractive industries where natural resources are publicly owned; (2) where capital markets are inadequate to permit private financing of enterprises essential to economic development; (3) to permit cyclical stabilization of investment outlays; (4) or, more dubiously, to use public enterprise as a source of monoply revenue for government. Unnecessary to add, public ownership may also result from bail-out operations where industries, if left to the accountability of the market, would not survive.

such loss may be met by subsidy. In the case of externalities, subsidies and taxes may be used to internalize external benefits and costs, and safety measures may be enforced by regulation. Indeed it might be argued that the distinction between public ownership and regulation is one of degree only. Private ownership in a publicly regulated enterprise is only semi-private, since the power to control usually associated with ownership is limited. Similarly, it might be argued that employment in a strictly controlled enterprise is semi-public, especially if controls (directly or indirectly) extend to employment conditions.

Public Production Due to Product Characteristics

All this has been discussed at length and I need not dwell on it here. More interesting to this conference is whether there are certain goods and services the intrinsic quality of which calls for their being produced by government. For lack of a better term I shall refer to this as "publicness in production."[3]

The most obvious case is given by the services of the legislator or other elected officials of government. These services by their very nature cannot be purchased from private firms. Next, the services of the judiciary may be placed in this category. Although there are historical instances in which judiciary functions were farmed out (leased) to private suppliers, the administration of justice is generally regarded as having to be performed publicly. Similar considerations apply to the exercise of law enforcement and the military establishment (with mercenaries the exception rather than the rule) also belongs in this category. Beyond this, public administration can be put into the public production category, at least insofar as it involves the supervisory function needed to assure the implementation of public policy.

Next, there comes a category of goods and services the nature of which may, but need not, call for public production. Suppose for instance that government wishes to provide for immunization of school children against a communicative disease. Giving the shots could be farmed out to a private clinic but this might require a costly system of inspection to assure the proper quality of service. It may then be cheaper for government to undertake the service itself. As in the previously considered case of natural monopoly, the choice between regulation and public operation becomes a matter of expediency.

At the other end of the scale there are many services which are produced by government, especially at the municipal level, which might just as well be produced privately. These services, such as street cleaning, do not require

3. As noted later in the text, the term "publicness in production" as here used should not be confused with the familiar concept of social goods which involve publicness (or non-rivalness) in consumption.

public production on grounds of innate quality, yet they account for a substantial part of public employment. The widespread practice of rendering such services publicly, especially at the municipal level, can hardly be rationalized on these grounds. Rather, it reflects traditional patterns, failure to recognize the distinction between public provision and public production, as well as political gains to be derived from the dispensing of public employment, and last but not least the power of public employee unions.

An especially interesting issue in production publicness arises in the case of education. Education may be made available free to the student either by government-operated schools which do not charge fees or by having the government assume the cost of private schools, whether via direct subsidies or through a so-called voucher system. The case for free education, therefore, is not to be confused with the case for public schools. The latter has to rest on the proposition that the inherent quality of the educational product supplied by the public school differs from and in some sense is considered superior to that provided by the private school. The public school may be considered more democratic, more compatible in the U.S. case with the tradition of the melting pot, or more unifying in its effect on the social structure. On the other hand, availability of private schools may offer more diversity and greater competitiveness in assuring quality of performance. These tradeoffs involve considerations of social choice which have direct bearing on who should produce.

Although it is difficult to define the specific qualities which make for publicness in production, it may be noted that most instances where public production seems called for relate to services rather than to goods. This suggests that a case for publicness arises where personal contact, intangible qualities and variable adaptation to personal circumstances are involved.[4] Strangely this is an interesting question which appears to have been overlooked in public finance literature. To avoid confusion with the familiar distinction between social and private goods, let me add that the quality of publicness in production may apply to rival (social) and non-rival (private) goods alike. Non-rivalness in consumption is not a function of *who* produces, whereas publicness in production deals with the quality of the product as a function of where it is produced. Public production enters as an argument in the product's production function.

II. Public Employment qua PUBLIC Employment

So far I have viewed public employment as simply a byproduct of public production. Emphasis, therefore, was on the nature of goods and services with which public employment is associated. I now turn to the intrinsic

4. I am indebted to Professor Ben Porath for this suggestion.

nature of public as distinct from private employment, and independent of what is produced.

Preference for Public Employment

A first rationale for public employment may arise where employees *prefer* to be employed publicly. Welfare maximization, based on a utility function which includes the quality of work environment or the structure of the work contract may call for public as distinct from private employment. Given this model, employees with such preferences will offer their services to public employers at a lower wage rate, whereas others will ask more than in private employment. There would thus be a market mechanism which allocates the division of employment between public and private firms in line with employee preferences. This, to be sure, is a somewhat paradoxical notion providing, as it were, for a market mechanism by which to determine the weight of public and private production within the economy, involving an employee referendum on the form of economic organization.

On a priori grounds it is not obvious whether such a model would lead to lower or to higher wage rates in the public sector. Some workers might prefer public employment because they believe it to provide a more congenial environment and greater security, and will thus be willing to accept public employment at a lower wage. Others will prefer the greater mobility and advancement prospects in the private sector and hence accept a lower private wage. Preference between "public service" and "competition" as a way of life may also be involved. In the actual setting, public wages, at least at lower levels of skill, tend to be higher but it is difficult to say whether this reflects a net preference for private employment or other factors. Thus, compensation for public employment may be higher because public employees as voters may vote themselves higher returns. Or, as noted before, public employment may be overexpanded because public employees vote for additional budget items which require their services.[5] Finally, and especially in developing countries, political patronage may cause over-employment in the staffing of public agencies.

Public Employment as Employment Creation

It remains to consider the more familiar role of public employment as an instrument of job creation. Provision for full employment may be likened to the provision of social goods. Beginning with a situation of unemployment,

5. See Bush and Denzau, 1977.

increased investment by an individual firm will generate beneficial employment externalities via multiplier effects which the firm cannot internalize. Thus public direction through appropriate monetary or fiscal policy is needed. Moreover, provision for full employment resembles provision for social goods in that the gain may be enjoyed by all concerned. Whereas having a job is a rival good under conditions of unemployment, this is not the case in a full employment setting.

But though it is evident that full employment is a desirable goal of public policy, it is not at all obvious what role public employment has to play in this endeavor.[6] When stabilization policy was first discussed in the early stages of Keynesian economics, emphasis was on public works to grant direct public employment to the unemployed. This was preferred to purchases from private firms which would draw on inventories and thereby reduce the multiplicand. A larger deficit would be required to achieve a given result. Restatement of stabilization theory later on noted that aggregate demand may be raised not only by increasing public expenditures but also by reducing taxes. This further weakened the need for public employment as an instrument of employment creation. Efficient resource allocation between outlays on public and private goods should be with reference to consumer preference at a level of full employment income. A situation in which aggregate demand is deficient should be no excuse for an overexpansion of the public sector, just as a situation of excessive demand should be no excuse for its over-restriction. According to neo-classical doctrine, all three objectives (full employment, price level stability, and efficient division of output) can be achieved by an appropriate mix of tax, expenditure, and monetary policies.

Given a state of widespread and sustained unemployment due to deficient demand, public employment thus plays only a minor role in a well-designed stabilization policy. But the situation may differ in dealing with shortrun fluctuations and where unemployment is selective. In such a setting, public employment can provide additional jobs more quickly, especially so if there is a shelf of public works ready for introduction. Moreover, unemployment may vary sharply by industry and location. In such cases job creation may be targeted more effectively through public employment than through tax reduction and even through public purchases. Where pockets of unemployment coexist with a generally high level of employment, the public employment approach may also reduce the conflict between raising employment and worsening inflation, as it reduces the required level of outlay.

6. I am aware, of course, that the precise meaning of "full employment" is controversial, that full employment is not the only policy objective, and that a tradeoff with moderating inflation may be called for. These issues, including the now popular concept of "natural" (by whose nature or in what set of institutions?) rate of unemployment fall outside the realm of this paper except for their relation to *public* employment in particular. This will be noted further later in the text.

This suggests that public employment through targeted public works may well assume a larger role in the current setting of stagflation than it deserved in the earlier context of Keynesian unemployment and output expansion along a horizontal supply schedule. The greater the risk that expansion of demand adds to inflation, the more important it becomes that additional jobs are provided with a minimum increase in aggregate demand. This adds to the importance of targeting and thereby the case for public works which may be located where unemployment occurs and where its burden is most severe.

But there are also considerations which may point in the other direction. It is argued that to overcome stagflation a more rapid rate of productivity growth is needed; and that to raise productivity the share of public employment should be reduced. This is based on the assertion that public employment (or public production) is inherently less productive than private employment, or on the more interesting point that publicly produced goods lend themselves less to productivity growth than do private goods. Indeed it has been argued (not quite convincingly to my mind) that this has been a major factor in the growth of the public sector share in GNP. Moreover, an expansion of public employment calls for a higher level of taxation than does the tax reduction alternative. This may increase cost pressures on inflation, especially so if commodity taxation is used or if wage demands are related to after-tax income. Finally, a larger public employment sector may make the economy more inflation prone. Due to tenure and seniority rules, the fear of layoffs is less likely to dampen wage demands and the time-lag typically involved in wage indexing may be reduced. In all, the share of public employment has a bearing on where the so-called natural rate of unemployment lies. On balance, I would expect stagflation to call for a higher level of public employment, but there are two sides to the argument and the outcome is uncertain.

There remains the proposition that government should be the employer of last resort. That is to say, people who cannot get a job elsewhere should be offered public employment—simply because entitlement to a job is a basic element of social justice if not a precondition for a democratic society. The basic entitlement is to a useful job. It cannot be suspended by substitution of relief or, for that matter, by a doctrine which holds that sustained unemployment to some must be accepted as the price of operating a market economy. I have no difficulty in accepting the obligation of government to serve as employer of last resort, but without further specification this obligation has little content. What wage rate is to go with the entitlement? Is the entitlement to a job in a particular location, a particular line of activity? How long a period of temporary unemployment or job search must lapse before a public job can be claimed? How intensive a search for private employment must there be? All these questions must be answered before the obligation of government to serve as employer of last resort is defined. Depending on the answers, the requirement may emerge as either a strong or a weak condition.

Public Employment and the Structure of Labor Markets

Finally, I note the role of public employment in dealing with structural problems of unemployment, that is, conditions which arise not because aggregate demand is deficient but because there is a mismatch between the type of labor and skills that are supplied and those that are demanded. These frictions are also involved in the problem of stagflation, but will exist where some of the important features of stagflation such as wage indexing are absent.

My reference is to sectors of the labor force which for structural reasons do not find their way into private employment. In the U.S., for instance, this is a major problem with regard to youth employment and employment of some minority groups. In other instances, the problem may relate to potential workers who do not readily fit the ordinary employment pattern, such as the aged, the institutionalized, and the handicapped. With regard to some groups, temporary public employment for the purpose of training and retraining may play an important part although once more it may be possible to meet this task by subsidizing private firms to undertake it. For other groups, special working conditions may have to be provided to permit employment, conditions which it may be difficult to create for private firms.

Employability is a matter of degree and a function of the institutional arrangements under which employment occurs. Where private employment is not feasible, public employment in lieu of relief will not only increase the well-being of the recipient but in most cases it will also raise GNP. Last but not least, the provision of public employment opportunity in lieu of relief will bypass, or at least narrow, the conflict between society's obligation to adequately care for the unemployed and the disincentive effects which income-support by transfer is bound to generate.

III. Conclusion

I have tried to show in these remarks how the rationale for public employment differs with the context in which public employment arises. It may be called for (1) as a mere byproduct of public production undertaken as an alternative of regulating natural monopolies or of correcting for externalities; (2) because the very quality of the desired output requires public production; (3) because workers prefer public to private employment; (4) as an instrument of job creation; or (5) as a way of dealing with structural

18   R. A. MUSGRAVE

maladjustments in the labor market. Public production, of course, may also
occur where none of these justifications applies. Public production may simply reflect institutionally embedded practices or, not infrequently, the interest of politicians, and of public employees voting their self-interest.

With the latter in mind, have I not been naive to address the problem of
public employment by analyzing the conditions under which efficient government calls for such employment? Would it not be better, as hard-nosed
observers of public mismanagement would do, to postulate from the outset
that public employment results because it adds to the power of politicians
and because those already on the public payroll wish to enhance their jobs?
In other words, why not explore the expansion of public employment in
terms of a class struggle between public and private employees, with the
former emerging as the victors?

Such an analysis is of interest and is pursued in other papers in this
volume. It also fits the pattern of recent public choice literature, where
government is viewed as a public-sector maximizing monopolist who preys
on the people. While I consider this an exaggerated image, I do not deny the
role of bureaucratic expansion or the importance of voting power of public
employees as a factor in expenditure analysis.[7] However, let me note that
public employment in most countries has risen at a considerably slower rate
than the budget share. Using the U.S. as an illustration, the ratio of public
expenditures to GNP rose from 10 percent in 1920 to 18 percent in 1940, 27
percent in 1960 and 32 percent in 1970. Thereafter, it declined to 30 percent
in 1980. Over the same period, the share of public in total employment
moved from 9 percent to 13 percent, 15 percent, 21 percent, and 19 percent.
For the 60 year period (1920–1980) as a whole, the expenditure to GNP ratio
tripled while the employment ratio only doubled. Only during the 1960s did
the employment share rise more rapidly. This, of course, reflects the fact that
the driving force in budget expansion has been in the transfer sector and not
in public goods and services. Moreover, as I have tried to show in this
discussion, there are many conditions under which public employment *is*
called for as a matter of efficient policy, and the economist's first task, as I see
it, is to identify the circumstances under which such is the case. Only after
standards have been set for the efficient scope of public employment can one
determine whether the existing scope is appropriate.

References

Bird, Richard M. 1979. *The Growth of Public Employment in Canada.* Toronto: Institute for Research
    on Public Policy.
Bush, W. and Denzau, D. 1977. "The Voting Behavior of Bureaucrats and Public Sector

7. See my article in H. Ladd and N. Tideman, eds. *Tax and Expenditure Limitations,*
Washington, D.C.: The Urban Institute, 1981.

Growth." In T. Borcherding (ed.), *Budgets and Bureaucrats: The Sources of Public Sector Growth*. Durham: Duke University Press.

Musgrave, Richard A. 1981. "Leviathan Cometh, or Does He?" In H. Ladd and N. Tideman (eds.), *Tax and Expenditure Limitations*. Washington, D.C.: The Urban Institute.

Résumé

Parce que le contexte dans lequel l'emploi public se situe échappe à une analyse raisonnée, on ne peut donner aucune théorie générale de l'emploi public (similaire à la théorie des biens publics). L'emploi public peut être conçu:

(1) comme un pur dérivé de la production publique chargé d'offrir une alternative pour contrôler des monopoles naturels ou pour apporter une correction à des externalités;

(2) parce que la qualité même de la production désirée nécessite une production publique;

(3) parce que les ouvriers préfèrent un emploi public à un emploi privé;

(4) comme instrument de création d'emploi;

(5) ou comme un moyen de régler des désajustements structurels sur le marché du travail.

L'emploi public, bien sûr, peut aussi se produire là où aucune de ces justifications ne s'applique. Il peut simplement réfléchir des pratiques institutionnelles ancrées ou, ce qui est assez fréquent, refléter les intérêts des politiciens et des fonctionnaires qui votent en raison d'intérêts propres.

8243
6211
MDCs

Public Finance, Public Employment, and Income Distribution

Wassily Leontief

There exists no better means to trace the changing role of government in modern market economies—and to a great extent in present day socialist countries as well—than to observe the rising level and changing structure of public expenditures and of public revenues.

The functions and, consequently, the financial transactions of public bodies can be viewed as serving two distinct sets of aims: First, *provision of common goods and services* that are not, and in many instances cannot, be produced or allocated through the operation of the market mechanism; second, *redistribution of income*—to the extent to which the distribution resulting from unconstrained interplay of impersonal forces of supply and demand is judged to be unsatisfactory, such redistribution is affected indirectly through regulation of (some call it interference with) these market forces, or directly by means of secondary transfers.

Policy measures designed to provide common goods are bound to affect to some extent the income distribution and, on the other hand, the measures intended primarily to redistribute income—such as large-scale public works—as a rule contribute to the supply of so-called public goods. The existence of public goods is recognized to be due primarily to the peculiar nature of benefits accruing from clean air, control of infectious diseases or national defense (which ironically turns out to be the most expensive of all public goods), that cannot be supplied or appropriated privately.

Primary income distribution, which the secondary transfers are intended to correct, is embedded deeply in the institutional structure of the society. One does not have to be a dogmatic marxist to recognize that social and, particularly, economic institutions must of necessity be in their turn attuned to the technological conditions under which the society exists.

In the historical past, successive phases of technological advance were accompanied by a corresponding change in social institutions. Needless to say, such adjustment usually occurs with delay and not without some fric-

Public Finance and Public Employment. Proceedings of the 36th Congress of the International Institute of Public Finance. Jerusalem, 1980.

tion. In the area of public goods, government concerns can be expected to be dominated for some time by their responsibilities for protecting the environment and managing scarce natural resources. In the field of income distribution government will have to meet the challenge of computer age technology, which unlike the technology of the passing machine age that enhanced the productive power of human labor seems to be able to replace it. The effect of technological advance on employment has been debated for over 168 years, since desperate workers in the textile town of Nottingham, England, led by a certain Ned Ludd wrecked newly invented knitting machines that threatened—so they thought—their livelihood. The mill owners of course disagreed and were supported by economists who proceeded to "prove" once and for all that unemployment caused by technology can be nothing but an illusion.

There were, however, notable exceptions, among them John Stuart Mill (the author of "On Liberty") who, after arguing first that workers displaced by machines in one line of production would necessarily find equally good employment opportunities in some other, later changed his mind and admitted that both the introduction of machines and their increase in numbers and efficiency can, indeed, depress the aggregate demand for labor.

Thirty years ago, it took several thousand switchboard operators to handle one million long-distance telephone calls; 10 years later, it took several hundred operators; and now, with automatic switchboards, only a few dozen or so are required. The productivity of labor—that is, the number of calls completed per operator—is increasing by leaps and bounds; it will reach its highest level when only one operator remains, and become infinite on the day that operator is discharged.

Technological advance is uneven. Some sectors of the economy are more affected by it than others, some types of labor replaced faster than others. Less-skilled workers, in many instances but not always, go first; skilled workers later. While in many operations even dirt-cheap labor could not compete effectively with very powerful or very sophisticated machines, a drastic general wage cut would temporarily arrest the adoption of labor-saving technology. But unless the introduction of the cut was interdicted by specially erected barriers, the old trend would be bound to recur. Even a most principled libertarian might hesitate to have the wage question settled by cut-throat competition among workers under continued pressure of steadily improved labor-saving machines.

Some advocates of full-employment policies have proposed that labor-intensive processes be given preference over labor-saving technologies. If administered persistently, such Luddite medicine would slow down technical progress and bring about difficulties even more menacing to the health of our economic and social system than the disease it is intended to cure.

Stepped-up investment can certainly provide additional jobs for people who otherwise would be unemployed. However, under conditions of labor-saving technological advance, creation of one additional job that 20 years ago might have required $10,000 today would cost $20,000 and 20 years from now easily $50,000, or more, even if inflation is controlled. A high rate of investment is indispensable to satisfy the expanding needs of a growing society. But it can make only a limited contribution to solution of the problem of involuntary technological unemployment, particularly since the greater the rate of capital investment, the higher the rate of introduction of new labor-saving technology.

From the time that the steam engine was invented, successive waves of technological innovation have brought about an explosive growth of total output accompanied by rising per capita consumption and, up until the middle 1940s, a progressive shortening of the normal working day, working week and working year. Although increased leisure (and for that matter cleaner air and purer water) is not included in the official count of goods and services used to measure the gross national product, it has certainly contributed greatly to the well-being of blue-collar workers and salaried employees. Moreover, the reduction of the average work week in manufacturing, from 67 hours in 1870 to 42 hours in the middle 1940's, combined with longer schooling amounted to a large-scale withdrawal from the labor market of many millions of working hours. At the end of World War II, the situation changed. Technological innovation continued as before and the real-wage rate continued to go up, but the length of the normal work week today is practically the same as it was 35 years ago. In 1977, the normal work week (adjusted for growth in vacations and holidays) was still 41.8 hours. One must conclude that it would be sensible to explore the possibility of resuming the interrupted process of the gradual reduction of the length of the labor day, labor week and labor year—or even labor life.

Once, voluntary sharing of technological unemployment—that is, progressive shortening of work time—was accompanied by a steady rise not only of hourly-wage rates and monthly salaries but also of total annual, and even lifetime, take-home income. Up to the middle 1940s, wage earners chose, as their real income rose, to enjoy it not only through increased consumption but in the form of a shorter work week and more leisure. Without the increase in leisure time, the educational and cultural advances that have marked the first 40 years of the 20th century would not have been possible. Americans probably would have continued to absorb potential technological unemployment in this voluntary way had real wages risen during the next 40 years even faster than they have. But because of the greatly expanded opportunities to replace labor by increasingly sophisticated machinery, the impersonal forces of the market will not favor this solution any more. Humans are not horses however,—they can reason, and in our democratic society they can vote.

Government policies designed to bring about a steady rise in real wages sufficiently large to induce workers and employees to resume continuous voluntary reduction in the length of the normal work week once could have been considered. Under present conditions, such policies would require so large an increase in labor's share of the total national income that there would be a decline in productive investment, resulting in an unacceptable slowdown of economic growth. The other alternative policy is a two-pronged approach combining direct action toward progressive reduction in the length of the normal work week with income policies designed to maintain and steadily increase the real family income of wage earners and salaried employees.

Recent studies sponsored by the U.S. Department of Labor (Best, 1980) seem to indicate that a significant further voluntary reduction of the total number of working hours offered by the existing labor force could be brought about by a more flexible scheduling of the labor time. Depending on the age group to which they belong, the family status, occupation, etc., some workers would be prepared—if offered a choice—to sacrifice a certain fraction of their current income by working four and a half instead of five days a week, by extending their annual vacation, or by an earlier retirement or arrangement that would permit them to enjoy a sabbatical leave every seven years. Reducing the standard length of the labor day by, say, fifteen minutes, proves to be one of the less desirable alternatives.

Tentative, and obviously somewhat speculative, computations based on a combination of the most desirable trade-off choices for different groups lead to the conclusion that the average U.S. worker could forego some 4.7 percent of his or her current earnings for free time. In the year 1978 the average worker's total annual work week would be reduced under these conditions from 1,910 to 1,831 hours. That is equivalent to a 7½-hour work day, a 37-hour week or about 11½ added days of paid vacation. While certainly deserving serious consideration, such measures cannot, however, provide a final answer to the long-run problem of enabling modern industrial society to derive all possible benefits from continued technological advance without experiencing involuntary technological unemployment and the resulting social disruption.

Before they were expelled from Paradise Adam and Eve enjoyed a very high standard of living without working. Their successors have been condemned to eke out a miserable existence engaged in heavy toil and trouble, working from dawn to dusk. The history of technological progress over the last 200 years is essentially a story of the human race working its way slowly but steadily back into Paradise. But what would happen if we suddenly found ourselves in it? With all goods and services "produced" without any work, no one would be gainfully employed and being unemployed means receiving no wages. Consequently, unless new income policies were appropriately formulated to fit the changed technological conditions, there would be starvation amid plenty.

If and when technological unemployment threatens to be transformed out of a theoretical possibility into reality, the relationship between employment policies and income policies becomes critically important. In the case of a typical American farmer whose income consists in part of wages for his and his family's labor, and in part of interest and profits on capital invested in the land used by his enterprise, the adjustment to progressive mechanization and automation proceeds naturally and simply. The number of labor hours devoted annually to farm work goes gradually down. But even while the imputed labor income of the farmer and his family diminishes, its shrinkage is more than compensated by an increase in the capital and rent income. No problems of income distribution arise, however, because all three different kinds of income land in the same pocket.

But this is an exceptional situation. What is now threatening not only the developed, but even to some extent the less developed countries is, *involuntary* technological unemployment. Under the present institutional set-up, a rational response to the essentially beneficial process of progressive replacement of labor by machines should consist of a gradual, mandatory reduction in the standard length of the labor day, labor week and even labor life, combined with income policies designed to compensate all wage earners for the resulting loss of income.

We are already practicing such income policies by gradual changes in the structure of our tax system and through Social Security, medical insurance, welfare payments and unemployment benefits. The system will have to be redesigned and expanded so as to reduce the contrast between those who are fully employed and those who are out of work. Let us remember the widespread European practice of payment of supplemental benefits to wage earners who work less than the normal number of hours per week. A reasonable and effective response to the incipient threat of involuntary unemployment should aim at bringing about an equitable distribution of jobs and income without, howevever, obstructing, even indirectly, technological advance.

But would not the admittedly far reaching measure proposed above contribute to inflation? Such a question is being asked nowadays whenever one speaks of better environmental protection, improved transportation or simply of resetting the clock to wintertime next Sunday. The inflation that has been plaguing this and several other (but not all) advanced free market economies for some time is, in my opinion, not primarily a technical economic problem, but a deep seated social problem. Although an effective combination of fiscal and monetary policies is indispensable for effective management of a modern economy, its success is predicated not only on tacit mutual understanding, but institutionalized day-by-day cooperation between business and labor.

I could have entitled this paper, "Public Finance and New Income Policies." However, the latter term has been used so much as a euphemism for wage and price controls that it has nearly lost its original meaning. Long after price and wage controls are recognized for what they are—a noble, but in the long run harmful, experiment—genuine income policies will remain a foremost subject of public concern and a major issue in public finance.

References

Best, Fred. *Exchanging Earnings for Leisure: Findings of an Exploratory National Survey on Work Time Preferences*. U.S. Department of Labor, Employment and Training Administration. R&D Monograph 79. U.S. Government Printing Office, 1980.

Bird, Richard M. 1979. *The Growth of Public Employment in Canada*. Toronto: Institute for Policy Analysis.

Bush, W., and Denzau, D. 1977. "The Voting Behavior of Bureaucrats and Public Sector Growth," in T. Borcherding (ed.) *Budgets and Bureaucrats: The Sources of Public Sector Growth*. Durham, N.C.: Duke University Press.

Musgrave, Richard A. 1981. "Leviathan Cometh, or Does He?" In H. Ladd and N. Tideman (eds.) *Tax and Expenditure Limitations*. Washington, D.C.: The Urban Institute.

Résumé

Dans le passé, les phases successives de l'avance technologique s'accompagnaient de changements correspondants dans les institutions sociales et les fonctions étatiques. La croissance de l'Etat–Providence et l'adoption de règlements sociaux (par exemple en ce qui concerne l'environnement) en sont deux exemples.

Dans l'avenir, il est probable que les préoccupations de l'Etat seront dominées par la protection de l'environnement et la gestion de ressources naturelles rares. Dans le domaine de la distribution des revenus, l'Etat aura la tâche difficile de faire face au défi de la nouvelle technologie de l'ère de l'ordinateur. A la différence de la technologie dépassée de l'ère de la machine qui rehaussait la puissance productrice du travail humain, il est probable que des changements technologiques imminents rendront la main-d'oeuvre trop abondante.

Autrefois, un partage volontaire du chômage technologique, c'est-à-dire une réduction progressive du temps de travail, était accompagné d'une hausse régulière, non seulement des taux de salaire horaire et des traitements mensuels, mais aussi d'un revenu global annuel ou même pour la durée d'une vie.

A cause des occasions beaucoup plus répandues qui s'offrent de remplacer le travail par des machines de plus en plus élaborées, il est peu probable que les forces impersonnelles du marché offrent cette solution.

Ce qui menace aujourd'hui les pays développés, mais aussi, dans une certaine mesure, les pays sous-développés, c'est un chômage technologique involontaire. Dans les conditions institutionnelles actuelles, une réponse rationnelle au processus éminemment bénéfique du remplacement progressif de la main-d'oeuvre par les machines, devrait pouvoir consister dans une réduction graduelle, obligatoire, de la durée moyenne de la journée de travail, de la semaine de travail et même de la vie de travail, combinée à des politiques des revenus ou de l'emploi public, afin de compenser pour les salariés la perte de revenu qui en résulterait.

Une réponse raisonnable et efficace à la menace contenue dans le chômage involontaire devrait viser à créer une distribution équitable des emplois et des revenus sans cependant gêner, même de façon indirecte, l'avance technologique.

Public Sector Employment Trends in Western Industrialized Economies

*John P. Martin**

I. Introduction

One of the most striking features of economic growth in the OECD area over the past twenty years has been the persistent rise in the share of the services sector in total employment. For example, the annual average employment growth rates over the period 1960–1978 for the three broad sectors were as follows: agriculture (−2.9 percent), industry (0.8 percent), and services (2.4 percent).[1] In the 1970s the role of the services sector in providing for *net* growth in employment has been even more pronounced. While agricultural employment continued to decline over the period 1970–1978, and industrial employment was virtually stagnant, employment in the services sector continued to grow at 2.5 percent per annum. Although it has often been suggested that continued expansion of the public sector has played a leading role in the growth of services employment, it has been impossible to verify this observation due to the lack of reliable comparative data on public sector employment.

Public sector employment should also be viewed in the wider context of concern in many OECD countries about the size and rate of growth of the public sector in recent years.[2] However, arguments about the appropriate size of the public sector have typically been conducted in terms of trends in public expenditure and/or public sector deficits.[3] Little attention has been paid to public sector employment even though this is clearly an alternative measure of the size of the public sector.[4] Indeed, as much of public expendi-

---

*I am indebted to Robert Haveman for helpful comments on an earlier draft. The opinions expressed are my own and should not be attributed to the OECD.

[1]Growth rates are calculated from *Labour Force Statistics* (OECD, various issues).

[2]For a discussion of these issues see OECD (1978).

[3]For example, see Beck (1979) or Nutter (1978).

[4]There are a few exceptions. See Economic Commission for Europe (1979) and Bird *et al.* (1979).

Public Finance and Public Employment. Proceedings of the 36th Congress of the International Institute of Public Finance. Jerusalem, 1980.

ture represents direct purchases of labour inputs, any attempt to restrain public expenditure is likely to involve control over the numbers employed in the public sector as well as their wage rates.

This paper aims to remedy some of the gaps in our knowledge of public sector employment growth in the OECD area. The structure of the paper is as follows. First, an operational definition of the public sector is specified. Second, trends in public sector employment since 1960 are analyzed. Third, data are also presented on some key disaggregations of the employment data for a smaller subset of countries. Finally, there is a review of several hypotheses which have been put forward to explain the growth of public employment.

II. Definition of the Public Sector

For this exercise the public sector was defined as the range of activities covered by *general government*. This sector, as defined in the System of National Accounts (SNA), covers the various departments and agencies at central, state, provincial and local level which produce *non-market* goods and services. The main exclusions from a comprehensive coverage of the public sector are government-owned firms and public corporations which produce and sell goods and services on a market. However, since some small-scale government enterprises are included in general government,[5] the boundary line in the SNA between general government and public enterprises is often difficult to establish in practice.

Clearly there are advantages and disadvantages to any working definition of the public sector. However, for the purposes of this study, data availability dictated limiting the coverage to general government.[6] Thus, the data presented here fail to give a complete picture of the size and growth of public sector employment in two respects.[7] First, many public corporations are excluded from general government, though in a few cases it was possible to collect employment data on this sector as well. Second, the hiving-off of some activities (which were previously included in general government) as public corporations may impart a downward bias to the figures over time.

[5]The SNA includes in general government those public enterprises "which mainly produce goods and services for government itself or which primarily sell goods and services to the public, but do not operate on a large scale" (UN, 1968, p. 79).

[6]I also exclude a variety of non-governmental activities, mainly in the "non-profit" sector, which produce close substitutes for public goods and services. See Weisbrod's contribution to this volume for an analysis of the size of this sector in the United States.

[7]The ECE (1979) study also restricted coverage to general government. This exercise differs from the ECE study in two respects. First, a larger sample of countries is included and the data are more up-to-date. Second, the ECE data were compiled from several different national sources. The data in this study were compiled in almost all cases from national accounts sources with the aid of national statistical agencies to ensure a minimum of international comparability.

III. Trends in Public Sector Employment Since 1960

A recent OECD (1978) study shows a rising trend of public expenditure to GDP in all Member countries since 1960, even though there were wide variations in the rate of increase across countries. Is a similar tendency observable for a growing public sector share in total employment? The data in

Table 1

Share of the Public Sector in Total Employment, 1960–1978

Country	1960	1965	1970	1975	1978
Australia[a]	n.a.	22.2	22.9	25.5	26.0
Austria	10.8	12.0	14.1	16.9	18.3
Belgium[b]	12.2	13.2	13.9	15.2	16.9
Canada[c]	n.a.	17.9[d]	19.8	20.4	20.0
Denmark	n.a.	13.3[d]	16.9	23.2	24.5
Finland	n.a.	n.a.	12.0	14.8	17.9
France	12.3	11.7	12.4	13.8	14.3
Germany	8.0	9.8	11.2	13.9	14.5
Ireland	n.a.	n.a.	11.2	13.6	15.1
Italy	8.1	9.9	10.9	13.4	14.2
Japan	n.a.	n.a.	5.8	6.5	6.4
Luxembourg	n.a.	n.a.	9.7	10.0	11.0
Netherlands[e]	11.7	11.5	12.1	13.5	14.6
New Zealand	17.9	17.9	18.2	18.9	19.6[j]
Norway[e]	12.7[f]	13.8	16.4	19.3	20.8
Portugal	n.a.	n.a.	7.3[i]	8.1	8.1[j]
Spain	n.a.	6.6	7.1	10.0	12.3
Sweden	12.8	15.3	20.6	25.4	29.0
Switzerland	6.3	6.7	7.9	9.4	10.1
United Kingdom	14.9[h]	15.7	18.0	21.0	21.3
United States	15.7	16.7	18.0	18.0	16.7
Mean (unweighted)[g]	12.0	12.9	14.5	16.6	17.5
		(12.8)	(14.5)	(16.8)	(17.8)
Coefficient of Variation (%)	28	25(28)	26(29)	26(28)	27(27)

[a] Australian data not directly comparable since the coverage is somewhat broader than general government. Figures adjusted for breaks in the series in 1966 and 1971.
[b] Figures adjusted for a break in the series in 1970.
[c] Figures adjusted for a break in the series in 1975.
[d] 1966.
[e] Data are in man-years.
[f] 1962.
[g] Summary statistics are calculated for a sample of 12 countries (excluding Australia), for which data were available for all years. Figures in parentheses are for a sample of 15 countries.
[h] 1961.
[i] 1971.
[j] 1977.
n.a.: not available.

Table 1 clearly give an affirmative answer to this question.[8] Excluding a few
countries where the data are either not entirely comparable or are only available for some years, the unweighted mean share of the public sector increased
from 12 percent of total employment in 1960 to almost 18 percent in 1978.[9]
There was a slight tendency for the inter-country dispersion, as measured by
the coefficient of variation, to decline between 1960 and 1965; since then
there has been no further change in the dispersion of public sector employment shares across countries.

There are very noticeable variations between countries in the size of the
public sector's share. The largest shares tend to be clustered among the
Scandinavian countries (excluding Finland) where general government currently accounts for 20–30 percent of total employment. Canada, New Zealand and the United Kingdom are three other countries where the public
sector employs at least 20 percent of the workforce. At the other extreme,
Japan, Portugal and Switzerland have the lowest public sector employment
shares, accounting for only 7–10 percent of total employment in 1978. Austria, Belgium, Finland and the United States have public sector employment
shares which are clustered about the OECD average while France, Germany,
Ireland, Italy, the Netherlands and Spain all have below-average shares in
recent years.

The largest absolute increase was recorded in Sweden, where the share
more than doubled between 1960 and 1978. Indeed, the other Scandinavian
countries also recorded very rapid growth in the public sector's share. There
are a few cases—Japan, New Zealand, Portugal—where the public sector's
share has been very stable over time. In the United States the public sector's
share has risen by only one percentage point over the entire period. However, this small increase covers two separate periods of expansion and subsequent decline. In the mid-1960s the share rose rapidly to a record level of
18 percent in 1968–69, remained at this level for several years and then
declined in 1973–74. After a sharp recovery in 1975 the share has sub-
sequently declined steadily by more than one percentage point.

Finally, there appears to be a levelling-off of the public sector's share in
several countries since the mid-1970s which may partly reflect growing pressure on public sector budgets following the 1974–75 recession. This tendency

[8]See Appendix Table A1 for data on numbers employed in the public sector. Detailed
source notes to all the tables are available from the author on request.
[9]The weighted mean shows less growth in the public sector's share. Here are the results for
the 12-country sample:

1960	1965	1970	1975	1978
12.8	13.9	15.5	16.8	16.7

The apparent stability in the weighted mean since 1975 reflects the declining public sector's
share in the United States over the past four years.

Table 2

Share of Employment in Public Corporations in
Total Employment
for Selected Countries, 1960–1977

Country	1960	1965	1970	1975	1977
Canada	3.8[a]	3.5	3.3	3.5	n.a.
Denmark	n.a.	n.a.	n.a.	3.3	3.3
France[b]	5.1	5.0	4.6	4.5	4.4[c]
Italy	n.a.	n.a.	n.a.	6.4	6.3
Norway[d]	4.2[e]	4.1	4.1	4.2	4.2
Sweden	n.a.	n.a.	6.6	7.6	8.1
United Kingdom	9.0[a]	8.0	8.2	8.2	8.4
United States	1.5	1.6	1.6	1.7	1.5

[a] 1961.
[b] Includes only eight large enterprises which in 1969 accounted for about 60 percent of the value added of public enterprises.
[c] 1976.
[d] Data are in man-years.
[e] 1962.
n.a.: not available.

towards stability, or even a decline in the public sector's share is most noticeable in North America,[10] but there also appears to be some evidence of it in Germany, Japan and the United Kingdom (since 1976).

Employment in Public Corporations

General government does not include many public corporations which are typically regarded as part of the public sector in most countries. Thus, the data in Table 1 are underestimates of the size of the public sector and an attempt was made to quantify the magnitudes involved across countries. Unfortunately, it is impossible to give a very precise answer since data could only be collected for eight countries (see Table 2). Moreover, there are comparability problems with this data which make intercountry comparisons especially fragile.[11]

With this caveat in mind, the data suggest that employment in public corporations typically accounts for a much smaller share of total employment

[10]The slowdown in Canada appears to date from the end of the 1960s. For further confirmation of this, see Bird *et al.* (1979, pp.27–51).
[11]For example, the current convention in the French national accounts only distinguishes a limited subset of public enterprises, what are termed "les grandes entreprises," from the rest of the private sector.

Table 3

Average Annual Growth Rates of Public and Private Sector Employment, Selected Periods (in percentages)

Country	1960–1965 Public Sector	Industry	Private Services	Private Sector	1965–1970 Public Sector	Industry	Private Services	Private Sector
Australia	2.6	n.a.	n.a.	n.a.	3.6	n.a.	n.a.	2.1
Austria	2.0	0.2	1.8	−0.4	2.5	−0.9	0.4	−1.2
Belgium	2.5	1.7	1.5	0.7	1.8	0.4	2.2	0.5
Canada	n.a.	n.a.	n.a.	n.a.	(4.8	n.a.	n.a.	1.7)^a
Denmark	n.a.	n.a.	n.a.	n.a.	(6.7	0.6	0.1	−0.5)^a
Finland	n.a.	n.a.	n.a.	n.a.	n.a.	n.a.	n.a.	n.a.
France	−0.5	n.a.	n.a.	0.7	2.2	n.a.	n.a.	0.7
Germany	4.6	1.3	0.5	0.1	2.5	−0.1	0.6	−0.5
Italy	3.2	n.a.	n.a.	−1.2	2.2	n.a.	n.a.	0.1
Japan	n.a.	n.a.	n.a.	n.a.	n.a.	n.a.	n.a.	n.a.
Luxembourg	n.a.	n.a.	n.a.	n.a.	n.a.	n.a.	n.a.	n.a.
Netherlands^c	1.0	2.1	2.5	1.5	1.9	−0.9	3.5	0.7
Norway^c	(3.5	n.a.	n.a.	0.4)^d	4.2	n.a.	n.a.	0.1
Portugal	n.a.	n.a.	n.a.	n.a.	n.a.	n.a.	n.a.	n.a.
Sweden	4.5	1.5	1.1	0.2	6.9	−0.3	1.1	−0.5
Switzerland	3.5	3.0	3.3	2.1	3.9	−0.2	2.5	0.5
United Kingdom	(2.0	0.6	1.6	0.5)^a	2.5	−0.8	−0.4	−0.9
United States	2.9	3.6^h	2.1	1.5	3.9	1.5^h	2.9	1.9

^{a} Rates are 1966–1970.
^{b} Rates are 1973–1977.
^{c} Data are in man-years.
^{d} Rates are 1962–1965.

than general government. This is especially so in North America but is the case in Denmark and Norway as well: In none of these countries did employment in public corporations in 1977 exceed 20 percent of general government employment. In France, Sweden and the United Kingdom, however, employment in public corporations was equivalent to 30–40 percent of employment in general government in 1977, while the 1977 figure for Italy was almost 50 percent. Thus, employment in the public sector (*including* public corporations) accounted for 30 and 36 percent of total 1977 employment in the United Kingdom and Sweden, respectively, compared to only 18 percent in the United States.

Unlike employment in general government, there is no general trend for employment in public corporations to grow faster than total employment over the same period. The share of employment accounted for by public corporations remained relatively stable in all countries except France, Sweden and the United Kingdom. Sweden appears to be the only country in this

Table 3 (*continued*)

1970–1973				1973–1978				
Public Sector	Industry	Private Services	Private Sector	Public Sector	Industry	Private Services	Private Sector	Country
2.8	n.a.	n.a.	2.1	2.9	n.a.	n.a.	−0.1	Australia
4.5	1.6	1.8	0.6	3.8	−0.8	1.8	−0.3	Austria
2.4	−0.4	2.2	0.5	2.9	−2.5	1.2	−0.7	Belgium
3.8	n.a.	n.a.	3.3	2.6	n.a.	n.a.	2.6	Canada
7.1	−0.8	0.7	−0.5	4.8	n.a.	n.a.	−0.2	Denmark
5.0	2.7	2.3	0.4	5.0	−1.8	0.2	−1.7	Finland
2.5	n.a.	n.a.	0.5	1.9	n.a.	n.a.	−0.1	France
3.8	−0.5	0.9	−0.4	1.8	−2.1	0.1	−1.6	Germany
5.0	n.a.	n.a.	−0.6	3.1	n.a.	n.a.	0.3	Italy
3.1	2.7	2.8	1.0	1.7	−0.5	2.4	0.7	Japan
2.7	4.2	3.6	3.2	(3.1	−0.4	1.2	−0.2)[b]	Luxembourg
2.3	−2.1	1.4	−0.4	2.4	−2.2	1.0	−0.5	Netherlands[c]
4.5	n.a.	n.a.	−0.3	3.6	n.a.	n.a.	0.8	Norway[c]
(3.0	1.6	−0.8	−0.9)[e]	(0.9	−1.5	0.3	−0.2)[f]	Portugal
5.2	−1.5	−0.5	−1.2	5.1	−0.9	0.5	−0.2	Sweden
3.6	−0.4	2.5	0.6	1.7	−3.7	−0.3	−2.0	Switzerland
3.1	−1.2	1.0	−0.3	1.7	−1.4	0.6	−0.5	United Kingdom
(1.0	2.7	3.4	3.5)[e]	1.3	0.9	3.1	2.2	United States

[e] Rates are 1971–1973.
[f] Rates are 1973–1976.
[g] Rates are 1961–1965.
[h] For the years 1960–1970 mining and quarrying are included in Industry.
n.a.: not available.

sample where the employment share of public corporations has risen over time.[12]

Growth Rates of Public vs. Private Sector Employment

In the introduction to this paper I drew attention to the unresolved issue of the relative contributions of the public and private sectors to the observed growth in service sector employment. Table 3 attempts to clarify this issue by presenting data on employment growth rates by broad sector for selected time periods. First, the growth rates for both public and private sectors are

[12]The United Kingdom data are particularly affected over this period by transfers of activities from general government to the public corporations sector, as well as by the nationalization of some private sector industries. For details, see Semple (1979).

compared where the latter is simply defined as total employment less employment in general government. Second, within the private sector so defined, an attempt was made to split out industry and private services wherever possible.[13]

The results clearly establish the major role of the public sector in sustaining employment growth in most countries. There is only one recorded instance where public sector employment actually declines—France over the period 1960-1965.[14] The contribution of the private sector to employment growth is much more variable. More than half the countries have recorded declines in private sector employment since 1970 and only in the United States has there been sustained growth since 1960. Employment in industry has declined in all countries since 1973 with the sole exception of the United States. Employment in private services has tended to grow over the whole period just as in the public sector.

Moreover, a comparison of sectoral growth rates suggests some tendency for the public sector to expand employment faster than private services. More rapid growth of public rather than private services has been recorded in Austria, Denmark, Finland, Germany, Sweden and the United Kingdom. The United States is the only country in question where private services have generally expanded employment faster than the public sector, the only exception to this being the period 1965-1970. In the remaining five countries there appears to have been no persistent tendency for employment growth in the public sector to outstrip growth in private services or vice versa.

Public Sector Employment Adjusted to Full-Time Equivalents

Thus far the discussion of public sector employment has concentrated on the *number* of employees without any attempt to adjust the data to full-time equivalents. Several commentators have argued that failure to adjust for part-time working is likely to exaggerate the growth of public sector employment. For example, with reference to the United Kingdom, Jackson (1979) has argued that "When account is taken of the importance of part-time employment in the public sector, it appears that many of the conclusions

---

[13]Industry comprises manufacturing, electricity, gas, water and construction. Private services includes all employment, excluding those of producers of government services, in ISIC divisions 6-9: wholesale and retail trade, transport and communication, finance, insurance, real estate and business services, and community, social and personal services. Producers of private non-profit services to households and domestic servants are also included in private services. The sum total of employment in industry and private services does not fully exhaust private sector employment which also includes employment in agriculture, mining and quarrying.

[14]The decline in France appears to reflect the very rapid rundown in the size of the armed forces in the early 1960s.

Table 4

Alternative Measures of the Share
of Public Sector Employment
in Total Employment, 1977

Country	*Persons*	*Full-Time Equivalents*
Denmark	24.1	21.8
Norway	21.1	20.0[a]
Sweden	27.5	26.5[b]
United States	17.1	15.9

[a] Data in man-years.
[b] Data refer to total hours worked.

drawn by some commentators about the growth of public sector employment are misleading" (p. 53).

It is impossible to give a categoric answer on this issue since the necessary data could only be assembled for four countires: Denmark, Norway, Sweden and the United States. The data for Denmark (1975–1977 only) and the United States are on a full-time equivalent basis, whereas the Swedish data refer to hours worked and the Norwegian data are on a man-years basis. Estimates of the share of public sector employment in 1977 for these four countries, in terms both of numbers employed and full-time equivalents, are presented in Table 4.

The public sector's share of total employment is lower when measured in full-time equivalents: the divergence is greatest in Denmark (10 percent) and least in Sweden (4 percent). Thus, discussions about the size of public sector employment which ignore the phenomenon of part-time work are likely to overstate the absorption of labour by that sector.

IV. Characteristics of Public Sector Employment in OECD Countries

This section attempts to put some flesh on the broad picture of public sector employment growth by analyzing trends in some important disaggregations of the totals. Unfortunately, the relevant data are only available for a few countries so that the force of the subsequent conclusions is more limited.

Female Employment in the Public Sector

Some commentators have related the persistent rise in female participation rates, especially among married women, to the continued expansion of

Table 5

Female Share of Public Sector Employment
in Selected Countries, 1965–1977
(in percentages)

Country	1965	1970	1975	1977
Australia	19.7%	23.9%	32.1%	33.9%
Austria	n.a.	39.9	44.2	45.3
Denmark	61.3^a	64.5	66.7	n.a.
Japan	n.a.	28.4	29.6	31.8
Norway	n.a.	n.a.	64.4	65.7
Sweden	65.8	70.8	72.5	73.6
United Kingdom	n.a.	48.8^b	53.4	54.3
United States	40.9	45.4	47.5	49.5

^{a} 1966.
^{b} 1971.
n.a.: not available.

employment opportunities in the public sector. The greater flexibility of the
public sector in creating part-time jobs is stressed as a major factor in enabling the public sector to tap this source of labour force growth.[15]

Data on the female share of public sector employment in eight countries
(see Table 5) throw some light on these issues. Several points can be noted.
First, there is a wide differential between the female-intensity of public
sector employment across countries. Typically, the public sector is very
female-intensive in the Scandinavian countries where seven out of every ten
workers are female, whereas Japan and Australia are at the other extreme
with a ratio of two males to every one female employed in the public sector.
Indeed, for this sample of countries there is a positive correlation between the
female-intensity of public sector employment and the size of the public sector: The larger the share of public employment in total employment, the
greater the female-intensity of the public sector.[16] Second, the data show
clearly that the public sector is also becoming more female-intensive over
time. In all eight countries the percentage of public sector employment accounted for by females has increased with the most rapid growth in the
female share in Australia.

[15]For example, the Economic Commission for Europe (1979) concludes that "in a number of
countries part-time female employment has played an important part in the expansion of government employment in the last decade and a half" (p. 66).
[16]Using 1977 data in every case except Denmark where 1975 data were used, a value of 0.62
was calculated for Spearman's rank correlation coefficient, which is almost significant at the 5
percent level.

Table 6

Proportion of Part-Time Workers[a]
in Public Sector Employment, 1965–1977

Country	1965	1970	1975	1977
Spain	24.0	28.3	26.2	20.6
Sweden	25.7	29.7	32.2	34.2
United Kingdom	n.a.	23.5[b]	27.7	27.4
United States	12.4[c]	13.3	14.5	14.5

[a] In both Sweden and the United States, part-time workers are defined as persons who work less than 35 hours a week. In the United Kingdom the definition covers persons normally working for not more than 30 hours a week. In Spain the definition of a part-time worker has changed over the period as follows: 1964–1971—persons who worked less than 40 hours a week; 1972–1975—persons who worked less than 37 hours a week; 1976—persons who worked less than 33 hours a week.
[b] 1971.
[c] 1968.

Part-time Work in the Public Sector

Since it appears that many females in the public sector are employed in part-time jobs, I monitored this by gathering data on the number of part-time workers in the public sector. Data were only available for four countries (see Table 6). But even in this small sample there appear to be wide divergences in the share of part-time working in the public sector, though some part of this simply reflects different national definitions of part-time work. It is noticeable that Sweden, which has the largest share of employment in the public sector among OECD countries, also has a very high proportion of part-time workers in this sector. Part-time workers in Sweden account for one-third of all public sector employees in recent years, compared to one-quarter in the United Kingdom, one-fifth in Spain and one-seventh in the United States.

The public sector in these countries is also more intensive in its use of part-time work than the private sector. In 1977 part-time workers only accounted for one-sixth of private sector employment in Sweden and one-fifth of private sector employment in the United Kingdom. There also appears to be an increasing trend towards more part-time work in the public sector. Finally, growth in part-time employment is mainly concentrated among females. In the United Kingdom females accounted for 91 percent of all part-time work in the public sector in 1977 whereas the corresponding figure for the United States was 74 percent.

V. Possible Explanations for the Growth of Public Sector Employment

Clearly, explanations of the growth of public employment cannot be divorced from the political process and it is unrealistic to analyze this phenomenon in purely economic terms. Nevertheless, there is a growing literature on the causes of public sector growth which seeks to draw useful insights based on economic analysis. For example, one hypothesis stresses the role of demographic factors and rising real incomes in generating greater demand for public goods and services. Yet another hypothesis builds on the assumption of lower productivity growth in the public sector relative to the private sector to demonstrate that this can lead to a growing public sector employment share over time.

It is commonly argued that income elasticities for many public goods and services are greater than unity. In these circumstances increased public expenditures are a natural outcome of the general rise in living standards. Indeed, with greater than unitary elasticities, demands for such services as education and health have risen more than proportionately to real incomes. In these circumstances one would expect such expenditure increases to be matched by growing public employment. There is an additional factor which may serve to reinforce this income effect. If the public sector is more labour-intensive than the private sector, any increase in public sector output will require relatively more labour input than an equivalent increase in private sector output. Thus, over time there may be a tendency for the public sector employment share to increase due to the interaction of rising real incomes with the greater labour-intensity of public sector production.

Demographic factors could also exert significant influence not only on the level of public expenditure but also on trends over time since the needs for different goods and services are heavily dependent on the size of client groups. For example, a rise in the population of school-going age is likely to be positively correlated with an increase in educational expenditures in much the same way as an aging population is likely to place greater demands on health expenditures. The OECD (1978) has recently analyzed the relative importance of demographic changes and increases in program coverage to growth in public expenditures on the so-called "welfare programmes"— education, income maintenance and health. The main conclusion was that "the greatest contribution to rising expenditures comes from an increase in programme coverage" (p. 26).[17] Demographic factors, while not negligible, especially in the case of health expenditures, were a much less significant influence.

---

[17]For a similar conclusion based on several Canadian studies, see Bird et al. (1979, pp. 126–127).

In an attempt to establish whether there is any statistical association between the share of public employment in total employment, rising real incomes, and changing demographic patterns, cross-section regressions were estimated by ordinary least squares for the years 1970, 1975 and 1978. The sample was all the countries in Table 1 (excluding Australia). Real income was proxied by GDP per capita in U.S. dollars at 1975 prices and exchange rates, the dependency ratio (the ratio of the non-working to the working population) was used as a measure of the differing demographic structures across countries. The prior expectation was that both explanatory variables would have positive coefficients. The female activity rate was also included in the set of regressors. Since the public sector is a major employer of female labour, one would expect an expanding public sector to have a positive impact on female activity rates.

The econometric results (see Table 7) lend some limited support to these hypotheses. There is a positive relationship between real income per capita and public employment shares in these cross-section regressions; however, the coefficient of real income is never well determined. The evidence is somewhat stronger in favour of a link between demographic structures and public employment shares across countries. The coefficient on the dependency ratio is often significant at the 10 percent level or above, especially when it is combined with the female activity rate. The latter variable dominates the other regressors in terms of explanatory power: Its coefficient is

Table 7

Cross-Section Regression Results

Equation No.	Dependent Variable	CONST.	GCAP	DEPR	FEMA	$\bar{R}^2$	S.E.E.
1.	PESH70	−48.938	0.0008	0.248	0.542	0.42	3.40
		(2.80)	(1.65)	(3.22)	(3.13)		
2.	PESH70	−48.412		0.249	0.620	0.36	3.57
		(2.64)		(3.08)	(3.55)		
3.	PESH75	−37.684	0.0009	0.176	0.501	0.34	4.15
		(1.75)	(1.59)	(1.93)	(2.58)		
4.	PESH75	3.013	0.0007		0.179	0.24	4.47
		(0.66)	(1.11)		(1.69)		
5.	PESH75	−28.986		0.144	0.518	0.28	4.33
		(1.33)		(1.55)	(2.56)		
6.	PESH78	−38.328	0.0007	0.173	0.543	0.34	4.38
		(1.68)	(1.27)	(1.85)	(2.66)		
7.	PESH78	−29.324		0.141	0.539	0.32	4.46
		(1.33)		(1.54)	(2.60)		

t-ratios are shown in parentheses. Symbols are as follows: PESH70 = share of public sector in total employment in 1970; GCAP = GDP per capita in U.S. dollars at 1975 prices and exchange rates; DEPR = dependency ratio; FEMA = female activity rate.

always significant at the 5 percent level. However, the overall explanatory power of these equations is rather weak. Even the best determined equation still leaves almost 60 percent of the residual variance unexplained.

An alternative hypothesis, associated with Baumol (1967), concentrates on the role of productivity differentials in a simple model of unbalanced growth. The central assumption is that the economy can be classified into two sectors: (1) a technologically progressive sector which experiences rapid rates of productivity growth, and (2) a non-progressive sector which is only able to realize limited productivity gains. With the aid of some subsidiary assumptions, Baumol arrives at two striking results. First, if the ratio of outputs in the two sectors is to remain relatively constant, the non-progressive sector must absorb a growing share of total employment. Second, this shift of labour will be accompanied by a falling real growth rate.

The literature on this hypothesis explicitly identifies the public sector with the non-progressive sector despite the difficulties of measuring productivity.[18] It is argued that the workings of the political-bureaucratic system will tend to produce at least a constant, if not rising, ratio of public to private goods and services. In addition, once allowance is made for the linkage through the labour market between wages in the two sectors, unit labour costs in the public sector will tend to increase over time.

Two clear predictions follow from this hypothesis: (1) the share of the public sector in total employment will tend to increase over time, and (2) a rising share of the wage and salary bill in total government expenditure. The evidence in Section III shows that the first prediction is consistent with the "stylized facts" since 1960 in many OECD countries. As for the second prediction it was possible to calculate the share of employee compensation in government final consumption expenditure for thirteen countries (see Table 8). Although there are marked inter-country differences in the wage and salary share, there also appears to be a general tendency for the wage and salary share to increase over time though there are a few exceptions.

The Baumol model seems to accord reasonably well with the empirical evidence in this paper, but one must be careful not to press this too far. There is, after all, the inherent difficulty in defining and measuring public sector output. In addition, one should be very cautious about predictions derived on the basis of an excessively simple two-sector model which rests on several very strong assumptions. Finally, while this thesis is noticeable for its stress on the role of the underlying technological structure in generating public sector growth, by the same token it appears deficient in giving little or no weight to the political process.

---

[18]For example, see Spann (1977) and Gramlich's paper in this volume.

Table 8

The Share of Employee Compensation[a]
in Government Final Consumption Expenditure

Country	Time Period	Average Share	Percentage Increase over the Period
Denmark	1970/71–1975/76	70.5	5.9%
Finland	1970–1978	69.1	−3.6
France	1975–1976	74.2	0.4
Germany	1960–1978	53.4	8.6
Italy[b]	1970–1978	74.0	−1.6
Japan	1970–1978	81.9	5.2
Netherlands	1969–1978	73.8	0.7
Norway	1967–1978	75.0	5.4
Portugal	1968–1976	60.6	30.9
Spain	1968–1977	82.4	6.8
Sweden	1963–1978	66.8	15.2
United Kingdom	1970–1978	63.3	1.6
United States	1970–1978	63.4	−0.5

[a] Employee compensation includes in addition to wages and salaries the employers' contribution to social security schemes and private pension insurance.

[b] Break in series at 1975; figures for 1970–1974 have been adjusted in line with later years.

In line with the latter argument, it seems difficult to disagree with the following conclusion of one writer on this topic: "We are as yet, however, far from having a sufficiently satisfactory theory of what gets done politically, and why, to permit us to reach any firm conclusions about the relative merit of the various explanations of government growth" (Bird et al., 1979, p. 152).

VI. Main Findings

The main findings of the paper are as follows:

1. The share of public sector employment (excluding public corporations) in total employment differs widely across OECD countries, ranging from about 7 percent in Japan to almost 30 percent in Sweden in 1978.
2. With only a few exceptions, the public employment share has tended to increase since 1960, though the rate of increase varies widely across countries, with particularly rapid growth in the Scandinavian countries.
3. In some countries, especially in North America, the share of public employment has tended to stabilize or even decline since the early 1970s.

APPENDIX: Table A1

Public Employment in OECD Economies, 1960–1978 (in thousands)

Country	1960	1961	1962	1963	1964	1965	1966	1967	1968	1969
Australia	844.9	870.2	890.2	911.8	935.2	960.8	1013.8 (1029.8)	1064.3	1100.8	1129.6
Austria	346.8	354.7	363.8	368.7	377.8	382.0	390.7	401.1	412.6	423.3
Belgium	405.4	407.5	424.1	446.5	448.2	459.1	472.2	483.1	489.0	494.4
Canada	..	..	..	..	..	..	1255.0	1319.0	1387.0	1460.0
Denmark	..	..	..	..	..	..	296.2	318.2	340.3	362.3
Finland	..	..	..	..	..	..	..	..	..	..
France	2391.0	2414.0	2412.0	2340.0	2321.0	2333.0	2372.0	2424.0	2471.0	2528.0
Germany	2098.0	2228.0	2348.0	2444.0	2540.0	2628.0	2706.0	2777.0	2803.0	2859.0
Ireland	..	..	..	..	..	..	..	..	..	..
Italy	1633.0	1688.0	1759.0	1823.0	1880.0	1912.0	1945.0	1991.0	2032.0	2091.0
Japan	..	..	..	..	..	..	..	..	..	..
Luxembourg	..	..	..	..	..	..	..	..	..	..
Netherlands	490.0	497.0	505.0	509.0	512.0	516.0	528.0	537.0	544.0	558.0
New Zealand	156.7	156.9	160.8	167.9	172.1	177.0	181.4	186.4	190.6	193.8
Norway	..	..	186.0	193.0	201.0	206.0	211.0	221.0	232.0	243.0
Portugal	136.0	145.0	123.0	133.0	140.0	150.0	161.0	173.0	186.0	200.0
Spain	..	..	..	..	833.2	785.3	801.0	816.5	792.9	805.4
Sweden	461.6	478.1	492.4	527.6	555.9	576.3	603.9	642.4	691.3	741.9
Switzerland	171.2	176.7	181.8	188.1	196.2	202.8	208.3	213.6	222.3	234.4
United Kingdom	3978.0	3643.0	3708.0	3778.0	3859.0	3947.0	4078.0	4236.0	4329.0	4369.0
United States	11317.0	11652.0	11995.0	12229.0	12655.0	13066.0	14224.0	15044.0	15506.0	15789.0

4. Employment in public corporations does not appear to exhibit the same trend towards an increasing share in employment as the general government sector. Sweden is one of the few exceptions; indeed the public sector (including public corporations) accounted for 37 percent of total employment in Sweden in 1978.

5. Since 1960 employment has generally grown more rapidly in the public sector than in industry. Employment in the public sector also appears to have expanded faster than in private services in some countries.

6. When public sector employment is adjusted to a full-time equivalents basis, it is clear that data on the numbers employed tend to exaggerate the share of total labour input in public production.

7. The public sector is a major employer of female labour. The share of females in public sector employment has also increased significantly over time.

8. There is some evidence that many of the females employed in the public sector are in part-time jobs.

9. Econometric evidence suggests that demographic structures and female activity rates are more significant variables explaining cross-country differences in public employment shares than real income per capita. However, the "best" equations only explain about 40 percent of the residual variance.

1970	1971	1972	1973	1974	1975	1976	1977	1978	*Country*
1162.9	1192.3	1328.4	1362.0	1404.0	1506.1	1502.1	1533.9	1586.4	Australia
	(1286.4)								
432.4	452.4	478.1	493.5	515.9	540.9	560.4	581.9	594.8	Austria
500.7									Belgium
(513.1)	(523.7)	(538.2)	(550.4)	(563.6)	(573.2)	(592.5)	(604.7)	(634.3)	
1514.0	1613.0	1647.0	1695.0	1757.0	1829.0				Canada
					(1897.0)	(1908.0)	(1978.0)	(1994.0)	
384.4	412.1	439.8	472.7	505.6	538.6	553.6	573.5	598.5	Denmark
255.4	265.6	277.9	295.4	313.2	331.2	350.3	363.7	377.8	Finland
2597.0	2668.0	2740.0	2797.0	2861.0	2917.0	2969.0	3030.0	3077.0	France
2978.0	3093.0	3233.0	3328.0	3441.0	3512.0	3558.0	3575.0	3638.0	Germany
118.3	120.9	125.0	130.9	136.0	142.9	148.4	152.7	158.2	Ireland
2130.0	2236.0	2355.0	2466.0	2568.0	2656.0	2713.0	2819.0	2870.0	Italy
3147.0	3228.0	3322.0	3445.0	3560.0	3646.0	3677.0	3726.0	3750.0	Japan
13.4	13.5	14.2	14.5	15.0	15.5	15.7	16.3	16.5	Luxembourg
567.0	584.0	601.0	607.0	617.0	630.0	650.0	668.0	681.0	Netherlands
198.8	203.0	210.3	209.4	215.0	228.2	233.9	234.0	240.4	New Zealand
253.0	265.0	277.0	289.0	298.0	308.0	320.0	331.0	344.0	Norway
216.0	233.0	241.0	247.0	250.0	251.0	254.0	254.0	..	Portugal
875.1	958.3	954.7	1181.9	1186.1	1245.8	1342.1	1354.0	1481.6	Spain
804.9	859.3	904.2	937.2	994.7	1045.9	1095.8	1141.3	1200.0	Sweden
245.3	253.5	263.7	272.9	280.3	284.4	288.8	294.2	297.3	Switzerland
4464.0	4591.0	4750.0	4888.0	4932.0	5235.0	5337.0	5304.0	5322.0	United Kingdom
15801.0	15810.0	15880.0	16114.0	16405.0	16709.0	16760.0	16902.0	17174.0	United States

10. There is some empirical evidence to support the Baumol thesis that the growth of the public sector reflects underlying technological forces.

References

Baumol, W. J. (1967), "Macroeconomics of Unbalanced Growth: The Anatomy of Urban Crisis," *American Economic Review*, Vol. 57, pp. 415–426.

Beck, M. (1979), "Public Sector Growth: A Real Perspective," *Public Finance*, Vol. 34, pp. 313–356.

Bird, R. M., Bucovetsky, M. W. and Foot, D. K. (1979), *The Growth of Public Employment in Canada*. IRPP series on public sector employment in Canada. Toronto: Butterworth.

Economic Commission for Europe (1979), "Employment in General Government in Industrial Market Economies," *Economic Bulletin for Europe*, Vol. 30, pp. 55–78.

Jackson, P. M. (1979), "Comment," in *De-Industrialisation* (ed. F. Blackaby), pp. 49–55, London: Heinemann.

Nutter, W. (1978), *Growth of Government in the West*. Washington, D.C.,: American Enterprise Institute.

OECD, (various issues), *Labour Force Statistics*. Paris: OECD.

OECD (1978), *Public Expenditure Trends*. Paris: OECD.

Semple, M. (1979), "Employment in the Public and Private Sectors 1961-78," *Economic Trends*, No. 313, pp. 90–108.

Spann, R. M. (1977), "The Macroeconomics of Unbalanced Growth and the Expanding Public Sector," *Journal of Public Economics*, Vol. 8, pp. 397–404.

UN (1968), *A System of National Accounts*. New York: UN.

Résumé

L'accroissement continu de la part du secteur des services dans l'emploi total constitue l'une des caractéristiques les plus marquantes de la croissance économique dans la zone OCDE au cours de l'après-guerre. Bien qu'on avance souvent que l'expansion continue du secteur public a joué un rôle majeur dans cette évolution, l'absence de données comparatives sur l'emploi dans le secteur public n'a pas encore permis de vérifier ce fait. Le problème de l'emploi public doit être aussi envisagé dans le cadre des préoccupations récentes exprimées dans les pays de l'O.C.D.E. relatives à l'importance et au taux de croissance du secteur public. Cependant, le débat a porté essentiellement sur la question de l'évolution des dépenses publiques et assez peu porté sur celle de l'emploi public. Cet article se propose de combler quelques unes des lacunes dans la connaissance que l'on a de la croissance de l'emploi public dans la zone OCDE. Le secteur public est défini ici comme couvrant toute la gamme d'activités du gouvernement et exclut la plupart des activités des entreprises publiques. Les résultats montrent que la part de l'emploi public dans l'ensemble de l'emploi diffère largement d'un pays à l'autre, variant d'un minimum d'environ 7 % au Japon à presque 30 % en Suède en 1978. Dans la plupart des pays, la part de l'emploi public a augmenté rapidement depuis 1960 bien que dans quelques cas, elle se soit stabilisée au cours des dernières années. L'emploi public s'est aussi accru plus rapidement que l'emploi dans les services du secteur privé dans de nombreux pays. Le secteur public constitue la source principale de l'emploi féminin notamment en offrant des emplois à temps partiel. Enfin, les résultats d'une recherche économétrique des causes de la croissance de l'emploi public suggèrent que les structures démographiques sont plus significatives que le revenu réel par tête dans l'explication des différences entre les pays des parts de l'emploi public. Ce résultat semble aussi apporter une certaine confirmation à la thèse de Baumol.

Trends and Determinants in Public Employment in Denmark, 1921–1977

Niels Westergaard-Nielsen*

Introduction

One of the striking features of postwar economic growth in most West-ern countries has been the persistent rise in the relative size of the public sector, as measured both by share of GNP and share of the labor force employed in the public sector. This increase has probably been made possi-ble by high economic growth and a substantial rise in the labor force partici-pation rate for married women.

Although the situation has been parallel in many countries, very few longitudinal studies of the growth of public employment drawing on national or international statistics have been conducted to date. One probable expla-nation is that statistics describing public sector employment are inadequate as a basis for studies covering several decades. This study will try to remedy that situation for Denmark since 1921.

After a brief description of the data, this study examines trends in the demand for public employees between 1921 and 1976. We attempt to esti-mate the impact on the demand for labor of an increasing tendency of work-ers to work part-time and a concomitant decline in the number of hours that individuals work. In particular, the excessively high growth in demand for labor in the last two decades is discussed and analyzed. A second aspect of this growth is the source of the increased labor supply. It appears that the main source of employees for the Danish public sector has been women who formerly were homemakers only.

Another peculiarity of the growth of the public sector is that the eco-nomic framework that can explain its development and the rising public share

*The author is grateful to B. Rold Andersen, T. Borcherding, R. Norstrand and P. J. Pedersen for helpful comments on an earlier version. This paper, prepared while the author was visiting the Institute for Research on Poverty at the University of Wisconsin—Madison, was made possible through administrative and financial support provided by the Institute.

Public Finance and Public Employment. Proceedings of the 36th Congress of the International Institute of Public Finance. Jerusalem, 1980.

of labor, service, and commodity markets has yet to be constructed. One approach in the existing economic literature has been to explain the size and the composition of the public sector as a result of consumer demand in the same sense as consumer demand for other goods. Such demand models have previously been estimated using cross-sectional data. (See, for example, Borcherding and Deacon, 1972; Bergstrom and Goodman, 1973; Deacon, 1978; and Pommerehne, 1978.) In this study we shall investigate how well those models describe the Danish time-series data on public employment.

Data Sources and Definition of the Public Sector

One difficult problem in studying trends over time is the construction of consistent data series. Because special censuses of the number of employees within the public sector in Denmark do not exist prior to 1975, the data for this study originate in population censuses and employment surveys. Population censuses were made up to 1970 at intervals of 5 to 10 years; the employment surveys began in 1969 and are carried out yearly. From these two sources it is possible to construct the necessary data series; unfortunately, however, the results for overlapping years are not identical, as can be seen in Figure 1.

Figure 1. Trends in Employment in the Public Sector, 1921–1976.

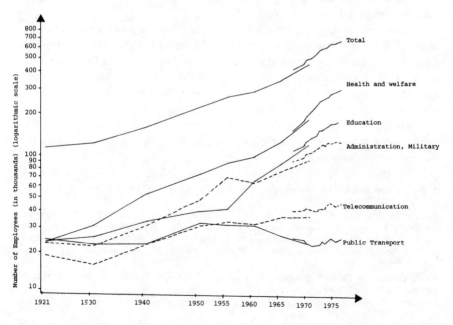

One of the difficulties in constructing the data series is that the definition of the public sector has to follow the one the Danish Statistical Bureau uses in its employment surveys. This definition includes employees in public administration, police, defense, welfare, health, education, churches and museums, as well as those in semiprivate (i.e., subsidized) institutions. It also covers general practitioners, dentists, veterinarians, midwives, and the like. For some purposes, railroads (now mostly state-run), other public transportation, and the state-run mail and telephone services are included in the public sector. In the education, health, and welfare sector there has been a substantial change from private to public ownership and entrepreneurship. Such changes do not reflect real changes in the utilization of resources; these groups are nevertheless included in the public sector, whatever the pattern of ownership has been in the past.

The Trends in Public Employment

Figure 1 graphs trends in the number of public employees for the period 1921 to 1976. The gaps for the years before 1970 reflect the differences between the two statistical sources. The curve for total employment shows a sixfold increase in the number of public employees—from 114,000 in 1921 to 700,000 in 1976. The curve also reveals that two periods of relatively rapid growth (1930–1955 and 1960–1972) and three periods of slower growth (1921–1930, 1955–1960, and 1972–1976). The highest growth rate for the whole period is that for the years 1960–1972.

Purely by chance, the different sectors were the same size in 1921. The curves demonstrate relatively moderate growth rates in all subsectors until the 1960s. Thereafter the growth rates increase, culminating in 1969–1972, and then slowing down. In the welfare sector, annual growth rates reached a record of 26% for the years 1970 and 1971 (Westergaard-Nielsen, 1979a).

The Impact of Increasing Part-Time Work

To obtain a more appropriate expression for the growth in demand, the rise in part-time work that we have already noted (see Table 1) must be taken into account. Unfortunately, data on part-time work in the public sector are not complete for a longer period, but it is clear that the number of employees in this case overestimates the real growth in the public sector. Two calculations can be made to show the effect of this tendency.

The first calculation demonstrates how the total public staff (excluding railroads, postal services, and telecommunications) would have grown if the

Table 1

Percentage of Labor Force Working Part-Time

Year	Total Labor Force	Education	Health and Welfare	Administration	Total Public Sector
1969	14.58	23.9[a]	27.2[b]	—	—
1970 S	15.67	—	—	—	—
1971 S	16.92	31.6	33.8	11.1	27.8
1972 S	17.51	33.7	35.9	—	—
1972 F	17.33	32.8	36.7	12.3	30.2
1973 F	18.75	36.0	38.2	11.9	31.8
1974 F	19.41	36.1	39.4	11.6	32.8
1975 F	20.03	35.3	41.1	12.8	33.2
1976 F	20.17	36.2	43.2	14.1	35.7

Source: See References, "Statistical Sources."
Note: S = spring, F = fall.
[a] Only teachers.
[b] Only health.

percentage of the labor force that worked part-time had remained the same as in 1969. This calculation shows a growth of 43,300 persons in the public sector from 1969–1976 arising from the increasing propensity to part-time work—in other words, it shows that 18.2% of the growth in public sector employment is caused by that higher propensity to part-time work. The second calculation transforms the number of employees to full-time equivalents, and adjusts for the increasing unemployment among those whose last job was in the public sector and who are encountered in the public sector labor force. The latter group totaled 11,000 in 1976. Unfortunately, no statistics exist on the total number of part-time workers in the public sector prior to 1970, but it is possible to make an estimate for the years 1950–1970 based on the increase in the propensity of all married women in the labor force to work part-time and on the number of married women employed in the public sector. Following the practice of the Danish Statistical Bureau, it is further assumed that part-time workers, on average, work half a normal working day. The results of this calculation are shown in Table 2. It appears that there is a substantial difference between the growth rates in numbers of persons and in full-time equivalents, especially around 1970. On average, the staff in 1976 has .82 full-time employment compared to 1.0 in 1950–1955.

Another change over the period has been a steady decrease in number of hours worked daily. If we ignore growth in productivity per hour because of decreasing number of hours worked per year, we can calculate how much new staff is necessary to maintain the same level of service, defined as hours worked. The result shows that hours worked per full-time employee have decreased by 25.3% between 1950 and 1976.

Table 2

The Demand for Persons and Full-Time Equivalents in the Public Sector, 1950–1976[a]

	Persons		Full-Time Equivalents		Hours Worked	
	Number	*Annual Growth*	*Number*	*Annual Growth*	*Number (1000s)*	*Annual Growth*
1950	165,559		165,348		385,592	
		4.5%		4.3%		3.8%
1955	206,300		203,765		465,399	
		2.7		2.4		1.1
1960	235,716		228,943		491,541	
		5.3		4.7		3.7
1965	304,468		287,880		589,866	
		6.5		5.0		4.6
1970	416,172		367,332		737,603	
		—		—		—
1970[b]	440,800		398,150		799,485	
		7.1		5.8		4.9
1972	540,379		458,764		900,554	
		3.9		3.1		1.7
1976	630,042		517,523		963,110	
1950–76		5.27		4.49		3.58

Source: See References, "Statistical Sources."
[a] Excluding public transport, telecommunications, and unemployment.
[b] In this and the following years the data from the employment surveys are used.

The combined effect of a higher percentage engaged in part-time work and the general shortening of the working day (partly in the form of longer vacations) is that the growth rate in number of hours worked is two-thirds of the growth in number of employees.

If there were no increases in production per hour worked, the growth rates in the last column of Table 2 would describe the growth in the production of public sector goods and services. Because that premise is not realistic, these growth rates must be taken as a minimum expression for the growth in the public sector. Additionally, the growth rate between 1950–1976 is very near the growth rate of GNP in the same period. Similar relations will be discussed later.

The Supply of Labor

The other side of growth in the public sector is the source of the necessary labor input and how this has affected the public share of the labor force.

Sources for labor supply, 1921–1976. The primary source of supply to the total labor market has obviously been the demographically determined growth in groups fit for work. But for women, the main sources have been shifts away from homemaking and from occupations such as housemaid or other domestic service. (These groups are not generally considered as belonging to the labor market.) At its highest point in 1930, this group numbered 211,000, as much as 70% of the women who were in the labor market. (Assisting wives are not included in the labor market in this study.) In 1970, there were only 20,000 left in this group. Among married women, only 14,966 were in the labor market in 1921. In 1976 the number was 583,000, and more than half of these were employed in the public sector.

The public share of the new supply of workers. The public sector has throughout the period employed an increasing fraction of the new supply of workers to the labor market. Since the mid fifties the dominant demand for

Figure 2. The Ratio of Public Employees to the Total Labor Force, 1921–1976

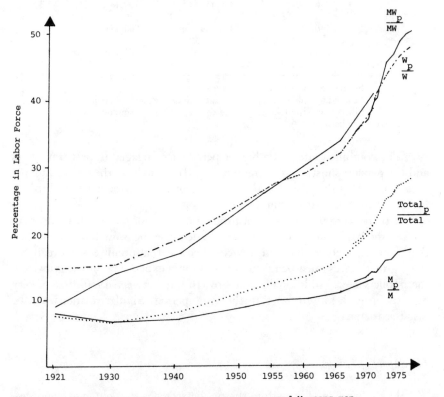

Note: MW means married women; W means women, and M means men.
Subscript p means public employees.

the labor of married women has come from the public sector. For men and unmarried women, the dominance of the public sector occurred first in the late sixties, when public demand often was so strong that there was a net shift from private to public employment. There are several reasons for the employment of married women above all in the public sector:

1. The public sector has many jobs that require no special skills. Census data from 1970 show that 32.9% of married women in the public sector were unskilled workers, whereas the figure within other service trades was 9.1%.

2. A high fraction (about one-half) of the increase of married women in the public sector has occurred in the health and welfare subsector, which traditionally has many jobs for women. Furthermore, the necessary condition for attracting married women to the labor market has presumably been that the public sector assumed the burden of caring for children and the elderly by providing day care for children and various kinds of assistance and housing for the elderly. Both these preconditions meant further demand for women.

3. The public sector has been able to offer part-time work (for example, 4 to 6 hours per day) and has attracted a great number of married women who previously might have left the labor market, after having had their first child, to become homemakers.

The result of this pattern in demand and supply is that the public sector (including public transport and telecommunications) in 1976 employed about 50% of all married women in the labor force and 28.25% of the total labor force. (See Figure 2.)

Models Describing the Growth of the Public Sector

In the preceding sections we have attempted to describe and analyze the growth in the Danish public sector, measured by the number of employees. The explanations have clearly been ad hoc. Here we investigate the extent to which a more general approach can be employed to describe the growth of the Danish public sector. Earlier, we noted the traditional view, that the nature of demand for publicly provided goods does not differ from the demand for private goods, and that the basic results from consumer theory are also valid for publicly provided goods and services. Most important is that the elasticity of (compensated) price changes of publicly provided goods is negative, and that the demand function "is zero" in all prices and income.

According to this view, the mechanisms of collective choice, for instance politicians, are considered as doing only what the consumers want them to do. This is probably a very crude assumption. Given that politicians are elected for a period of 3 to 4 years, that they have personal preference functions which might differ from those of their constituencies, and that consumers do not have full information, it seems likely that politicians have substantial latitude in deciding the size of the public sector. Add to this the role of government in pursuing countercyclical policy and the fact that public employees themselves may be able to pursue their own aims by influencing voters and politicians because of their allegedly higher information level. (See, for example, Courant et al., 1979; Borcherding, 1977; and Dich, 1973.)

In this study we shall, however, concentrate on the economic models for growth in the public sector. We attempt to see how well a demand model of the type that previously has been utilized to describe cross-sectional data can describe time-series data.

The Model

Assume that labor is the only input factor in public production and that production in the public sector is given by the production function

$$X = aLe^{\pi t}, \tag{1}$$

where X is the output of the public sector, L is the labor utilized and π the rate of productivity growth in the public sector, t is time, and a is a constant.

Further, assume that the demand for public sector services is given by the constant elasticity of demand function

$$\frac{X}{N^\alpha} = K \left(\frac{P_{pub}}{P_{priv}} \right)^\eta \left(\frac{Y_r}{N} \right)^\delta, \tag{2}$$

where α is a crowding parameter, N the size of the population, K a constant, P_{pub}/P_{priv} the relative price of public goods to private goods, Y_r the real income, and η and δ the demand and income elasticities of public prices and real income. α is defined in the range $(0,1)$: if X is a private good, α takes the value 1; and if X is a pure public good, α takes the value 0.

Taking the logarithms of (2), we get

$$\ln X = K_1 + (\alpha - \delta) \ln N + \eta \ln \left(\frac{P_2}{P_1} \right) + \delta \ln Y_r, \tag{3}$$

where $K_1 = \ln K$.

By using (1), (3) can be changed to

$$\ln L = K_2 + (\alpha - \delta) \ln N + \eta \ln \left(\frac{P_{pub}}{P_{priv}} \right) + \delta \ln Y_r - \pi t, \tag{4}$$

where $K_2 = K_1 - \ln a$.

This equation will now be estimated on the data series described above and on data which are available upon request from the author.

It is, however, obvious that the data series have several shortcomings when it comes to the specification and estimation of the demand function (4). First, no data exist on productivity growth in the public sector, and second, the data series are highly multicollinear. Neither of these is, however, unique to this study; both can be found in other studies (for example, Deacon, 1978; Norstrand, 1976).

Estimation

Various specifications of the relation in (4) have been estimated. A typical result looks like

$$\ln L = -10.82 + .51 \ln Y_r + 2.68 \ln N + .22 D_{69} + \epsilon, \tag{5}$$
$$(-1.87) \quad (1.78) \quad\quad (2.50) \quad\quad (2.70)$$

where ϵ is $N(0,\epsilon)$, R^2 (adjusted for degrees of freedom) $= .99$, and Durbin Watson statistics $V = 1.44$. T-statistics in parentheses. A dummy variable, D_{69}, is included to pick up the shift in data in 1969.

The coefficient to N is here α, which has been calculated from $\alpha - \delta$. It is found that the income elasticity is reasonably close to the findings of other authors (Borcherding and Deacon, 1972; Bergstrom and Goodman, 1973; Pommerehne, 1978; and Norstrand, 1976). The α coefficient is found to be far above the defined range. Conceivably, there is an overall trend in the size of public sector development which is related to the size of the population. The relative price has also been used as an explanatory variable. The estimated sign appears to be positive, in contrast to the predicted sign. This suggests that we are dealing with the supply curve, not the demand curve, and indicates that the necessary number of employees has to some degree been forthcoming as a response to increasing salaries. An alternative explanation is that the price factor measures change in quality and that consumers or politicians demand at the same time both high quality and greater quantity.

So far the results have not supported the crude consumption analogy in any convincing way. We shall, therefore, allow for changes in tastes and other similar things that might influence the consumption function. To get around the problems with α we shall keep α constantly equal to 1. The most simple equation now becomes

$$\ln \left(\frac{L}{N} \right) = 2.65 + 1.14 \ln \frac{Y_r}{N} + .13 D_{69} + \epsilon, \tag{6}$$
$$(29.69) \quad (11.30) \quad\quad (1.58)$$

with R^2 (adjusted for degrees of freedom) $= .97$ and DW $= 1.85$.

An extended version includes the average unemployment rate over the last 5 years, and the number of married women in the labor force:

$$\ln \left(\frac{L}{N} \right) = \underset{(21.61)}{2.65} + \underset{(5.77)}{.87} \ln \frac{Y_r}{N} + \underset{(2.75)}{.23 D_{69}} + \underset{(1.12)}{.06 U} \tag{7}$$

$$+ \underset{(2.38)}{.02 MW} + \epsilon,$$

where R^2 (adjusted for degrees of freedom) $= .98$ and DW $= 2.28$.

This suggests that in periods with higher unemployment politicians have increased public employment more than in periods with less unemployment. The relation between the growth of public employment and the number of married women in the labor force may be explained via the increasing need for care for children and the elderly that arises when married women join the labor force.

Several other plausible factors were unsuccessfully tried in the regression. One was the dependency ratio—the ratio of those below 16 years of age and those above 65 years of age to the total population. This ratio should reflect changes in the group that consumes most of the production of the education and the welfare sectors. Neither this ratio nor the absolute number gave any reasonable statistical explanation. Finally, the number of taxpayers was incorporated, but also without success.

The main problem with the above regressions is the high degree of multicollinearity, which means that the estimates unfortunately are unreliable although unbiased. Although the multicollinearity problem is serious, it is not different from that which occurs in other similar studies. One way of dealing with the problem would be to estimate the model on first differences, but the number of observations does not favor such a regression.

Summary and Conclusions

The growth in public sector employment is related both to the changing role of women in the labor force and to the increasing number of married women who now remain in the labor force. Thus, a substantial part of the public sector is occupied in taking care of children and the elderly, tasks which were earlier to some extent done within the household and, in particularly, by housewives. Part of the growth in the public sector consists, therefore, of moving activities from the household, where by convention they did not count in the National Income Statistics, into the public sector, where they do count.

The public sector itself is shown to have attracted the necessary labor force by offering part-time jobs to married women who otherwise would have left the labor force; 38% of the public labor force in 1976 was working part-time.

To obtain a more general view of the growth of the Danish public sector, a demand-type model was estimated using data for that sector. In an attempt to incorporate the above findings in the estimations, it was found that the change of tastes involved in the increasing number of two-earner families, as measured by the number of married women in the labor force, has indeed influenced the size of the public sector with a positive coefficient.

Finally, we have investigated the role of unemployment. The results suggest that the politicians have exercised some latitude in using the public sector to achieve countercyclical policy.

(Note: Data used in the regressions are available from author.)

References

Bergstrom, T. C. and R. P. Goodman. "Private Demands for Public Goods," *American Economic Review*, 63 (1973):280–296.

Borcherding, T. E. and R. T. Deacon. "The Demand for the Services of Non-federal Governments," *American Economic Review*, 62 (1972):891–901.

Borcherding, T. E. (ed.). *Budgets and Bureaucrats*. Duke University Press, Durham 1977.

Courant, P. N., E. M. Gramlich, and D. L. Rubinfeld. "Public Employee Market Power and the Level of Government Spending," *American Economic Review*, 69 (1979):806–817.

Deacon, R. T. "A Demand Model for the Local Public Sector," *Review of Economics and Statistics*, 60 (1978):184–192.

Dich, J. S. *Den Herskende Klasse*. Gyldendal, Copenhagen, 1973.

Norstrand, R. "Prognoser for Offentlige Udgifter." University of Copenhagen, Institute of Economics, Memo No 48, 1976.

Pommerehne, W. W. "Institutional Approaches to Public Expenditure," *Journal of Public Economics*, 9 (1978):255–280.

Westergaard-Nielsen, N. C. "The Demand for Labor in the Public Sector" (in Danish with English summary), in I. Henriksen et al., *The Unemployment Surveys 1*. Danish National Institute of Social Research, Publication No. 91, Copenhagen, 1979a.

Statistical Sources

Statistical Yearbooks. 1967–1978, Danmarks Statistik (The Danish Statistical Bureau).

Hansen, S. A. *(Okonomisk Vaekst i Danmark*. Bind II. Akademisk Forlag, Copenhagen, 1974.

Westergaard-Nielsen, N. C. "Den Offentlige Sektors Arbejdsstyrke 1921–1976," in *Vaekst og Kriser i Dansk Okonomi*. Institute of Economics, University of Aarhus, Aarhus, 1979b.

Résumé

L'une des principales caractéristiques de la croissance économique d'après-guerre dans la plupart des pays de l'ouest est la croissance continue de la taille relative du secteur public, en ce qui concerne à la fois la part du PNB et la part de la force de travail employées dans le secteur public. En dépit des similarités nationales, à ce jour, on a fait très peu d'études longitudinales de la croissance de l'emploi public basées sur des statistiques nationales ou internationales. Cette étude va essayer d'y remédier pour le Danemark à partir de 1921, en considérant surtout la forte croissance de la demande et la source première d'offre, constituée par le travail à temps partiel des femmes mariées.

Dans cette étude, nous utilisons un modèle de demande pour décrire les données danoises des séries temporelles de l'emploi public. Nous trouvons qu'un modèle, qui comprend le revenu par tête et la participation à la force de travail des femmes mariées, donne une assez bonne description du développement du secteur public danois. Nous trouvons aussi qu'une politique contra-cyclique semble jouer un rôle important dans la détermination de la part publique de la force de travail à différentes époques.

Manpower Demand in the Public Sector:
A Sectoral Approach

Hans de Groot
Jozef M.M. Ritzen

1. Introduction

In the short- and medium-term, full employment in the traditional sense is not considered feasible in the Netherlands, as in many other industrialized countries, given the effect of institutional limitations which the minimum wage and the social security system place on the flexibility of labour prices and the mobility of labour. As a result political pressure is mounting to expand the public sector in order to confine unemployment. This pressure is closely related to what often seems to be the ideology of "unfulfilled needs":[1] In modern industrial society many needs remain unfulfilled by market production and are as yet not satisfied by the present state of public production.

Against this background, the study reported in this paper has been undertaken. It presents an exploration of past and future employment in the public sector. The approach can be compared with other attempts to reveal the structure of the demand for public services (e.g., the papers of Pommerehne and Schneider, Gramlich, and Westergard-Nielsen, included in this volume; for a review, see Borcherding, 1977). However, instead of the usual assumption of a general demand function, we specify a collective welfare function for different age groups of the population which benefit from different public services and for private commodities. Maximization of the welfare function with national income as the boundary constraint produces demand equations. Time-series of expenditure and data on the population can

---

[1] The concept of "need" is not an economic one according to Williams (1978, p. 32), "A need exists so long as the marginal productivity of some treatment input is positive. Only when the efficacy of treatment has become zero at the margin does need disappear. People may still be sick, but since there is nothing we can do for them, the implication is that they are not in need." In other words "need" is interpreted to indicate that certain services can be advantageous to someone. But advantageous is not an objective concept. Symbolical treatment can be advantageous as well. The concept of need then is no more than an indication of a positive marginal utility for certain goods.

Public Finance and Public Employment. Proceedings of the 36th Congress of the International Institute of Public Finance. Jerusalem, 1980.

be used to estimate revealed preferences. With some additional assumptions on population and preference changes, estimates of future public consumption and public employment can be derived.

The limitations of the approach are connected with the interpretation of the collective welfare function.

The latter embodies the effects of the bureaucratic decision making process which is not however considered explicitly.[2] Also the static character of the welfare optimization approach with a given national income forms a limitation. Present research by the authors is concerned with a dynamic approach.

2.   Trends in Public Sector Employment in the Netherlands

The term public sector is used in many different ways. Musgrave (1978, p. 8) refers to it as "the provision of public services which are made available free of charge and financed by tax (or loan) revenue", adding that these services have been the classical concern of the theory of public finance. In such a definition at least two types of Government activity are excluded from the public sector, i.e., public enterprise and public regulation. When considering public sector *employment* this definition is both too wide and too narrow, since the term "services" is not understood in the sense of a final product, but rather in a financial sense. The subsidy of health services is considered a service, not the final product of the health service itself. An income transfer is a service, yet it only creates the basis for the purchase of final products. Our definition of public services is focussed on the consumption-side. Hence, income transfers are excluded but services which are partly subsidized are included. This definition is based on our preoccupation with employment. Employment in subsidized activities can be controlled to a considerable degree by public decisions. For the purpose of this paper, those activities should be included in the public sector. The tertiary sector of the economy is then split up into a tertiary sector *sec* and a quaternary or public sector in which all economic activities are financed to a large extent (at least 50%) by tax (or loan) revenue or social security premiums.[3] Moreover, the budgetary provision should be structural, that is, lasting for an indefinite period to exclude, for example, economic activities in the industrial sector which receive government subsidies for investments or incidental sub-

[2]Dr. C. B. Blankart gave helpful suggestions for incorporating the median voter analysis in our approach.

[3]The term quaternary sector will not be used in this paper since it has been used by others in a different sense. Lengellé (1966, p. 48) uses the term to indicate general government services (including military personnel) which do not have any direct relation to the agricultural, industrial or service sector. For a general analysis, see Wolfe (1955).

sidies to industries which run a deficit. As a result of this definition of the public sector, a public enterprise, the National Railways—like all public personal transport—has been included in the public sector insofar as it concerns the transport of persons, since it is allowed to run structurally with a considerable deficit. All other public enterprises are excluded because they usually break-even. The fact that they are owned by the public is not relevant in our delineation: Public ownership should not be confused with public provision or public steering of private provision (as proxied by at least a 50% public participation in the expenditure).

Public sector employment is a derivative of the size of public sector production. There are many ways to explore the rate of growth of the public sector. Nominal expenditure per capita is of little relevance because it is influenced by such factors as the growth of Net National Income (NNI), population, and inflation. The share of NNI accounted for by public expenditure is neutral with respect to these factors. It presents an ex-post measure of the distribution of NNI. In Table 1 the development of government and social security expenditure for the public sector is presented as a percentage of NNI. Compatible figures for direct private expenditure for public services are not available.

The table shows that by comparison with other public expenditure, such as transfers, the average income elasticity—calculated on the assumption of a zero price elasticity—of expenditure for the public sector in the period 1963–1979 is low. It should be noted, however, that net capital formation is included in this expenditure, which showed a decrease from 4.8% of NNI in 1963 to 2.8% in 1979.

An alternative measure of the growth of the public sector is the development of the ratio of public sector production to private sector production. For a correct insight into the percentage of private sector production to be surrendered, *net* expenditure for the public sector should be used, that is, gross expenditure minus the income tax paid by public sector employees and the indirect taxes on material public sector purchases or on public sector services rendered. Skolka (1977) has emphasized this and the Dutch Socio-Economic Council has put it into practice in its reports (Sociaal Economische Raad, 1979). Application of this indicator, however, renders the same conclusions as derived from Table 1.

Now we turn to employment. In Table 2 the development in the period 1969–1977 is presented. The table shows that the ratio of public to private sector employment increased monotonously in the period under observation by 3.7% annually on the average,[4] while labour productivity in the private sector increased annually by about 4%. The explanation of the shift from

[4]Note that the traditional definition of public employment—general government and defense—comprises only 40% of the public sector as defined here.

Table 1

Public Sector Expenditures as a Percentage of NNI Compared to Other Government Expenditure

Type of Expenditure	Year							Average Income Elasticity[a]			
	1963	1971	1976	1977	1978	1979	1963–1971	1971–1976	1976–1979	1963–1979
Expenditures for the public sector (material and personnel)	23.9	28.2	30.5	30.4	30.6	30.8	1.17	1.12	1.04	1.14
Transfers to households[b]	11.1	15.6	20.7	21.0	22.0	22.5	1.35	1.45	1.35	1.37
Other expenditure[c]	7.6	9.4	11.0	11.0	11.4	12.9	1.22	1.25	1.68	1.29
Total	42.6	53.2	62.2	62.4	66.2	66.2	1.23	1.25	1.26	1.24
Rate of growth of NNI	5.3	3.2	5.1	2.5	2.5	2.5				

Source: Sociaal-Economische Raad, 1979.

[a] Calculated on the assumption of a zero price elasticity.

[b] Includes family-allowances, scholarships, rent-relief, etc.

[c] Includes commodity-subsidies, capital transfers to firms, transfers abroad, interest on government debt and financing expenditures.

Table 2

Employment in Public[a] and Private Sector, 1969–1977

Year	Employment Percentages					Average Annual Growth Rate		
Total	1969	1971	1973	1975	1977	1969–1973	1973–1977	1969–1977
	100	100	100	100	100	0.2	−0.2	0
Private	80	79	78	76	75	−0.5	−1.1	−0.8
Public	20	21	22	24	25	+3.1	+2.6	+2.8
Total public	100	100	100	100	100	3.1	2.6	2.8
Medical services	19	20	21	22	22	5.5	3.9	4.7
Culture and recreation	3	3	3	3	4	3.9	4.0	4.0
Education	18	19	19	20	20	4.2	3.7	4.0
General government and defense	41	40	38	37	37	1.1	1.7	1.4
Other services[b]	19	18	19	18	17	3.4	1.4	2.4

Sources: Central Bureau of Statistics, Statistical bulletins 78 (1974), 60 (1976), 58 (1979).
[a] Excluding public transport.
[b] Estimate.

private to public employment must be sought in the production technology and the demand structure. The production technology of economic activities within the public sector has had little attention in the literature on production functions.[5] A major contribution in this respect has been Baumol's anatomy (1967) of the service sector and Fuchs's general analysis (1968) of the production characteristics of that sector. Baumol suggests that economic activities can be considered in two groups: service activities with a low rate of growth of productivity, and other activities with a high rate. In the high growth sector, innovations, capital accumulation and economies of scale yield an increase in output per worker. Because of its high service content, the public sector may show little or no technological progressivity. Considering the private sector as the high productivity sector a constant ratio of production of both sectors implies a growing ratio of public to private employment at the rate of the difference in productivity between both sectors. The empirical observations are then consistent with a low or zero productivity increase in the public sector. Only if one assumes an increasing volume of public sector production relative to private production could the results be consistent with a productivity increase in the public sector.

To test the assumptions regarding public sector productivity, measurement of the product of the public sector is required. Two different approaches can be followed. One approach consistent with the measurement of the product of the private sector measures the services performed in terms of the units offered to the consumer. An alternative and more sophisticated approach is based on the *effects* the services have on individuals; for example, the provision of health services is not an end in itself but is undertaken to improve people's health, whether measured by life expectancy, the expectation of years in good health, or otherwise. The "product" of the first approach becomes an intermediate good in the second approach. The second approach, although elegant at first sight, need not necessarily be followed within the context of public sector employment where optimality in the provision of services is assumed. Its practicability is limited. The approach assumes a utility-maximizing indiviudal for whom the arguments of the utility function are private sector quantities and "final products" of the public sector, such as improved health, acquired skills, justice, or peace achieved. The individual is faced with a (for each individual possibly different) set of production functions by which intermediate outputs, like years of education or health consultancies, are transformed into final products.[6]

---

[5]Considerable literature exists on production functions in education (see, e.g., Cohn, 1975; Bowles, 1970). The product to which these functions refer—achievement or attitudes—is not marketed as such and therefore not a product in the same sense as product in the private sector.

[6]Mathematically this can be represented as follows:
The individual utility function is
$$U = U (q_1 , q_2'),$$
where q_1 represents private sector commodities and q_2' final products of the public sector, so

First, the possibilities for measurement of the final products of the public sector are limited. At best ordinal scales can be constructed with agreeable properties for their measurement. The ordinality of the scale is a major hindrance for any statistical estimation of the production function. Second, we have learned from econometric evidence on these production functions that indeed the production functions differ between individuals because of personal characteristics (e.g., age in assessing the effects of healthcare, and family background, which is important in educational production functions). Also, we have learned that other factors such as time spent in study (for education), or general living habits (for health), are at least as important in the production of the final products as the purchased inputs. Third, we must ask ourselves whether production functions which are internalized should explicitly be considered in studies where the *effects* of services rendered are not of central concern. Why not leave it to the individual to value the intermediate outputs directly in the utility function, summarizing the valuation of the final product and the assessment of the production function thereof?[7] In this way a study of employment in the public sector can limit itself to the use of intermediate products, like the number of children in school or the number of consultancies.

Productivity is then simply described in terms of personnel (manpower) and services rendered (in volume) with average productivity as the ratio between services rendered and manpower involved in that process. The limitations of the approach are apparent since the quality of the services is not taken into account.

In most subsectors it is possible to relate productivity to crude indicators of the services rendered, such as the number of pupils, patients, clients, visits. This has been done for about twenty subsectors of the public sector, comprising about 80% of total employment. Details can be found elsewhere (Sociaal en Cultureel Planbureau/Centraal Planbureau, 1980). It turns out that only 40% of the employment growth of the Dutch public sector in the mid-seventies can be attributed to the growth of the services rendered.

3. Public Sector Employment and Collective Preferences

The size and composition of the public sector can be considered to be the result of a collective decision making process. Collective preferences are

---

that
$$q_2' = f(q_2),$$
where q_2 denotes the intermediate products of the public sector.
    [7]In terms of note 6, insert the production function for q_2 in the utility function
$$U = U(q_1, f(q_2))$$
and rearrange
$$U = U'(q_1, q_2).$$

formed in a complicated process in which individual preferences of citizens are weighted in the democratic process, but where the preferences of the government bureaucracy and pressure groups like trade-unions and professional organizations are also included. In this analysis, we assume that the government maximizes a collective welfare function with national income as a boundary constraint.[8] Dynamic interactions between the collective choices for public versus private consumption are ignored in this analysis: National income is considered to be exogeneous. In reality, the boundary constraint of national income itself is, over time, influenced by the decisions concerning the distribution of national income over public and private sectors of the economy. Roughly speaking, a higher preference for private versus public sector consumption implies higher growth rates of national income and vice versa, due to the difference in productivity, if one ignores the possible contribution of the public sector to growth.

The assumptions concerning the demand structure can be summarized as follows:
—Collective welfare is the sum of the logarithms of individual welfare
—Individual welfare functions are of the Cobb-Douglas type
—Within the age groups (0–19, 20–64, and 65 years and older) individual welfare functions are considered to be the same for all individuals
—Preferences are not only considered to cut across different goods but also across groups of consumers distinguished by age (0–19, 20–64, and 65 years and older)

With these assumptions one can derive relative preferences by type of public sector consumption, as is shown in the Appendix. The distinction of preferences by age group is motivated by the fact that many public goods have age-specific allocations: For instance, most educational services are provided for the younger part of the population, homes for the elderly are provided for the aged.

With data on the period 1969–1977, relative preferences have been calculated for the following types of public sector consumption by means of the measures indicated:
—Hospitals (excluding mental hospitals)—consumption is measured by the number of patient-days by age-group
—Nursing homes—all expenditures are assigned to the 65+ group in view of the age-distribution of the patients
—Home-help services—the hours of home-help provided for families and for the aged are used to assign expenditures to the 20–64, and 65+ group respectively

---

[8]A comparable approach has been used to study the economic evaluation of the quality of the physical environment (see Nijkamp and Paelinck, 1973). The extraction of implicit government preferences in economic policy follows similar lines (see Ancot and Hughes Hallett, 1978; Friedlaender, 1973).

—Homes for the aged—expenditures are assigned to the 65+ group
—Primary and secondary education—expenditures are assigned to the 0-19 group

For other services, no specific age-group can be considered as the "target-group." Therefore, consumption is assigned to the whole population as "other consumption in the public sector." Private consumption is used as the numeraire. Private goods and services are not differentiated in view of the focus of this analysis on the public sector.[9] In Table 3, the relative preference coefficients obtained for the goods and services mentioned above are listed for 1969 and 1977 by "commodity" and age group. The coefficient for a particular commodity and age group is equal to the ratio of the per capita expenditure on that commodity of the age group and private consumption per capita of the total population. The relative preferences by age group are obtained by adding up over commodities. It appears that in the period 1969-1977 the relative preferences for all public services and age groups considered here have become stronger. Also, a preference shift from the younger to the older target-groups is apparent. However, the data show that in the period 1975-1977 a small shift of relative preferences took place towards private goods, except for the public services provided for the elderly. This could be connected with the decreasing growth of the national income since 1973 and the government policy to restrict the increase of the share of government and social security expenditure in the national income.

The preference-drift might well be interpreted as an income elasticity and/or a price elasticity for public sector consumption greater than, respectively, one and minus one. The average price elasticity in the period 1969-1977 was about 0.1 if the income elasticity were one. Conversely, if the price elasticity were minus one the income elasticity would have been 1.8.[10] Multiple regression does not produce statistically significant results for income and price elasticities. The tentative conclusion is that the apparent range of the price elasticity is between—1 and 0.1 and that of the income elasticity between 1 and 1.8.

In this analysis, the productivity decrease in terms of services rendered per manyear mentioned earlier is implicitly considered as a quality improvement and not accounted for as a productivity decrease in terms of the volume index used here. Income transfers from government or social security funds to households are not included in this analysis. It is conceivable that the

[9]Private consumption as defined here contains fewer items than in the usual definitions in the National Accounts. This is a direct consequence of our broad definition of the public sector.

[10]The price index of public sector services used here is a weighted index of the wage index (weight 0.75) and the consumption price index (weight 0.25), assuming a constant ratio of labour and material inputs as in 1975. The volume of public services in terms of required inputs has been estimated by deflating nominal expenditure with the price index mentioned. The real price of public sector services is determined with respect to the price index of national income.

Table 3

Relative Preferences for Public Consumption Relative to Private Consumption by Target-Group ($\times 10^2$)

Year	Hospitals			Nursing Homes	Home-Help		Homes for the Aged	Education (prim./sec.)	Other Public Sector Goods	Total Public Consumption
	0–19	20–64	65+		20–64	65+				
1969	2.6	3.2	8.1	5.9	0.4	0.9	11.1	23.9	20.7	34.8
1977	3.0	4.6	13.9	13.4	0.8	3.2	18.3	29.9	23.9	43.1
Average annual increase (%)	1.5	4.7	7.0	10.9	8.5	18.2	6.4	2.8	1.8	2.7

Age Group	1969	1970	1971	1972	1973	1974	1975	1976	1977	Average Annual Increase (%)
0–19	47.2	48.3	50.8	52.3	52.3	55.5	58.0	57.4	56.7	2.3
20–64	24.3	25.3	26.7	27.2	27.1	28.5	29.3	29.1	29.2	2.3
65+	46.6	50.6	55.6	59.8	62.3	67.1	72.0	72.2	72.6	5.7
Total public consumption	34.8	36.1	38.3	39.4	39.6	41.9	43.7	43.3	43.1	2.7

Table 4

Development of Public Consumption
as Percentage of Total Consumption

	1977	1980	1985	1990	Average Annual Increase (%)
Fixed preferences	30.1	29.9	29.6	29.3	−0.2
Extrapolated preferences	30.1	32.3	34.6	36.8	1.6

increasing burden of income transfers on the government budget induces preference changes leading to decreasing expenditure on public services.

To gain insight into possible developments of public expenditure and employment in the future, the following two alternatives are considered:

1. Aggregate preferences by age-group are frozen at the level of 1977. The level of public expenditure is then determined by demographic changes and the level of total consumption.

2. Aggregate preferences by age-group are extrapolated using the "preference-drift" observed in the period 1969–1977.[11]

The population forecast of the Central Bureau of Statistics (alternative 2) is used. Total consumption as well as the national income is assumed to grow at a rate of 2% per year (constant prices). As in the revelation of preferences, national income is considered as exogenous and not influenced by the distribution of resources between the public and private sector, despite evidence to the contrary.

The results for the relative share of public sector consumption are given in Table 4. If relative preferences remain the same, a small decrease in the consumption of public services relative to total consumption results. This happens despite increased expenditures on the aged. However, decreasing expenditures on education compensate this increase. Extrapolated preferences produce a yearly increase in the share of public consumption somewhat smaller than the average increase in the period 1969–1977 (1.9%). This result may be an overestimation in view of the apparent shift of preferences in the 1975–1977 period in favor of private goods and services.

Future public employment depends on the absolute level of public expenditure and the ratio between expenditure and employment. The level of public consumption can be calculated from Table 4 and the assumptions on

[11]Since this drift could possibly also be explained by an income elasticity greater than one or a price elasticity greater than minus one, extrapolation of the preference-drift is equivalent to extrapolation of the growth of national income in a constant income elasticity (>1) − constant preference model.

Table 5

Development of Relevant Public Employment (man-years × 1000)

	1977	1980	1985	1990	Average Annual Increase (%)
Fixed preferences and wages	923	972	1062	1159	1.8
Fixed preferences, growing wages	923	917	908	898	−0.2
Extrapolated preferences, fixed wages	923	1050	1241	1456	3.6
Extrapolated preferences and wages	923	990	1061	1128	1.6

the growth of national income mentioned above. The ratio between expenditure and employment is determined by the ratio of wage to other expenditure on the one hand and the wage level on the other. Wage levels in the public sector follow private sector wages in the Netherlands. We consider two alternatives in Table 5: constant real wages, or wage levels following the assumed rate of growth of the national income. The ratio between wage and other expenditures is determined by the production structure. Let us assume that for public sector activities a Cobb-Douglas structure applies so that expenditure shares are constant, which is in fact close to reality. Only current expenditure is considered. From Table 5 we see that, except in the case of linearly extrapolated preferences and fixed real wages, the growth of public sector employment is considerably less in the eighties than in the seventies. The conclusion then is that only under rather unlikely conditions will employment in the public sector increase in the near future as it did in the seventies. A similar conclusion is suggested by a study of the future development of more than fifty services in the Dutch public sector, based on extrapolation of the volume of services per capita for relevant population groups and accounting for demographic changes (Sociaal en Cultureel Planbureau/Centraal Planbureau, 1980).

Derivation of Relative Preferences

The general form of the utility function of the members of age group j can be written as follows:

$$U_j = \prod_{\substack{i \in I \\ r \in J}} (q_{ir}/N_r)^{\alpha_{irj}} \tag{1}$$

in which q_{ir} is the total national consumption of commodity i by the age group r ($r \in J$), N_r is the number of potential consumers in group r, and α_{irj} is the preference-coefficient for average consumption of commodity i per head of group r for members of group j ($j \in J$). The demand structure inherent in this utility function is one of constant budget shares. The utility function exhibits collective elements since individuals of group j can have a non-zero preference for consumption by group r ($\alpha_{irj} \neq 0$ for $r \neq j$).

Total collective welfare is taken to be the weighted sum of the logarithms of individual welfare. The weights (β_{ij}) are specific by age group and commodity and can be considered as imposed by "paternalistic" decisionmakers in the allocation of public funds. The logarithmic addition is consistent with the Cobb-Douglas utility function, in which utility per good is logarithmically added up. The welfare function is then as follows:

$$W = \prod_{\substack{i \in I \\ j,r \in J}} (q_{ir}/N_r)^{\alpha_{irj}\beta_{ij}N_j}. \tag{2}$$

When excluding direct externalities ($\alpha_{irj} = \alpha_{ij}$ if $r=j$, $\alpha_{irj} = 0$ if $r \neq j$), but including paternalistic collective elements the welfare function is more simply written as

$$W = \prod_{\substack{i \in I \\ j \in J}} (q_{ir}/N_j)^{\gamma_{ij}N_j} \tag{3}$$

where $\gamma_{ij} = \beta_{ij}\alpha_{ij}$.

Maximization of the welfare function of Eq. (3) with the boundary constraint of total national consumption gives the following expression for the preference coefficient:

$$\frac{\gamma_{ij}}{\gamma_0} = \frac{p_i q_{ij}}{p_0 q_0} \bigg/ \left(\frac{N_j}{N} \right), \tag{4}$$

where the index o refers to private sector consumption taken as the numerary good, consumed by the population as a whole, and where p_i is the price of commodity i. The equation indicates, for example, that public sector consumption for an age group has to rise if the relative size of that group increases and relative preferences are kept constant. It also implies that—all other things remaining constant—quantities decline if relative prices increase.

References

Ancot, J. P. and Hughes Hallett, A. J. (1978) "A General Method for Estimating Revealed Preferences," Discussion paper 7817/G, Rotterdam, *Institute for Economic Research, Erasmus University.*

Baumol, W. J. (1967) "Macro-economics of Unbalanced Growth: The Anatomy of Urban Crisis," *American Economic Review*, 57 (3), pp. 415-428.
Borcherding, T. E. (1977) "The Sources of Growth of Public Expenditures in the United States, 1902-1970," In T. E. Borcherding (ed.) *Budgets and Bureaucrats: The Sources of Government Growth*, Durham, Duke University Press.
Bowles, S. S. (1970) "Towards an Educational Production Function," in W. L. Hansen (ed.) *Education, Income and Human Capital*. New York, NBER, Columbia University Press.
Cohn, E. (1975) *Input-output Analysis in Public Education*. Cambridge, Mass.: Ballinger Publishing Co.
Friedlaender, A. F. (1973) "Macro-policy Goals in the Postwar Period: A Study in Revealed Preference," *Quarterly Journal of Economics*, 87, pp. 25-43.
Fuchs, V. R. (1968) *The Service Economy*. New York: NBER/Columbia University Press.
Lengellé, M. (1966) *Le Revolution Tertiaire*. Paris, Génin.
Musgrave, R. A. (1978) "Growth of the Public Sector," in *The Future of Fiscal Policy: A Reassesment*. Leuven, Leuven University Press.
Nijkamp, T. and Paelinck, J. (1973) "Economic Evaluation of the Environment," *Regional and Urban Economics*, 3, (1), pp. 33-62.
Skolka, J. V. (1977) "Unbalanced Productivity Growth and the Growth of Public Services," *Journal of Public Economics*, 7 (2), pp. 415-528.
Sociaal en Cultureel Planbureau (1980), *Social and Cultural Report 1980*. Den Haag, Staatsuitgeverij.
Sociaal en Cultureel Planbureau/Centraal Planbureau (1980), *De Kwartaire Sector in de Jaren Tachtig*, Den Haag, Staatsuitgeverij.
Sociaal-Economische Raad (1979) *Advies inzake het sociaal-economische beleid op de middellange termijn*. Den Haag, Sociaal-Economische Raad.
Williams, A. (1978) "Need, an Economic Exegesis," in Culyer, A. J. and K. G. Wright, *Economic Aspects of Health Services*. London, Martin Robertson.
Wolfe, M. (1955) "The Concept of Economic Sectors," *Quarterly Journal of Economics*, p. 406.

Résumé

Cet article est consacré au développement de l'emploi dans le secteur public. Ce secteur public a été délimité de façon à comprendre toutes les activités économiques qui sont (a) par leur structure, c'est-à-dire, en principe, pour une période de temps indéterminée, autorisées à présenter un déficit d'au moins 50 % des dépenses et (b) pendant laquelle ces déficits sont couverts par des impôts, des primes de Sécurité Sociale ou des prêts publics. On interprète la croissance récente de l'emploi public par rapport à l'emploi privé selon le modèle de productivité différentielle de Baumol. On explore le développement possible de l'emploi public dans l'avenir d'une façon originale. On considère que l'attribution des services publics est basée sur une fonction de bien-être collectif appartenant au type Cobb-Douglas. On calcule les préférences révélées pour différents services à partir de données historiques. Pour étudier l'emploi dans l'avenir, nous utilisons 4 alternatives : 2 selon lesquelles les préférences sont fixées au niveau de 1977, et 2 où les séries temporelles de préférences sont extrapolées. Pour chacune des préférences, on suppose que les salaires du secteur public sont soit constants, soit suivent la croissance du revenu national réel. Les résultats suggèrent une croissance relativement modérée de l'emploi du secteur public dans l'avenir comparée aux années 70. Cela est dû à une décélération de la croissance de la population et à une diminution attendue de la croissance des préférences relatives pour les services publics.

6360, 8243
6140
8226
U.S.

Growth of the Nonprofit Sector: Implications for Public Employment and Public Finance

Burton A. Weisbrod*

I. Introduction

The size of the public sector has long interested economists and political scientists, and, indeed, politicians and citizens.[1] Employment in the public sector is one measure of this size. Although there are other dimensions in which size could be gauged, I want to focus not on the measurement of size but on the ambiguity of the concept of employment "in the public sector" and on the relationship between the public and the private nonprofit sectors.

If a person works for, and is paid by a governmental agency (case 1), that worker would be defined by most people as being employed in the public sector. Such a sharp distinction, however, between government employees and private-sector employees is not likely to be useful for most purposes. If, for example, a government agency were to write a check to a private firm for the expressed purpose of that firm's hiring someone to work for the government agency (case 2), we would probably not find it meaningful to call this "private-sector" employment, although customary usage does exactly that. In either case 1 or 2, government pays for the employment and the workers involved perform virtually the same tasks. An economics approach to the definition of "government" employment would suggest that close substitutes be recognized and, depending on the purpose at hand, either that they be encompassed in a single definition or that attention be directed to a broader concept of employment which encompasses governmental and "near-

*I thank Calla Wiemer for imaginative and perseverant research assistance, and the Ford Foundation, the National Science Foundation and the University of Wisconsin Institute for Research on Poverty for supporting various portions of my research on the nonprofit sector. Sheldon Danziger, Robert Haveman, David Merriman and Mark Schlesinger made helpful comments on an earlier draft.

[1]See, for example, articles by Bird (1971), and Peacock and Wiseman (1979) on the "Wagner's Law" literature. See also Ginzburg et al. (1965), and Hiestand (1977).

Public Finance and Public Employment. Proceedings of the 36th Congress of the International Institute of Public Finance. Jerusalem, 1980.

governmental," just as we have done with various measures of the "money supply."[2]

Close substitutes for government employment take still other forms. One involves employment in private firms that are either heavily subsidized by government (e.g., Lockheed or Chrysler—case 3) or that sell much or all of their output to government (e.g., a firm that collects garbage under contract with a municipal government, or a munitions producer that deals exclusively with a government military agency—case 4).

The distinction between governmental *production* of a commodity and governmental *finance* through nongovernmental enterprises can be illustrated for the case of research and development (R&D). Analysis of the flow of funds to R&D in the United States highlights the distinction between the source of funding of production and the sectoral locus of employment. In 1975, the United States federal government financed $18,160 million of R&D, but only $5,200 million—29 percent—of the funds were actually spent within the federal government (*Statistical Abstract of the United States*). Thus, assuming that the distribution of employment can be approximated by the distribution of expenditures, only some 29 percent of the employment to which the federal government's support of R&D gave rise actually occurred *in* the federal government. Half of the federal support led to employment in the private for-profit sector ("industry"). An additional 18 percent of the federal funds manifested themselves as employment in the private nonprofit sector ("universities and colleges" plus "other nonprofit institutions"), although some portion of that led to employment in universities and colleges that are governmental.

There are still other means available to government to affect the allocation of resources, including employment. Government can provide tax subsidies which, by reducing tax liabilities, encourage private provision of goods as an alternative to governmental provision (case 5). Government can also *regulate* the private sector (case 6), as it does, for example, in the environmental and occupational safety and health areas, where it requires (or precludes) adoption of particular usages of labor inputs.

A final example of close substitutes for public provision of goods and services is the subject of this paper. This involves activities in the private nonprofit sector (case 7). In earlier work I set forth and tested a model in which heterogeneous demands for public ("collective") goods led a demo-

---

[2]The division between "governmental" and other activities, and the conceptual problem of how to make the distinctions, is analytically similar to the well-known problems of defining an "industry" or an "occupation." A cross-elasticity of substitution either among outputs or inputs generally provides the conceptual foundation for drawing distinctions. Operationally, of course, determining which substitutes are close enough to be grouped and which are different enough to be distinguished is difficult. This is what is involved as we consider here the question of which employment should be regarded as governmental and which as nongovernmental, recognizing the kinds of borderline cases already referred to.

cratic government to provide less than the amounts wanted by the high demanders, and this "undersatisfied demand" gave rise to nonprofit sector provision (Weisbrod, 1975). The present paper, building on this foundation, attempts to show the extent to which recognition of employment in the nonprofit sector is relevant to a full understanding of the status of, and changes in, governmental employment. The connection between the two sectors is important for two reasons: First, there exists a variety of nongovernmental, private-sector firms—in the United States they are largely in the nonprofit sector, but in other countries they may have other designations and forms—that produce *close substitutes for governmental goods and services.*

Second, decisions by government can greatly affect the distribution of employment among sectors. Governmental decisions on whether to produce particular goods and services, to purchase them from nongovernmental firms, or to regulate, mandate, tax or subsidize private firms to produce them, can all achieve the same output results,[3] but the resulting distribution of employment among the government, the private proprietary (for-profit), and the private nonprofit sector can differ enormously. Thus, while the concept of governmental employment is subject to a variety of reasonable and useful interpretations, the narrow concept of persons "on a government payroll" is of limited value.

The private nonprofit sector's goods and services are often financed by government but even when financed by other sources they are often close substitutes for direct governmental provision in the areas of education, health, charity, scientific research and other social welfare activities.[4] Focusing on the nonprofit sector is designed to show that when we consider the activities of this sector we obtain a rather different impression of the size and growth rate of public employment.

II. The Nonprofit Sector and the Government

There are a number of industries that include both nonprofit firms and governmental organizations. Education, hospitals, nursing homes and charity are but a few examples of such industries. Previous research suggests that governmental and nonprofit organizations in these industries produce similar outputs.[5]

---

[3]Both the nature of what is produced and the techniques of production are encompassed by the references to the "goods and services" that are produced.

[4]In 1976, nonprofit organizations in the United States had aggregate revenues of $142 billion, of which 29 percent went to organizations operating in the area of education, 35 percent to organizations engaged in health activities, and 7 percent to welfare organizations. (Source: My calculations are from Internal Revenue Service tax forms, Form 990.)

[5]See, for example, Bendick (1978) on schools, and Lee and Weisbrod (1978) on hospitals.

In this section I assemble a variety of data intended to shed light on the importance of employment in the nonprofit sector relative to the governmental employment for which it is, in significant measure, a substitute. Regretably, employment data for the nonprofit sector are extremely scarce: Thus, I infer such data from a variety of types of incomplete data. I utilize data on revenues and assets, and on employment for particular industries as a basis for inferring aggregate employment in the nonprofit sector. No one form of the data described below presents a clear picture, but together they show the sizable and growing importance of nonprofit firms' activities and employment.

A.   Assets of Nonprofit Organizations—The National Income Accounts

Raymond Goldsmith has estimated the assets of nonprofit organizations annually for 1953 through 1975, using the U.S. national income accounts definition of that sector. Not all of the organizations included are providers of substitutes for governmental goods and services, but until more detailed data become available, Goldsmith's data can help to develop the picture of the nonprofit sector's importance. Assets of the nonprofit sector have grown at a more rapid rate than GNP, rising from 11.5 percent of GNP in 1953 to more than 15 percent by 1973, and from 1.5 percent to 1.8 percent of total national assets (Goldsmith, forthcoming, Table 53). Relative employment in the nonprofit sector is also likely to have increased in at least a roughly similar degree.

With the nonprofit sector contributing less than 2 percent of national assets, one might be tempted to dismiss the sector as inconsequential. That would be an error. The evidence that nonprofit organizations own 1.8 percent of U.S. assets takes on added importance when it is realized that the federal government "owned" 3.9 percent of U.S. assets at the end of 1975, and state and local governments owned some 8.5 percent more (p. 178). Thus, assets of the nonprofit sector equal 15 percent of all government assets in the U.S. and nearly 50 percent of those of the federal government.

While the nonprofit sector has been growing relative to the aggregate economy, the federal government has been declining. Controlling 7.5 percent of national assets in 1953, the federal government's share fell steadily and by 1975 it was 3.9 percent (p. 178). Even when the growing state-local government sector is considered, we still find that the assets of the aggregate federal-state-local governmental sector declined from 13.1 percent of national assets in 1953 to 12.4 percent in 1975, whereas the nonprofit sector's share was growing. If changes in employment are approximately proportional to changes in assets, the nonprofit sector's employment is growing relative to the economy as a whole, and it is already large compared to employment in the federal and state and local government sectors.

Table 1

Assets of Nonprofit and Proprietary Organizations,
United States, 1971–1975 (in billions)

| | *Assets* | | | |
| | *Nonprofit* | | *Proprietary* | |
Year	*Total*	*Tax Deductible*	*Corporations*	*Partnerships*
	(1)	(2)	(3)	(4)
1971	$127.1	$74.4	$2,889	$135.4
1972	136.7	87.4	3,257	176.9
1973	157.2	88.2	3,649	185.1
1974	176.3	98.6	4,016	283.4
1975	195.6	106.6	4,287	235.5

Sources: Columns 1, 2—Tabulated from IRS Form-990 data.
Column 3—*Statistical Abstract of the United States*, 1975,
p. 497; 1979, p. 563.
Column 4—Department of the Treasury, 1971, p. 153;
1972, p. 96; 1973, p. 200; 1974, p. 199; 1975, p. 310.

*B. Number and Assets of Nonprofit Organizations—Internal Revenue Service (IRS)
Tax Return Data*

Each organization that has tax-exempt, nonprofit status in the U.S. is required to file a tax return (unless it is a church with no "unrelated business income," or unless it has revenue under $5,000 in the given year—$10,000 beginning in 1977). Table 1, derived from the IRS tax files, shows not only the growth of assets of all nonprofit organizations (col. 1) but also the assets of the subset of those organizations for which donations are deductible on income tax returns (col. 2). The latter groups, judged to be providing services having a particularly large public-good component, are likely to provide particularly close substitutes for the collective-type (public) goods of the government sector. A comparison of the assets of the tax-deductible organizations with the assets of the private corporate and partnership sector of the economy (cols. 3 and 4) shows that these nonprofits have grown at essentially the same rate over the 1971–1975 period, the only years for which comparable data are available.[6]

Not only are the assets of the nonprofit sector growing rapidly, but the number of organizations is growing even faster, and this may be a harbinger

[6]The absolute level of assets in the nonprofit sector is larger according to Goldsmith's estimates than it is according to the IRS data, in Table 1—$243 billion vs. $196 billion for 1975. The principal reason may well be the exclusion from IRS data of most churches; another contributor to the discrepancy is the exclusion of all nonprofit organizations with less than $5,000 of revenue and disbursements.

of an accelerated growth rate of employment in the years ahead. Over the decade 1967–1976, the total number of nonprofit organizations (including nonfilers) increased from 309,000 to 763,000—by 118 percent—the number of proprietary corporations increased by 37 percent, and the number of partnerships and proprietorships increased by 24 percent (IRS, *Tax Commissioner's Annual Reports; Statistical Abstract of the United States*, 1973, Table 684, 1979, Table 509).

Between 1969 and 1978 the number of nonprofit organizations for which tax-deductible status was given went from 137,500 to 293,900—an increase of 114 percent (IRS *Tax Commissioner's Annual Reports*). These are the organizations whose public interest (collective-good) activities presumably gave rise to the special tax treatment. Thus, the associated increase in employment is likely to be a substitute for governmental employment. If employment in the nonprofit sector grew at even roughly the same rate as the increase in the number of organizations, the growth of that sector would have made direct governmental employment lower than it would otherwise have been. (During the decade 1969–1978 direct governmental employment increased by 23 percent, from 12.7 million to 15.6 million, full time plus part time—*Statistical Abstract of the United States*, 1973, Table 684; 1979, Table 509.)

C. Inferring Employment in the Nonprofit Sector from Revenue and Asset Data

Methodology employed in this section is as follows: Ratios of (1) employment to organizational revenue, and (2) employment to organizational assets are estimated for various sectors of the economy; then those ratios are used as multipliers of corresponding revenue and asset data for the nonprofit sector to obtain estimates of employment in the nonprofit sector. The ratios I have been able to estimate are in Table 2. Use of revenue data is dictated by its availability together with the belief that the level of employment of a firm or sector bears some reasonably consistent relationship to revenue.

If the nonprofit sector has the employment-revenue ratio of the economy as a whole, the sector's 1976 revenue of $143 billion[7] would imply full-time equivalent (FTE) employment of 7.9 million persons. If the nonprofit sector had the higher employment-revenue ratio of the service sector of the economy, this would imply nonprofit sector employment of 10.3 million. Either employment figure is at least 60 percent of the total federal, state and local government civilian FTE employment of 13.1 million in 1976, and two and a half times or more the level of federal government civilian employment, 2.8 million (Survey of Current Business, 1978, p. 55).

It is likely, however, that the nonprofit sector has a lower ratio of employment-to-revenue than does the service sector as a whole (7.19 employees per $100,000 revenue) and, thus, the 10.3 million figure is probably

[7]Tabulated from IRS Form - 990 data.

Table 2

Revenue, Assets, and Full-Time Equivalent Employment,
Various Economic Sectors, United States, 1976

Sector, Industry or Ownership Type	Ratio of Employment to Revenue (in hundreds of thousands of dollars/year)	Ratio of Employment to Assets (in hundreds of thousands of dollars)
	(1)	(2)
I. Economy as a whole	5.50	
II. Service sector	7.19	
III. Government enterprises	6.31	
IV. Health	6.33	
A. Hospitals		4.85
1. Government		5.92
2. Proprietary (for profit)		4.78
3. Nonprofit		4.38
B. Nursing Homes	9.29	
1. Government	9.42	
2. Proprietary	8.71	
3. Nonprofit	10.10	
V. Education	5.03	
1. Government	5.35	
2. Private (proprietary and nonprofit)	3.69	
VI. Social services	12.16	
VII. Legal services	11.22	
VIII. Art museums	5.73	
1. Government	5.91	
2. Nonprofit	5.41	

Sources for Table 2:
Rows I–IV: *Survey of Current Business*, 1978, pp. 53, 55.
Row IV-A: American Hospital Association, 1977, pp. 6–9.
Row IV-B: Calculated from data in *Wisconsin's Nursing Homes, Facility Characteristics.*
Row V: National Center for Education Statistics, 1977–1978, Table 16; Bendick, 1975, Table 2.5.
Rows VI–VII: *Survey of Current Business.*
Row VIII: *Statistical Abstract of the United States*, 1978, Table 409.

high. This tentative conclusion is generally consistent with the limited industry data available by ownership type, which is presented in Table 2.

Among hospitals (panel IV-A), the nonprofit sector has the lowest ratio of employment to assets—4.38 employees per $100,000 assets, compared with 4.78 in the proprietary sector and 5.92 in the government sector. Similarly, the nonprofit sector in art museums (panel VIII) has a lower ratio of employment to revenue. The data for schools (panel V) do not distinguish between nonprofit and private for-profit schools, but the private schools as a whole have a markedly lower ratio of employment to revenue than do the government schools. On the other hand, nursing homes (panel IV-B) display the opposite picture, the nonprofit sector having a higher ratio of employment to revenue than either the governmental or private for-profit sectors.

It is dangerous to generalize from this limited number of industries, although the nonprofit components of the hospital, education and nursing home industries are substantial. Nonetheless, given the paucity of employment data for the total nonprofit sector, I judge it probable that the nonprofit sector as a whole has fewer employees relative to revenue than does the service sector as a whole.

If the nonprofit sector had the lower employment intensity (i.e., ratio of employment to revenue) of government enterprises, 6.31 in 1976 (Table 2), then aggregate employment in the nonprofit sector would still have equalled 9.0 million—12 percent of the 1976 FTE labor force, 74.4 million.[8]

D. Volunteer Labor

If a count were taken of those members of the labor force who were employed in the nonprofit sector, it would result in a substantial under-enumeration of actual labor inputs. Volunteer labor—because it receives no explicit wage—is not included in labor force statistics; yet the bulk of this labor goes to the nonprofit sector and particularly to that component of the sector that is most closely substitutable for governmental employment. Thus, the analyst who is interested in public-sector employment and its close substitutes should recognize these forces.

In 1973, the latest year for which data on volunteer labor are available, about 6 billion hours of labor were volunteered in the United States with a market value of $29 billion (Morgan et al., 1976, p. 160). By 1976 the hours volunteered had a market value that could be estimated conservatively at $30 billion. If this imputed value of labor were added to the total explicit revenue of the sector, then the employment calculations in section C, above, would imply an additional 1.8 million FTE workers—about 20 percent of the total nonprofit sector employment of 9.0 million estimated above using the "government-enterprises" basis. Alternatively, if all the volunteer labor were donated directly to nonprofit organizations, the 6 billion hours would constitute some 3 million FTE workers each working 2000 hours per year. Using

[8]Substantial relative growth of employment in the nonprofit sector has been found by Hiestand (1977, Table 4). He reports, "based on data from the U.S. Department of Commerce and American Hospital Association" (but with no more precise information on the source or the estimation methodology), that employment in nonprofit institutions grew from 3.0 percent of FTE employment in 1950, to 4.3 percent in 1960, 5.5 percent in 1970, and to 5.9 percent in 1973.

Hiestand's data on the absolute level of employment in nonprofit institutions indicate, however, a lower level of total employment than we have estimated. For 1973, the latest year for which he presents an estimate, total FTE employment was reported to be 5.0 million, substantially less than the 9.0 million presented for 1976. Some growth doubtless occurred between 1973 and 1976, but the bulk of the discrepancy remains. The precise definition used by Hiestand of "nonprofit institutions" is not given; he may have used a narrower definition.

either calculation we conclude that attention solely to market labor leads to a significant understatement of total employment in the nonprofit sector.[9]

Not all volunteer labor goes to private nonprofit organizations, but even if it did, all of that labor would not substitute for governmental employment. A considerable portion of volunteer labor goes to churches, which have no governmental counterparts in the United States. According to the 1973 survey cited earlier, 43 percent of all volunteer time went to churches (Morgan *et al.*, Table 50).

A few words are in order about the relationship between the uncounted volunteer labor and the estimate of 9.0 million total employment in the nonprofit sector, as presented in section C, based on ratios of employment to revenue. It is not appropriate simply to add the quantity of volunteer labor to the quantity of labor inferred from the data on nonprofit sector revenue. If organizational outputs generate the revenue examined in section C, and given that inputs generate those outputs, then a given level of revenues implies a quantity of inputs. Only insofar as a person-hour of market labor and of volunteer labor are not perfect substitutes would the previous estimates of employment based on organizational revenue need to be corrected to account for volunteer labor. There are some reasons to believe that volunteer labor is inferior to market labor—for example, it is harder to discipline and organize—but in other respects it may be superior—for example, more dedicated to the organization's "cause."

E.   *Employment in the Public and Nonprofit Sectors in Selected Industries*

Industry data on employment by "ownership" sector are extremely limited. Some revealing data, however, are presented in Tables 3 and 4 for hospitals and schools in the United States.

The hospital industry provides a particularly powerful illustration of the incomplete picture of employment that one obtains by overlooking the private nonprofit sector. Indeed, the bulk of hospital employment is in the private nonprofit sector. Table 3 shows the growth of employment in governmental and private nonprofit hospitals between 1950 and 1977. Aggregate employment in nonprofit short-term hospitals has been relatively stable at approximately three times the level of employment in all state and local government hospitals, and approximately double the employment of all government hospitals, including federal.

---

[9]If, however, the market value of the time were donated, it is likely that less than all of it would be used to employ labor. As an approximation, my data suggest that about 60 percent would go to labor, for I estimated that the $30 billion of market revenue generated by the 3 million workers would, if given to nonprofits, generate some 1.9 million additional FTE employment, assuming the ratio of employment to revenue for government enterprises is 6.3.

Table 3

Full-Time Equivalent Employment
in Governmental, Private Nonprofit
and Proprietary Short-Term Hospitals,
U.S., 1950–1977 (in thousands)

| | *Type of Hospital* | | | |
| | | | *Governmental* | |
Year	*Private Nonprofit*	*Proprietary*	*State and Local*	*Federal**
	(1)	(2)	(3)	(4)
1950	473	41	148	169
1955	597	41	188	192
1960	792	48	241	186
1965	1,011	70	306	199
1970	1,387	97	444	216
1975	1,714	139	546	256
1977	1,863	159	559	278

Sources: Columns 1, 3, and 4—*Statistical Abstract of the United States*, 1975, Table 122; 1971, Table 173. Column 2—American Hospital Association, 1978, p. 6.

*Includes long-term, which constitute some 5 percent of the totals shown.

Table 4

Enrollments, Public and Nonpublic Schools, by Level of School,
U.S., 1930–1977[a] (in thousands)

Enrollments	*1930*	*1940*	*1950*	*1960*	*1970*	*1975*	*1977*
Grades 1–8							
Public	20,555	18,237	18,353	25,679	29,996	28,137	27,087
Nonpublic	2,255	2,096	2,575	4,286	4,100	3,700	3,400
Grades 9–12							
Public	4,399	6,601	5,725	8,485	13,022	14,132	14,310
Nonpublic	341	458	672	1,035	1,400	1,400	1,400
Higher Education							
Publicly controlled	533	797	1,355	1,832	5,112	6,838	7,275
Privately controlled	568	698	1,304	1,384	2,024	2,185	2,314
Expenditures (% of GNP)							
All Schools[b]							
Public	2.1	3.0	2.7	4.0	6.1	6.4	6.0
Private	0.4	0.5	0.7	1.1	1.4	1.5	1.3

Source: *Statistical Abstract of the United States*, 1975, Tables 175 and 176; 1979, Tables 213 and 214.

[a] Prior to 1960, excludes Alaska and Hawaii.

[b] Includes kindergarten and a variety of quantitatively-small types of schools not included elsewhere in this table.

Turning to the education sector, we see in Table 4 the quantitative importance of the private sector, the vast bulk of which consists of nonprofit organizations.[10] While not a *perfect* substitute for governmentally-provided education, private education is surely somewhat substitutable.

The top panel of Table 4 portrays enrollments rather than employment. Assuming, however, that the ratios of employment to enrollments are not greatly different,[11] the table suggests that total employment in the nonprofit sector (for which the "nonpublic" sector is a proxy) is about 13 percent as great as governmental employment for grades 1–8, about 10 percent as great for grades 9–12, and 30 percent for higher education.

The bottom panel of table 4 shows the growth of schools in terms of expenditures as a percentage of GNP. Between 1930 and 1977 the share of GNP taken by education tripled from 2.5 percent to 7.3 percent; the relative size of the public and nonprofit sectors, however, changed little, being on the order of 4 or 5 to 1 (public to nonprofit) throughout.

III. Conclusion

Employment in the public sector cannot be understood apart from the employment in the part of the private nonprofit sector that provides collective-type goods. Research should go forward to detect the varied forms that private nonmarket organizations take in each country. In other countries the institutional forms may differ and the term "nonprofit" may not be used, but private nonmarket organizations that provide goods similar to those of government do exist, and they may well be more important than is commonly realized. In a previous study of nonprofit sector activity in the area of legal representation we were repeatedly told that there were no counterparts outside the United States to the nonprofit "public interest" law firms. Our survey, however, turned up rather similar organizations in France, Italy and Japan (Sward and Weisbrod, 1980). Other examples have appeared in a recent newspaper account which reported on private consumer-protection organizations in nearly every developing country, including, for example, Barbados, Bangladesh and Malaysia. These organizations keep track of water pollution, "bogus" job agencies, flammable toys, "unsafe" drugs and, in general, the shortcomings of governmental and private-market "consumer-protection" efforts (Newman, 1980).

[10]Bendick (1978, p. 130) estimates that for 1970, 14.7 percent of "all conventional instruction"—measured in dollars of revenue—was in the voluntary nonprofit sector and 1.3 percent in the for-profit sector. Thus, for the two sectors combined, 92 percent of the revenue was in the nonprofit sector.

[11]It was shown in Table 2 that the ratio of employment to *revenue* differed between the government and private sectors in education; however, the ratio of employment to *enrollment* is a somewhat independent matter.

Further attention is needed to identify other nonprofit forms of organizations that provide collective-type goods. With forms of social institutions, as with nature more generally, sharp distinctions are less to be expected than more continuous gradations. The conventional dichotomy between government and the private sector is too simple. The private nonprofit sector, while not formally part of government, bears important relationships to it. Employment in the nonprofit sector often substitutes for direct government employment. The nonprofit sector exists in significant part because of governmental decisions that encourage this alternative to increased direct governmental provision.

The estimate developed in this paper has employment in the private nonprofit sector of the U.S.A. equal to some 8–10 million full-time workers. This is about 12 percent of total full-time equivalent employment in the country, about two-thirds of total government employment, and well over twice the level of employment in the federal government.

Government may, and in the United States does, grant tax advantages to nonprofit organizations and to donors to many of those organizations. The proportion of individuals who utilize the tax advantage of donating by itemizing on their income tax returns has been declining in the United States, and this implies that the government tax subsidy operating through donors is of diminishing importance. An unintended side-effect is, quite likely, a decrease in revenue to nonprofit organizations and a resulting increase in the pressure on government to provide substitutes. Government then finds itself raising taxes in order to finance expenditures previously being made by the nonprofit sector. Thus, the traditional public finance problem of raising revenue is entwined with the activity level of the nonprofit sector in any economy.

Recognition of the relationship between the government and nonprofit sectors also highlights the choice that exists for consumer-citizens; they are not limited to government as the institutional mechanism through which to obtain collective-type goods. The evidence examined here, which indicates substantial growth of the nonprofit sector, suggests that reliance on the nonprofit sector is growing. Is confidence in government declining? Might economic research within a comparative economic systems framework benefit from attention to the variety of institutional mechanisms that exist not only among countries but also within any particular country?

References

American Hospital Association. *Hospital Statistics*, 1977.
Bendick, Mark, Jr. "Education as a Three Sector Industry," in B. Weisbrod, *The Voluntary Nonprofit Sector*. Lexington, MA: D. C. Heath, pp. 101–142, 1978.
Bird, Richard M. "Wagner's Law of Expanding State Activity," *Public Finance Quarterly*, Vol. 26, No. 1 (1971), pp. 1–26.

Department of the Treasury, Internal Revenue Service. *Business Income Tax Returns*, various years.

Ginzburg, Eli, Hiestand, Dale L. and Reubens, Beatrice J. *The Pluralistic Economy* (New York: McGraw Hill, 1965).

Goldsmith, Raymond. *The National Balance Sheet of the United States, 1953-1975*, National Bureau of Economic Research, forthcoming.

Hiestand, Dale L. "Recent Trends in the Not-For-Profit Sector," in U.S. Department of Treasury, *Research Papers Sponsored by the Commission on Private Philanthropy and Public Needs*, 1977, pp. 333-337.

Internal Revenue Service, U.S. Department of Treasury, *Annual Report of the U.S. Tax Commissioner*, Washington, D.C., various years.

Lee, A. James and Weisbrod, Burton A. "Collective Goods and the Voluntary Sector: The Case of the Hospital Industry," in Weisbrod, *The Voluntary Nonprofit Sector* (Lexington, MA: D. C. Heath, 1978), pp. 77-100.

Morgan, J., Dye, R., and Hybels, J. "Results from Two National Surveys of Philanthropic Activity," in U.S. Department of the Treasury, *Research Papers Sponsored by the Commission on Private Philanthropy, and Public Needs*. Washington, D.C., 1977, pp. 157-324.

National Center for Education Statistics. *Digest of Education Statistics, 1977-1978*, Washington, D.C.

Newman, Barry. "Watchdogs Abroad: Consumer Protection is Underdeveloped in the Third World," *Wall Street Journal*, April 8, 1980, p. 1.

Peacock, Alan T. and Wiseman, Jack. "Approaches to the Analysis of Government Expenditure Growth," *Public Finance Quarterly*, Vol. 7, No. 1, January 1979, pp. 3-23.

Statistical Abstract of the United States. See U.S. Department of Commerce, Bureau of the Census.

Survey of Current Business. See U.S. Department of Commerce, Bureau of Economic Analysis.

Sward, Ellen and Weisbrod, Burton A. "Public Interest Law: Collective Action in an International Perspective," *Urban Law and Policy*, 3 (1980) 59-98, North-Holland Publishing Co. Revision of "Public Interest Law Activities Outside the U.S.A.," in Weisbrod, in collaboration with Joel F. Handler and Neil Komesar, *Public Interest Law* (Berkeley: University of California Press, 1978), pp. 502-531.

U.S. Department of Commerce, Bureau of the Census. *Statistical Abstract of the United States*, various years.

U.S. Department of Commerce, Bureau of Economic Analysis. *Survey of Current Business*, Vol. 58, No. 7, July 1978, pp. 53, 55.

Weisbrod, 1975. "Toward a Theory of the Voluntary Nonprofit Sector in a Three-Sector Economy," in E. Phelps (ed.), *Altruism, Morality, and Economic Theory*. New York: Russell Sage Foundation, pp. 171-195.

Wisconsin's Nursing Homes, Facility Characteristics. Madison, WI: Division of Health, various years.

Résumé

Cet article suggère que la reconnaissance de l'emploi dans le secteur sans but lucratif relève d'une compréhension complète du statut de "l'emploi public" et des changements qui y sont intervenus. Le rapport entre ces deux secteurs est important pour deux raisons : premièrement, il existe une catégorie d'entreprises non-publiques, du secteur privé (aux Etats-Unis, on les trouve principalement dans le secteur sans but lucratif, mais dans les autres pays elles peuvent avoir d'autres appellations et d'autres formes) qui produisent de proches substituts aux biens et services publics. Deuxièmement, des décisions du gouvernement peuvent grandement affecter la répartition de l'emploi entre secteurs. Les biens et services du secteur privé sans but lucratif sont souvent financés par le gouvernement, mais même lorsqu ils sont financés par d'autres sources, ils se substituent, d'une façon très voisine à une prestation publique directe, dans les domaines de l'éducation, la santé, l'assistance, la recherche scientifique et autres activités de "bien-être social"; grâce à la mise en lumière de ce secteur, nous obtenons une impression assez différente quant à la dimension et au taux de croissance de l'emploi "public."

Il est nécessaire d'apporter davantage d'attention encore pour identifier d'autres formes d'organisations sans but lucratif fournissant des biens de type collectif. La dichotomie conventionnelle entre état et secteur privé est trop simple. Le secteur privé sans but lucratif, bien que ne faisant pas formellement partie du secteur public, lui est étroitement lié. L'emploi, dans le secteur sans but lucratif, se substitue souvent à l'emploi public direct. L'estimation utilisée dans cet article montre que l'emploi dans le secteur privé sans but lucratif équivaut, aux Etat-Unis, à environ 8 à 10 millions d'ouvriers à plein temps. Il s'élève donc à environ 12 pour cent du total de l'emploi plein temps équivalent dans le pays, soit 2/3 environ de l'emploi public total et largement deux fois plus que le niveau d'emploi du gouvernement fédéral.

8226, 8243
LDCs

Public Employment in Developing Countries: Evidence from Latin America

Fernando Rezende
José Cezar Castanhar

Introduction

Studies of the employment problem in Latin America emphasize the relatively slow rate of growth in employment as compared to high postwar rates of growth in GDP. A 1975 publication of the Regional Program of Employment for Latin America and the Caribbean (PREALC) shows a low rate of growth of industrial employment in the last 30 years (3% on the average), but a much faster growth rate of industrial output (7% on the average) over the same period (PREALC, 1975, pp. 1–2).

An earlier study (Turnham, 1970) points to identical discrepancies by analyzing a broader sample of developing countries for a shorter period of time. According to Turnham, between 1955 and 1965 the average annual growth rates of product and employment in manufacturing were 7.4% and 4%, respectively. In the same ten-year period, the average rate of industrial growth in Latin American countries was 5.9%, while employment grew at an annual rate of only 2.3% (Turnham, 1970, Table 1).

The widening gap between industrial growth and employment creation leads to further difficulties in the choice of policy alternatives to deal with the employment aspect of economic development. It should be stressed that, in most of Latin America, past development has not contributed to lowering prevailing levels of unemployment or underemployment,[1] thus depriving a sizable portion of the population of the benefits of economic growth. The situation is potentially dangerous in urban areas, where unemployment is especially high. Household surveys conducted by PREALC in 1973 showed, for instance, that unemployment reached 12% in Assunción, 20% in Santo

---

[1]Turnham (1970) gathered data showing reasonable stability in the rate of unemployment for most developing countries during the period 1957–68. The same data show higher rates of unemployment for some Latin American countries: Argentina had the lowest rate (5%) and Colombia, Puerto Rico, and Trinidad and Tobago the highest (12% to 14%).

Public Finance and Public Employment. Proceedings of the 36th Congress of the International Institute of Public Finance. Jerusalem, 1980.

90	F. REZENDE AND J. C. CASTANHAR

Domingo, and 31% in the poorest sections of Managua (PREALC, 1975, pp. 2-3). PREALC studies conclude that in addition to remaining at high levels, the rate of unemployment fell in only six out of eighteen countries in the last ten years (PREALC, 1979, Quadro 10).[2]

The present and prospective problems of jobs in the region underline the importance of studies of public employment. At the onset it is important to analyze past trends and present levels of job creation in the public sector, to provide an empirical basis for evaluating public employment as an instrument of public policy.

Level and Trends in Public Employment

Data Problems and Limitations

Empirical studies of public employment in Latin America suffer from the traditional limitation of the available data: lack of homogeneity for inter-country comparisons, insufficient disaggregation of the relevant variables, and absence of an adequate time horizon. Our analysis is conducted within those constraints.

The main source of international data on the composition of the economically active population (EAP), the ILO *Yearbook of Labour Statistics*, does not identify the private or public nature of a particular job.[3] At best, the information permits us to measure the amount of employment in activities

---

[2]The data are for Argentina, Bolivia, Brazil, Colombia, Costa Rica; Chile, Ecuador, El Salvador, Guatemala, Jamaica, Mexico, Nicaragua, Panama, Paraguay, Peru, Dominican Republic, Uruguay, and Venezuela. Of these, only Argentina, El Salvador, Nicaragua, Paraguay, the Dominican Republic, and Venezuela experienced a decline in the rate of unemployment during the 1966-78 period. With the sole exception of Argentina, however, the rate remained high in these countries, reaching 9.6% in Nicaragua, 8.6% in El Salvador and the Dominican Republic, and 6.7% in Paraguay.

[3]The yearbook provides data on the composition of the EAP by activity and by occupation. Activity classifications are agriculture, forestry, hunting, and fishing; mining and quarrying; manufacturing; construction; electricity, gas, water, and sanitary services; commerce (which includes finance and insurance); transportation, storage, and communication; services (which includes personal, social, and community services); "activities not adequately described." Occupational categories are employers and workers on own account; salaried employees and wage earners; family workers; others and status unknown.

The composition of the economically active population is not entirely homogeneous. National practices vary among countries with regard to the treatment of such groups as the armed forces, inmates of institutions, persons living on reservations, persons seeking work for the first time, seasonal workers, and persons engaged in part-time economic activities. In general, however, the data refer to the total of employed and unemployed persons, excluding students, women occupied solely in domestic duties, retired persons living entirely on their own means, and persons wholly dependent upon others.

where public involvement is high: electricity, gas, and water; transportation and communications; and personal, social, and community services. Total employment in these activities therefore constitutes the first step toward measuring employment in the public sector.

Estimates of public employment may be improved by exluding the number of private employers, self-employed, and family workers from the labor force engaged in activities where public production predominates. Given the predominance of government-owned enterprises in the economic infrastructure and public utilities in Latin America, the number of salaried workers is roughly equal to public employment in electricity, gas and water and transportation and communications.

Merely excluding all nonsalaried workers does not provide a satisfactory solution for estimating the share of public employment in the provision of personal, social, and community services. We would also have to exclude salaried workers in personal and recreational services, which may represent a sizable portion of the wage earners in this category. Since available data do not furnish a detailed breakdown of employment, it is usually impossible to obtain more accurate estimates of public sector employment for a broader sample of countries. Fortunately, however, we were able to rely on special tabulations of the latest population censuses for 14 Latin America countries, which allowed us to estimate the share of the public sector in service employment.[4]

Share of Public Employment in Urban EAP

Estimates based on census data around 1970 for 14 countries showed that, on average, the public sector accounts for about one-half of total service employment and for one-fifth of the urban EAP. That is, one out of five in the urban labor force is a government employee.

An average of 20% for public employment in the urban EAP seems to contradict the usual claims about excessive job creation by government in less developed countries. In fact, this ratio appears modest if we take into consideration the increasing economic intervention of governments for the purpose of fostering industrialization and development.

Table 1 presents estimates of the ratio of public employment to urban EAP for each of the 14 countries in the sample. Intercountry differences are reasonably explained by the level of development. Regression analysis shows a positive correlation between the relative size of public employment and per

[4]These tabulations were organized by the Centro Latino Americano de Demografía on the basis of the latest population census and refer to the years around 1970.

Table 1

Public Employment in the Urban
"Economically Active Population"
in Latin American Countries, 1970

Countries	Percentage of Public Employment among EAP
Argentina	23.7
Bolivia	17.8
Costa Rica	25.3
Chile	25.0
Ecuador	18.1
El Salvador	14.3
Guatemala	16.8
Honduras	19.3
Mexico	14.0
Nicaragua	16.9
Panama	24.6
Paraguay	20.5
Peru[a]	16.8
Brazil	22.4
Average	20.0

Source: Estimates based on special tabulations of population censuses for 1970 by the Centro Latinoamericano de Demografía.

[a] From PREALC, *Situacion y Perspectivas del Empleo en Peru* (Santiago: PREALC, 1975).

capita GDP,[5] following Baumol's (1967) hypothesis concerning the growth of government.

The growth in public employment as an accompaniment of economic development may also be found by looking at the historical record. The data in Table 2 show that employment in predominantly public activities grew faster in countries which had higher rates of growth.[6] On the average, from the beginning of the 1950s to the end of the 1960s, employment in predominantly public activities grew at a rate of 3.9%, almost the same rate of growth observed for the urban EAP.[7] Due to the relatively rapid urbanization during

[5]The following variables were alternatively used in the regression analysis: per capita GDP, total GDP, rate of urbanization, total population, urban population, and size of country. Better results were obtained when per capita GDP was the independent variable in the regression. This variable explained 50% of the observed variation in the size of public employment. The correlation coefficient was 76, statistically significant at less than 5%.

[6]The main exception was Mexico, whose low rate of growth in public employment can be explained by a low ratio of public expenditure to GDP (see the next section, "Constraints").

[7]Annual rates of growth in urban EAP were practically equal to growth in employment in predominantly public activities for every country in the sample. On the average, urban EAP in Latin America grew at an annual rate of 3.7%.

Table 2

Employment Growth in Public Sector Activities and in Urban EAP, 1950–1970

Countries	Period	Annual Percentage Growth in Period				Urban EAP
		Utilities	Transportation	Services	Total	
Argentina	1947–70	5.3	1.3	1.9	1.9	2.0
Bolivia	1950–76	1.5	3.3	3.0	3.1	2.8
Brazil	1950–70	—	2.8	4.5	4.7	4.4
Colombia		—	—	—	—	3.9
Costa Rica	1950–73	6.1	4.1	5.2	5.0	4.8
Cuba	1953–70	—	—	—	3.9[2]	2.8
Chile	1952–70	0.6	3.1	2.2	2.3	1.8
Ecuador		—	—	—	—	—
El Salvador	1950–71	6.1	4.7	5.3	5.3	3.9
Guatemala	1950–73	—	—	—	3.5[2]	3.4
Honduras	1950–74	5.8	3.8	4.7	4.5	4.8
Mexico	1950–70	—	—	3.4	3.4	4.0
Nicaragua	1950–71	—	—	—	5.0[2]	4.3
Panama	1950–70	6.3	3.2	5.1	4.9	5.0
Paraguay	1950–72	—	—	—	2.9[2]	2.9
Peru		—	—	—	—	—
Dominican Republic	1950–70	—	—	—	4.8[2]	4.0
Uruguay		—	—	—	—	—
Venezuela	1950–71	—	—	—	—	—
Average		4.5	3.3	3.9	3.9	3.7

Sources: See text.
Note: Public sector employment includes only salaried employees and wage earners; EAP employment includes self-employment and family workers.

this period, the relative size of public employment (measured by the ratio of employment in predominantly public activities to urban EAP) remained stable.[8]

Trends in Public Employment: Selected Cases

More accurate information for analyzing trends in public employment comes from case studies of Chile, Peru, Brazil, and Panama. For Peru and Panama, the individual studies refer to the period 1960–70; for Chile, the

[8]We may be underestimating actual growth in public employment because we could not remove personal services, including domestic service, from total service employment under "predominantly public activities." Since domestic employment represented about 30%, on average, of employment in personal, social, and community services, actual growth of public employment would be higher if we took it for granted that domestic employment decreases with the level of development.

Table 3

Growth in Public Employment in Selected Countries

Countries	Public Employment (in thousands)			Annual Rate of Growth	Share of Public Employment in EAP		
	1950	1960	1970		1950	1960	1970
Brazil	1,027.0	—	3,351.0	5.3%	19.3%	—	19.4%
Chile	—	267.1	366.8	5.4	—	15.0%	18.4
Panama	—	36.0	65.6	6.2	—	24.0	23.9
Peru	—	238.8	351.7	4.0	—	15.7	16.0
Average				5.2		18.3	19.4

Sources: *Brazil:* Fernando Rezende and Flávio Castelo Branco, "O Emprego Público como Instrumento de Política Econômica," in Rezende *et al.*, *Aspectos du Participação do Governo na Economia,* serie monográlica (Rio de Janeiro: IPEA/INPES, 1976), n. 26. *Chile:* Oscar Muñoz, "Crescimento y Estimativa del Empleo Estatal en Chile, 1940–1970" (Santiago: PREALC, December 1978), mimeo. *Panama:* International Labor Office, *Situación y Perspectivas del Empleo en Panama* (Geneva: ILO, 1974). *Peru:* PREALC, *Situación y Perspectivas del Empleo in Peru, 1971* (Santiago: PREALC, 1975).

period 1958–70; and for Brazil, 1950–73. The data provided by these studies are given in Table 3.

During the 1960s, the annual rates of growth in public employment in the four countries were higher than the rates of increase in employment in the public sector activities shown in Table 2. This confirms our hypothesis that taking aggregate data on service employment (plus other public activities) as a proxy for employment in the public sector underestimates the actual growth in job creation by the government. We can infer, therefore, that during the 1960s employment in government grew faster than employment in the public activities studied, a result that reinforces the hypothesis of a rising trend in public employment with the development of the economy.

Increasing public employment, however, was not sufficient to overcome the increasing supply of labor in the urban areas, due to population growth and internal migration. In general, the individual country studies verify the conclusion of relative stability in the ratio of public employment to urban EAP.[9]

In sum, two main conclusions may be drawn from the evidence presented in this study: (1) the share of public employment in urban EAP is about 20% on average in 14 Latin American countries; (2) despite higher rates of growth, the relative size of public employment remained practically stable over recent decades due to faster urbanization.

[9]The exception is Chile, where the share of public employment in urban EAP increased from 15% in 1964 to 18.4% in 1970. In this case, however, the rise in public employment could be explained by political reasons.

Table 4

Growth of Formal and Informal Sectors in Selected Countries, 1960–1970

Countries	EAP in Formal Sector			EAP in Informal Sector			Ratio of Formal to Informal Sector Growth (B/A)
	1960 *(in thousands)*	1970	Rate of Growth (A) *(percent)*	1960 *(in thousands)*	1970	Rate of Growth (B) *(percent)*	
Argentina	5,178	5,900	1.3%	926	1,605	5.7%	2.7
Chile	1,293	1,543	1.8	412	513	2.2	1.2
El Salvador							
Guatemala	313	426	3.5	115	240	5.0	1.4
Mexico	3,742	5,454	3.8	1,166	1,726	4.0	1.1
Nicaragua	134	184	4.0	58	86	5.1	1.3
Trinidad and Tobago	171	244	2.8	52	75	2.9	1.0
Venezuela	1,169	1,631	3.4	392	670	5.5	1.6
Total or Average	12,000	15,382	2.5%	3,121	4,915	4.6%	1.8

Source: PREALC, *Employment in Latin America* (New York: Praeger, 1978), Table 1.8, p. 24.

Employment in the Informal Sector

The imbalance between the increase in labor supply and creation of new jobs in urban areas has worsened the employment gap in the last decades. A sizable amount of the urban EAP that could not find regular jobs ended up in informal occupations as a strategy of survival.

In fact, PREALC surveys show that, during the 1960s, the so-called "informal" sector[10] grew, on the average, at an annual rate of 4.6%, almost twice as fast as the 2.5% rate of growth of the formal sector. The results of these surveys, shown in Table 4, indicate that higher rates of growth for the informal sector are the rule for 7 of the 8 countries studied, the only exception being Trinidad and Tobago, where the two sectors grew at about the same pace. In Argentina, the informal sector grew three times faster than the formal sector.

The growth of the informal sector is the result of the low priority that employment received in the region's development policy. Emphasis on output growth did not favor labor absorption in manufacturing and was not compensated by direct job creation in publicly owned activities. The mounting social problems and increasing urban poverty that result from lack of

[10]The informal sector includes those that work in small traditional activities, independent workers (with the exception of university professionals) and those in domestic service. Its main characteristics are ease of entry, family ownership, low-skill requirements, small-scale operation, use of domestic products, labor-intensive technology, and predominance of perfect competition in both the product and factor markets. See PREALC (1978).

regular jobs urge a reappraisal of the role of the government in providing
alternative solutions to the employment problem.

Constraints on Growth of Public Employment

Proposals to give more emphasis to employment in the design of public
policy may prompt the usual claims of probable loss of efficiency. To respond to this point, it should be stressed that we are not talking about simply
adding jobs in the public sector, but of reappraising the potential for efficiently creating new jobs in designing the public production of urban services. First, the possibility of using labor-intensive technologies in public
service production should be considered. Second, the generation of more jobs
within the government ought to result from a change in the product mix in
the context of a new development strategy aimed at adjusting the production
structure to the basic needs of the population.

Direct employment in the public sector is subject to two main constraints: (a) continuing concern over reducing state intervention in the economy; (b) technological sophistication in provision of public services, following efforts to increase efficiency in public administration.

Concern over size of the government led to institutional changes in
public production, to avoid more rapid increases in public expenditures. We
have mentioned before that the ratio of public employment to urban EAP
seemed unrelated to the growing role of the government in development
policies. The same can be said if we look at the ratio of public expenditures to
GDP. For Latin American countries, the available data shows an average of
15%, a surprisingly low figure.

It is true that the ratio of public expenditures to GDP does not measure
the actual size of the government, due to a growing decentralization of public
activities. In some countries the recent growth of independent agencies and
public enterprises reduced the public budget to one-third of the public sector
as a whole (Rezende, 1978).

Decentralization of public activities also meant specialization in public
production. The traditional functions of the government have been kept
within the boundaries of the budget, whereas capital intensive developments
in economic infrastructure, production of basic inputs, and provision of
urban services are the responsibility of independent agencies and government
enterprises. In other words, the more labor-intensive activities (production of
public and merit goods) are those which remain subject to the tighter controls
through the tax burden and the government budget. At the same time, the
faster-growing "development" programs are less subject to budget controls
since they can rely on alternative methods of financing.

The hypothesis to be tested, then, is that, for a given level of development, the ratio of public employment to urban EAP is associated with the

share of the budget in the consolidated public sector. Unfortunately, the available data did not allow this hypothesis to be tested. It is worth noting, however, that the most deviant cases in the regression analysis of public employment and level of development are the ones in which this relationship is clearly affected by the size of the budget. This is, for instance, the case of Mexico, where the lower ratio of labor absorption in government is associated with a below-average ratio of budgetary expenditures to GDP.

Decentralization in government activities contributes also to the introduction of capital-intensive technologies in the public provision of urban services, where the potential generation of new jobs is usually high. The public enterprises in charge of producing such services are induced to adopt labor-saving techniques that may reduce production costs and improve their financial position. As a consequence, the social benefits of creating more jobs is usually disregarded.

Garbage collection provides a good example. Evidence from the city of Brasília, for instance, is impressive. During the period 1966–71, the amount of garbage collected rose from 15 to 75 thousand tons per year, whereas employment fell from 1,340 to 1,303. These figures are proudly cited in official reports as the "result of a more intensive use of capital which increased productivity" (Governo do Distrito Federal, 1972). It should be stressed, however, that indiscriminate modernization of urban public services contributes to further aggravating the imbalance between supply and demand of unskilled labor, adding to the already high social pressures in the cities.

Concluding Remarks

If we put aside the belief in a "natural" solution to the employment problem in developing countries as a by-product of higher rates of growth, discussion of alternative policy measures will bring to light the almost untouched question of direct employment in the public sector. It will consequently be necessary to abandon the contradictory situation of waging intensive debate over the appropriate means of inducing higher rates of labor absorption in the private sector while public agencies try to reduce the amount of labor employed in providing public services.

The growth of the informal sector, noted above, is clear evidence of the widening gap between the rate of urbanization and the creation of new jobs. And there is no evidence that this situation can be significantly changed in the near future unless a high priority is given to employment in the design of development policies. It should be noted that the burden of increasing unemployment will then fall upon society as a whole.

A simple exercise may serve to call attention to the dimensions of the problem. Projecting the trends of the last decades into the near future, we come up with a total deficit of 33 million jobs at the beginning of the next decade for the countries in our sample.[11] It is worth noting that PREALC projections, using a model of the Latin American economy developed by the Economic Commission for Latin America, put the rate of total underemployment around 45% of the labor force for the year 2000 (PREALC, 1978, Chap. 3).

In this context, increasing employment opportunities deserves top priority. Planned expansion of public employment is one alternative. Besides generating employment opportunities for unskilled labor, the expansion of public services may produce important side-effects from the viewpoint of reducing poverty and controlling internal migration. We know that rural to urban migration has been a major cause of difficulties in the urban labor market. Geographical dispersion in the provision of public services and the possibility of creating additional jobs in small and medium-size cities adds to the possibility of public employment also being used to reduce the inflow of rural migrants in the large metropolitan areas.

Increasing public revenues to cope with a rise in public employment is an obvious implication of creating more jobs within the public sector. It should be noted, however, that there are trade-offs to be considered. The first is the growing financial pressures on social security systems as a result of the aggravation of the employment crisis. Because social security systems are usually financed by payroll contributions, further increases in the relative size of social-security financed programs in the total government budget[12] will have a negative effect on employment by raising the relative price of labor.

The second trade-off is the negative effect of decreasing urban safety. In this case, as individuals become aware of their own insecurity, the government will be pressured to increase taxes to finance higher expenditures on public safety. Ironically, rapid growth of labor-intensive public safety programs would increase labor absorption in the government, contributing to a reduction of underemployment in the cities.

References

Baumol, William. 1967. Macroeconomics of unbalanced growth: the anatomy of urban crisis. *American Economic Review*, 57 (3).
ILO (International Labor Office). 1979. *Yearbook of Labour Statistics*. Geneva: ILO.
PREALC (Programa Regional del Empleo para America Latina y el Caribe), Oficina Internacional del Trabajo. 1975. *Políticas de empleo en America Latina*. Santiago: PREALC.

[11]These projections are based on the average growth rates of the urban labor force and of salaried employment in the period 1950-70 for the 14 countries listed in Table 1.

[12]According to available data, the relative size of social security systems is already high. The average for thirteen developing Latin American nations was found to be 17.2% in the period around 1974.

PREALC. 1978. *Employment in Latin America.* New York: Praeger.
PREALC. 1979. *Archivo de datos ocupacionales sobre America Latina y Caribe.* Santiago: PREALC.
Rezende, Fernando. 1978. El sector público y los gastos por concepto de educación en America Latina. Paper presented at Seminar on Financing Education in Latin America, Mexico City.
Turnham, David. 1970. *The employment problem in less developed countries: a review of the evidence.* Paris: OECD Development Center.

Résumé

La situation actuelle et les développements à venir des problèmes de l'emploi en Amérique latine soulignent combien l'étude de l'emploi public est importante. Les chiffres disponibles montrent un écart grandissant entre la croissance industrielle d'après-guerre et la création d'emploi ; il en est résulté des taux élevés de chômage urbain et une augmentation du secteur "informel" à l'intérieur du marché du travail urbain. Selon les études PREALC, le secteur informel a progressé, en moyenne, à un taux annuel qui atteignait presque le double du taux du secteur formel.

Pour l'emploi du secteur public, les données montrent une stabilité relative de la part des fonctionnaires dans la force de travail urbain, à cause des taux d'urbanisation rapides. On montre que la part moyenne s'élève, pour 14 pays, à 20 % environ.

Les tendances d'après-guerre de l'emploi ont contribué à nous faire refuser de croire à une solution "naturelle" du problème de l'emploi dans les pays en voie de développement, en raison de taux de croissance plus élevés. La croissance du secteur informel montre de façon évidente un écart grandissant entre le taux d'urbanisation et la création de nouveaux emplois. De plus, rien ne laisse prévoir que cette situation puisse changer de façon significative dans un avenir prochain étant donné l'absence d'une forte priorité à l'emploi dans la formulation des politiques de développement. Cet article soutient qu'une expansion planifiée de l'emploi public est l'une des alternatives à considérer. Cette alternative demanderait une évaluation du potentiel de création d'emploi dans les services publics grâce à l'utilisation plus poussée de technologies nécessitant plus de travail et à une augmentation dans la satisfaction des besoins de base.

3 7 1 2
322 /
8 2 4 2
/ 3 4 0
8 2 2 6
U. K.

The Effects of Public Employment and Other Government Spending on the Rate of Wage Inflation

Robert W. Bacon*

Introduction

The central theme of this book is public employment and this paper aims to explore the link between spending on public employment and the rate of wage inflation. Since the principal link between the two is contained within the relation between total public spending and wage inflation, the analysis concentrates on the microeconomic foundations of the hypothesis that increases in public spending (whether on employment, materials or transfers) will increase the level of money wages.

In 1974, Bacon and Eltis (hereafter BE) drew attention to the particularly rapid shift away from industrial employment and into non-industrial non-agricultural employment that had been recently occurring in the U.K. At that date, before the oil-price rise, the U.K. was "deindustrializing" much more rapidly than other industrial nations. It was suggested that one of the main net importers of labour was the public sector.

In 1975 the discussion by BE was broadened. Attention was switched to the broader category of total public expenditure. They showed that the ratio of general government spending to the GNP of the non-government "market" sector had risen from 43.9% in 1962 to 61.0% in 1974 (the figure of 60% has been used by later commentators). It was argued that the increases in spending produced higher average (and marginal) tax rates which had eventually met with worker resistance leading to wages being pushed up faster than would otherwise have happened.

The macroeconomic effects of an internally generated increase in wages are controversial and complex (see BE, 1978, for one account of their effects on the U.K. economy). It is not the purpose of this paper to analyze these effects.

*I am grateful to Walter Eltis and Jim Mirrlees for comments but responsibility for errors is entirely the author's.

Public Finance and Public Employment. Proceedings of the 36th Congress of the International Institute of Public Finance. Jerusalem, 1980.

In this paper it will be assumed for simplicity that all government spending is tax financed (as indeed the great majority is in most countries). Even in such a simplified situation, increased public spending can "crowd-out" employment in several different ways. The main distinction is between "demand crowding out", which is familiar from macro-economic textbooks, and "supply crowding out" (Taylor, 1979). Supply crowding out has two distinct aspects:

1. Out of a given total factor supply, the state may directly use some factors to produce more social output and so the supply left for the market sector decreases.
2. The effect of the higher tax rates required to pay for the public spending may shift the total supply curve to the left thus reducing the supply for the market-sector further still.

All categories of public spending can produce the second type of effect but the first effect results solely from increases in public employment. Most of the paper is concerned with the second effect, which raises some new problems beyond those of dividing supply between competing demands.

The shifting of the aggregate supply schedule by tax changes is not a new idea, although standard macroeconomic analysis usually ignores this aspect of fiscal policy. There are three separate bodies of literature which can be brought together in order to analyze the inflationary aspects of public spending. The first is the econometrically dominated literature relating wage increases to changes in direct and indirect taxes. The second area is that of the microeconomics of the supply of effort which links taxes to individual labour supply. The third area is the public finance topic of the optimum combination of public and private goods. A brief review of each area is given and then a synthesis is attempted in order to show how a changed public provision of goods alters the labour supply curve of the individual and hence the macroeconomic wage rate. From this approach, a framework emerges for understanding the various effects public spending can have on wages.

Taxes and Wage Inflation

The hypothesis that direct taxes are passed on in part or completely is a common feature of recent empirical studies of the wage equation.[1] Particular emphasis has been placed on this in the U.K., but a study by the OECD published in 1978 concluded that this effect was significant for all the industrial countries except France. Surprisingly, in the light of much earlier discussions of tax rates and the supply of effort, this factor appears to have been

[1]Early studies are listed in OECD (1978).

completely ignored in empirical wage equations before about 1970. It had been accepted very much earlier that indirect taxes do affect wages, via their effect on prices (e.g., Klein *et al.*, 1961).

The wage-tax literature has relatively little microeconomic underpinning and this may account for the diversity of models that have emerged, which fall into two opposing views: (1) that the worker bargains for a desired real net of tax wage and so the effects of a 1% rise in prices or in direct taxes would produce the same money wage reaction; (2) that direct taxes have some effect on wages but not necessarily related to the size of the effect of prices on wages.

Studies in the U.K. began with the observation of Wilkinson and Turner (1972) that the percentage of earnings deducted for taxes and social security had accelerated very sharply (i.e., the retention ratio had fallen) in the U.K. for all classes of worker. This pointed toward the hypothesis that these tax changes had led to increased union militancy and hence to increased money wages.

The first to test this hypothesis for the U.K. were Johnston and Timbrell (1973), who said

> We have not felt it plausible or realistic to postulate any specific collective utility function to be maximised by the unions. All we assert is that adverse movements in taxes and/or prices will lead to wage demands pitched at a higher level and pursued with greater force and vigour than would otherwise have been the case.

Accordingly, prices and the retention ratio were entered separately into the wage equation—the retention ratio variable was significantly different from zero.

Parkin, Sumner and Ward (1976) hypothesized that the supply of labour depends on the net real wage whereas demand depends on the gross real cost of labour. This produced equal coefficients for the price and tax terms in their wage equation. As they point out, their model implies "that economic agents are unaware of, or disbelieve, the benefit theory of taxation; otherwise the supply of labour would depend on the pre-tax real wage."[2] Their econometric estimates did not support the hypothesis that direct taxes affect wages.

Henry, Sawyer and Smith (1976) argued that workers bargain in money wages to attain a target real net earnings figure. Although the mechanisms for forming expected prices and expected retention ratios are different, so that the short-run effects of price changes and tax changes are different, the long-run impact of direct taxes and of prices are constrained to be equal. The authors claimed that their results support the hypothesis that taxes affect

---

[2]As shown later, belief in the benefits of taxation does not necessarily imply that the coefficient on taxes should be zero, but rather that it could be less than the coefficient on prices.

wages, but in fact it is doubtful that their significance tests actually relate specifically to this part of their hypothesis. Henry and Ormerod (1978) used the same formulation and also concluded that direct taxes are significant.

The study by the OECD (1978) had relatively little theoretical under-pinning and included price and tax terms separately. Both were significantly different from zero for all countries and the tax coefficient actually supported the hypothesis of full passing on for the U.K.

This brief survey illustrates the current view that direct taxes do affect wages while highlighting the range of views of the mechanism. The view that direct taxes are fully passed on (people attach no value to the associated benefits) is the polar case from earlier studies where no passing on was assumed. The view that the degree of passing on of taxes may be less than that of prices appears to be a compromise without any secure theoretical foundations.

Taxes and the Supply of Effort

There is a well-established theoretical and empirical literature on the effect of direct taxes on the supply of effort by individual workers (Godfrey, 1975). It is, nevertheless, useful to rehearse the simplest aspects of this theory. The worker must choose between private goods and leisure. If the tax system is a single average tax payable on all income, then a change in the tax rate has exactly the same effect on the choice between leisure and consumption as a change in prices.

This seems to be the proper starting place for the hypothesis that the passing on of direct taxes and of prices is equal—both shift the aggregate supply of labour curve in the same fashion. Although the passing on of prices and taxes are predicted to be equal by this model, there is no reason to suppose that they will be fully passed on. This will be determined by the wage determination mechanism and may well depend on the elasticity of the demand and supply schedules.

An important extension to this model was made by Scitovsky (1952), who recognized that taxes provide benefits and hence affect the labour supply analysis in two ways. The benefits were assumed to be distributed as lump sum payments and could be analyzed as if they were unearned income. Since this is effectively a positive "real income effect" then it will tend to counter the negative income effect of the increased tax and the substitution effect is more likely to dominate. In this model the effects of price increases and tax increases on an individual worker are likely to be different. Mirrlees (1978) generalized this by considering the case where some benefits are income related whereas others are of a lump sum nature. At the same time, he assumed that amounts of pure social goods (which cannot be thought of as affecting the individual's command over goods or leisure) do not affect his choice between goods and leisure. Since in Mirrlees' calculations about one-third of public spending is of this nature, and it clearly affects utility, it is worth considering the case where the choice between goods and leisure is affected by the provision of such goods.

The Optimum Combinations of Public and Private Goods

It is standard in the theory of public finance to treat private goods and public goods as the two arguments of the individual and collective welfare functions. At any point in time there is an optimal mix of the two relative to the output of the economy. The share of public spending in total output has received much attention, being the subject of "Wagner's Law." The usual view (Musgrave and Musgrave, 1976) is that this share will rise with the level of national income, but in a recent study Chrystal and Alt (1979) have suggested that the share has an asymptotic value.

If we use the elementary notions of demand analysis to investigate this topic we can imagine a utility map for society drawn between private goods and public goods. The budget line is provided by the current output of the economy. The slope of the budget line depends on the relative price of the two goods, that is, the rate at which taxes can be converted into an output of public goods.[3] If the price ratio does not change over time,[4] and if there is a mechanism making sure the optimum mix is attained continuously, then the "income expansion" path will reveal the optimal level of public spending as a proportion of output. If the income elasticity of demand for public goods is unity then the share of public goods will be constant. If the income elasticity for public goods is greater than unity then the share will rise with output (private goods would then be income inelastic). Increases in the share caused by changes in relative prices must however not be attributed to income.

If the general form of Wagner's Law is true, that the income elasticity is greater than unity, it follows that it is not possible to assess whether an economy is out of line with regard to its share of public spending in national income unless the level of income is taken into account. For example, attempts to argue that the U.K. is not a particularly high spender on public goods compared with her continental neighbours usually omit to note that

[3]From now on the term "public goods" will be used as a shorthand for all items of public spending so that it includes transfers as well as pure public goods.

[4]This is a strong assumption. The relative costs may change over time in the two sectors as seems to have happened in the U.K. (Dean, 1977; Price, 1979), or the efficiency of provision of public goods may change.

the U.K. has a lower *per capita* income and therefore would be expected to spend a lower proportion of output on public goods (rather than the higher proportion that she actually spends).

Taxes, Public Spending and Wages

In order to make the simplest possible synthesis of the preceding material it is useful to make two preliminary assumptions, which do not affect the main burden of the argument:
1. All public spending is financed by taxes (direct or indirect). This is not a bad approximation and removes the difficulties associated with deficit finance.
2. All public spending is converted into public goods (the so-called "social wage"). The benefits of the social wage felt by the typical worker are then proportional to the level of spending.

The central hypothesis of this paper, aimed at unifying the material of the three previous sections, is that the utility of an individual worker depends on the amounts of private goods, public goods and leisure he can consume. This hypothesis, which was the basis of Winston's criticism (1965) of Scitovsky's model, produces a more complex supply of labour function than that of the models discussed above. The utility surface is assumed to be convex and all three arguments are assumed to be "normal" (positive real income elasticity).[5] In his treatment of the budget surface Winston assumed that the provision of public goods did not affect the individual's command over marketed goods and so the wage planes (before and after tax) are parallel to the public goods axis—the constraint on the individual's consumption of public goods is simply the amount of such goods available (which is not assumed to vary with taxes). For our purposes this breaks the macroeconomic links between taxes paid and benefits received.

It is necessary to recognize that, even for the individual, as he pays more taxes he will receive increased benefits because everyone else is paying more taxes too. In such a model the budget surface intersects all three axes—on the leisure axis it is at 24 hours, on the private goods axis it is at the maximum output ("full income") the typical worker can produce, and on the public goods axis it is at the amount of public goods that could be produced if a worker worked all day and was taxed at 100%. The two price ratios determining the slope of the surface are the wage rate in terms of the price of private goods and the cost of public goods in terms of the price of private goods. The optimum is where the utility surface is tangent to the budget surface. One

[5]Mirrlees' model could be fitted into this utility framework using the assumption that the utility function is weakly separable in its three arguments (Phlips, 1947).

feature that distinguishes this model (and that of the previous section) from most consumer choice models, and also from Winston's model, is that the worker is constrained to a sub-space of the budget surface by a given tax rate. This fixes the proportion of private to public goods available, whereas the general level of the two together can be varied against leisure. The government can set the tax rate (or public spending) too high or too low and a corner solution can occur.

This model also shows a very clear difference between changes in prices (not caused by indirect tax shifts) and changes in indirect taxes and direct taxes. The former moves the budget surface along the private goods axis but keeps the proportion of public to private goods on offer as before. Increases in direct or indirect taxes both have the same effect as a price rise of the private goods in rotating the surface towards the origin along the private good axis but also both increase the proportion of public to private goods on offer (hence changing the relative position of the constraint on the new budget surface).

With such a complex shift it is not surprising that general conclusions do not emerge unless a specific utility function is utilized. However, this simple framework makes it clear that, unless a mechanism is known to exist which automatically achieves an optimum level of public spending, in order to discuss whether the share of public spending in national output is optimal, it is necessary to know the shape of both utility function and the budget constraint.

BE (1978) identified two other reasons why there might be too high (or low) a share of public spending. Their first case resulted from generalizing to more than one category of public spending (which increased the number of arguments in the utility function). The mixture of spending on public goods could be incorrect even though the total corresponded to the optimal spending and tax rate. This situation would be exemplified by a propensity to spend lavishly on politically prestigious projects (of a nature unattractive to workers) in an economy where there was a great need for spending on health and education. This is in effect imposing a further constraint on the feasible region of the budget surface. The second case resulted from specifically making a distinction between public spending and public output.[6] If there is technical inefficiency in the provision of public goods, then the tax rate, which would be optimal if they were efficiently produced, could be suboptimal in practice. Such a fall in efficiency is in effect a rise in the price of public goods. The optimal demand for public goods falls (both by the income and substitution effects). If this effect is strong enough, the optimum tax rate can fall. If public goods are indeed income elastic, as suggested by versions of

---

[6]Conventionally, public output is valued at cost but such an assumption allows neither for variations in productivity or in technical efficiency.

Wagner's Law, then the probability that the optimal tax rate will fall is strengthened.

If the labour market is perfectly competitive then the position of the aggregate supply of labour curve, as I have argued above, may be affected by the magnitude of the tax financed government spending program. In such a framework increases in taxes can in certain circumstances lead to higher money wages. If instead the labour market were monopolistic then the attitudes of the unions to the trade-off between social goods and private goods would also be important. The union utility function which traditionally has had as its arguments real wages and employment would have to be augmented to include the level of public spending (Oswald, 1976). An increase in the tax rate could lead to a decrease in employment being sought because of a strong desire for private consumption for those who are left in work. The effect will again not in general be the same as that caused by a rise in the price level.

The U.K. Economy, Wagner's Law and the Rate of Wage Inflation

A full statistical test of even the above simplified framework would be a considerable task and well beyond the scope of this paper. However, two areas have emerged as suitable for empirical investigation. The first is the extent to which it is plausible that public spending has risen above an optimum in any economy and the second is whether such a rise, if it can be identified, is associated with stronger tax pressure on wages.

The classic study of the share of public spending in national income for the U.K. is by Peacock and Wiseman (1961), but their study terminates at 1955 and does not cover the recent years which led authors such as BE (1975) to claim that the increasing share of public spending has had damaging effects on the U.K. economy via the inflation rate.

Table 1 presents data on general government spending and relates this to gross marketed output (GDP less general government spending on wages and salaries),[7] and also to GDP.[8]

[7]As was done in BE (1978, Table 12.1). BE have given two estimates (1978, Table 23; 1979) of the effects on final demand of government spending. This is of course a different magnitude from an indicator measuring the tax burden of government spending.

[8]Chrystal and Alt (1979) in concluding that the income elasticity was unity for the U.K. relate just current consumption of the government to GDP. This is because they argue that transfer spending is determined by a different mechanism and that to include it would raise the possibility that government spending could be larger than GDP. Since they claim that this would be nonsense transfers are omitted. In fact in a situation where transfers and government employees' wages are taxable and are partly saved it is quite feasible (but unlikely) that government spending could be larger than GDP.

Table 1

The Share of Government Spending in GDP for the U.K. (in £ millions)

	Total General Government Spending (GGS)	GGS on Wages and Salaries	GDP at Factor Cost	Share of Total GGS in GDP	Share of GGS in GMO*	Share of Wages in GDP	Real GDP
1955	6455	1698	16894	38.2%	42.5%	10.1%	57165
1956	7029	1866	18289	38.4	42.8	10.2	58233
1957	7619	1987	19390	39.3	43.8	10.2	59361
1958	7954	2092	20206	39.4	43.9	10.4	59157
1959	8432	2212	21239	39.7	44.3	10.4	61195
1960	8914	2338	22616	39.4	44.0	10.4	64027
1961	9725	2501	24203	40.2	44.8	10.3	66327
1962	10368	2717	25254	41.1	46.0	10.8	66951
1963	10954	2923	26886	40.7	45.7	10.9	69585
1964	11988	3154	29208	41.0	46.0	10.8	73317
1965	13309	3466	31219	42.6	48.0	11.1	75352
1966	14448	3770	33120	43.6	49.2	11.4	77007
1967	16672	4084	34925	47.7	54.1	11.7	78995
1968	18289	4382	37554	48.7	55.1	11.7	81659
1969	18984	4690	39616	47.9	54.4	11.8	83091
1970	20867	5394	43460	48.0	54.8	12.4	84822
1971	23445	6351	49428	47.4	54.4	12.8	87051
1972	26316	7425	55147	47.7	55.1	13.5	88385
1973	30503	8739	64154	47.6	55.0	13.6	95634
1974	39146	10486	74073	52.8	61.6	14.2	94313
1975	51642	14759	93502	55.2	65.6	15.8	93502
1976	58362	16841	110268	52.9	62.5	15.3	96958
1977	61738	18085	125211	49.3	57.6	14.4	98417
1978	71351	20044	141999	50.2	58.5	14.1	100825

Sources:
Total general government spending: *National Income and Expenditure* (NIE) (1979, Table 9.4); *Economic Trends* (ET) (1979, Table 13.5).
General government spending on wages and salaries: NIE (1979, Table 9.6) and earlier issues.
GDP at factor cost: NIE (Table 1.1); ET (Table 34).
GDP at factor cost and constant 1975 prices: NIE (Table 2.1); ET (Table 1).
*GMO (gross marketed output) is GDP *less* GGS on wages and salaries.

The table shows a complex picture. From 1955 to 1964 there is a slow increase in the ratio of government spending to GDP as the level of real GDP increases. There are also minor fluctuations which appear to be of a counter-cyclical nature (the ratio increases strongly in years of below average growth and increases less than normal in years of more rapid growth). After 1964 the spending ratio increases much more sharply with increases in real GDP and the counter-cyclical variations (in 1974 and 1975 in particular) are much

Table 2

The Relation Between the Share of Government Spending and Real GDP in the U.K., 1955–1978

Period	a	b	c	R^2	DWS
1955–1978	20.4	0.00033	−0.559	0.91	1.20*
	(10.5)	(14.0)	(3.30)		
1955–1964	27.3	0.00021	−0.222	0.92	2.54
	(19.9)	(8.91)	(3.13)		
1965–1978	24.6	0.00029	−0.597	0.67	1.27*
	(4.0)	(4.14)	(2.25)		

Note: Figures in brackets are t ratios and all coefficients are significantly different from zero. F ratio for equality of the last two regressions is 44.4 with a critical value at 5% of 3.6.
  *Inconclusive at 5%.

stronger. Even without formal testing it seems overwhelmingly clear that the ratio of public spending to GDP has risen steadily as the U.K. has become richer. Moreover the income elasticity (which is thus greater than unity) appears to be increasing.[9] These hypotheses are tested using a regression model. Variables are needed, both for the long-term share and for the short-run counter-cyclical effects. The second is approximated by the % change of real output since the previous year,[10] and so the regression is of the form

$$R_t = a + b\,O_t + c\,\dot{O}_t,$$

where R is the ratio of GGS to GDP
  O is real GDP
  $\dot{O}$ is % change in O.

The results of OLS estimation are shown in Table 2. The results for the whole period and for the two sub-periods support the hypothesis that the share of spending increases with real output. The regressions for the separate periods also support the hypothesis that the relation between the share of spending and real output intensified after 1964. Moreover, the effects of growth on the share (via counter-cyclical policy) are significant and have intensified.

The evidence so far cited is consistent with the view that the share of government spending rose abnormally rapidly relative to real output in the U.K. from the mid-1960s. Whether or not this was purely an enforced substitution for private consumption or was complicated by shifts in leisure

[9]As pointed out, this may be due to a price effect or to some interaction with the demand for leisure.
  [10]Ideally deviations from a trend are needed, but this trend depends on government stabilization policy and would be difficult to establish.

(labour supply) is too complex to answer here. Two pieces of evidence can be produced to support the view that the share of public spending was too high for the income available. The first is the evidence emerging from the interchange between Hadjimatheou and Skouras (1979) and BE (1979) on the effect of public spending on private consumption. Although private consumption initially took a lower share of output as public spending rose, this was not sustained from 1969 to 1973 and during the early years of the world recession. The share of private consumption rose (via the mechanism of functional income redistribution and balance of payments deficits) despite a concomitant rise in the savings ratio. This is consistent with the share of public spending being too high for workers to voluntarily accept.

The other evidence comes from the econometric studies cited earlier. Taxes, both direct and indirect, appear to have been passed on in whole or part. A simple exercise is to see whether there is any evidence that the post-1964 increase in the share of government spending in the U.K., which appears to be much greater than pre-1964 values would have suggested was optimal, coincided with a strengthening of the impact of direct taxes on wages.[11] The simplest model to use is that of the OECD. This model, based on annual changes, is relatively unsophisticated but showed strong effects of prices and of taxes on wages for the period 1964–1975. The model is of the form

$$\dot{W} = A + B\,(PC/W_{-1}) + C(Ty),$$

where W is the unit cost of labour

$\dot{W}$ is the rate of change of W

PC is the private consumption deflator

Ty is average tax and social security payments of households.[12]

Results are shown in Table 3 for generalized least squares using the Cochrane-Orcutt procedure for treating first-order serial correlation.

The results for the whole period 1955–1978 show both prices and direct taxes having a positive effect on wage costs. The coefficients are not directly comparable with the OECD estimates because the price index used is a 1975 rather than 1970 deflator. The coefficients are both significantly greater than zero (using a one-sided 5% test). In the period after 1964 the re-estimated equation shows an almost identical coefficient for prices but a very much larger coefficient for the effect of direct taxes. The coefficient on prices remains significant but the coefficient on taxes just fails to be significantly different from zero using a one-sided 5% test. Thus the equations are very suggestive that the impact of direct taxes on wages not only was positive throughout the period but indeed strengthened considerably in the post-1964

---

[11]There was no overall shift to indirect from direct taxation over the period so that it is safe to identify an increase in government spending with an increase in the average deduction from income.

[12]See OECD (1978) for further details of the variables.

period. In order to subject these hypotheses to more stringent testing it would be necessary to provide a more carefully specified supply/demand/wage setting model.

Public Employment and the Rate of Inflation

This paper has attempted to show that increases in public spending will have variable effects on money wages depending in part on the desirability of the spending as seen by those workers who pay taxes to finance the spending. A situation where it was accepted that more "social output" was required would not lead to higher wages via a shift in labour supply but would merely allow private consumption to fall, thus presenting no strain for the macroeconomy. Where, on average, spending was seen as being on undesirable objects or on inefficient public services then tax resistance would shift the supply of labour curve and push up wages, setting off an inflationary spiral. Since any part of public spending cannot be identified with any particular tax increase the taxpayer will be solely concerned with the general level of social benefits. To him what matters is the total cost per unit of social benefits. As Table 1 shows, the expenditure on wages and salaries by the government in the U.K. has increased particularly rapidly and will have more than played its part in raising taxes above the willingness-to-pay level if there has been a degree of "passing-on." This, in turn, might depend on whether the rapid increase in wage and salary expenditure was in response to a widely felt increase in demand (e.g., caused by demographic factors) at the same level of provision for all entitled individuals, or was to provide an increase in the level of provision to the same group of individuals.

It may well have been that expenditure rising at this rate was itself sub-optimal. However, added to this possibility is the charge of inefficiency in the provision of public goods. Transfer payments are not likely to be inefficient as regards spending because all the money goes to a recipient who is likely to spend it efficiently on consumption goods.[13] However, in the provision of health, education and administration there is plenty of scope for inefficiency and only rather weak mechanisms for producing the maximum social output from any level of social expenditure. To the extent that there was a *growth* in the inefficiency of such activities then the trade-off between private goods and public services was even more likely to be sub-optimal. A great deal of private goods (with high taxes to finance high expenditure) might have been given up in exchange for too little an increase in actual benefits felt by the taxpayers.

---

[13]Of course there can be further shifts in the labour supply curve caused by benefit induced unemployment.

Such arguments on crowding out via the shifting of the aggregate supply curve apply to all items of public spending which must be analyzed in the aggregate for this effect.

It is important to recognize that in an economy with a degree of monopoly power arising from the existence of trade unions the effect of raising taxes and social spending past the optimal point can be to increase the amount of collective voluntary unemployment. The effect of the higher tax is to make those unions with a strong preference for private goods and a low preference for public goods and for employment push for higher money wages and hence accept the unemployment this creates for other workers. This type of shift can be seen as increasing the natural rate of unemployment and it follows that attempts to cut actual unemployment to any given level will be more inflationary than before. If this phenomenon was important in the U.K. during the late 1960s and in the 1970s the mere existence of unemployment cannot be used as a counter-factual argument to deny the possibility of crowding out (see BE, 1978, p. 197).

However, it is important to remember that public employment can create another sort of crowding out. The supply of labour available to the private sector is reduced and, if the economy is near the natural rate of full employment, this will present difficulties because the government may be changing the pattern of supply (marketed versus non-marketed goods) without changing the pattern of demand. Civil servants want the same mixture of private and public goods as equivalent private sector workers. A balance of payments problem could ensue although the relative wage rate of the two sectors may be able to negate such effects.[14] A subsidiary aspect of this argument, much voiced by British industrialists (with little firm evidence), is that public employment crowds-out certain categories of labour. Potential managers became civil servants being attracted by the wage/pension/job security/working conditions combination offered by the government. With a segmented labour market this could occur even though there were a substantial overall level of unemployment. More research would be needed to substantiate such an argument.

Conclusions

This paper has shown that, by integrating macroeconomic theories of wage determination with microeconomic models of choice between private goods and leisure and between private goods and public goods, a generalized supply of labour function can be derived. Such an approach shows the following:

[14] A problem could arise if the government attempted to fix both the volume of labour and its price in terms of private wages (or goods).

Table 3

The Effect of Direct Taxes on Wages
in the U.K.

Period	B	C	R^2	DWS
1955–1978	1.002	0.599	0.83	1.67
	(7.01)	(1.80)		
1965–1978	1.090	1.235	0.82	1.73
	(5.27)	(1.75)		

Note: Figures in brackets are t values.

1. Direct taxes can be expected to affect wage settlements but with varying strength, depending on the trade-offs between public goods, private goods and leisure in individuals' utility functions.
2. Increases in direct and indirect taxation are both likely to be inflationary in any given situation since they have identical effects on the supply of labour curve.
3. Increases in indirect taxation are not necessarily as inflationary as price increases for other reasons (which do not bring offsetting increases in the provision of social goods).
4. Changes in the efficiency of providing social goods can by themselves increase wages by affecting the supply of labour curve.
5. Only in very special cases is the ratio of public spending to output, in an optimal situation, invariant with respect to the level of output. This means that comparisons of this ratio over time or over space without reference to real output levels, need not reveal whether observations are atypical.
6. Attempts to compare ratios of public spending to output also need to take into account the consumption of leisure and the relative prices of private goods to leisure and private goods to social goods: A low ratio of public spending to output can nevertheless be optimal because of a high relative price of public spending to the other two factors.
7. The effects of increases in public spending on employment not only need to take into account any demand creation effects plus the effects on the existing patterns of supplies of factors to marketed and non-marketed goods, but also the possibly substantial effects on the aggregate supply curve.
8. The U.K. experience supports the view that public spending (as a share of GDP) increased far faster than the level of GDP safely permitted in the late 1960s and the 1970s, with the effect that a far larger part of direct taxation was passed-on into wages in this period compared with pre-1965.

Many of the above conclusions must be regarded as tentative since the aim of the paper has been to outline possible links between public spending and wages rather than to provide a full test of the model sketched above. Nevertheless the generality of the approach and the support of the crude tests carried out do indicate that this aspect of public spending is well worth further study.

References

Bacon, R. W. and W. A. Eltis (1974) "A Budget Message for Mr. Healey: Get more People into Factories," *Sunday Times*, 10 November.

Bacon, R. W. and W. A. Eltis (1975) "The Great Debate on Declining Britain," *Sunday Times*, 2 November.

Bacon, R. W. and W. A. Eltis (1978) *Britain's Economic Problem: Too Few Producers.* London: MacMillan, 2nd rev. ed.

Bacon, R. W. and W. A. Eltis (1979) "The Measurement of the Growth of the Non-Market Sector and its Influence: A Reply to Hadjimatheou and Skouras," *Economic Journal*, Vol. 89, June, pp. 402–415.

Chrystal, A. and J. Alt (1979) "Endogenous Government Behaviour: Wagner's Law or Götterdämmerung?," in S. T. Cook and P. M. Jackson, eds., *Current Issues in Fiscal Policy*, Martin Robertson.

Dean, A. J. H. (1977) "Public and Private Sector Manual Worker's Pay 1970–1977," *National Institute Economic Review*. November.

Economic Trends, Annual Supplement 1979. HMSO.

Godfrey, L. (1975) *Theoretical and Empirical Aspects of the Effects of Taxation on the Supply of Labour*. OECD.

Hadjimatheou, G. and A. Skouras (1979) "Britain's Economic Problem: The Growth of the Non-Market Sector?" *Economic Journal*. June.

Henry, S. G. B., M. C. Sawyer and P. Smith (1976) "Models of Inflation in the United Kingdom," *National Institute Economic Review*. August.

Henry, S. G. B. and P. A. Ormerod (1978) "Incomes Policy and Wage Inflation: Empirical Evidence for the U.K. 1961–77," *National Institute Economic Review*. August.

Johnston, J. and M. Timbrell (1973) "Empirical Tests of a Bargaining Theory of Wage Rate Determination." *Manchester School*.

Klein, L. R. *et al.* (1961) *An Econometric Model of the United Kingdom*. Oxford: Blackwell.

Mirrlees, J. A. (1978) "Arguments for Public Expenditure," in M. J. Artis and A. R. Nobay, eds., *Contemporary Economic Analysis*. Croom Helm.

Musgrave, R. A. and P. B. Musgrave (1976) *Public Finance in Theory and Practice*. McGraw Hill. 2nd ed.

National Income and Expenditure 1979. HMSO,

OECD (1978) *Public Expenditure Trends*. O.E.C.D.

Oswald, A. J. (1979) *Wage Determination in a Partially Unionised Economy*. Mimeo.

Parkin, M., M. Sumner and R. Ward (1976) "The Effects of Excess Demand, Generalized Expectations and Wage-Price Controls on Wage Inflation in the U.K.: 1956–71," in K. Brunner and A. H. Meltzer, eds. *The Economics of Price and Wage Controls*. North Holland. Carnegie Rochester Series on Public Policy, Vol. 2, pp. 193–222.

Peacock, A. T. and J. Wiseman (1961) *The Growth of Public Expenditure in the U.K.* Princeton.

Phlips, L. (1974) *Applied Consumption Analysis*. North Holland.

Price, R. W. R. (1979) "Public Expenditure: Policy and Control," *National Institute Economic Review*, November.

Scitovsky, T. (1952) *Welfare and Competition: The Economics of a Fully Employed Economy*. Unwin.

Taylor, C. T. (1979) "Crowding Out: Its Meaning and Significance," in S. T. Cook and P. M. Jackson, eds., *Current Issues in Fiscal Policy*. Martin Robertson.

Wilkinson, F. and H. A. Turner (1972) "The Wage-Tax Spiral and Labour Militancy," in D. Jackson, H. A. Turner and F. Wilkinson, eds., *Do Trade Unions Cause Inflation?* Cambridge.

Winston, G. (1965) "Taxes, Leisure and Public Goods," *Economica*. February.

Résumé

Cet article étudie quels sont les fondements théoriques du lien qui existe entre le niveau des dépenses publiques et la position de la courbe de l'offre globale. On obtient ceci en généralisant les modèles existants de translation de l'impôt par les salariés. On pose que la demande de travail dépend non seulement du taux de salaire réel après-impôt mais aussi du niveau de la production publique de biens et services non marchands. Sur la base de cette hypothèse on soutient que si l'Etat essaie de fournir un niveau trop élevé de biens publics (et delà un taux d'impôt trop élevé) pour ce niveau donné de production nationale, les salariés peuvent essayer d'augmenter leur niveau de consommation privée en obtenant une augmentation de leurs rémunérations, ce qui peut produire une augmentation du chômage.

Des tests exploratoires sont menés pour l'économie britannique, ils confirment la thèse selon laquelle l'augmentation plus rapide de la dépense publique par rapport au produit national après 1964 s'est accompagnée d'un plus haut degré de translations des impôts directs dans les salaires.

Cet article montre, en conclusion, que des augmentations d'impôts peuvent, selon les préférences pour la consommation privée par rapport à la consommation publique, conduire à des augmentations de salaire. Un important corollaire existe cependant, à savoir que ce lien peut varier en force dans le temps en fonction de la situation économique. L'éventualité d'une augmentation des salaires sous l'effet de la majoration des impôts directs peut encore dépendre du degré d'efficacité des dépenses publiques : des augmentations de l'inefficacité moyenne des dépenses publiques sont équivalentes à des augmentations des prix des biens publics et peut nécessiter de plus faibles taux moyens d'imposition et de niveau de dépenses pour répondre aux préférences des salariés.

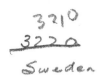

The Expansion of the Public Sector in Sweden: 1964–1977

*Jiří Skolka**

Certain aspects of the rising share of public services in the GDP were treated in an earlier paper by this author (Skolka, 1977), in which a simple model, based on Baumol's hypothesis (1967) about differential productivity growth, was used. Similar studies were published soon after (Peacock, 1979; Smith, 1978; Spann, 1977). I return to this problem here, using empirical data for Sweden taken mainly from the OECD (1979) national accounts statistics and from the Swedish medium-term Survey (Ministry of Economic Affairs, 1979).[1]

1. Concepts and Measures

Economic Activities of the Public Sector

Economic activities of the public sector can be defined in several ways, as illustrated by Swedish data for 1965 (see Tables 1 and 2). Public services is one of the economic branches (industries). It employs a labour force (14.2 percent of total labour in 1965), and its output involves services such as public administration, defense, education, health care, social care. The value of the output can be measured either by value added (13.1 percent of GDP), or by gross output, which is the sum of value added and of deliveries of other industries to public services. The gross output value is not published in national accounts, but can be found in input-output tables (see, e.g., UN Economic Commission for Europe, 1977). It is, however, almost always

*The author acknowledges the benefit of discussions with Mr. Bengt Olof Karlsson. The views expressed herein are those of the author.

[1]After this paper was finished, the author found a recent international comparative study by Beck (1979). Some of the conclusions of that study are very close to those of this paper.

Public Finance and Public Employment. Proceedings of the 36th Congress of the International Institute of Public Finance. Jerusalem, 1980.

Table 1

Government Receipts, Outlays, Final Consumption Expenditure
and Public Services in Sweden, 1965–1977
(shares in GDP and annual rates of growth in percentages
at current and 1975 constant prices, employment in number of persons)

Item		1965		1970		1974		1977
						Years or periods		
Gross domestic product	(nom.)			8.46		10.12		12.09
	(real)			3.93		2.23		−0.22
Current receipts	(nom.)	39.08		46.73		49.84		60.88
			12.48		11.67		19.82	
Savings	(nom.)	9.22		9.70		5.24		5.28
			9.64		−5.81		4.25	
Current disbursements	(nom.)	29.86		37.03		44.60		55.60
			13.30		15.12		20.64	
Final consumption by government	(nom.)	17.65		21.34		23.69		25.78
			12.74		12.78		18.73	
	(real)	21.63		23.69		23.60		25.36
			5.80		2.13		4.65	
Public services	(nom.)	13.05		17.15		19.47		24.41
			14.18		13.87		20.67	
	(real)	16.80		18.69		19.48		22.28
			6.10		3.40		4.02	
Employment in public services		14.25		19.57		24.04		27.08
			7.39		5.82		5.06	
Total employment			0.79		0.51		0.97	

equal to the final consumption by government (17.6 percent of GDP). Government not only has to finance its final consumption of services and goods, but it is also the vehicle for various transfer payments to households and enterprises. Consequently, its total disbursements (29.9 percent of GDP) are higher than its consumption and are met by its revenues (39.1 percent of GDP). The difference is savings (9.2 percent of GDP), created in Sweden mainly in the public pension system. This short explanation shows that the various indicators of the economic activities of the public sector differ strongly and have to be used according to the purpose of the particular investigation.

Total Consumption of the Population

A part of current disbursements by government and a part of its final consumption flow back to households: social security allowances (8 percent of GDP) are paid in cash, and are a part of households' net income; whereas

Table 2

Elements of Income Redistribution through Government, Sweden 1965–1977

Item		1965	65–70	1970	70–74	1974	74–77	1977
		\multicolumn{7}{c}{Years or Periods}						
Direct and indirect taxes & social security contribution	(nom.)	34.97	12.04	41.28	12.59	45.20	20.71[a]	53.63[a]
Social security benefits & social assistance grants	(nom.)	8.40	13.21	10.38	19.76	14.65	19.96[a]	17.96[a]
Redistributed final government consumption	(nom.)	10.51	14.76	15.43	12.84	15.56	19.98	16.89
	(real)	13.12	7.33	15.43	2.48	15.56	5.08	16.98
Private consumption	(nom.)	56.60	7.56	54.12	9.34	53.06	14.34	53.58
	(real)	54.40	3.07	52.28	1.71	51.23	3.50	53.85
Total consumption of the population	(nom.)	67.11	8.82	68.02	10.08	68.52	15.67	70.75
	(real)	67.52	3.93	67.51	1.91	66.81	3.87	70.74

[a] 1976.

Table 3

Deflators of GDP, Public Services,
Government Consumption and Productivity in Sweden,
1965–1977 (average annual rates of change)

Item	Period		
	'65–'70	'70–'74	'74–'77
GDP	4.36	7.72	12.34
Public services	7.62	10.13	16.00
Final gov. consumption	6.56	10.43	13.46*
Redistributed gov. consumption	6.92	10.11	14.18*
Private consumption	4.36	7.50	10.47*
Total consumption of the population	4.70	8.02	11.36*
Labour productivity total	3.12	1.71	−1.18
public services	−1.21	−2.28	−1.00
industries	3.93	3.08	−1.30

* 1976.

education, health care, social security, welfare services, housing and community amenities (10.5 percent of GDP) are provided in-kind and can be added to private consumption. The total of the latter item and of private consumption is the total final consumption by the population (the exact definition of which is still open to discussion; see, e.g., Cao-Pinna and Foulon, 1975; Foulon, 1976; Saunders, 1980). In Sweden in 1965 the share of private consumption in GDP was 56.6 percent and the share of total consumption by the population in GDP was 67.1 percent.

Redistribution of government revenues can also be compared with tax receipts. In Sweden in 1965, total direct and indirect taxes (paid both by households and enterprises) and total social security contributions amounted to 35 percent of GDP. The sum of social security benefits, social assistance grants and the part of governmental final consumption redistributed in-kind to households was equal to 18.9 percent of GDP. More than half of the tax and social security revenues was thus redistributed back to households.

The Relative Tax Burden

The relative tax burden is not a very exact concept, since it can be measured at least in the following three ways: (1) as the share of taxes and social security contributions in GDP (35 percent); (2) as their ratio to the "marketed" GDP (i.e., GDP less value added of the public services) at market prices (40.2 percent); or (3) as their ratio to the marketed GDP at factor costs (67.3 percent). However, the level of the relative tax burden can be biased upwards due to the "self-taxation" of the public sector: income taxes and social security contributions are paid by public employees and indirect taxes levied on purchases by public bodies. The exact size of this double-counting of taxes cannot be easily estimated from national accounts data; it depends, in general, on the relative size of the governmental consumption on the one hand and on the rates of direct and indirect taxes on the other hand.

Public Services at Constant and Current Prices

Various measures of the economic activities of the public sector in Sweden in 1965 have been illustrated in the previous paragraphs by their nominal values (i.e., at current prices); but they can also be measured in real terms (i.e., at constant prices). The deflation of nominal values into real ones is difficult for most service activities. The methods used differ from country to country and the results are not always reliable. The recent national accounting data for Sweden (OECD, 1979) base the real values on the 1975 prices. The ratio of nominal and real figures gives values of deflators, which are presented in Table 3.

2. Development of the Public Sector in Sweden from 1965 to 1977

The Period under Investigation

The analysis refers to data for the period between 1965 and 1977, which is subdivided into three subperiods, identical with those used in the Swedish medium-term survey (Ministry of Economic Affairs, 1979). Economic growth was rather high and inflation relatively low during the first period (1965 to 1970). In the second period (1970 to 1974) the GDP growth rate declined and the rate of inflation increased. Both tendencies ended in a "stagflation" during the third subperiod (1974 to 1977).[2]

Important Aspects of the Development of the Public Sector

Productivity, real output and allocation of labour. Between 1965 and 1977 public service employment in Sweden almost doubled: Its share in total employment rose from 14.2 percent in 1965 to 27.1 percent in 1977. Labour productivity growth in all three subperiods was slightly negative. Swedish statistics use the working hypothesis of a zero productivity growth in public services. Figures presented in Table 3 differ from zero due to some inconsistencies in data on output and employment available for this paper.[3] The real growth of output (i.e., of value added) is then given by the product of employment and productivity growth. It was positive during the whole period and even higher than the real rate of growth of GDP.

The pattern of final consumption by government. Output of public services can be measured either by value added or by gross output (which is the sum of value added and of goods purchased by public bodies). Gross output is almost exclusively (in Sweden by 93 percent in 1964) purchased by the government which, however, channels a large part of it to households as various provisions in kind.

Changes in the relations of the three items just mentioned are of interest. The share of value added of public services in government's final consumption increased (in real terms) from 0.77 in 1965 to 0.83 in 1974 up to 0.89 in 1977. This means that the public services expanded relatively to goods pur-

---

[2]Average growth rates in the tables were calculated as a geometric mean of the first and last value in each time interval.

[3]The negative (but small) figures are the result of a combination of data on real output from OECD (1979) national accounts and on employment from the Swedish medium-term survey (Ministry of Economic Affairs, 1979). The latter publication also contains the following information about the rates of labour productivity growth in public services (measured by value added at constant prices per hour) during the three subperiods: -0.0, -0.1 and $+0.1$. The decline in the productivity growth measured per man-year in Table 3 was probably also due to the reduction of working time between 1965 and 1977.

chased by the public sector. The part of government's final consumption further redistributed remained nearly stable; its share increased (in real terms) from 0.65 in 1965 to 0.67 in 1977.

Total consumption by the population. The share of government's final consumption in GDP (in real terms) rose from 12.7 percent in 1965 to 18.7 percent in 1977. A relatively constant share of government's final consumption was further redistributed, so that the share of redistributed goods and services in GDP increased in the same way as the total. At the same time, the real share of private consumption in GDP declined. These two complementary tendencies resulted in an almost stable share of total consumption of population in GDP: 67.1 percent in 1965, 68.0 percent in 1970 and 68.5 percent in 1974. The sudden rise in 1977, however, deviates from the previous trend. The composition of total consumption, of course, changed; goods and services provided by public bodies free of charge expanded at the expense of purchases for money on the market.

Value of public activities in nominal terms. Data on public activities in real terms help to explain shifts in the allocation of output and labour between the public and private sectors. But the financial problems of the public sector can be understood only with data in nominal terms, related by deflators to the real values. These deflators are shaped by productivity development. Contrary to the fast productivity increase in production for the market (which was seriously retarded, only by the recession after 1974), labour productivity in the Swedish public service was stagnating. This can be simply the result of statistical conventions used, but the consequence of this productivity differential was that the deflator of public services was permanently higher than the GDP deflator. The differential is even reflected in the relations of the deflators of public services and of total and redistributed government consumption (which include goods and services produced in the private sector). The nominal data on the public sector then reflect both the shifts in real terms and relative price changes. Between 1965 and 1977, the fastest growth was recorded by public services: Their nominal share in GDP almost doubled (rising from 13.1 percent in 1965 to 24.4 percent in 1977). The rise in nominal shares of total and redistributed government final consumption was slower due to both slower real expansion and lower deflators. They increased by 46 and 62 percentage points. The nominal share of total consumption by the population in GDP remained almost constant.

Government expenditures, receipts and redistributive flows. The rapid rise in government final consumption in nominal terms cannot fully explain the expansion of public expenditure between 1965 and 1977. On the contrary, the share of consumption expenditures (on goods and services, including public services) in total current disbursements by government declined from 59 percent in 1965 to 46 percent in 1977. Other spending, in particular social security benefits and social assistance grants, increased much faster, doubling in these twelve years. Consequently, the share of government expenditure in total nominal GDP rose from 29.9 percent in 1965 to 55.6 percent in 1977, that is, by a factor of 1.86. Higher public expenditures called for higher government revenues. Due largely to savings (mainly in the public pension system), revenues were higher than the current disbursements and amounted to 39.1 percent of GDP in 1965 and to 60.1 percent of GDP in 1977 (i.e., they increased by a factor of 1.56 during that period).

It is reasonable to assume that redistribution from households through government back to households, both in cash and in kind, was an important cause of the rapid increase in both government spending and receipts and also in the output of public services. This hypothesis can be further supported by the following figures. The main source of government revenues was direct and indirect taxes and social security contributions. Their share in GDP (at current prices) rose from 35 percent in 1965 to 53.6 percent in 1977. They were levied mainly on households income (directly or indirectly through purchases of goods), but a large part was channeled back to households. If social security benefits, social assistance grants and the nominal value of government final consumption redistributed back to households are added together, their share of nominal GDP rose between 1965 and 1977 from 18.9 percent to 34.8 percent (i.e., by a factor of 1.84) and their share in total tax and social security revenues increased from 54 percent to 65 percent.

Two Important Causes of the Growth of the Public Sector in Sweden between 1965 and 1977

As the figures which have been presented show, the expansion of the public sector in the sixties and seventies has dramatically changed the structure of the Swedish economy. The following data show perhaps most clearly the magnitude of shifts which have taken place during the twelve years between 1965 and 1977: The share in total employment of employment in public services rose from 14.2 to 27.1 percent and the share of government total current disbursements in nominal GDP increased from 29.9 to 55.6 percent. Both shares—which were not low in 1965—almost doubled in this relatively short period. A far reaching and profound reallocation of both physical and financial resources must therefore have been under way. The national accounts data used in this paper indicate that the following two factors played an important role in that process: the difference in productivity growth rates between the public and market-oriented (private) sectors, and the tendency to redistribute more and more goods, services, and money through public institutions. The impact of the traditional functions of the government, like administration, defense or justice, was, on the contrary, almost negligible.

The Slow Productivity Growth in Public Services. The rise in the share of
public services in total employment is caused both by the increase in the real
share of the output of public services in GDP and by the difference between
the rates of productivity growth in public services and in market (private)
production. The relative importance of these two factors can be estimated as
follows: between 1965 and 1977 the share of public employment in total
employment increased by a factor of 1.90, and the share of value added of
public services in GDP (in real terms) increased by a factor of 1.33; the ratio
of both factors is then equal to 1.40. This means that (1) had there been no
increase in the share of public services in GDP, the productivity gap alone
would have caused an increase in the share of public employment in total
employment by a factor of 1.40; (2) had there been no productivity gap (i.e.,
had the rise in the productivity in the public and private sector been equal),
the increase in the output share of public services alone would have caused an
increase in the share of public employment by a factor of 1.33; and (3) the
joint effect of both factors is responsible for the near doubling of the employment share.

The productivity growth rates are also related to price increases as depicted by the values of deflators. The deflator of the public services was in all
three subperiods (see Table 3) roughly 3 percent higher than in the whole
economy. The labor productivity growth (except in the last stagflationary
subperiod) was roughly 4 percent lower in the public services than in the
whole economy. Such inverse relationship between price and productivity
development is not surprising. It cannot, however, be more thoroughly investigated on the basis of national accounts alone. Other information, in
particular on the relation of the wage increase in the private and public
sector, would be needed.

Redistributive activities. The growing tendency to redistribute more and
more goods and services through public institutions is another important
cause for the expansion of public activities in Sweden in the sixties and
seventies. In all countries, a part of government revenues (mainly taxes and
social security contributions) is redistributed to households either in-kind
(e.g., health and educational services) or in cash (social security benefits,
social assistance grants). This utilization of public revenues increased in
Sweden at the expense of the share of "traditional" activities of the government, like administration, defense and investment in public utilities. The
Swedish data would then support the hypothesis that the growing consumption of public services in-kind by households was a compensation for the
decline in the share of private consumption in GDP. The share of total
consumption of the population in the GDP remained at a more or less constant level. The steadily growing share of payments in cash cannot be explained by data from national accounts alone. One plausible hypothesis
would be to assume a rise in government outlays in response to political

demands or as consequence of promises made by politicians. The increased outlays were then balanced by higher government revenues.

3. Concluding Remarks

Good Swedish statistics, available internationally, was one reason why data for Sweden were used in this paper. The other reason was the fact that Sweden is one of the most developed countries with a high standard of living and an extensive social security system. The present structure of its economy can be in many respects considered as a model of a situation in which other industrial countries may soon find themselves if they follow a similar path of development and/or similar economic and social policy.

The dramatic increase in the size of the public sector in Sweden in the twelve years between 1965 and 1977 is a unique event in the history of economic development. The national accounts data would largely support two parallel explanations of the far reaching shifts in the structure of the economy and in the resource allocation which were caused by this development. The first one was the productivity gap of the public services, which was to a great degree responsible for the increase in public employment and also for the rise in the deflators of public activitites. The second one was the expansion of income redistribution (in cash or in-kind) from households through public bodies back to households, which was mainly responsible for the increase in the share of government revenues and expenditures in GDP.

Data presented in this paper allow me to make a very simple prediction: The development which took place between 1965 and 1977 cannot be repeated in another twelve years. A simple extrapolation of past trends until 1989 leads to the conclusion that government revenues should be almost equal to GDP and that the public sector should employ about one-half of the total labour. Both cases are unlikely. The relative size of the public sector will therefore probably stabilize around a certain level, which may not necessarily be as high as the present one.

Several other important questions arising from the Swedish development between 1965 and 1977 remain open. The living standard in Sweden is no doubt high, the personal income distribution (even before tax) relatively egalitarian. This does not mean that there is no need for collective measures aiming at more social justice and a better social security system. But is it necessary, in order to achieve this target, to redistribute about a third of GDP from households back to households and to have about a quarter of the labour force employed in the public sector? Has the doubling of the relative size of public activitites and the extensive shifting of burdens and benefits brought the desired social effects (Eltis, 1979) or has it had certain negative consequences not only for the economy, but also for the morale of the people? Could such growth be responsible for the recorded decline in public sector productivity or for the expansion of the "shadow" or "black" economy (Stuart, 1979)?

References

Baumol, W. J. (1967), "Macroeconomics of Unbalanced Growth: The Anatomy of Urban Crisis," *American Economic Review* 3, 415–426.

Beck, M. (1979), "Public Sector Growth: A Real Perspective," *Public Finance* 3, 313–356.

Cao-Pinna, V., and A. Foulon (1975), "A Comparative Analysis of Household Consumption Financed by Individual and Collective Resources in France and Italy (1959, 1965, 1969)," *Review of Income and Wealth* 1, 53–79.

Eltis, W. (1979), "How Rapid Public Sector Growth Can Undermine the Growth of the National Product," in Beckerman, W. (ed.), *Slow Growth in Britain: Causes and Consequences,* Oxford, Clarendon Press, 118–139.

Foulon, A. (1976) "A Preliminary Assessment of the Redistribution of Public Funds in France in 1965," in Solari L., and J. N. du Pasquier (eds.), *Private and Enlarged Consumption,* Amsterdam, North Holland, 127–164.

Ministry of Economic Affairs (1979), *The Medium-Term Survey of the Swedish Economy,* Stockholm.

OECD (1979), *National Accounts of OECD Countries: 1960–1977,* Paris.

Peacock, A. (1979), "Public Expenditure Growth in Post-industrial Society," in Gustafsson, B. (ed.), *Post-industrial Society,* London, Croom Helm 80–100.

Saunders, C. T. (1980), "Measures of Total Household Consumption," *The Review of Income and Wealth* 26, 351–356.

Skolka, J. V. (1977), "Unbalanced Productivity Growth and the Growth of Public Services," *Journal of Public Economics* 7, 271–280.

Smith, V. K. (1978), "Unbalanced Productivity Growth and the Growth of Public Services: A Comment," *Journal of Public Economics* 10, 133–135.

Spann, R. M. (1977), "The Macroeconomics of Unbalanced Growth and the Expanding Public Sector," *Journal of Public Economics* 8, 197–404.

Stuart, C. (1979), Swedish Tax Rates, Labor Supply, and Tax Revenues, *Mimes.,* Lund, Sweden, Economic Department, University of Lund.

UN Economic Commission for Europe (1977), *Standardized Input-Output Tables of ECE Countries for Years around 1965,* New York, United Nations.

Résumé

Cet article traite des différents indicateurs utilisés pour mesurer la taille du secteur public, la part des services publics dans l'emploi total et les parts dans le produit intérieur brut de la valeur ajoutée des services publics, la consommation finale de l'Etat et ses recettes et dépenses courantes. Ces mesures sont illustrées par des données concernant la Suède pour l'année 1965. Leurs valeurs diffèrent fortement avec leurs parts significatives qui sont respectivement de 14,2 - 13, 1 - 17,6 - 29,9 - et 39, 1 pour cent. Une grande partie de la consommation publique est cependant redistribuée aux ménages (par exemple éducation, santé) et devient ensemble avec la consommation privée, une partie de la consommation totale de la population; une grande partie des revenus de l'Etat est redistribuée en espèces aux ménages (par exemple les allocations de Sécurité Sociale). Les valeurs nominales et réelles des indicateurs des activités publiques diffèrent dans le temps, en grande partie à cause d'une augmentation rapide des coûts et prix, qui se retrouve dans les valeurs significatives des déflateurs. Les chiffres réels tout comme les chiffres nominaux montrent une expansion très rapide de la taille du secteur public en Suède, causée principalement par une croissance lente de la productivité dans les services publics, d'une part, et par une forte tendance à la redistribution des revenus, de l'autre. La première a été largement responsable de l'augmentation de la part de l'emploi public dans l'emploi total (de 14,2% en 1965 à 27,1% en 1977) et de l'augmentation des coûts de la consommation publique. La seconde a causé la croissance des dépenses publiques (de 29,9% du PIB en 1965 à 55,6% en 1977) ainsi que celle des revenus de l'Etat (de 39,1% du PIB en 1965 à 60,1% en 1977). Bien que la part de la consommation totale de la population dans le PIB soit demeurée constante, sa composition a changé en faveur de la consommation publique fournie gratuitement en nature aux ménages.

32/2
8210
8226

Efficient Public Employment with Labour Market Distortions

George E. Johnson
P. R. G. Layard*

1. Introduction and Summary

Everybody would agree that the public sector ought to be efficient, but what does efficiency mean? A common view is that the State should minimize the money cost of producing whatever level of public output is selected. This we call the Thatcher-Reagan (TR) criterion. In this paper we examine whether or not the view is valid. The answer depends of course on what constraints apply, and in many cases a second-best rather than first-best efficiency solution may be indicated. It is also important, both from a normative and a positive angle, to look at who gains and who loses from government intervention, and we therefore examine not only the efficiency but the incidence of public employment policies.

We consider an economy in which there are only two factors of production-skilled labour (A) and unskilled (B), with public and private output produced at constant returns to scale. Public sector output has been independently determined. In an undistorted economy, efficiency requires that the public sector choose its mix of workers so as to minimize the money cost of production—the TR view. We confirm this in Section 2, though we also point out that the As will always want the public employment of As to be pushed beyond the cost-minimizing level, and the Bs will likewise want public employment tilted in their direction. In each case the reason is that discriminatory hiring raises the real wage of the favoured group. But such discrimination is inefficient.

*We are grateful to the Esmee Fairbairn Charitable Trust and the Ford Foundation for financial support. Each of us has written on related topics before. Jackman and Layard (1980) showed that if there were unemployment benefits or rigid wages, social efficiency could be improved by wage subsidies or discriminatory public employment. Johnson (1980) examined the local impact of several labour market policies in the context of a model with several factors of production. Neither of these papers computed optimality conditions, and the model in the present paper is deliberately simplified in order to facilitate the evaluation of these conditions.

Public Finance and Public Employment. Proceedings of the 36th Congress of the International Institute of Public Finance. Jerusalem, 1980.

Suppose, however, that due to minimum wages, trade union pressure, convention, or other reasons, the wage of B workers is fixed higher than would prevail in an unconstrained equilibrium with the public sector following the TR principle. We consider this case in Section 3. If the public sector follows the TR principle now, there will be unemployment of B workers. It follows that, at that particular allocation, the marginal social cost of employing an extra B worker is zero, provided that (as we assume in this section) labour supply is given. It also follows that the marginal social cost of employing an extra A worker exceeds his wage in the private sector. For the real wage of B workers is fixed, which implies that the ratio of A workers to B workers in the private sector is fixed. Therefore if one less A worker is employed in the private sector, there will also be fewer B workers employed there. Thus TR hiring would be singularly inappropriate, since the money wage of B exceeds its shadow price, and the reverse applies to A.

What then is the optimum mix of workers in the public sector? For any given level of public output, the government should aim to bring about full employment by discriminatory hiring of B workers in lieu of A workers: B workers should be hired in the public sector even when their relative marginal product is less than their relative wage.

However, one naturally asks whether there will be public support for such a policy. The B workers will like it, of course. The A workers will also support the policy up to a point, if, as we suppose, unemployed B workers receive social benefits paid for by taxes levied on the A workers only. For this reason, even the A workers will not favour TR efficiency but will support policies leading to higher levels of private output (for any given level of public output). They may not, however, be willing to go the whole hog in supporting discriminatory hiring right up to the socially efficient level.

We next consider (in Section 4) a second major distortion to which modern economies may be prey—this time on the supply side rather than the demand side. The existence of unemployment benefits means some workers whose wages in work are not much higher than their income if unemployed may choose not to work; but this choice will itself depend on the wage. Thus we now assume that there is a rising supply curve of B workers, and that their level of employment is inefficiently reduced by unemployment benefits: They equate the marginal value of leisure not to the wage but to the gap between wages and benefits. Wages are now fully flexible and, as before, the supply of A is totally inelastic.

Once more the cost of a B worker employed in the public sector is less than his wage. At the limit as the supply elasticity tends to infinity, the cost tends to the value of leisure (i.e., the wage gap), for, since the wage of B workers is in effect fixed, there is no loss of private output when an extra B worker is employed in the public sector. But this is a very extreme case and we derive the relevant general expression of cost. Turning to the A workers, their cost is, once more, *greater* than their wage, since if A workers are substituted for B workers in government, the wage of B workers will fall and their already-distorted labour supply decrease.

Once we have expression for the marginal social cost of A and B workers in the public sector we can find the socially efficient employment mix by equating the ratio of marginal costs to marginal products. Once again the unskilled Bs will be employed more than the TR criterion would indicate. The interesting question now is how great is the difference between this outcome and the TR criterion. We present a series of estimates assuming the Bs are 10 per cent of the labour force, paid one half as much as the As; public employment is a quarter of the total. If the replacement rate is .8, the elasticity of substitution unity and the labour supply elasticity .25, the public employment of Bs should be expanded until their relative marginal product is 20 percent below their relative wage cost. This means expanding public employment of Bs by almost 14 percent beyond that indicated by TR.

Once again the Bs would prefer the matter to be taken further than this, and the As would prefer to stop short. We have already seen that with no distortions the As would like the public employment of Bs to be lower than the TR level. In other words the As, if left as decision makers, would wish to exercise the resulting monopsony to drive down the wages of the Bs. Even with no distortions there is a limit to this, since the As have to pay for the higher resulting cost of government output. If in addition there are labour supply distortions, the As also have to pay for the resulting unemployment benefits. This means they will prefer a higher level of Bs in the public sector than in the Section 2 case. They will prefer a higher level of Bs than indicated by the TR criterion only if the replacement ratio exceeds their monopsony power (as measured by the reciprocal of the Bs elasticity of supply).

We next (in Section 5) relax the assumption of fixed government output and ask how labour market distortions affect the optimal level of government output. We assume that both public and private sectors have the same production functions and both outputs are normal in demand. In this case a rigid wage (as compared with flexible wages) will reduce the optimal level of public (and private) outputs. But, if efficient policies are adopted to restore full-employment, the optimal level of public output will be higher than if the TR criterion of public hiring is used.

Finally, we turn in Section 6 to a rather disturbing thought. We have so far assumed that the distortions in question can only be offset by action in the public sector, with no action in the private sector. But suppose there was a wage subsidy to the Bs? Consider the rising supply curve issue. The simplest possible scheme would be to pay each employed B worker in both the public and private sectors a subsidy equal to the level of unemployment benefit. The public sector should now follow the TR criterion, and this will in fact (given inelastic supply of As) produce a first-best efficient outcome. So we see that the arguments for discriminatory hiring in the public sector are only valid if, for some reason, the legislature is unwilling to provide appropriate subsidies that cover both public and private sectors.

2. Model with No Distortions

In this section we set out the basic model, with no distortions, which will serve as the starting point for each of our two variants. There are two types of output in the economy: "private" output (the volume of which is Q) and "public" output (G). There are two types of labour input: A workers, who are skilled or "primary" in the convertional sense, and B workers, less skilled or "secondary". Throughout the paper we assume that the level of aggregate demand for private sector output just equals its supply. Total employment can therefore not be expanded by monetary or fiscal policy without violating inflationary and/or balance of payments constraints. This obviously abstracts from the set of questions dealing with the optimal public employment policy over the business cycle.

The following notation is used throughout the paper:

Q, G : Real output of the private, public sector
L_a, L_b : Aggregate potential labour forces of type A and B workers
E_a, E_b : Private sector employment levels
P_a, P_b : Public sector employment levels
W_a, W_b : Real wage levels (in terms of private output)

We assume that the output of each sector is a linear homogeneous function of the inputs of the two classes of labour, that is,

$$Q = F (E_a, E_b) \qquad (1)$$

and

$$G = G (P_a, P_b). \qquad (2)$$

A more realistic model would include capital as an input in each of the production functions, but this would complicate the story unnecessarily.

If the labour forces of each type of labour are inelastic with respect to their wage levels and both W_a and W_b are free to adjust to their full employment values, the loss in private sector output due to an increase in public employment is quite straightforward. First, the full employment assumption implies that

$$L_i = E_i + P_i \qquad (3)$$

for both types of labour ($i = a,b$). Since each of the labour forces is assumed to be fixed, an increase in the public employment of one of the types of labour decreases its private employment by one, i.e., $dE_i/dP_i = -1$. Second, profit maximization in the private sector implies that

$$W_a = \frac{\partial Q}{\partial E_a} = F_a\,(E_a,\,E_b) \qquad (4)$$

and

$$W_b = \frac{\partial Q}{\partial E_b} = F_b\,(E_a,\,E_b). \qquad (5)$$

Thus, an increase by one in the number of A workers in the public sector decreases private sector output by W_a; an additional P_b lowers Q by W_b.

In the absence of distortions, the efficiency of the public sector (producing a given value of G at its lowest cost in terms of market prices) requires that the ratio of the marginal products of the two factors in that sector equals their relative prices, or

$$\frac{\dfrac{\partial G}{\partial P_b}}{\dfrac{\partial G}{\partial P_a}} = \frac{G_b}{G_a} = \frac{W_b}{W_a}\,. \qquad (6)$$

This TR efficiency condition holds at all points on the production possibility frontier defining the feasible mixes of public and private output. What output mix is chosen depends upon social preferences but for simplicity (up to Section 5) we take the level of public output as given at G^*. This implies, for future reference, that since $G^* = G(P_a,\,P_b)$,

$$\frac{dP_a}{dP_b} = -\frac{G_b}{G_a}\,. \qquad (7)$$

We also assume that the distribution of the benefits from public output as between groups A and B is predetermined, independently of how it is produced.

We now make a very obvious point. Each group would like the government sector to employ more of their group than is warranted by the TR criterion, for this extra demand for their labour in the public sector will raise their scarcity and thus their wage. This is intuitively obvious, except perhaps for the problem of financing the additional money cost of government expenditure. We shall therefore confirm that, even if one group (a) bears the full cost of government expenditure, as we assume throughout this paper, it would still want the public sector to employ an inefficiently large number of its members. This analysis will also be useful in developing building blocks for the later sections of the paper.

The As pay the entire cost of government, which is $W_aP_a + W_bP_b$. The aggregate pre-tax earnings of the As are W_aL_a, so their net (after-tax) income equals

$$I_a = W_aL_a - W_aP_a - W_bP_b. \tag{8}$$

By Euler's theorem $Q = W_aE_a + W_bE_b$, and $L_i = E_i + P_i$ for both the As and Bs. These facts imply that the aggregate net income of the As is

$$I_a = F(L_a - P_a, L_b - P_b) - W_bL_b, \tag{9}$$

that is, total private output less Bs share of it. The optimal combination of P_a and P_b from the point of view of the As is that which maximizes I_a. Clearly an increase in the use of P_b (in place of P_a) will drive up W_b. Since we assume that $F(E_a, E_b)$ is homogeneous, the marginal product of B workers changes according to

$$d(\log W_b) = \frac{\alpha}{\sigma} \left[d(\log E_a) - d(\log E_b) \right]$$

$$= \frac{\alpha}{\sigma} \left[\frac{1}{E_aG_a} \frac{G_b}{} + \frac{1}{E_b} \right] dP_b, \tag{10}$$

where $\alpha = F_aE_a/Q$ is the output share of A workers in the private sector and σ is the elasticity of substitution between the two types of labour in that sector. The first-order condition for maximization of I_a requires that

$$\frac{G_b}{G_a} = \frac{\dfrac{F_b}{F_a} + \dfrac{W_bL_b}{\sigma Q} \dfrac{E_a}{E_b}}{1 - \dfrac{W_bL_b}{\sigma}}, \tag{11}$$

so long as σ is finite, this is satisfied only when $G_b/G_a > F_b/F_a$, i.e., there is greater use of A workers than would be consistent with the efficient allocation of resources in the sense of (6).

The point of the preceding exercise is that even in the absence of labour market imperfections the composition of public employment among skill groups will be a subject of political controversy. Each of the groups would be willing to let the economy get inside the production possibilities frontier so long as the misallocation is in favour of them.[1]

---

[1]All of this has been based on the assumption that the wages of public and private employees are equal. For a model that allows the public sector wage to exceed that in the private sector, see Courant, Gramlich, and Rubinfeld (1949).

3. Model with Fixed Real Wage of B Workers

The results in the preceding section are based on the assumption that the labour markets for both types of labour function quite smoothly. There are, however, reasons for believing that the markets for certain types of labour in many countries do not behave in this manner. We will distinguish two different types of labour market problems, which are assumed to apply only to the B workers. First, the wage of B workers may be institutionally fixed, either in (1) real terms or (2) relative to the wage of the higher-paid A workers. This rigidity would arise because of institutional "aberrations" such as trade union wage policy, legal minimum wage provisions, or a reluctance by employers to pay less than some customary wage. The implications of assumptions (1) and (2) for public employment policy are similar, so we confine our discussion to the former, that is, that $W_b = W_b*$, an institutionally fixed constant. We assume labour supply to be fixed, with the value of leisure zero.

Cost of Public Employment

If the fixed W_b* leads to greater than frictional unemployment of B workers, there is ample justification for expanding the use of Bs in the public sector, for the level of private sector employment of the Bs is given implicitly by the marginal productivity condition

$$W_b* = F_b(L_a - P_a, E_b). \tag{12}$$

The problem is illustrated geometrically in Figure 1. At the fixed wage, there is only E_b' private sector employment of B workers, and, with public sector employment of the Bs at P_b', there is substantial unemployment.[2] Some or all of these unemployed could be employed in the public sector without loss of private sector output. Thus, over the relevant range the opportunity cost of B workers is zero.

By the same argument, the opportunity cost of using A workers in the public sector is greater than their wage. Because of linear homogeneity of the production function, coupled with the fixity of W_b*, E_b is proportional to the private sector employment of A workers: $E_b = (E_b/E_a)*E_a$. Since $P_a = L_a - E_a$, each additional P_a reduces E_a by one and reduces E_b by $(E_b/E_a)*$ as well. Thus, the reduction in private sector output due to the hiring of one additional P_a is

---

[2]As P_b is increased As are released from the public sector and this raises the marginal product curve for B in Fig. 1—thus reducing somewhat the number of Bs who need to be absorbed into the public sector before full-employment is reached.

Figure 1.

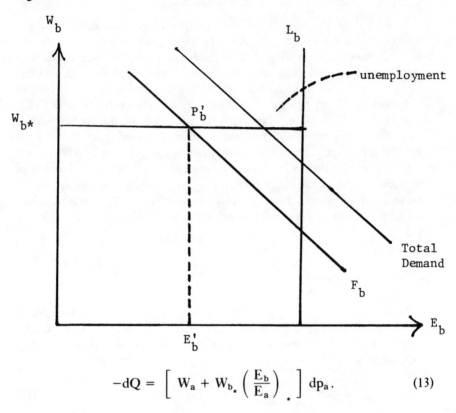

$$-dQ = \left[W_a + W_{b_*} \left(\frac{E_b}{E_a} \right)_* \right] dp_a. \qquad (13)$$

Optimal Public Employment Mix

The zero opportunity cost of the Bs and the higher-than-market-wage opportunity cost of the As suggests that, if there is this type of structural unemployment, society should employ all the unemployed Bs in the public sector, up to the maximum possible limit consistent with producing the predetermined level of public output.

There are two cases here. In one case there is limited scope for substituting B workers for A workers in the public sector ($\sigma < 1$), so that even if all B workers in the world were put into the public sector there would still need to be some A workers employed in the public sector as well. Thus the public sector can always fruitfully absorb more Bs and release some As. Given this, the case for moving to full-employment is cast-iron.

The second case is where the elasticity of substitution in the public sector is greater than unity ($\sigma > 1$). If this is so, it would be possible to produce the desired public output using only B workers, and the number of B workers needed might be smaller than the surplus left over by the private sector. In this case, of course, there would be an overwhelming case for expanding the level of public output, since this would be desirable given any positive marginal value of public output.

Let us suppose that, for our chosen level of public output, full employment is possible, and therefore socially second-best efficient. It is still not clear that this solution would receive the support of both groups A and B. Obviously the Bs would support it (so long as the income transfer payment (π) is less than the wage, $\pi / W_b < 1$). But it is not clear that the fully employed As would. If the latter pay all the taxes in the economy, their aggregate net income is (see equation 9)

$$I_a = F(L_a - P_a, E_b) - W_b^* (E_b + P_b) - \pi (L_b - E_b - P_b). \quad (14)$$

If this is maximized subject to the Bs not being over-employed ($E_b + P_b < L_b$) and if the solution is interior (i.e., with the inequality holding) the first order condition is[3]

$$\frac{G_b}{G_a} = \frac{F_b}{F_a} \left(\frac{1 - \rho}{1 + \rho \dfrac{1 - \alpha}{\alpha}} \right), \text{ where } \rho = \frac{\pi}{W_b}. \quad (15)$$

This condition could well obtain before full-employment is reached: $\dfrac{G_b}{G_a}$ could fall to the value of the right-hand side of (15) too quickly.

One final, and obvious, point. It is only because they are saving money on social benefits that the As are willing to support discriminatory hiring of Bs in the public sector. If $\rho = 0$, the As would prefer Thatcher-Reagan efficiency.

[3]To see this:

$$\frac{dI_a}{dP_b} = F_a \frac{dE_a}{dP_b} + F_b \frac{dE_b}{dP_b} - (W_{b_*} - \pi) \left(1 + \frac{dE_b}{dP_b} \right).$$

But $\quad \dfrac{dE_a}{dP_b} = \dfrac{G_b}{G_a}$ (from (7))

and $\quad \dfrac{dE_b}{dP_b} = \dfrac{dE_b}{dE_a} \cdot \dfrac{dE_a}{dP_b} = \left(\dfrac{E_b}{E_a} \right)_* \dfrac{G_b}{G_a}$

and $\quad F_b = W_{b_*}.$

Substituting, we find

$$\frac{G_b}{G_a} \left[F_a + \pi \left(\frac{E_b}{E_a} \right)_* \right] = W_{b_*} - \pi$$

$$\therefore \frac{G_b}{G_a} = \frac{F_b (1 - \pi/W_b)}{F_a \left(1 + \dfrac{\pi}{W_b} \cdot \dfrac{E_b W_b}{E_a W_a} \right)}.$$

4. Model with Rising Supply Curve of B Workers

A very different type of distortion arises from the existence of social benefits paid to the unemployed. In what follows we again assume that B workers can claim a transfer payment π per wage-period if they decide not to work at the prevailing wage. The replacement ratio for B workers is thus $\pi/W_b = \rho$. The higher W_b the more B workers choose to work, the labour supply function being

$$E_b + P_b = S(W_b) \tag{16}$$

with $\epsilon = d(\log S) \, / \, c \, (\log W_b)$ being the elasticity of supply.

We continue to assume that the labour supply of A is completely inelastic. This is clearly a simplification but has a good deal of truth in it. For although high-quality workers are generally entitled to unemployment benefit, the available evidence suggests that their elasticity of labour supply is much less than of unskilled workers (Jackman and Layard, 1980). This may be partly for behavioural reasons and partly because it may be more difficult for a skilled man to persuade the social security authorities that he cannot find a reasonable job. As far as the behavioural interpretation is concerned, this can easily be rationalized using a Cobb-Douglas utility function, in which case the supply elasticity tends to zero as the replacement rate tends to zero.[4] We shall assume that the supply elasticity of A workers is zero, since this greatly simplifies the analysis. If the supply of A workers changed, optimal policies would have to reflect not only the consumer surplus of the A workers but also the impact of changes in the tax rates on A workers' labour supply. We have derived many of our results in the presence of variable labour supply of the As but will not report them in this paper. The results are not very different from those reported below, provided the elasticity is, as the empirical evidence suggests, relatively small.

Cost of Public Employment

We can now examine the case for more public employment of Bs. The initial equilibrium of the B labour market is depicted geometrically in Figure

[4]Suppose, for example, that the underlying utility function for each individual is Cobb-Douglas, that is, $U = c^\alpha L^{1-\alpha}$, where $c = W_b h + \pi(1-h)$ is consumption per period and $L = T-h$ is leisure. The utility-maximizing supply of labour is then readily shown to be

$$h = \alpha T - (1 - \alpha) \frac{\rho}{1-\rho} ,$$

where $\rho = \pi/W_b$ is the replacement ratio. If there is no income transfer system, $h = \alpha T$ (or one in terms of the text) and the wage elasticity of labour supply is zero. For $\rho > 0$, ϵ is positive and increases to infinity as the replacement ratio increases toward some value less than unity (i.e., towards $\alpha T/[\alpha T + (1 \times \alpha)]$).

Figure 2.

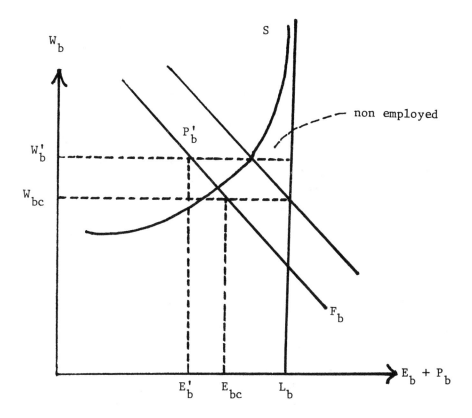

2. The aggregate supply curve is SS, and, given the level of public employment P_b, the market clearing wage is W'_b. If there were no income transfer program, the supply would simply be L_b,[5] and the equilibrium wage would be W_{bc}. Thus, the effects of this imperfection are (1) to lower private sector employment from E_{bc} to E'_b, and (2) to raise the wage rate of the Bs.[6]

An increase in the public employment of B workers (holding P_a and E_a constant) may be represented by a rightward shift in the total demand curve

---

[5]Figure 2 is drawn on the implicit assumption that in the absence of the income transfer program the labour supply function would be inelastic, as is true of the utility function in note 4. This is convenient for expositional purposes, but, qualitatively at least, the results in this section would apply equally under a more general specification.

[6]Under the specification of the supply function that S depends only on the ratio of W_b to π, an increase in the transfer payment increases the total labour earnings of the Bs if

$$\frac{\sigma}{\alpha} < 1 + \frac{P_b}{E_b}$$

where σ/α is the elasticity of the private sector employment demand for B workers. As public employment increases in relative importance, this condition is the more likely to be satisfied.

Figure 3.

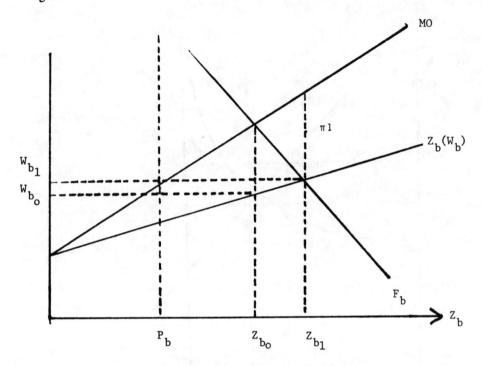

in Figure 3, and this obviously increases both the total employment of the Bs and their wage rate. But what does it cost?

The effect of an increase in P_b on private sector employment is[7]

$$dE_b = - \frac{\dfrac{E_b}{E_b + P_b}}{\dfrac{E_b}{E_b + P_b} + \epsilon \dfrac{\alpha}{\sigma}} dP_b, \qquad (17)$$

---

[7]If F( ) is homogeneous,

$$d \log W_b = \frac{\alpha}{\sigma}(d \log E_a - d \log W_b) = (\text{here}) - \frac{\alpha}{\sigma} \frac{dE_b}{E_b}.$$

Along the supply curve

$$\frac{dE_b}{E_b + P_b} + \frac{dP_b}{E_b + P_b} = \epsilon \, d \log W_b,$$

substituting

$$\frac{dE_b}{E_b} \left(\frac{E_b}{E_b + P_b} + \epsilon \frac{\alpha}{\sigma} \right) = - \frac{1}{E_b + P_b} dP_b.$$

which is negative but greater than minus one (given $0 < \epsilon < \infty$), i.e. there is incomplete offset. The effect of P_b on the wage rate is given by

$$d(\log W_b) = \frac{\dfrac{1}{E_b + P_b}\dfrac{\alpha}{\sigma}}{\dfrac{E_b}{E_b + P_b} + \epsilon \dfrac{\alpha}{\sigma}} dP_b \qquad (18)$$

which is positive so long as $\epsilon < \infty$. Notice that $\epsilon = \infty$ corresponds to the fixed real wage case in the preceding section.

The loss in private sector output due to the employment of one more B in the public sector, holding P_a and E_a constant, is simply W_b times the absolute value of the coefficient on dP_b in (17). For $0 < \epsilon < \infty$, $-dQ/dP_b$ is positive but less than W_b. Likewise the private output lost due to employing an extra A worker in the public sector (holding the Bs constant) is more than W_a, since this act reduces the marginal product of B and hence the labour supply of B.

However we also have to allow for the value of the leisure lost by the additional workers. Workers will at the margin be indifferent between work and leisure only if the value of leisure plus benefits (π) equals the available wage (W_b). So the value of leisure equals ($W_b - \pi$). Hence the true welfare change caused by additional public employment (excluding the value of the public output) is not $dQ = W_b dE_b$, but

$$dQ' = W_b\, dE_b - (W_b - \pi)\,(dE_b + dP_b). \qquad (19)$$

This will be smaller than dQ: In other words, the loss is greater.

Before examining the size of this welfare change, it is interesting, as usual, to break it down into the change for each of the two groups. For the A group, welfare is measured by private output *less* total wages of B workers, *less* benefit payments. Hence

$$dI_a = W_b\, dE_b - (E_b + P_b)\, dW_b - W_b(dE_b + dP_b) + \pi\,(dE_b + dP_b). \qquad (20)$$

For the B group the only change that matters is the change in wages for the employed:

$$dI_b' = (E_b + P_b)\, dW_b. \qquad (21)$$

This is because the workers who are induced to enter the labour force experience a negligible welfare change. Adding up the two changes we retrieve our initial expression for dQ'.

Turning to magnitudes, the total cost of one additional B used in the public sector is found by substituting (17) for dE_b in (19), that is

$$dQ' = -W_b \left[1 - \rho \frac{\epsilon \dfrac{\alpha}{\sigma}}{\dfrac{E_b}{E_b + P_b} + \epsilon \dfrac{\alpha}{\sigma}} \right] dp_b, \tag{22}$$

for $\epsilon = 0$, the cost of another P_b is simply W_b, but as ϵ gets very large the cost falls to $W_b(1 - \rho)$. In this latter case, private sector output does not change, but the Bs give up one unit of leisure worth $W_b - \pi$.

On the other hand, for positive but finite values of ϵ the cost of hiring an additional A in the public sector will exceed W_a. To show this, we first note that an increase in P_a changes E_b by

$$dE_b = - \frac{\dfrac{\alpha\epsilon}{\sigma}}{\dfrac{\alpha\epsilon}{\sigma} + \dfrac{E_b}{E_b + P_b}} \frac{E_b}{E_a} dP_a \tag{23}$$

which is obviously negative unless $\epsilon = 0$. It therefore follows that the value of private output plus leisure is changed by

$$dQ' = -W_a dPa + \pi dE_b$$

$$= -W_a \left[1 + \rho \frac{(1 - \alpha)\dfrac{\epsilon}{\sigma}}{\dfrac{\alpha\epsilon}{\sigma} + \dfrac{E_b}{E_b + P_b}} \right] dP_a \tag{24}$$

by the hiring of one more P_a.

Optimal Mix of Public Employment

The results concerning the opportunity costs of P_a and P_b given by (22) and (24) clearly suggest that public officials should be instructed, for any given level of public output, to use a more B-intensive technology than would be implied by the conditions for cost minimization at market prices. The social welfare-maximizing ratio of the marginal products of the two factors is given by the ratio of (22) to (24), or

$$\frac{G_b}{G_a} = \frac{W_b}{W_a} \left[\frac{\dfrac{E_b}{E_b + P_b} + (1 - \rho)\epsilon \dfrac{\alpha}{\sigma}}{\dfrac{E_b}{E_b + P_b} + \dfrac{\epsilon}{\sigma} (\rho + \alpha(1 - \rho))} \right] , \qquad (25)$$

the socially optimal value of G_b/G_a is less than W_b/W_a (i.e., the expression within brackets is less than unity) if both ϵ and ρ are positive. If, of course, either ϵ or ρ is zero, (25) reduces to (6), the conventional optimality condition.[8]

To see what this implies for the numbers of Bs hired and of As sacked to carry out this compensatory public employment programme, we first note that the proportionate change in the ratio of public sector marginal products is

$$d(\log G_b/G_a) = -\frac{1}{\sigma'} \left[d(\log P_b) - d(\log P_a) \right] , \qquad (26)$$

where σ' is the elasticity of substitution in the public sector. Since public sector output is fixed, the proportionate change in P_a is

$$d(\log P_a) = - \frac{1 - \alpha'}{\alpha'} d(\log P_b), \qquad (27)$$

where α' is the elasticity of G with respect to P_a. The proportionate reduction in G_b/G_a with respect to a proportionate change in P_b is found by substituting (27) for $d(\log P_a)$ in (26), so the increase in P_b necessary for a given decrease in G_b/G_a is given by

$$d(\log P_b) = - \alpha'\sigma' d(\log G_b/G_a). \qquad (28)$$

Similarly, the proportionate decrease in P_a associated with a decline in G_b/G_a is determined by

$$d(\log P_a) = (1 - \alpha')\sigma' d(\log G_b/G_a). \qquad (29)$$

For a numerical illustration of this, we take a set of parameters that approximate the situation in the United Kingdom. First, we assume (somewhat arbitrarily) that 10 percent of total employment are Bs and that W_b is

[8]If we had assumed that taxes were paid by both groups A and B, using an equiproportionate tax on the workers, then the required degree of discriminatory hiring would be still greater. The reason is that there is now a still greater distortion in the labour market for B workers.

Table 1

Optimal Compensating Distortion
in Public Sector, $(G_b/G_a)/F_b/F_a)$,
for Selected Values of ϵ, σ and ρ

ρ	ϵ	σ		
		0.5	1.0	1.5
.5	.00	1.00	1.00	1.00
	.10	.894	.941	.959
	.25	.798	.874	.909
	.50	.710	.798	.826
	1.00	.629	.710	.762
.8	.10	.891	.906	.935
	.25	.679	.799	.854
	.50	.553	.679	.753
	1.00	.413	.553	.622

half the value of W_a. On the assumption that the public and private sectors
are equally skill-intensive, the values of the share parameters are $\alpha = \alpha'$
$= .947$. Second, we will assume a range of values of the elasticities of substitution for both sectors ($\sigma = \sigma'$): 0.5, 1, and 1.5. Third, about a quarter of
total employment (25 million) in the UK is in the public sector, so, given the
assumption of identical factor proportions, $E_b/(E_b+P_b) = .75$. Finally, we
assume two different values of the replacement ratio of the income transfer
programme (ρ), .5 and .8. The resultant calculated values of $(G_b/G_a)/(F_b/F_a)$,
the expression within brackets in (25), are shown in Table 1.

We have assumed that 2.5 million of the UK's employment force are B
workers, and 625,000 of these are employed in the public sector; 5.625
million A workers are employed in the public sector. For $\rho = .5$, $G = .10$,
and $\sigma = 1.5$, the optimality condition requires that G_b/G_a be brought down
to .959 of W_b/W_a. Ignoring the effects of the policy on W_a and W_b, this
requires that $D(\log G_b/G_a)$ in (28) and (29) equal $-.042$. This requires a 6
percent increase in P_b, or 37,300 workers. P_a must decrease by 0.33 percent,
a fall of 18,800 workers. For larger values of ρ and ϵ and smaller values of σ,
the impact of the policy is much greater. For example, for $\rho = .8$, $\epsilon = 1$, and
$\sigma = 1$, the ratio must fall to .553, or $d(\log G_b/G_a) = -.592$. This is accomplished by increasing P_b by 350,400 and decreasing P_a by 176,500. It would
not, of course, be necessary to carry out quite so large a redistribution of the
public sector work force, because the resultant change in E_b/E_a would raise
the value of F_a/F_b. (Roughly, only ¾ of the above reallocation would be
required.)

There is, of course, no guarantee that all segments of society (in this case individuals who possess human capital endowments that place them in the two labour groups), will support this policy. Since the As are assumed to pay all the taxes and additional P_b drives up W_b, the Bs prefer as much public employment as possible to be filled by their own group. For the As, on the other hand, an increase in P_b, holding G constant, lowers W_a (by decreasing E_b/E_a), which lowers their income, but also increases E_b+P_b, which reduces taxes and raises their net income.

The aggregate net income of the As is

$$I_a = W_a L_a - (W_a P_a + W_b P_b) - \pi (L_b - E_b - P_b)$$
$$= Q - (W_b - \pi)(E_b + P_b) - \pi L_b. \qquad (30)$$

Maximization of I_a with respect to P_b for a fixed level of government output yields the same first-order condition as for the maximization of social welfare except that an additional expression,

$$- \frac{dW_b}{d(E_b + P_b)} (E_b + P_b) \left(1 + \frac{dP_b}{dE_b} \right) ,$$

which is negative for $\epsilon > 0$, is included. The resultant optimization condition for factor proportions in the public sector is

$$\frac{G_b}{G_a} = \frac{W_b}{W_a} \left[\frac{\dfrac{E_b}{E_b + P_b} + (1 - \rho)\epsilon \dfrac{\alpha}{\sigma} + \dfrac{\alpha}{\sigma}}{\dfrac{E_b}{E_b + P_b} + \dfrac{\epsilon}{\sigma}(\rho + \alpha(1 - \rho)) - \dfrac{1 - \alpha}{\sigma}} \right] . \qquad (31)$$

It is straightforward to show that the expression within brackets in (31) is (1) always less than the expression within brackets in (25) and (2) less than one if $\rho \epsilon > 1$. If the replacement ratio is less than the reciprocal of the elasticity, the As prefer that the public authorities use more As (fewer Bs) than is efficient in an accounting sense.

The reason for this somewhat curious result is that by this specification the As have an incentive to behave like monopsonists with respect to the Bs. To see this, assume that P_a and P_b are at the levels implied by minimization of the cost of government services in terms of market prices, say $\bar{P}_a$ and $\bar{P}_b$. The total supply of B labour is $E_b + P_b = Z_b$, $Z_b - \bar{P}_b$ of which is employed in the private sector. The net income of the As at this position is, by (30),

$$I_a = F[(L_a - P_a),(Z_b - \bar{P}_b)] - (W_b \times \pi)Z_b - \pi L_b. \qquad (32)$$

Maximization of this with respect to Z_b requires that

$$\frac{dI_a}{dZ_b} = F_b - \left[W_b + \frac{dW_b}{dZ_b} Z_b \right] + \pi$$

$$= F_b - W_b \left[1 + \frac{1}{\epsilon} \right] + \pi = 0. \tag{33}$$

This is shown geometrically in Figure 3. In the absence of an income transfer program (i.e., $\pi = 0$), the As would want Z_b to be that implied by the intersection of the "marginal outlay" curve, MO, and the marginal productivity schedule. This requires a reduction in P_b such that total employment of the Bs equals Z_{bo}. At a value of π just equal to the difference between MO and F_b, the As are happy with the efficient combination of P_b/P_a in terms of market prices. Notice that at this point $W_b/\epsilon = \pi$, or $\rho\epsilon = 1$. Finally, when π exceeds π_1 the As are willing to hire more P_b than is implied by the Thatcher-Reagan solution because the loss in their gross earnings is more than offset by the reduction in their taxes.

5. Optimal Size of Government Output

To this point we have shown that if there is some distortion in the labour market for B workers—caused either by real wage rigidity or by an income transfer program—it is socially optimal to use a more B-intensive technology than would be implied by the conventional efficiency criteria. This leaves open the question of whether the public sector would be larger or smaller if our optimizing conditions were followed.

The answer to this question is rather difficult, for it depends on, among other things, the nature of the production processes in the public and private sectors. To illustrate this difficulty, we shall attempt to answer the question for a relatively simple case. The specific assumptions underlying the model are the following:

1. W_b is fixed at a rate W_b* that is higher than would obtain at automatic full employment (the model of Section 3).
2. All surplus Bs are employed in the public sector, so $P_b = L_b - E_b$.
3. The production functions in the two sectors are identical, i.e., $Q = F(E_a, E_b)$ and $G = F(P_a, P_b)$.
4. The demand functions for public sector output are homothetic, that is, their income elasticity is unity.

In the absence of labour market distortions the trade-off between private and public production is given by the "flexible W_b" line in Figure 4. Since the production functions are identical, $E_b/E_a = P_b/P_a = L_b/L_a$, and private plus public output is given by

Figure 4.

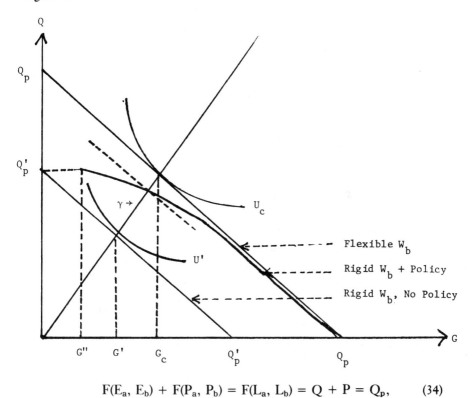

$$F(E_a, E_b) + F(P_a, P_b) = F(L_a, L_b) = Q + P = Q_p, \qquad (34)$$

where Q_p is potential output with automatic full employment. The wage of the Bs in this situation is

$$W_{bc} = F_b (L_a, L_b), \qquad (35)$$

which, because both sectors are assumed to have equally B-intensive production functions, is independent of the division of Q_p between Q and G.

We now introduce the distortion that the wage of the Bs is institutionally fixed at $1 + D$ of its competitive level. Thus, the ratio of E_b to E_a is higher than L_b/L_a. If the public sector also makes relative employment decisions on the basis of relative wages, the total employment of the Bs will be less than their supply. As an approximation, the proportionate reduction in potential output for a given wage distortion is[9]

---

[9]$d(\log E_b) = -\frac{\sigma}{\alpha} d(\log W_b)$ and $d(\log Q) = (1 - \alpha) d(\log E_b)$. Thus, $d(\log Q) = \frac{1 - \alpha}{\cdot \alpha} \sigma$ $d(\log W_b)$. A similar effect applies in the public sector.

$$-\frac{Q'_p - Q_p}{Q_p} \approx -\frac{1-\alpha}{\alpha}\sigma D. \tag{36}$$

The value of private sector output is now given by

$$Q = F\left(L_a - P_a, \left(\frac{E_b}{E_a}\right)_* (L_a - P_a)\right)$$

$$= (L_a - P_a) F(1, (E_b/E_a)_*) \tag{37}$$

and Q'_p is, of course, the value of (37) at $P_a = 0$. Government output is

$$G = F\left(P_a, \left(\frac{E_b}{E_a}\right)_* P_a\right) = P_a F(1, (E_b/E_a)_*), \tag{38}$$

so, as with the automatic full employment case, $Q + G$ equals potential output. The resultant transformation line is given by the "Rigid W_b, No Policy" line Figure 3.

Given the assumption of homothetic preferences for public and private output, the optimum level of government output is G_c in the automatic full employment case and G' in the Rigid W_b case. What remains to be shown is what happens to G when the government employs all the surplus Bs in the public sector. First, E_b is equal to $(E_b/E_a)^*(L_a - P_a)$, and Q is still given by (37). This means that the public sector employment of A workers is $P_a = Q/F^*$, where F^* is the (fixed) average product of E_a as determined in (37). Substituting for P_a in the public sector production function, we obtain

$$G = F(L_a - Q/F^*, L_b - (E_b/E_a)^* Q/F^*). \tag{39}$$

Differentiation (39) with respect to Q and inverting the result yields the slope of the trade-off between Q and G when the wage distortion is compensated for by a policy of full employment. This is

$$\frac{dQ}{dG} = -\frac{Q}{F_a{}^g E_a + F_b{}^g E_b}, \tag{40}$$

where $F_a{}^g$ and $F_b{}^g$ are the marginal products of the two types of labour in the public sector. The shape of the resultant production possibilities curve is shown by the "Rigid W_b + Policy" curve in Figure 4. When all A workers are hired by the public sector, government output equals Q_p as in the case of automatic full employment. When no As are hired by the public sector, G equals G'' (which is zero if the public sector elasticity of substitution does not exceed one) while Q equals its maximum value attained without a compensatory public employment policy. For values of G between G'' and Q_p, the sacrifice in Q per unit of G is less than unity, for (40) equals minus one only if the accounting cost of public sector output is minimized.

The tangency of an indifference curve with the Q-G compensatory curve will occur to the right of point γ in Figure 4, for the slope of the indifference curve at point γ is minus one. Hence the public sector is larger than it would be with TR policies applied to public hiring. We cannot tell, however, whether the optimum value of G is greater or less than G_c, its value under automatic full employment.

This result represents only one case of several that could be investigated. Another possibility is that (as is the case in most countries) the public sector is much more skill-intensive than the private sector. If this is so, it may be desirable to reduce public output and release as many As to the private sector as possible in order to increase the demand for Bs in that sector.[10] In any event, there is also the possibility of using labour market policy to increase E_b as well as P_b, to which topic we now turn.

6. Public Employment versus Subsidy Programmes

Throughout the preceding sections we have investigated the marginal social cost of additional public employment and the optimal combination of factors in the public sector on the explicit assumption that public employment is the only available instrument of labour market policy. If, on the contrary, there are other policies available, the results of Sections 3 to 5 do not necessarily apply.

To take the most simple case, suppose that in the fixed real wage model in Section 5 the government could, in addition to adjusting the proportions of A and B workers used in the public sector, provide a subsidy to private employers for hiring Bs. Then the level of private output, holding the level of public output at a fixed level G*, is

$$Q = F(L_a - P_a, L_b - P_b), \tag{41}$$

where $G* = G(P_a, P_b)$. The marginal product of B labour in the private sector is F_b, and the subsidy paid employers is $(W_b* - F_b)E_b$. Differentiating (41) with respect to P_b yields the equilibrium condition

$$\frac{G_b}{G_a} = \frac{F_b}{F_a} = \frac{W_b}{W_a} (1 - s), \tag{42}$$

where $s = (W_b - F_b)/W_b$ is the subsidy rate in the private sector.

---

[10] In the United States the public employment programs of the 1970s were, by and large, a failure because they attempted to prop up low-skilled employment by expanding the state and local government employment. But this is in fact the most skill-intensive sector in the U.S. economy, and local officials were quite inventive at circumventing regulations concerning whom to employ (see Johnson and Tomola, 1977).

In other words, if society can compensate for the relative wage distortion in both the private and public sectors, it should equate the ratio of the marginal products in the two sectors. If there is a commitment to full employment, as was assumed in Section 5, the levels of P_a and P_b will be chosen so that one reaches the same equilibrium point as would be reached at automatic full employment.

In the case of a distortion caused by an income transfer program the implications of the availability of a private employment subsidy are very similar. The level of private output plus leisure is

$$Q' = F(L_a - P_a, E_b) + V_b(E_b + P_b), \tag{43}$$

which is maximized subject to the constraint that $G* = G(P_a, P_b)$. The first-order conditions are

$$\frac{\partial Q'}{\partial E_b} = F_b - (W_b - \pi) = 0$$

$$\frac{\partial Q'}{\partial P_b} = F_a \frac{G_b}{G_a} - (W_b - \pi) = 0. \tag{44}$$

The first of these equations says that the optimal subsidy on B workers in the private sector is

$$s = \frac{W_b - F_b}{W_b} = \frac{\pi}{W_b} = \rho, \tag{45}$$

that is, the replacement ratio of the income transfer program. Similarly, the public authorities should be instructed to act as if there were a subsidy of on B workers, that is,

$$\frac{G_b}{G_a} = \frac{W_b}{W_a} (1 - \rho). \tag{46}$$

This could, of course, be accomplished just as readily by providing a subsidy directly to the Bs as a form of negative income tax.

References

Courant, P. N., E. M. Gramlich, and D. L. Rubinfeld, "Public Employee Market Power and the Level of Government Spending," *American Economic Review*, December 1979, 806–17.
Jackman, R. A., and P. R. G. Layard, "The Efficiency Case for Long-Run Labour Market Policies," *Economica*, August 1980.

Johnson, G. E., "The Theory of Labour Market Intervention," *Economica*, August 1980.
Johnson, G. E., and J. D. Tomola, "The Fiscal Substitution Effect of Alternative Approaches to Public Service Employment Policy," *Journal of Human Resources*, Winter 1977.

Résumé

Le but de cet article est d'établir les conditions d'une politique d'emploi public efficace lorsque des distorsions du marché du travail existent. Il y a deux aspects à cette question: a) Quelle combinaison des différents types de travail devrait-on utiliser? b) Quelle devrait être la taille du secteur public?

Les distorsions du marché du travail qui sont au centre du modèle comprennent: (i) des rigidités de salaires pour certains types de travail, (ii) des subventions aux loisirs par l'intermédiaire de programmes de transfert de revenu, (iii) des impôts sur les revenus du travail.

Ces distorsions mises à part, nous raisonnons sur une économie de plein emploi.

Les principales conclusions sont les suivantes:

Premièrement, la société maximise le bien-être social global en utilisant les facteurs qui sont sujets à la plus grande distorsion économique relative, plus intensivement qu'il ne résulterait d'une prise en compte de la minimisation des pertes.

Deuxièmement, il n'est cependant pas évident que la production publique devrait être d'autant plus grande que les marchés du travail sont plus soumis à des distorsions.

Troisièmement, si des subventions compensatoires peuvent être appliquées dans le secteur privé, les règles de décision publique et privées devraient suivre la même procédure.

Problems in the Evaluation of Job and Cash Approaches to Income Maintenance

Jack Habib
Haim Factor*

Introduction

Interest has been growing in job programs that expand employment opportunities and guarantee an adequate income to those who are able and willing to work. This paper focuses on the role of job-creation programs in pursuing income maintenance objectives and explores the relationship between job-conditioned (hence job) programs and transfer programs that are not conditioned on employment (hence cash transfer).

Two broad categories of job programs are usually distinguished (Haveman, 1979). (1) Direct public service employment programs make specially organized and administered jobs available to defined target groups. These may be viewed as temporary and transitional jobs, often with some element of training, or as permanent long-term positions. (2) Employment subsidy programs are designed to induce job creation and supplement earnings of workers with a particular emphasis on the private sector. Two main variants are the earnings and wage rate subsidies. Either of these variants may be paid to employers or to employees. Employer subsidies are usually designed so as to subsidize *new* workers for *limited* periods. They often are targeted on groups with high unemployment rates but do not target the subsidy by wage or earnings level. Employee subsidies tend to be *permanent* and targeted on *all* workers with earnings or wage rates below certain levels. They are often targeted on groups with primary family reponsibilities. As a result employer subsidy proposals and programs have had an employment focus, while employee subsidies have had more of an income maintenance focus (Lerman, 1980).

There is a broad range of cash transfer programs. We do not consider social insurance programs designed to replace earnings or that focus on spe-

*We would like to thank Robert Lerman for helpful discussions. A special note of thanks is due to Robert Haveman for his extensive help at various phases.

Public Finance and Public Employment. Proceedings of the 36th Congress of the International Institute of Public Finance. Jerusalem, 1980.

cial groups such as the aged and disabled. Our focus is on programs that provide a minimum income to the able-bodied population of working age. There are two main variants: selective transfers of the negative income tax (NIT) variety, and universal transfers of the tax credit or child allowance type.

The Comparison of Job and Cash Strategies

The empirical literature comparing job and transfer programs has focused on the comparison of a NIT with some form of wage or earning subsidy, and on the comparison of the effects on labor supply and on poverty. The most extensive quantitative comparison is that of Masters and Garfinkel (1977). Further estimates for wage subsidies were made by Barth (1972) and elaborated upon by Haveman (1973). The results for a range of program specifications that have appeared in the literature are in Table 1.

There are three programs that appear in the table. The wage subsidy is defined in terms of a target wage rate (W_t), subsidy rate (r), the minimum wage level (which may be zero) required for eligibility, and the definition of family types and members eligible for the program. It may also allow for variation in the benefits with family size or reduce benefits if the recipient unit has unearned income. The formula for the subsidy in its simplest form is $S = r(W_t - W)$, if $S > 0$, where S is the subsidy per hour and W the wage level. Benefits decline as the wage rate increases and rise with increases in labor supply. The results for a number of specifications are in the table. All have the same subsidy rate (r) of .5. The specifications vary in the level of the target wage, in the types of families that are eligible, and in the provision for family size.

In an earnings subsidy, benefits rise with earnings at a rate (r) up to an earnings level (E), referred to as the pivot point. After the pivot point the subsidy is reduced at a rate (t) in a fashion that parallels a NIT so that additional earnings in this range are taxed. There may be a minimum earnings level required for eligibility and unearned or family income may be subject to a means test. The subsidy may be confined to certain family members or types and variation may be introduced with family size. In the table there are two alternative specifications that differ in both the initial subsidy rate (r) and in the pivot point (E).

In a NIT program benefits are at a maximum for someone who does not earn (b) and are reduced as family income rises at a rate (t) after some initial disregard (D). The maximum benefit (b) typically varies with family size. A separate benefit reduction rate (t) may be applied to various income sources. The pure NIT considered here does not impose any work or job search requirements as a precondition for receiving benefits. A single specification is provided in Table 1 with a tax rate of .5 and a guarantee at the poverty line.

Table 1

Simulations of Wage and Earnings Subsidies and a NIT[a]

	Wage Subsidy (subsidy rate is .5)[b]								Earnings Subsidy		NIT
	All Family Members Eligible			Only Family Heads Eligible					Subsidy Rate		Poverty Line Guarantee; Tax Rate = .5
	Target Wage			Guarantee Constant				Guarantee Varies with Family Size			
				Target Wage							
Effects	$3.30	$2.50	$1.60	$3.30	$2.50	$2.00	$1.60	$3.30	.5[c]	1.0[c]	
ΔLS/LS (%)[d]											
Recipients	5.8	..	..	2.1	..	..	..	1.2	−7.0	−6.9	−12.0
Total	3.5	..	..	0.7	..	..	..	0.3	−1.3	−1.3	−2.5
Δ earnings/earnings (%)											
Total	1.2	..	..	0.3	..	..	..	0.1	−0.8	−0.8	−1.2
% reduction in poverty gap per billion dollars	1.08	..	..	1.97	..	..	..	2.93	4.16	4.21	7.04
Benefits going to poor (%)	11.2	14.2	23.1	18.0	27.8	39.5	52.6	26.3	24.9	35.6	50.4

Sources: Based primarily on Masters and Garfinkel (1977). Additional specifications are from Barth (1972). Some of Barth's results are found in Haveman (1973).
[a] Simulations based on Survey of Economic Opportunity 1967. All wage levels are in 1967 dollars. Specifications with labor supply effects are from Masters and Garfinkel. All others are from Barth.
[b] Simulations by Rea (1974b) of wage subsidies yield a reduction in labor supply for some specifications but are not included in the table as comparable target efficiency measures are not available.
[c] The pivot point equals the poverty line and 2/3 the poverty line for subsidy rates of .5 and 1.0 respectively.
[d] Percentage change in hours worked for recipients and for the entire labor force.

155

We begin by addressing several concerns related to the generation and interpretation of the outcome measures reported in the table. We then turn to the question of the basis of comparison for the various programs.

Employment Effects

One must distinguish between three concepts in discussing employment effects: the amount of labor that persons want to supply at given wage rates, the extent to which workers are able to find as much work as they want to offer at existing wage rates, and how much people actually work. The latter two will be a function of market conditions. We first consider desired labor supply.

The evaluation of the labor supply effects of income maintenance programs has received a great deal of attention. The most extensive evidence is available for selective cash transfers as a result of the series of negative income tax experiments conducted in the United States. The standard theoretical analysis of a NIT leads to the conclusion that labor supply will be reduced. The various experiments bear out this prediction. Until very recently a consensus had emerged as summarized by Bishop (1978): "Husbands in families receiving payments reduced their labor supply by 6 to 7 percent when the negative tax rate on earnings was 50 percent, and 11 or 12 percent when the negative tax rate was 70 percent. The wives in these families also reduced the amount of time spent working outside the home by approximately 22 percent when the tax rate was 50 percent, and 32 percent when the tax rate was 70 percent."

Most of the income maintenance experiments were run on a three-year basis. One of the concerns in interpreting the results has been whether the effects of a short-term program might be less than those of a permanent program. To test this some of the participants in the last of the experiments (Seattle-Denver) were provided benefits over a five-year period. Recent work, much of it still available only in draft form, suggests that for those in the experiments for five years, the effects may be twice as great. However, there have been conflicting findings and a number of basic methodological issues have been raised, so that no new consensus has as yet emerged (Bishop, 1980).

Wage subsidies are generally assumed to have a positive effect on labor supply. The theoretical prediction is, however, ambiguous, as there are conflicting income (negative) and substitution (positive) effects. The overall effects depend on whether the labor supply curve is positively or negatively shaped in the relevant range. Rea (1974a) and Kesselman (1976) take a more pessimistic view of the effect of wage subsidies on labor supply. The effects of an earnings subsidy are divided into two parts. Below the pivot, earnings subsidies, like wage subsidies, have positive substitution and negative income effects. The earnings subsidy resembles a NIT above the pivot point. The overall effect is obviously a weighted sum of these two sections. Some, such as Bishop (1979), take the view that the earnings subsidy will lead to labor supply reduction that differs very little from those of a NIT. Others, such as Haveman et al. (1973), argue that the earnings subsidy could have much less negative or even positive impacts.

There have not been any empirical experiments that have directly tested the effects of a wage or earnings subsidy. Theoretically, the estimates of income and substitution effects from the NIT experiments are equally applicable to wage and earnings subsidies. However, the findings with respect to the relative magnitude of income and substitution effects have varied considerably among the analyses of the experimental results. There has been even less consistent evidence as to how these relative effects vary as wages rise.

The labor supply estimates of Masters and Garfinkel (1977) in Table 1 are an attempt to apply a single set of labor supply equations to the three programs in a comparative framework. For a full poverty guarantee NIT, they find that the decline in labor supply as measured by hours worked is 12% for recipients and 2.5% in relation to the total labor supply. The earnings subsidy also is found to reduce labor supply by about 7% and 1.3% respectively. The wage subsidy raises hours worked, but the gains are modest. They are particularly modest when the subsidy is targeted on family heads.

The labor supply effects in the table are based on simulating cross-section estimates of labor supply functions rather than the experimental results. However, they are similar to the results obtained from simulations of a national NIT based on the results of the experiments. If the further analysis of the experiments should lead to a new consensus about the shape in the relevant range of the labor supply function, these comparative results could also be affected.

There are several additional difficulties that arise in evaluating the comparative effects on labor supply. The labor supply results are presented here and indeed in almost all studies in terms of the effect on average hours worked per year. One does not have any notion of what the distribution of the impact on hours might look like. Is it mainly overtime that is being reduced? Is it an extra week of vacation? Is it a shift to part-time work? An increase in turnover and extended search efforts? Or does it represent a tendency to drop out of the labor force and if so, on a short-run or a long-run basis? Indeed, the effects of changes in labor force participation are not even embedded in the estimates of hours as these shifts are ruled out for technical reasons in the simulation of the wage and earnings subsidies in Table 1.

The lack of information as to the substance of labor supply effects is a serious limitation on the ability to draw policy conclusions from existing estimates. These limitations are particularly bothersome in making comparisons of a NIT with job and subsidy programs where there is so much stress on the goal of encouraging the labor force participation of the poor. As Haveman (1973, p. 41) points out: "Under a negative income tax, some families might be given the incentive to withdraw totally from the labor force, subsisting on the income guarantee. Under an earnings supplement or a wage subsidy program the absence of an income guarantee would provide no incentive to withdraw from the labor force."

What can be learned or is known of the nature of employment effects from other sources? One source is surveys of the labor force characteristics of the lower income population. Reviews of such surveys tend to find little evidence of large-scale voluntary unemployment (President's Commission on Income Maintenance, 1969; Freidman and Hausman, 1977).

The primary public concern that motivated the NIT experiment was with persons who dropped out of the labor force on a long-term basis. Yet it is precisely this aspect of the labor supply response about which we have learned the least. Recent analyses of the experiment have focused more on weeks worked. Bishop (1980) argues, on the basis of estimates of Robins and West (1980) and West and Steiger (1979), that the major part of the labor supply response to a NIT is in the form of reductions in weeks worked. This is primarily due to people not working at all during the year. Yet the same study indicates that at least half of this decline in weeks worked may represent increased unemployment and job search rather than voluntary withdrawal. Increased job search will mean less time employed, at least in the short run, but may lead to jobs providing higher earnings, more job satisfaction, and a stronger attachment in the long run. About 15% of husbands in the 5-year experiment did not work at all during the year (West and Steiger). It does not point to a massive withdrawal from all employment in response to a NIT, and the percentage who stop working over the full life of the experiment would be even smaller. Similar evidence for subsidies is not available. Yet the estimates here provide upper bounds to the hard-core group that could potentially respond to positive incentives for labor force participation.

The second major issue that arises in interpreting the labor supply results lies in the assumption that all changes in labor supply represent changes in actual employment. The simulation results presented here are based on the assumption of perfectly elastic demand for labor and competitive markets that equalize the demand and supply for labor (no unemployment). If the demand is not perfectly elastic there will be a smaller labor supply increase for a wage subsidy and a smaller decrease for a NIT as wage changes serve to moderate the initial effects. In conditions of unemployment a NIT that reduces the supply of labor will not reduce actual employment but only the extent of unemployment. The effects of a wage subsidy will now depend on the details of the type of subsidy and the sources of unemployment. It will no longer be possible to assume that an increase in supply will be automatically translated into employment. There will now be a divergence between the effects of subsidies provided in the first instance to the employer and that provided to an employee. Employer subsidies may still be effective in promoting employment because they directly reduce labor costs, but they may do little or nothing to raise net wage rates to employees. Employee subsidies may increase wages without stimulating additional demand. The simplest illustration is when unemployment is due to wages that are too high to clear the market either because of a minimum wage or some other source of rigidity. There is thus a conflict in designing a wage subsidy between the goal of raising the income of the working poor and that of stimulating the employment of the poor.

This conclusion must, however, be qualified in two respects. There is a growing literature addressing the question of the effects of employer subsidies under various assumptions about the nature of unemployment. Lerman (1980) has extended these analyses to the evaluation of employee subsidies. He argues that for some sources of unemployment an employee subsidy may still be effective in raising employment. The second qualification is that all of the micro-based analyses of employment effects assume a single homogeneous type of unskilled labor and a single wage that is being affected (a few analyses, such as Bishop, 1979, have considered a two-sector model with skilled and unskilled labor). Even if wages at the bottom are fixed, the distribution of wage rates at the lower end could become more compressed. Moreover, the institutional forces leading to ratchet effects would still allow for changes in relative or real wages when all wages are rising due to inflation or growth. Macro-economic oriented approaches have assumed some translation of wage subsidies into both wage and employment effects for low income groups (Nichols, 1980). There thus remains considerable ambiguity with respect to the nature of wage and employment effects.

Poverty and Target Efficiency

Any income maintenance program may be designed to eliminate poverty in eligible groups. Of greater interest, therefore, is the relative effectiveness of programs in achieving a given proverty-reduction goal. Target efficiency is commonly defined as the relationship between poverty reduction and budgetary costs of the program. It is most accurately calculated as the reduction in the poverty gap (the total difference between the poverty-line income and the actual incomes of the poor) per dollar of budgetary expenditure. Yet it is often the case that studies do not report directly on this measure.

In the table, as we have noted, there are two other measures. The percentage reduction in the poverty gap per billion dollars of expenditure is a direct reflection of the target efficiency as defined above.

The share of benefits to the poor is related but not equivalent to target efficiency. It differs in several respects. Transfers that raise the poor above the poverty line are included in this measure while they are excluded from the target efficiency measure. Other differences between these two measures emerge when the possible impact of programs on labor supply and wage rates is considered. The decline in the poverty gap will reflect not only the direct effect of transfers, but all changes in the labor supply or wage rates of the poor as well, whereas the transfers going to the poor will not be directly influenced by these effects. This measure will therefore underestimate the relative efficiency of a program such as a wage subsidy designed to increase employment among the able-bodied poor. On the other hand, an opposite bias is introduced by reductions in wage rates that reduce the relative effectiveness of wage subsidies and are also not reflected in the share measure.

Comparing the programs in Table 1 on the basis of the available measures, it is apparent that the NIT dominates all programs except for one of the wage rate subsidy specifications. It is also apparent that the results for a wage rate subsidy are very sensitive to the specification that is chosen—the target efficiency declines as the target wage rises, and trageting on family heads and varying benefits with family size significantly raises the share going to the poor.

Aside from the biases inherent in the different outcome measures, the labor market assumptions on which the estimates are based clearly favor the wage subsidy. The assumption of full employment favors the wage subsidy as the full poverty effect of the increases in labor supply find full expression. The assumption of perfectly elastic demand also favors the wage subsidy as wage changes that reduce the poverty effect of the subsidy and improve that of a NIT do not find expression.

There are two additional limitations of the simulations results presented here that should be mentioned. A factor that complicates the design of transfer systems and increases the cost is provision for integration with the positive tax system. The failure to allow for integration can lead to exorbitant penalties on increases in income or wage rates. In the simulations reported in the table, no allowance has been made for the problem of tax integration. The simulations are also based on the assumption that all those eligible for benefits receive them. There is growing evidence of the failure to realize benefits at a significant rate in a wide range of transfer and subsidy programs. This evidence is so compelling that there would appear to be a definite need to begin to include attention to the pattern of utilization in simulations of alternatives. There is evidence that at least in selective cash programs the highest rates of non-receipt are among those eligible for only small amounts. As a result, the actual flow of benefits to the non-poor might be smaller than the formulas themselves would dictate and target efficiency considerably greater.

What conclusions may be drawn from these patterns? Focusing on various pieces of the results presented in the table, some have concluded that the NIT has a clear advantage in targeting benefits to the poor while others have argued that the difference is not great and may even favor subsidies. In order to assess this issue one has to address a number of methodological issues that relate to how these alternatives should be compared.

Comparable Alternatives

One of the key problems in evaluating income maintenance programs is to establish an appropriate basis of comparison. In our case, which of the wage subsidy options in Table 1 may be appropriately compared to the NIT option? The various specifications are associated with different budgetary costs and different guarantee levels. To standardize the comparison one could compare programs with equal costs or alternatively those that provide equal guarantees.

In a different context it has been argued that an equal cost basis is inappropriate for comparing selective and universal strategies (Kesselman and Garfinkel, 1978; Habib, 1979). A similar argument could be made in this context. The basic problem is that the NIT spreads a given amount between two groups, the non-working and the working poor. One would therefore expect that an equal cost NIT would provide more benefits to those below the poverty line. Thus an NIT that provided a full poverty line guarantee to the non-working poor would provide well beyond a full poverty guarantee to the working poor. If an equal amount were concentrated in a wage subsidy just on the working poor, the guarantees should be even higher. But with the subsidy one could achieve adequate guarantees at a much lower cost. The equal cost comparison would therefore not seem to be appropriate.

Consider comparisons based on equal guarantees. In a NIT the basic guarantee is generally defined to be the lowest post-transfer income level. It is uniquely determined by the level set for the parameter b in the NIT formula. In a job program and particularly a subsidy program, the problem is more complex. The lowest income for someone employed in a job program would be that of someone who works one hour at the lowest possible wage. This is obviously of little interest. Defining a more meaningful target depends on the goals of the program. One can assume that the program is concerned primarily with a guarantee to those fully employed. In addition, one needs to define a reference wage level. If there is a universal minimum wage, it may serve as the reference point. Otherwise one could choose a wage level that is representative of the lowest paid workers. There is obviously an arbitrary element in this choice. It will reflect the percentage of persons at various wage levels and, in effect, the choice of a minimum percentage has to be made.

Having defined a wage rate on which guarantees are to be based, one can specify the parameters of the subsidy. A crucial constraint is the relationship between the minimum wage and the poverty line. This will obviously vary with family size. Consider a family of four and actual values for 1967. In 1967 the poverty line was $3,400 for a family of four and the minimum wage was $1.25. The target wage (for r=.5) required to guarantee the poverty line to someone working full time at the minimum wage was about $2.15. Although this particular wage level does not appear in the table it is possible to estimate what the outcome of such a program would look like from the estimates for wage rates of $2.00 and $2.50. Thus the estimated share would be about 35% with a subsidy targeted on family heads and around 18% if it were not targeted. Both rates are considerably below that of the full poverty guarantee NIT. However, we are not able to assess the further improvement that introducing family size variation would bring at this wage level. If it were of the same order of magnitude as that for the $3.30 wage level available in the table, the end result could easily be a program that compares favorably with a NIT in its target efficiency.

In making this assessment it is necessary to keep in mind that there are several reasons why even a higher target wage might be required for a full poverty guarantee. One is that there may be a wage decline in response to the subsidy. In this case one would have to adjust the target wage or the subsidy rate so as to produce the desired net wage. Because of the progressivity of the subsidy formula, some of the wage decline would be offset by an automatic increase in the subsidy. Barth (1974) estimated the possible wage response to a subsidy for alternative wage and price elasticities and suggests that it might be considerable. Bishop (1979), by contrast, taking a more general equilibrium perspective, has suggested that the response would be small.

Because not everyone works full time or necessarily earns the assumed minimum wage, the wage subsidy will not fully reduce poverty even among those employed. If one were to make the guarantee more inclusive, such as of those employed at least half-time, the target wage would have to be more than double. By contrast a NIT with a full poverty line guarantee provides even more than a poverty line guarantee to anyone employed. It is thus not surprising that a wage subsidy compared on this basis might compare favorably in its target efficiency and perhaps surprising if it did not. If the guarantee in the NIT were to be made comparable for those employed full time it would be inadequate for those not employed. This is another sense in which comparisons based on equal guarantees are also problematic.

We are thus left with the question of how these programs might be appropriately compared. Before addressing this, let us consider another form of job programs.

Direct Public Service Employment

The one major job program not included in the table is subsidized direct public employment. The basic rationale for such a program is to provide jobs during periods in which regular public or private sector jobs are not available and in this way to provide some minimum income through employment. As such, there is considerable concern with targeting the program on those unable to find regular jobs, with encouraging turnover when regular jobs become available, and on limiting the attractiveness of these jobs relative to regular employment. Thus, wages are kept low. The programs typically require a waiting period defined in terms of a spell of unemployment. They may often set a limit to the length of stay and require additional waiting periods for reentry. In the interests of targeting on the poor, eligibility may be conditioned on family income or confined to specific family members. An additional design element is whether the financing is open- or close-ended, that is, whether all those meeting the eligibility criteria are assured of a job.

The basic wage level and the maximum hours allowed under public employment programs provide a guarantee to those fully employed in the program. Those who work part time are provided with a guarantee that is proportionally lower. The universality of the guarantee depends on whether the job program is budgeted on an open-ended basis or not. The provisions for initial and intermittent waiting periods significantly affect the continuity and reduce the adequacy of the guarantee. If included, they raise serious doubts about the ability of a public job program to provide a full alternative to a guarantee in a cash program.

Consider now the labor supply, employment, and poverty-reduction effects of direct public employment programs. Direct public employment programs can increase employment by providing jobs to those involuntarily unemployed. They may also encourage additional labor supply to the extent that wage rates are better than otherwise available. The nature of these effects (as with a subsidy) depends on the slope of the labor supply curve. However, it may be that the attractiveness of the jobs is viewed differentially so that a given rise in potential wages will elicit a different response. Of course the increase in employment and labor supply will be only some fraction of the total employment in this program as some workers leave or reduce their regular employment.

The efficiency of targeting benefits on the poor in a public job program is influenced by the wage level, which in turn will influence the level of support to poor recipients, the percentage of recipients who are poor, and the extent to which persons who would have been otherwise employed participate in the program. Clearly, the lower the wage, the greater the share of benefits to the poor for all the above reasons; however, the guarantees will be inadequate. The share of the poor, as in all job-creation programs, will be influenced by the extent to which eligibility is confined to specific family types or family members and by whether wages vary with family size. This is a case in which the share of the benefits going to the poor is particularly inadequate as a measure of efficiency in that the lost wages from the decline in regular employment will not be subtracted from total benefits.

There have been studies of the extent of participation in public job programs and how this relates to the wage rate and other program specifications. These studies suggest that participation by workers who would be otherwise employed might be considerable (Greenberg, 1978). The only study to focus directly on the effect of a job program on poverty reduction is Betson and Greenberg (1980). They argue that even a job program paying the minimum wage and limited to primary earners does no better than a NIT with a guarantee at 75% of the poverty line and t = .5 in targeting benefits on the poor. Their conclusions are based on the share of benefits to the poor which is biased in favor of the job program. We calculated from their data the percentage reduction in poverty per billion dollars and found that the advantage of the NIT is much greater—6% as opposed to 4%. (Betson and Greenberg, Tables 4 and 5). The advantage of the NIT is attributed to the large number of workers attracted out of private employment by the job program, and to the fact that a significant portion of these are not poor.

These estimates are not presented here as definitive. The specifications are not in any sense necessarily comparable (whether in terms of costs or guarantee). It would also be useful to test the sensitivity of these results to a number of possible variations in the programs, such as introducing family size variation in the public job wage. Even more basic difficulties with the comparison of job and cash programs are discussed in the next section.

Differences in the Populations Covered

The fact that there are certain groups provided for by a NIT and not eligible or adequately supported under a subsidy or job program brings us to the most fundamental problem in comparing these programs. Indeed, it raises the question as to whether they are at all comparable. Another way of putting the question is to ask: to the extent that a more complete empirical analysis would yield significant differences in target efficiency, to what structural differences between the programs may they be attributed?

1. A NIT can provide a full guarantee to all groups of poor. A public employment or subsidy program cannot. As we have noted neither equal cost based comparisons or equal guarantee comparisons can get around this basic difficulty.
2. Among the overlapping population that is served—that is, the working poor—the criteria for deciding the amount of support and which persons

among the working population are to be supported are fundamentally different. In a cash program the amount of support declines with earnings (or, as in a universal program, it may be constant) while in job programs it rises at least over some range with earnings.

3. The NIT considers family income from all sources while job programs usually do not (those simulated in the table do not).

All these differences influence the labor supply effects and target efficiency of the programs and it is not clear as to which is the critical factor. Moreover, they need not necessarily be combined. One can also have hybrid programs (such as the Family Income Supplement program in England) in which support is conditioned on employment but falls as earnings rise.

Aside from the empirical question of how these three factors shape the results, a methodological issue arises. Given the differences in the population receiving support under the programs, what populations should be included in the comparison and measurements of effects—any group covered by either program or those that overlap? Thus it could be argued that the NIT may have higher target efficiency because an additional population is being supported which has no earned income and all transfers to this group fully serve to reduce the poverty gap. Thus a fairer comparison would be to look only at the effects on the working poor even though the program serves additional groups. On the other hand one can argue that as the programs are expected to lead to shifts among categories by inducing people into employment (wage subsidy) or out of employment (NIT) one needs to measure the consequences for all these groups.

Even the comparison for the working poor raises some basic conceptual difficulties. It is necessary to distinguish between two reasons that the distribution of benefits would be different between a wage subsidy and a NIT also limited to those employed. One relates to the fact that there are differential sources of leaks to the non-poor. The second is that the wage subsidy implicitly defines the poor in terms of low wages while the NIT defines them in terms of low earnings. The question of which definition is the more equitable must be resolved before a basis of comparison can be determined.

The appropriate response to these issues is related to the broader question of the basic ideological thrust underlying the movement to income support through jobs. Is the thrust to increase incentives for employment and to assure adequate support for the working poor, or is it to support those deemed worthy of support while denying support to the undeserving? The NIT movement has been associated with the notion of support to all those without earnings no matter what the source. This was indeed the type of NIT on which the experiments were focused and which have been simulated in Table 1. But if the thrust of job programs is to deny support to those unwilling to work, it would seem appropriate to compare job programs with

Table 2

Alternative Job and Cash Transfer Strategies

I. Able Bodied Non-Employed Not Eligible for Support

Pure Job	Public Job, Subsidy and Work-Conditioned Cash Transfer[a]	Pure Cash[b]
1. *Only public jobs* which guarantee employment but may not provide poverty-line wage level. Measures to reduce shifts out of regular employment diminish continuity of guarantees. 2. *Public job and subsidy.*[c] Subsidy increases incentive for regular employment and supplements incomes of working poor. Makes possible a higher wage or more continuous employment in the job program. Because of public job, subsidy could focus on those fully employed.	Public job guarantees employment. Cash transfer may be universal or income-tested. Designed to introduce family size variation and/or raise guarantees. Because of cash transfer supplement, subsidy may have low target wage and still guarantee poverty line.	The work test denies support to those unwilling to work and avoids recourse to a guaranteed job. Key consideration is the extent to which the willingness to accept available jobs can be accurately determined. Offer of a public job puts this willingness to a more direct test.

166

II. Able Bodied Non-Employed Eligible for Support (Cash Component Required)

Only Cash Transfers[a]	NIT and Job Program[e]	Universal Cash and Job Program
Three variants:	Two major variants:	Universal cash transfer designed to provide fully for working poor or alternatively to supplement support provided by job programs by introducing family size variation and reducing required subsidy parameters. Universal transfer could also provide for non-working poor with children if desired guarantees to these groups are modest. Otherwise a combined universal/NIT cash component is desirable. The NIT would be confined to non-working poor.
1. *NIT* that provides for working and non-working poor.	1. NIT has limited role of providing for those not employed. Job component will provide for working poor. Guaranteed job may be included to assure opportunities and increase incentives.	
2. *Universal allowance credits* that provide for working and non-working poor-high allowances required.	2. NIT provides for those not employed and for working poor. Case for guaranteed jobs as above and case for subsidy based on desire to limit further disincentive effects of a NIT or to create incentive for regular as opposed to subsidized public employment.	
3. *Mixed universal allowances/NIT.* NIT provides for non-working poor and allowances supplement earnings of the working poor. Low allowances are sufficient and provide for family size variation in benefits in NIT. In universal or mixed, allowances could replace tax exemptions and progressivity of marginal income tax rates is reduced.		

[a] Variant with selective transfer, proposed by Haveman (1973); with universal by Garfinkel (1977).

[b] For a critical review of work-tests, see Freidman and Hausman (1977).

[c] Bishop and Lerman (1977).

[d] See Kesselman and Garfinkel (1978) for a comparison of NIT and universal schemes. Mixed scheme is emerging in Europe and has become official policy in Israel. The three options are compared in Habib (1979).

[e] For combined job and NIT, see Kesselman (1973), Betson and Greenberg (1980), and Carter's Program for Better Jobs and Income; with added subsidy see Lerman (1974).

167

a NIT that includes a work test. Yet even this comparison would not be appropriate unless a direct job and wage subsidy were viewed in combination so as to provide for those not able to find work as well as those employed. Alternatively, if support is to be provided to those who do not work for whatever reason, the only appropriate comparison will be between a NIT and some combination of cash and job programs. Whereas analyses of individual programs are necessary to provide the basis for their design, only combinations of programs may be meaningfully compared.

In Table 2 we have tried to provide some sense of the ways in which various job and cash components may be combined in an overall income maintenance strategy. The table is divided into two halves, emphasizing the key role in shaping the options of the decision as to whether those who do not want to work should be supported. Space does not permit us to elaborate upon the various options presented in the table. We do want to call attention to the fact that the possible roles of universal cash transfers are emphasized in our description of the various options and that we indicate the possible advantages of combining a universal component with a selective cash or job program. This is consistent with the growing emphasis upon and proliferation of child allowance programs in European countries (Messere and Owens, 1979).

Suggestions for Future Research

Our review of the existing analyses of job and cash programs has revealed many gaps in our knowledge. To deal with some, such as the allowance for market imperfections or the extent of benefit take-up, will require considerable advances in existing simulation methodology and in the knowledge base. Others may be addressed within existing models. Thus full poverty line guarantee job programs appropriately targeted with adequate variation in benefits with family size and provision for integration with the tax system have not been simulated. As a result, we do not have sufficient insight into the relative budgetary and real costs of job programs providing full poverty-line guarantees that can serve as a basis for an evaluation of these programs. Similarly, we do not have a sense of the way in which the outcomes of a full guarantee job program vary with alternative specifications of other program parameters, or of how the performance of programs varies with the guarantee level. Aside from the need to examine a wider range of specifications, available simulations have not provided sufficient and consistently comparable data on the substance of labor supply effects, on the reduction in the poverty gap, or on the distribution of benefits to the non-poor.

If our knowledge of these individual programs is limited, our knowledge of the mixed strategies reviewed in Table 2 is even more so. Relative to the broad range of options, policy analysis has had a very limited focus. There is need for research that will elaborate the design issues involved in integrating these programs into an overall strategy, evaluate the performance of the alternative specifications of these mixed strategies, and provide a framework for comparing them. It would seem safe to say that while some work of this kind has been done, the basic arithmetic of these mixed strategies has not been worked out. The research on the way in which universal transfers and selective cash or job programs may be combined would seem to be particularly limited. At the same time this is an area in which there is a rich and developing international experience. This suggests a third area of research that would focus on the way many of these basic issues have been addressed in a comparative perspective. There are few studies that provide a sense of how different countries have placed themselves on the spectrum suggested by Table 2. In Europe little or no attention has been given to the role of job programs in guaranteeing a minimum income to those unemployed or to the working poor. These different emphases could be purely coincidental or related to differences in values, the nature of the underlying problems, or the context of overall social policies. Unravelling these differences would certainly provide important insights.

References

Barth, Michael C. "Universal Wage-Rate Subsidy: Benefits and Effects." In *The Economics of Federal Subsidy Programs*, Part 4, pp. 497–540. Joint Economic Committee, 92nd Cong., 2nd sess. Washington, D.C.: Government Printing Office, 1972.
———. "Market Effects of a Wage Subsidy." *Industrial and Labor Relations Review* (1974) 27:572–585.
Betson, David, and Greenberg, David. *A Simulation Study on the Interaction Between Transfer Policy and Employment Programs*. Mimeograph. Paper prepared for the Middlebury College Conference on Welfare Reform, 1980.
Bishop, John. "The Welfare Brief." *The Public Interest* (1978) 53:169–175.
———. "The General Equilibrium Impact of Alternative Anti-Poverty Strategies: Income Maintenance, Training and Job Creation." *Industrial and Labor Relations. Review* (1979) 32:2.
———. *Reactions to the Latest Sime/Dime Labor Supply Results*. Mimeograph. 1980.
Bishop, John, and Lerman, Robert. "Wage Subsidies for Income Maintenance and Job Creation." In *Job Creation: What Works?*, edited by R. Taggart. Washington, D.C.: National Council on Employment Policy, 1977.
Freidman, Barry, and Hausman, Leonard. *Work, Welfare and the Program for Better Jobs and Income*. Joint Economic Committee, 95th Congress, 1st sess. Washington, D.C.: Government Printing Office, 1977.
Garfinkel, Irwin, and Haveman, Robert. "Earnings Capacity and the Target Efficiency of Alternative Transfer Programs." *American Economic Review, Papers and Proceedings* (1974) 64:196–204.
Garfinkel, Irwin, with Skidmore, Felicity. *Income Support Policy: Where We've Come from and Where We Should be Going*. Discussion Paper no. 490–78. Madison, Wis.: Institute for Research on Poverty, 1978.
Greenberg, David H. "Participation in Public Employment Programs." In *Creating Jobs*, edited by J. Palmer, pp. 323–368. Washington, D.C.: Brookings Institution, 1978.
Habib, Jack, *An Integrated Approach to Taxes and Transfers*. Jerusalem: The Maurice Falk Institute for Economic Research in Israel, 1979.

Haveman, Robert H. "Work-Conditioned Subsidies as an Income Maintenance Strategy: Issues of Program Structure and Integration." In *Studies in Public Welfare*, Paper no. 9, Part 1, pp. 33–67. Joint Economic Committee, 93rd Cong., 1st sess. Washington, D.C.: Government Printing Office, 1973.

———. *Direct Job Creation: Potentials and Realities*. Discussion Paper no. 570–79. Madison, Wis.: Institute for Research on Poverty, 1979.

———, Lurie, Irene, and Mirer, Thad. *Earnings Supplementation Plans for "Working Poor" Families: An Evaluation of Alternatives*. Discussion Paper no. 175–73. Madison, Wis.: Institute for Research on Poverty, 1973.

Kesselman, Jonathan R. "A Comprehensive Approach to Income Maintenance: SWIFT." *Journal of Public Economics* (1973) 1:59–88.

———. "Tax Effects on Job Search, Training, and Work Effort." *Journal of Public Economics* (1976) 6:255–272.

——— and Garfinkel, Irwin. "Professor Friedman Meet Lady Rhys-Williams: NIT vs. CIT." *Journal of Public Economics* (1978) 10:179–216.

Lerman, Robert I. "JOIN: A Jobs and Income Program for American Families." In *Studies in Public Welfare*, Paper no. 19, pp. 3–67. Joint Economic Committee, 93rd Cong., 2nd sess. Washington, D.C.: Government Printing Office, 1974.

———. *Employer Versus Worker Wage Subsidies: A Comparison of Their Effects on Employment*. Mimeograph. Paper prepared for The Brookings Conference on Categorical Wage Subsidies, 1980.

Masters, Stanley, and Garfinkel, Irwin. *Estimating the Labor Supply Effects of Income Maintenance Alternatives*. Institute for Research on Poverty Monograph Series. New York: Academic Press, 1977.

Messere, Kenneth, and Owens, Jeffrey. "The Treatment of Dependent Children Under Income Tax and Social Welfare Systems." *International Social Security Review* (1979) 1:50–59.

Nichols, Donald. *Reducing the Non-Inflationary Unemployment Rate with a Targeted Wage Subsidy*. Mimeograph. University of Wisconsin, 1980.

President's Commission on Income Maintenance Programs. *Poverty Amid Plenty: The American Paradox*. Washington, D.C., 1969.

Rea, Samuel A. *Investment in Human Capital and Income Maintenance Programs*. Institute for the Quantitative Analysis of Social and Economic Policy, Working Paper no. 7404. Toronto, 1974a.

———. "Trade-Offs between Alternative Income Maintenance Programs." In *How Income Supplements Can Affect Work Behavior*, Studies in Public Welfare Series, Paper no. 13. Joint Economic Committee, 93rd Cong. 2nd sess. Washington, D.C.: Government Printing Office, 1974b.

Robins, Philip K., and West, Richard. *Labor Supply Response to SIME/DIME: Analysis of Six Years of Data*. Mimeograph. 1980.

West, Richard and Steiger, Gary. The Effects of the Seattle and Denver Income Maintenance Experiments on Alternative Measures of Labor Supply, *Mimeo.*, Nov., 1979.

Résumé

A la lumière de l'importance croissante attachée au maintien d'un revenu des défavorisés capables de travailler et en âge de le faire, cet article étudie la méthodologie employée pour évaluer ces approches et les comparer à celles en termes de transferts monétaires. Deux aspects sont considérés: d'une part, la façon selon laquelle les effets sur l'emploi et la capacité à réduire la pauvreté sont mesurés, d'autre part le cadre permettant de choisir les normes comparatives des programmes alternatifs. La conclusion à laquelle nous arrivons est que l'éventail des normes pour lesquelles nous disposons de renseignements convenables quant à leurs conséquences est bien trop étroit pour faire des comparaisons valables entre les programmes. Il resterait un énorme travail à faire pour éclairer ces différences. Il y a toutefois des problèmes conceptuels inhérents à la comparaison de simples programmes en terme d'emploi ou de transfert monétaires; par conséquent, il convient de considérer toutes les stratégies qui s'occupent de ces différents groupes qui doivent être aidés et qui peuvent combiner des programmes d'emploi et de transferts monétaires. Cet article essaie de dresser l'éventail des principales stratégies avec, d'un côté, les stratégies monétaires pures, de l'autre, les stratégies en termes purs d'emploi, et au milieu, un éventail d'options qui les combinent. Ce que l'on sait actuellement du succès relatif et des problèmes de structure propres à des stratégies combinatoires est encore plus limité. L'expérience internationale suggère que les transferts monétaires pour les défavorisés capables de travailler pourraient être intégrés dans une stratégie globale en combinaison avec des programmes sélectifs en termes de transferts monétaires. Des recherches centrées sur ces possibilités et sur la réalité de l'expérience internationale seraient tout à fait intéressantes.

The Design of Employment Subsidies:
The Lessons of the U.S. Experience

John Bishop

The industrialized West is finding it increasingly difficult to reconcile the twin objectives of low rates of inflation and low rates of unemployment. Monetary and fiscal policy seems to be unable to reduce unemployment below unacceptably high levels without accelerating an already unacceptably high rate of inflation. Employment subsidies have been proposed as a potentially effective mechanism for dealing with this problem. They lower the cost of labor and the marginal cost of extra output and thus they should simultaneously increase employment and lower prices. The purpose of this paper is to assess employment subsidies as a remedy for stagflation and to examine in the context of this objective, how they are best designed.

The U.S. experience with New Jobs Tax Credit (NJTC), the WIN Tax Credit, the Targeted Jobs Tax Credit (TJTC) and Comprehensive Employment and Training Act (CETA) on-the-job-training subsidies has much to say about how employment subsidies should be designed. The main body of this paper describes these programs, summarizes the studies that have been done of their effectiveness and explores how the design characteristics of each program influenced its success or failure. The most successful of the U.S. employment subsidies, the New Jobs Tax Credit, is discussed in the first section. The more targeted programs are discussed in section II. The final section of the paper applies the lessons developed earlier to the design of a prototype employment subsidy.

There are at least five questions I would like this review of each of these programs to answer:

1. Is there significant employer participation?
2. Does the subsidy induce the employers that receive the subsidy to increase employment of workers eligible for subsidy?
3. Does total employment in the industry or nation increase? To what extent does the subsidy of certain workers and firms cause unsubsidized workers and firms to suffer declines in employment?

Public Finance and Public Employment. Proceedings of the 36th Congress of the International Institute of Public Finance. Jerusalem, 1980.
Copyright © 1982 by Wayne State University Press, Detroit, Michigan, 48202.

4. Does the subsidy produce a reduction in product prices?
5. Do subsidized workers get higher wages and does this tend to promote inflationary wage increases?

The first question is the easiest to study. If a program does not succeed in attracting significant employer interest (this can be either many employers using the subsidy intermittently or a few employers using it extensively), it is a failure and there is no point in addressing any of the other questions. The second question can be addressed by interviewing employers that have received the subsidy and comparing them to other similar employers. If these firms are expanding employment of subsidized workers, we have not established that total employment is rising—a constant level of employment may just be redistributed. The other three questions are the hardest ones to answer. Answers are necessary, however, before a definite judgment can be made that employment subsidies are an effective way of dealing with stagflation. With one exception the empirical work on the U.S. experience does not address the last three questions. The burgeoning theoretical literature on employment subsidies has addressed these questions, however and is referred to where appropriate.

I. The U.S. Experience with the New Jobs Tax Credit

Signed into law in May 1977, the New Jobs Tax Credit (NJTC) offered firms a tax credit against corporate or personal income tax liability for expansions in employment in 1977 or 1978. NJTC was a marginal subsidy of 50% of the increase in an employers wage base under the Federal Unemployment Tax Act above 102% of the previous year. The scheme was only mildly targeted but simple enough in administration for employers to calculate their own eligibility on their tax forms.

Despite the fact that public agencies made very little effort to advertise or promote NJTC and that many small firms had not yet heard of it in February 1978, use of NJTC was quite extensive. In 1977 its first year of operation $2.3 billion of NJTC were claimed on a total of 610,000 tax returns. In 1978 $4.4 billion of credits were claimed on a total of 1,107,000 tax returns. In 1979 $1.6 billion were claimed on 300,000 returns with tax credit carry overs or with fiscal years that overlapped 1978. Since the firm's deductions for wages must be reduced by the amount of the credit, revenue costs (assuming no direct effects on before tax profits) were approximately $5.0 billion. While roughly one-third of the returns claiming a credit were corporate returns, two-thirds of the dollars claimed were on these returns. Since the credits due to a partnership or Subchapter S corporation may show up on more than one individual return, the total number of businesses claiming the credit is smaller than the number of tax returns claiming it. Nevertheless, more than 30% of the nation's 3.5 million employers claimed the credit in 1978. A lower bound estimate of the number of workers whose employment received subsidy can be obtained by dividing the dollars of credit claimed by the $2100, the maximum credit an employer can receive for one worker. This calculation implies that during its 2-year period of operation at least 3.95 million employees were subsidized. By comparison, total private nonagricultural employment grew 2.8 million in 1977 and 3.6 million in 1978.

A. The Impact of NJTC on Subsidized Firms

To date there have been three studies of the New Jobs Tax Credit. Two have focused on the differential impact of NJTC on the firms that knew about it or said they responded. The other studied the credits impact on total employment and on inflation.

The first study is based on a mail questionnaire survey of a sample of the membership of the National Federation for Independent Businesses (NFIB) (McKevitt, 1978). The first survey to ask questions about NJTC was conducted in January 1978. Of the employers responding, 43% knew about NJTC and 1.4% reported that the credit had influenced them to hire extra workers (the number averaged 2.0 per firm). The April survey found that 51% knew of NJTC's existence and that 2.4% had increased hiring by an average of 2.3 employees as a result. In the July 1978 survey 58% were aware of the credit and 4.1% of the firms reported they had increased hiring as a result. An increase in employment of 2.3 employees by over 4% of all employers is not a small response. If the NFIB survey is representative, and other firms are not hurt by the expansion of subsidized firms, these responses imply that in the second quarter of 1978 there were more than 300,000 extra jobs directly created as a result of the NJTC at a tax expenditure of roughly $8500 for each job created.

The second study (Perloff and Wachter, 1980) is based upon the survey conducted by the Bureau of the Census. Perloff and Wachter compared rates of employment growth between 1976 and 1977 for firms that knew about the credit and those that did not. Holding employment size, class, region, form of organization, type of industry, and the growth rate of sales constant, they found that the employment of firms that had heard of the credit before February 1978 had grown 3% faster. Firms that reported they made a conscious effort to expand employment because of the credit grew 10% faster than firms that knew about the credit but did not report making any special effort. Since firms may learn about the credit because they are growing fast, Perloff and Wachter conduct a Wu test for simultaneity and find themselves unable to reject the hypothesis that knowledge of the credit wa uncorrelated with the error term of the employment change regression. If one were to assume that NJTC caused the 3% higher growth of the small and medium-sized firms that knew about the credit (about a quarter of total employment is in these firms) and that NJTC left the rest of the economy unaffected, the total number of extra jobs in 1977 would be roughly 700,000. Tax expenditure per job created would be $3500 per job.

B. The Impact of NJTC on Total Employment

Studies like those just reviewed are measuring the differential impact of NJTC across firms and not the net impact of NJTC on the total economy. Since firms compete with each other in both labor and product markets, the increases of employment in subsidized firms may cause decreases of employment in their unsubsidized competitors. Alternatively, an NJTC-induced expansion by one firm may cause that firm's suppliers to expand as well. The direction of NJTC's impact on nonsubsidized firms is not known a priori for it depends upon the relative size of offsetting effects. We suspect, however, that the first effect is larger than the second. If so, simple extrapolations from measured impact of the credit on firms to impacts on the economy like those in previous paragraphs will exaggerate the true impact. Since most of the displacement effects that may bias estimates of net job creations when the firms are the unit of observation are netted out when the industry is the unit of observation, studies of NJTC's impact on an entire industry's employment would seem to be able to resolve this issue.

The third study (Bishop, 1980) has attempted to address the displacement and inflation effects of the NJTC by examining its effect on two of the industries—construction and distribution—in which one would expect the largest response. Non-seasonally adjusted monthly data on employment and man-hours in these industries were regressed on seasonal dummies, trends on the dummies, and three-year distributed lags of input prices and retail sales (or construction put in place). With few exceptions, the lag structures were freely estimated with each input price or price ratio being represented by its contemporaneous value, and that of each of the previous four quarters and four half-years. All models were estimated using two-stage least squares.

The NJTC variable was an average over the past six months of the proportion of firms (weighted by employees) that knew about the credit. It had a value of .057 in June 1977 and rose at an average rate of .0424 per month, reaching .343 in January 1978 and .572 in June 1978. Most of the coefficients on the NJTC variable were positive and significant. Across all of the regressions the average NJTC employment stimulus over the 12-month period from mid-1977 to mid-1978 ranges from 150,000–670,000 depending on specification. Hours worked per week declined so total hours worked rose proportionately less.

C. The Impact of NTJC on Price Inflation

Employment subsidies lower both the average and marginal costs of production and sales. In competitive industries output will expand and prices will fall. Given the wage level, supply curves of most competitive industries are quite flat so if the subsidy does not raise wage rates, the price reduction should be nearly as large as the downward shift of the supply curve. A marginal employment subsidy like the NJTC lowers the marginal costs of existing firms and the marginal and average costs of new firms by a lot more than it lowers the average costs of existing firms. Consequently, a marginal subsidy may induce price reductions in competitive industries that in the short and medium run are substantially larger than the total dollar amounts of subsidy paid out.

The unsettled nature of the theory of oligopolistic pricing makes infeasible definitive theoretical predictions of how oligopolistic industries will respond to marginal employment subsidies. Some theories predict a price decline that is equal to the reduction in average costs of existing firms. If, however, the oligopoly is setting its price just low enough to forestall or limit entry of new competitors into the industry, their response will depend on the subsidy's impact on the average costs of new entrants. Having a zero threshold, a new entrant receives subsidy on all of his workers. Consequently, a marginal employment subsidy with a fixed threshold that is perceived to be permanent should cause the entry forestalling price to decline by the full amount of its subsidy of marginal costs. A smaller decline will occur if the threshold will be revised in the future, if the subsidy is not viewed as permanent, or if, as with the NJTC, limitations are placed on the subsidy that new firms can receive. Nevertheless, here again theory predicts that the short and medium run price decline may be substantially larger than subsidy induced reduction in the average costs of existing firms.

An examination of the behavior of prices during the NJTC's period of operation tends to support the hypothesis that a marginal employment subsidy can temporarily slow inflation. A number of the features of the NTJC—the $100,000 per firm limitation, subsidizing only the first $4200 of wages, and its temporary nature—should have focused the subsidy and stimulus to production on sectors of the economy with high rates of employee turnover and large numbers of small and medium sized firms. The distribution sector—trucking, wholesale, and retailing—fit this description so it was hypothesized that NJTC would tend to compress the margin between retail prices and manufacturer's prices of finished consumer goods. Preliminary support for this hypothesis is provided by the fact that between May 1977 and June 1978 nonfood commodity retail prices rose only 4.73% while manufacturers prices of nonfood, consumer finished goods were rising 6.56%.

The hypothesis was tested statistically by regressing the monthly rate of change of retail prices on current and lagged changes in a number of distribution industry cost variables (wage rates, wholesale prices, the rental price of capital, and excise taxes), the unemployment rate, seasonal dummies, and trends on the seasonal dummies. Coefficients on NJTC were negative and statistically significant for the nonfood commodities aggregate and for restaurant and tavern prices. The size and statistical significance of the NJTC coefficients were robust to a variety of changes of specification. The 5–7% reduction in marginal costs induced by the credit seems by June 1978 to have lowered prices of nonfood commodities by nearly 2% and all commodities by roughly 1%. The compression of the margin is all the more remarkable when one remembers that retail price indexes include imported goods whose relative price was rising while wholesale prices do not.

The savings to the consumer from the compression of retail margins seems on its own to have been roughly comparable to the face value of tax credit claims. Tax credit claims in 1977 were $2.4 billion: The coefficients imply consumer savings were between .5 and 1 billion dollars. In 1978, claims were $4.5 billion and consumer savings were estimated to be between $3.8 and $7 billion. If the prices of services and some manufacturing goods were forced down as well, the NJTC induced price reduction during its second year could well have been two, three or four times the size of the tax subsidy. Although this result is predicted by theory, it is nevertheless quite remarkable that a marginal employment subsidy handicapped by a two year life and limited to $100,000 per firm should have had so large an effect.

D.   The NJTC's Impact on Wage Inflation

The primary concern economists have had about marginal employment subsidies is that when labor markets are tight the subsidy may tend to accelerate the rate of wage increase and thus raise the underlying rate of inflation. When it was initiated NJTC was seen as a temporary countercyclical employment stimulus. It was phased out on schedule in December 1978 primarily because the economy was perceived to be already at the point where further reductions in unemployment rates would result in accelerating wage increases.

Whether employment subsidies do in fact have an impact on wage rates has not yet been formally tested. In Table 1 the annual rates of change of wage rates for a variety of industries is tabulated for the period May 1975 through April 1980. Wage rates rose more rapidly during the phase-in period of the NJTC—May 1977-December 1978—than in the previous years. During this period, however, unemployment rates were lower than previously and the minimum wage was rising more rapidly so the increase in rate of wage inflation may have been a response to these phenomena and not a direct response to the NJTC. More to the point, however, is what appears to be a

Table 1

Annual Rate of Change of Wage Rates

		Phase In of NJTC Impact			Phase Out	
	5/25 to 5/76	5/76 to 5/77	5/77 to 5/78	12/77 to 12/78	12/78 to 12/79	12/79 to 4/80
Minimum Wage	9.5	0.0	15.2	15.2	9.4	6.9[a]
Wholesale & Retail	6.2	7.6	8.7	9.8	8.7	6.9
Construction	7.0	4.0	6.9	7.6	6.8	5.3
Service	8.2	6.5	7.1	7.5	8.1	7.0
Manufacturing[b]	6.9	9.1	8.2	9.2	9.0	9.7
Total Private	8.0	7.4	8.1	9.2	8.1	6.1
Unemployment Rate of 20–65 Males	6.5	5.8	4.8	4.1	4.1	4.8

[a] Annual rate of change for 12/79–12/80.
[b] Excludes the effects of overtime and interindustry shifts.

deceleration of wage increases in wholesale, retail, construction and the total private economy during the phase-out period December 1978 to December 1979 when unemployment remained low. Careful econometrics is required to sort all these factors out but this cursory examination of the evidence certainly provides no evidence that a reduction in unemployment induced by a marginal employment subsidy is less wage inflationary (as distinct from price inflationary) than reductions in unemployment engineered by other policy interventions. Consequently, it would seem prudent to either avoid operating a marginal employment subsidy during tight labor markets or to redesign the scheme so that wage increases are discouraged at the same time that employment is stimulated. (Such a redesign is described in Section III.)

II.   U.S. Experience with Targeted Programs

The United States has experimented with a variety of targeted employment subsidies. These programs—WIN tax credit, JOBS contracts, CETA On-the-Job Training Subsidies, and Targeted Jobs Tax Credit (TJTC)—have all been targeted on highly disadvantaged workers and have as a consequence been quite complicated to administer. In each of these programs certification of a worker's eligibility has required separate application by and certification of both the worker and his employer. Although these programs may have helped specific individuals to find jobs and get off welfare, they have not yet achieved significant scale and consequently have not had an

appreciable impact upon the number of people on welfare or the unemployment rate of people in the target group.

A. NAB-JOBS

The first of the subsidy programs was the National Alliance for Business
JOBS program's contract placements effort in which the government issued
contracts that reimbursed employers for part of the costs of hiring and training disadvantaged workers. To qualify for the program a worker had to be a
high school dropout, less than twenty-two or more than forty-five years old,
handicapped or in a family with below poverty level income. Contract
placements grew from 8400 in fiscal 1967 to 93,000 in fiscal 1971 and thereafter declined. Thus at its peak JOBS contracts were subsidizing only 1/10 of
1% of the nation's workers. Tight budgets were not responsible for the small
scale of the program, for the administrators of the program were consistently
unable to expend the funds programmed for JOBS contracts. In 1969 for
instance, only $49 million of the $210 million programmed for JOBS contracts was expended.

Also significant is the fact that only one-third of the employers that
hired JOBS enrollees went to the trouble of establishing a contractual arrangement and thus receiving a subsidy for what they were doing. This
reveals that the problem is not just one of employers being reluctant to hire
stigmatized individuals. Many employers seem to find the delays and red
tape of arranging a contract and the potentially greater vulnerability to affirmative action complaints so potentially costly that they do not apply for the
50% subsidy of the first six months of a worker's wages for which they are
eligible.

B. CETA-OJT

With the reorganization of manpower services mandated by the Comprehensive Employment and Training Act of 1973, the JOBS program
evolved into what is now called CETA On-the-Job Training (OJT) contracts.
The OJT program has not developed an effective local constituency because
many small businessmen have an ideological aversion to handouts and because the perceived benefits of participating are so small. Seldom does a firm
receive more than one subsidized worker and the maximum payment is
generally less than 25% of a year's wages. Thus despite Congressional man-
dates to expand the scale of the program, only 1% of the nation's employers
participated during 1979. Contracts are typically written for only one worker
even when the participating firm is large. As a result, OJT subsidies account
for only a tiny proportion of total employment.

C. The WIN Tax Credit

For nearly ten years employers that hire recipients of Aid to Families with Dependent Children have been eligible for a tax credit. Despite increases in the rate of subsidy from 10 to 20% and now to 50% and other liberalization of the terms of the subsidy, claims for WIN tax credits have remained at a level of only 30 to 40,000 FTE workers for a number of years. This implies that less than 5% of each year's new WIN registrants, less than 2% of adults receiving AFDC benefits and less than 10% of working welfare recipients have been aided by the WIN tax credit. As with JOBS, only a small proportion of the firms that hired WIN eligible workers applied for the tax credit for which they were eligible. Either the firms did not know they were eligible or they found the paper work too burdensome and the benefit too small to warrant applying. Of those firms that have received a WIN credit, less than 10% attributed their hiring of the WIN enrollee to the credit.

D. The Targeted Jobs Tax Credit (TJTC)

Beginning in 1979 employers outside the personal service sector have been able to obtain a tax credit of 50% of the first $6,000 of wages per employee for the first year of employment and 25% of such wages for the second year of employment for the hiring of certain categories of workers. These include high school students in cooperative education (coop-ed) programs, economically disadvantaged youth (18–24), veterans, ex-convicts, Supplementary Security Income, general assistance recipients, and the handicapped.

It is too early in the life of the program to predict what its eventual scale will be. Already, however, it has surpassed the scale of the JOBS, CETA-OJT and WIN Credit programs. The program started slow; the cumulative total number of certifications was only 13,677 by the end of July 1979. The rate of new certifications (jobs obtained by vouchered workers) was 9200 in August, 21,000 in October, 31,000 in December 1979, 33,000 in February 1980, and 21,000 in April during our precipitous descent into recession. In the latter half of 1980 roughly 200,000 workers were in subsidized jobs (adjusted for attrition). The comparative success of TJTC is due to three features:

1. It is an entitlement. Reluctance on the part of local agencies to administer it cannot prevent a persistent employer from obtaining certification of employees that are eligible. In fact, a recent study of early implementation of TJTC found "the rather limited vouchering and certification activity that had taken place by then was largely in response to employer and applicant inquiries rather than active promotion by their staff." (ETA, piv)

2. At least one target group—the Co-op-Ed students—was defined by a characteristic that does not carry stigma. For this group, student and employer certification was made into a one step process and responsibility was centralized in the hands of a person—the high school official responsible for Co-op-Ed—who was being judged by his supervisors on the basis of the number of jobs he found for his target group. As a result, roughly half of all jobs certified for TJTCs have been for Co-op-Ed students.
3. Participation in TJTC requires less paper work than CETA-OJT or the JOBS and early WIN programs did and requires fewer contacts between government agencies and the employer.

Nevertheless, TJTC is currently helping less than 10% of the pool of young people eligible for the program.[1] In contrast, NJTC attracted in its second year the participation of 50 to 70% of all eligible firms. There are three basic causes of TJTC's low participation rate:

1. Most job seekers and most employers are not aware or only vaguely aware of the program. A recent survey of employers found that only 20% of all employers reported being "familiar" with TJTC.
2. There is a stigma attached to being a member of most of the TJTC's target groups. This reduces the likelihood that employers will ask CETA or the Job Service to refer TJTC eligible workers to their firm. Furthermore, many applicants feel that telling prospective employers of their eligibility for TJTC may hurt their chances of getting the job.
3. In most cases, employers are unable to identify who is eligible on their own. Government certification of employee eligibility is necessary and this has three consequences: (a) it often introduces red tape and delays into the hiring process, (b) it often forces a firm out of its traditional recruitment channels, and (c) it makes the program's success depend upon the enthusiasm and competence of government bureaucrats.

The first problem can be overcome by publicity and aggressive promotion of the program. Much greater efforts are possible in this area so hopefully this problem is temporary.

The other two problems, however, arise from a mismatch between the structure of the employment subsidy scheme and the recruitment processes that predominate in the relevant labor markets. Each month the typical employer is hiring one employee for every ten they have on board (Cohen and Schwartz, 1979). The probability that a new hire will still be with the firm a few months later is less than 50%. As a result, employers try to keep

[1]There are 7 to 9 million new hires every month and 55% of these are under age 25 (Cohen and Schwartz, 1979). Certainly at least 10% of the age group is eligible so the average of monthly certification rates, from October 1, 1979 to September 30, 1980 of 22,000 implies a participation rate of 6% or less.

the costs of searching for new employees to a minimum. Studies of how people have obtained their last job show that 35% of all jobs were found by applying directly at the firm without suggestions or referrals and that another 26% were obtained by apply directly at the firm at the suggestion of a friend or a relative (Rosenfeld, 1975). Most firms prefer to hire people who are recommended by current employees or who have shown their desire for the job by personally coming to the establishment and applying. Two-thirds of the employers in the EOPP survey had not listed a job with the employment service in the previous year. As a result, even though 34% of all workers had checked with the employment service during their last period of job search, only 5.1% had gotten their job through an employment service referral. Employers prefer informal recruitment channels because (a) they are faster, (b) they do not become inundated with job applicants who must be interviewed, (c) pre-screening is possible so the number of applicants who are turned down is minimized, and (d) they can avoid dealing with government.

This preference acts to limit the market penetration of any program for finding jobs for the disadvantaged that depends upon a labor market intermediary—Job Service, or a CETA subcontractor like Urban League. Such programs can overcome their inherent structural weakness only when unusually dedicated and competent people are running the labor market intermediary. With only ordinary leadership such a program is bound to be only partially successful—helping some of the people who approach the agency for help but failing to reach most of the eligible population. This structural weakness is exacerbated by the adversarial relationship between government and business. A recent study (Employment and Training Administration, 1979) found that many Job Service and CETA staff "doubt the value of the tax credit in increasing job placement among the targeted groups or in netting hires among them that would not have taken place anyway." (ETA, pivii) The comments of staff seem to reflect a lack of desire to help firms receive a tax benefit to which they are entitled unless the firm reciprocates by changing its behavior (something the tax law does not require).

The targeted employment subsidies that preceded TJTC all necessitated agency referrals of eligible job applicants. With TJTC there are two alternate ways of bringing subsidy, employer, and job seeker together. Job seekers may inform employers of their eligibility. This does not now occur to a significant degree because most eligible workers are unaware of TJTC's existence and because most Employment Service offices do not routinely inform the eligibles that do come to it for assistance that they are eligible. The other barrier to this mechanism becoming important is the reluctance of many job applicants to advertise their TJTC eligibility for fear they will be stigmatized.

The second alternate mechanism assigns the initiative to the one who most directly benefits from the tax credit, the employer. This scenario envisions employers' screening job applications for eligible individuals and then sending them down to Job Service for vouchering and certification before or after they are hired. Presumably, anticipating that A may be eligible for subsidy and B not eligible, will increase the probability that A is offered the job. The use of family income and participation in welfare programs as targeting criteria, however, makes it difficult for employers to know who is eligible and thus prevents many employers from taking the tax credit into account when hiring. Sending job applicants over to the Employment Service prior to hiring does not seem to have become popular for it delays the hiring process, risks losing the worker altogether, and is thought to be unethical by many employers.

III. Lessons and Recommendations

Although more time and more research is required before final judgments can be made about the overall effectiveness of NJTC and TJTC, there is sufficient experience to draw on for some very important lessons:

1. A tax credit for general expansions in employment for which employers can calculate and certify their own eligibility will very quickly achieve a very high participation rate.
2. Employers do expand employment and cut prices in response to such a tax credit.
3. There is a danger, however, that the employment and output expansion induced by such a credit will cause an acceleration of the rate of wage increase even while price increases are slowing down.
4. A subsidy or tax credit for employing stigmatized target groups will not attract the participation of many employers.
5. The necessity of government certification of a worker's eligibility (rather than employer certification with audit) is a substantial barrier to employer and employee participation in an employment subsidy program.

While TJTC is a far superior way of stimulating employment than CETA-OJT contracts or public sector employment, and improved administration should increase its impact, it is not an answer to the stagflation problem. Wage subsidies can be major instruments for dealing with stagflation only in the following cases:

1. all or almost all employers are eligible (Perloff, 1980)
2. employers are able to certify their own eligibility
3. the target group is large enough to encompass all or almost all job seekers needing assistance (Johnson, 1980)
4. the target group is defined by non-stigmatizing criteria that are visible to employers.

Such a subsidy will maximize its cost effectiveness, if it is marginal—that is, paid for by increases in employment above a threshold. If a wage subsidy is to be marginal, however, care must be exercised in selecting the target group, and in defining the subsidized activity and the threshold at which the subsidy begins (Bishop and Haveman, 1978; Bishop and Wilson, 1980).

Our experience with NJTC suggests that a marginal wage subsidy with these qualities can succeed in stimulating employment and lowering prices. But in a pure form such a subsidy may promote wage inflation. This tendency can be forestalled, however, by reducing the tax credits a firm is eligible for it its wage increases exceed some wage increase standard. Such a subsidy can be very simple to administer. To calculate its subsidy the firm would need four numbers: total wage bill this year and in the base year and total hours worked this year and in the base year.

How such a scheme would work is most easily understood by examining a specific proposal. (The specific parameters of this proposal are illustrative). Firms and nonprofit entities would receive a tax credit against social security taxes of $1.00 per hour for every hour by which total hours worked (including those worked by salaried management) at the firm in 1982 exceed total hours worked in 1980. A tax credit would also be provided in 1983 for increases in total hours worked over the higher of 1982 or 1980's hours worked. In 1984 the tax credit would be for increases in total hours worked over the highest of 1983, 1982 or 1980 hours worked. The tax credit the firm would be eligible for is reduced if its average wage (calculated by dividing total compensation by total hours worked) in 1982 was more than 17% greater than its 1980 wage. The threshold for the take back might be 24% in 1983 and 32% in 1984.

A general formula for the tax credit is

$$TC = s \sum_i \Delta H_{i_t} - u \sum_i (W_{i_t} - g\overline{W}_0) H_{i_t}$$

subject to the constraint that if $TC \geq 0$ and $\sum_i (W_{i_t} - g\overline{W}_0) H_{i_t} \geq 0$

where H_i = hours worked by people in the "i"th job during time period "t"

ΔH_{i_t} = growth of employment in the "i"th job above the threshold
W_i = hourly wage rate of the "i"th job
$\overline{W}_0$ = the firm's average wage in the base period
s = hourly tax credit
g = wage growth standard, $g > 1$
u = take back rate

An increase in the wage rate is taxed at the rate u. This discourages wage increases above the standard. An expansion of hours that leaves the composition of employment unchanged is subsidized at the rate of s dollars per hour.

Where expansions are not proportional and the firm is in the take back region, the tax benefit depends upon the wage rate of the jobs that are expanded:

$$\frac{dTC}{dH_i} = s - u(W_{i_t} - g\overline{W}_o)$$

If for instance s = $1 per hour, u = .1 and $g\overline{W}_o$ = $8.00 an hour, expanding a job paying $4.00 an hour would generate a tax credit of $1.40 per hour, expanding a job paying $12.00 would generate a credit of $.60 an hour and expanding a job paying $18.00 an hour would generate no credit.

This pattern of declining subsidies as wage rate rise creates an incentive for the firm to focus its employment expansion in the labor markets with the greatest surplus of workers.

This type of a marginal employment subsidy has a number of attractive features:

1. Firms are encouraged to increase employment by hiring inexperienced workers and training them rather than by increasing overtime work or bidding experienced workers away from other firms by raising wages.
2. Within each firm it tends to target the employment stimulus on the least skilled workers. (This occurs because hiring extra low wage workers lowers the average wage of the firm and this helps the firm meet the wage increase standard). The increase in demand at the unskilled end of the labor market should produce large reductions in the unemployment of youth and the disadvantaged.
3. Targeting on less skilled workers is accomplished without giving low wage firms a proportionately larger subsidy.
4. Firms are encouraged to slow the rate at which they increase wage rates.
5. Both marginal and average costs of production are reduced while simultaneously wage increases above the standard are taxed. Penalty TIP's in contrast, have the disadvantage of raising marginal and average costs and, therefore, prices of firms that violate the wage standard.

It is a balanced anti-inflation program. The subsidy component lowers price inflation and the takeback lowers wage inflation.

References

Bishop, John. "Employment in Construction and Distribution Industries: The Impact of the New Jobs Tax Credit." In *Studies in Labor Markets*, edited by Sherin Rosen (University of Chicago Press, Chicago, 1981).
Bishop, John and Haveman, Robert. "Targeted Employment Subsidies: Issues of Structure and Design," contained in volume from Conference on Creating Job Opportunities in the

Private Sector, sponsored by the National Commission for Manpower Policy, Washington DC, October 19–20, 1978.

Bishop, John and Wilson, Charles. "The Impact of Marginal Employment Subsidies on Firm Behavior," Social Systems Research Institute Workshop Series, University of Wisconsin, January, 1980.

Cohen, Malcolm S. and Schwartz, Arthur R. "New Hire Rates by Demographic Group," Institute of Labor and Industrial Relations, University of Michigan, Ann Arbor, Michigan, July, 1979.

Employment and Training Administration, Office of Program Evaluation, Division of Staff Evaluation Studies. "Evaluation Study of the Early Implementation of the Targeted Jobs Tax Credit Program," Report Number 51, December, 1979.

Johnson, George E. "The Allocative and Distributive Effects of a Categorical Employment Subsidy Program," prepared for Brookings Institution Conference on Categorical Employment Subsidies, Washington, DC, April 2–3, 1980, January, 1980.

McKevitt, J. "Testimony Before the Senate Finance Subcommittee on Administration of the Internal Revenue Code and Select Committee on Small Business," July 26, 1978.

Perloff, Jeffrey M. "The Micro and Macro Effects of the Targeted Jobs Tax Credit," prepared for the Brookings Institution Conference on Categorical Employment Subsidies, Washington DC, April 2–3, 1980, January, 1980.

Perloff, Jeffrey and Wachter, Michael. "A Re-evaluation of the New Jobs Tax Credit," Department of Economics, University of Pennsylvania, Philadelphia, 1980.

Rosenfeld, Carl. "Jobseeking Methods Used by American Workers," *Monthly Labor Review*, Volume 98, #8, August, 1975.

Résumé

L'expérience américaine des crédits d'impôts liés à la création d'emplois a montré une distanciation entre la définition et la mise en oeuvre. Le Crédit d'Impôt attaché aux nouveaux emplois, subvention à objectif modéré pour l'expansion générale de l'emploi, était réclamé en 1978 par plus de 1.100.000 d'entreprises, soit plus de 30% de tous les employeurs du pays et, plus de la moitié de tous les ayants-droit. La participation à des programmes destinés à des catégories particulières d'ouvriers, qui demandent que l'état certifie l'éligibilité de l'employeur et de l'employé est minime; les taux de participation des ayants-droit sont de moins de 20% dans le système de crédit de l'impôt WIN qui est vieux de dix ans, et moins de 10% dans le système TJTC, vieux de deux ans.

Des études sur le NJTC ont montré qu'il avait des effets significatifs sur l'économie. Les trois études sur le NJTC ont toutes montré qu'il augmentait l'emploi de 200.000 à 700.000 postes. La seule étude qui ait considéré son influence sur les prix a trouvé qu'il réduisait de 1% la marge entre prix de détail et prix de gros des produits. Aucune étude formelle n'a été faite de l'influence du NJTC sur les taux des salaires mais un résultat préliminaire laisse penser que l'expansion de l'emploi accélère l'augmentation des salaires même si les augmentations de prix diminuent. Les conclusions finalisées ne sont pas encore connues mais puisque ces programmes sont si petits, leurs impacts sur l'emploi global ne peuvent pas avoir été importants.

   Les leçons à tirer de cet examen de l'expérience américaine se résument
au fait qu'une subvention de l'emploi du secteur privé n'atteindra une efficacité d'échelle et de coût suffisante pour ouvrir une brèche dans le chômage
structurel que si:

1. Les employeurs sont capables de démontrer aisément leurs droits à subvention
2. L'influence sur le comportement désiré des employeurs doit être évidente
   et simple pour eux à mettre en oeuvre
3. Tous ou presque tous les employeurs peuvent en bénéficier (autrement le
   résultat est une redistribution de l'emploi entre les employeurs.)
4. Un objectif est essentiel, mais il est plus important d'inclure tous les
   ouvriers nécessitant de l'aide plutôt que d'exclure les ouvriers ne nécessitant pas d'aide.
5. Le groupe visé est défini par un critère non stigmatisant, visible pour
   l'employeur (une caractéristique de l'emploi, comme le taux de salaire, est
   meilleure que des caractéristiques portant sur l'ouvrier).
6. La subvention est marginale—payée pour des augmentations d'emploi
   au-dessus d'un seuil comme dans le NJTC.

8226
8225
8243
3230
~~West~~ Germany

Public Finance Measures to Generate Employment for Hard-to-Place People: Employer Wage Subsidies or Public Employment Programs?

Günther Schmid

Introduction

The following paragraphs describe and analyze in detail two types of employer wage subsidies and public employment programs in Germany. Emphasis is on the employment and distributional impact of those "structural measures." Both quantitative and qualitative evaluations lead to disappointing results, and arguments are developed to explain this outcome. The study ends with perspectives and conditions of an integrative employment strategy which combines selective demand management with supply oriented measures in such a way that the real bottlenecks of the labor market are dealt with.

The Effectiveness of Employer Wage Subsidies in Germany

The Instrument of "Eingliederungsbeihilfen"

The most important employer wage subsidy program in Germany is the job creation subsidy for hard-to-place people (*Eingliederungsbeihilfen*). The purpose of this program is to promote the hiring of unemployed people who are hard to place, that is of long-term unemployed, older people, young people without professional skills, generally people with restricted work achievements. The program is part of the Labor Promotion Law (*Arbeitsförderungsgesetz*), and although a permanent program the rules of application have been adjusted several times to the changing labor market situation. At the moment, the program provides the employer with a wage cost subsidy of up to 80% during the starting period of employment; the maximum period is

Public Finance and Public Employment. Proceedings of the 36th Congress of the International Institute of Public Finance. Jerusalem, 1980.

2 years, with the average period of subsidization about 9 months. The following observations are the result of my own evaluation study with K. Semlinger (1980) on this type of job creation subsidy. The study consisted of a quantitative analysis for all 142 employment agencies and of a qualitative interview study in nine selected employment agencies.

Explaining the Take-Up of the Scheme

West Germany is divided into 142 employment agencies which register unemployment, pay unemployment benefits, provide placement services and counseling, and implement selective employment policies. The starting point of our quantitative analysis was the different take-up of employer wage subsidies in 1978: What factors influence the take-up of a specific scheme? The answer to this question will give us clues as to whether or not a program meets with the causal structure of the situation and with the behavior of labor market participants, especially of the employers.

The variation of the take-up between 142 local employment agencies is fairly high: Some local employment agencies place only 1% of their clients with the help of *Eingliederungsbeihilfen*, others up to 20%. This drastic difference might be explained by the difference in the local labor market situation, but it might also be explained by the different administrative strategies of the employment agencies. We therefore asked which factors were responsible for the different take-up, and tried to find indicators for these factors. The comprehensive model and the underlying theory of the selected indicators is described elsewhere.[1]

Table 1 summarizes the most important results of a multiple regression analysis, and contains only those variables of the total model that have a significant influence in the take-up of *Eingliederungsbeihilfen*. The model explains 74% of the total variance, which is quite good for this type of cross-section analysis. Assuming that we included all important non-administrative variables which potentially influence the take-up, we can say that about 25% of the variance is due to different administrative practices or circumstances. But in the present state of the model we can not say which of the potential administrative factors are responsible for the differences in the take-up. In future work, we will try to develop indicators for the administrative structure, such as qualification of personnel, availability of training capacities and so on.

The first expected result shown in Table 1 is that the average unemployment rate explains most of the variance (38%). The second expected result is the influence of the percentage of young people in the unemploy-

[1]Schmid/Semlinger, 1980; Schmid/Wilke, 1980.

Table 1

Variables, Regression Coefficients (b), and Explained Variance
of the Multiple Regression Analysis with the Dependent Variable
"Eingliederungsbeihilfen 1978"

	Independent Variables	*Regression Coefficient* b	*Explained Variance in* %	*F- Value*
V14	Unemployment rate, Sept. 1977	0.192	38.0	21.7[a]
V19	Proportion of longterm unempl., Sept. 1977	−0.042	5.9	19.5[a]
V05	Proportion of labor force in the three largest manufact. ind.	−0.013	0.4	8.5[a]
V01	Proportion of labor force in tertiary sector, 1977	−0.010	2.2	6.7[b]
V08	Proportion of labor force in labor intensive industries, 1977	0.005	0.2	4.9[b]
V15	Proportion of youth unempl. > 20, Sept. 1977	0.025	11.0	4.6[b]

[a] = Significant at the 1% level.
[b] = Significant at the 5% level; RSQ = 74%; 120 cases (employment agencies).

ment stock: the higher this percentage, the higher the take-up. This result can be explained by the fact that wage costs play a higher role with young people who are relatively inexperienced than with older people who are experienced and whose wages are strongly influenced by institutional rules, especially seniority. An additional explanation is that youth unemployment is politically much more sensitive, and employers put a great deal of pressure on the exchange officers to pay the subsidy if hiring young unemployed people, especially young people without training. It is very doubtful, however, if the hiring of unskilled teenagers should be promoted by wage subsidies without any guarantee of training and career promotion. The unfavourable employment effect (discussed later) supports this argument.

Another expected result is the influence of employees in labor intensive industries: the higher the percentage of dependent labor force in labor intensive industries, the higher the take-up of *Eingliederungsbeihilfen*. This result is compatible with the theory that the sensitivity of firms to a wage subsidy is high where the production factor "labor" plays an important role in the budget calculations.

Three target groups, however, are not reached as would be expected from the program design. Old people, long-term unemployed, and women are explicit target groups; but female and old-age unemployment do not influence the take-up in a positive sense (as might be expected), and long-term unemployment even shows a strong negative sign—the higher the percentage of long-term unemployed, the lower the take-up of the subsidies. These results can be interpreted in the following way: In opposition to the aim of the policy the target group with the highest priorities, namely the long-term unemployed, did have a negative effect on the take-up. It is obviously difficult to place long-term unemployed persons even with the offer of a substantial wage subsidy.

The qualitative interviews in the employment agencies came up with a very clear and plausible explanation for this: It is not the wage cost which is the bottleneck, but qualifications in the broad sense of the term. Employers are reluctant to hire people with a high risk of work stability, or lack of skills or work experience. We were told that for persons with unstable job records or long unemployment histories even a subsidy of more than 100% will not help to place them. But the reluctance to hire such people comes not only from the employer or the personnel management, but also from the staff or the working group in which the "outsiders" have to be integrated. There are simple social and economic reasons for this behavior. The isolated "homo economicus" of the neoclassical theory, who seems to form (at least partly) the background of pure employer wage subsidy programs, is seldom found in reality. The wages are not only determined by the individual's productivity, the lack of which is intended to be compensated for by the subsidy. Often such productivity cannot be isolated because of work interdependence. Piece-work wages, for example, are often determined by the group performance as well as by the individual performance. If a low-performing individual enters the group, the group performance will be affected and thus the commonly determined part of wages. Hence, it is rational for a group to reject a low performer, a "problem case," an apparent "drunkard," etc.

The "victims of the labor market" therefore need a much more intensive placement service; they especially need pretraining and training courses, social, psychological and technical counseling and aid. The majority of present employer wage subsidies for hard-to-place people should be paid for building up a training and counseling infrastructure, and not for subsidizing wage costs of which the financial incentive proves rather weak.

Observing and Explaining the Employment Effect

The second important problem connected with almost every kind of subsidy is the question of whether employers taking the subsidy really change their behavior according to the aims of the policy, or if they manage to claim the subsidies without really changing their behavior. The question of the effectiveness is closely connected with the question of "windfalls" or the net impact on employment. With respect to our example, the one extreme would be a 100% windfall, that is, every recruitment in connection with *Eingliederungsbeihilfen* would have taken place without the subsidy; the other extreme would be that every subsidy case induces an additional recruitment which would not have taken place without subsidies. The reality, of course, is something between the two, and other side-effects such as displacement and multiplier effects have to be considered.

The basic model for measuring the net impact on employment is explained elsewhere.[2] As a dependent variable we used the change in the unemployment rate, because every case of *Eingliederungsbeihilfen* should have induced an additional exit from the unemployment stock into employment. One of the independent variables influencing the unemployment change is, of course, the take-up of the subsidy.

The results of four independent multiple regressions are summarized in Table 2. The interesting results here are the beta coefficients related to the four independent variables: total job creation subsidies or *Eingliederungsbeihilfen* (V20), subsidies for unemployed people aged 45 and above (V24), subsidies for unemployed people aged 24 and below (V25), and subsidies for long-term unemployed (one year and longer, V26). The first beta coefficient for *Eingliederungsbeihilfen* in total is negative as expected, but not significant; this means—if our model is correct—that *Eingliederungsbeihilfen* in total had no impact on the reduction of unemployment. The beta coefficient for young people is positive but not significant either. Only *Eingliederungsbeihilfen* for old people, and to a lesser extent for long-term unemployed, have a significant negative sign which corresponds to the expectation connected with this policy instrument. All other things being constant, *Eingliederungsbeihilfen* for long-term and especially for old unemployed people produced an additional reduction in unemployment.

To summarize the main results of the quantitative and qualitative evaluation of *Eingliederungsbeihilfen* as an example for employer wage subsidies old and long-term unemployed are hard to place even with a relatively generous wage-cost subsidy, but once placed a clear employment effect can be observed. Young unemployed people are more easily placed with a wage-cost subsidy, but the employment effect is dubious because of "windfalls," displacement effects, or sheer rotation.[3] The qualitative interviews in the employment agencies support this observation. There is also a clearly decreasing gross effect of every additional Mark spent on this type of employer wage subsidy: The average expenditure per person in *Eingliederungsbeihilfen* in wages of 1973 was 1,341 DM in 1973, 2,457 DM already in 1976, and it

---

[2]Schmid/Wilke, 1980.

[3]"Rotation" refers to the practice whereby either a subsidized person is dismissed and replaced by another subsidized person, or the dismissed person finds another subsidized job after a period of unemployment.

Table 2

Variables, Regression Coefficients (b), F-Values and Explained Variance of the Multiple Regression Analyses with the Dependent Variable "Change of the Unemployment Rate between Dec. 1977 and Dec. 1978" (V23)

Independent Variables	b	F	b	F	b	F	b	F
V20 Total *Eingliederungsbeihilfen* as a % of labor force	-0.016	0.0						
V24 *Eingliederungsbeihilfen* for unemployed aged > 45			-1.553	6.4[a]				
V25 *Eingliederungsbeihilfen* for unemployed aged < 25					0.122	0.2		
V26 *Eingliederungsbeihilfen* for longterm unemployed							-1.582	3.3[b]
V01 Proportion of labor force in tertiary sector	-0.004	0.7	-0.007	1.9	-0.003	0.4	-0.005	1.0
V02 Proportion of labor force in construction, 1977	-0.042	4.0[c]	-0.047	5.1[c]	-0.041	3.8[c]	-0.038	3.3
V03 Proportion of labor force in small firms, 1970	-0.001	0.0	-0.001	0.0	-0.001	0.0	-0.003	0.2
V04 Proportion of labor force in large firms, 1970	0.004	1.6	-0.002	0.4	0.004	1.3	-0.004	1.2
V05 Proportion of labor force in the three largest manufact. industries, 1977	-0.002	0.2	-0.004	0.4	-0.002	0.1	-0.002	0.1
V06 Proportion of labor force in shrinking industries, 1977	0.007	4.6[c]	0.006	4.3[c]	0.007	4.7[c]	0.006	4.1[c]
V07 Proportion of labor force in growth industries, 1977	-0.006	2.4	-0.005	2.1	-0.006	2.4	-0.005	2.1
V08 Proportion of labor force in labor intensive ind., 1977	-0.002	0.5	-0.001	0.2	-0.002	0.8	-0.001	0.2
V09 Proportion of male white collar workers in the manufact. ind., 1977	-0.016	1.1	-0.014	0.9	-0.015	1.0	-0.019	1.6
V10 Proportion of female blue collar workers in the manufact. ind., 1977	-0.023	9.2[a]	-0.027	13.0[a]	-0.022	8.4[c]	-0.026	11.7[a]
V11 Proportion of foreign labor in manufacturing, 1977	-0.006	0.4	-0.009	1.1	-0.005	0.3	-0.005	0.3
V22 Unemployment rate, Dec. 1977	-0.185	19.2[a]	-0.184	20.8[a]	-0.189	20.1[a]	-0.172	16.8[a]
V21 Persons in job creation, 1978, as a % of labor force	-0.263	4.1[c]	-0.235	4.0[c]	-0.291	5.1[c]	-0.231	3.7
V12 Inflow of unemployment, 1978, as a % of labor force	0.061	11.8[a]	0.074	17.2[a]	0.060	11.7[a]	0.063	13.1[a]
Explained Variance in %	45		48		45		47	

[a] = Significant at 1% level.
[b] = Significant at 7% level.
[c] = Significant at 5% level.
120 cases (employment agencies).

almost doubled again in a few years to 4,669 DM in 1979! Employer wage subsidies aimed at hard-to-place people obviously have to be redesigned or replaced by other measures.

The Effectiveness of Public Employment Programs in Germany

The Instrument of ABM (Allgemeine Arbeitsbeschaffungsmaßnahmen, or General Work Creation Measures)

Although Germany shares with most other countries a tradition of public relief projects, the present general work creation program is of rather recent vintage. With the passing of the Employment Promotion Law in 1969, the older program, which was oriented toward emergency relief projects, was transformed into an effective instrument of modern labor market policy. ABM is intended to create temporary employment for unemployed persons by providing financial assistance (in the form mostly of grants, sometimes of loans) to sponsors who carry out projects which provide jobs for persons assigned by local employment agencies. These projects must be such that they are carried out *in addition* to normal activities of the sponsor, in the sense that without this financial assistance they would not have been carried out at all, or at least not at this time or to this extent. The projects must also be *in the public interest*. In principle, any projects meeting these criteria can be assisted. However, in line with the new function of work creation measures in dealing with structural features of unemployment, preference is given to those projects which are aimed at creating conditions for the overall permanent employment situation by contributing to the improvement of the economic structure of the region or by providing permanent work for hard-to-employ individuals, especially older workers who have been unemployed for a long time. Depending on the labor market significance of a given project, the financial assistance until 1979 could range from a minimum of 60% to a maximum of 120% (in the case of particularly significant projects) of the total wage costs of those workers assigned by the employment agency; the grants and loans together could not comprise more than 90% of the total costs of the projects, which means that the sponsors always had to contribute at least 10% of the costs. In some cases, where the projects were of particular significance for the labor market, the *Länder* and the Federal Government provided supplemental assistance over and above the aid given by the Federal Employment Agency.

ABM played a marginal role before the recession of 1974/75, but have expanded considerably in recent years.[4] The expenditures of the Federal

[4]For tables including time series, see Schmid (1980b).

Employment Agency, including grants by the Federal Government, rose from 19 million DM in 1972 to 1.575 billion DM in 1979, and the average number of persons in ABM rose at the same time from 1,500 to 50,000 persons. The composition of project types as well as of unemployed persons involved in these projects also changed during this time: During the recession, ABM was clearly used as a counter-cyclical instrument, especially in traditional relief-type projects in agriculture, coastal protection and land reclamation, forestry, road building, and construction. But ABM was still a modest program, involving only about 0.14% of the dependent labor force.

After the recession and because of the changing structure of unemployment (increasing white collar and female unemployment), ABM composition moved gradually toward office and clerical work, and—as an innovation—toward social services: More than 50% are now in these public service projects (in 1976 about 20%), and 90% of the women in ABM are in office or clerical or social service activities (in 1979). The strong resurgence of projects in the agriculture, parks and landscaping category up to a steady level of about 20%, and the relatively steady position of forestry projects (around 10%) reflects the use of traditional outdoor relief measures for providing work for unemployed young and unskilled men, another problem group receiving increased attention. More than 50% of the males in these projects were below the age of 25 in 1979.

The Global Employment and Unemployment Effects

In judging the impact of ABM on labor markets, three different kinds of employment effects must be taken into consideration (see Table 3): the take-up, the employment impact, and the unemployment impact. First of all there are the numbers of unemployed persons in ABM projects. This effect is calculated either in average man years throughout the year (here the average number of persons in ABM projects) or in the total number of unemployed assigned by local employment agencies. The latter figure is about three times higher because the average period spent by each person in ABM projects is 17 weeks. Thus the average number of persons in ABM was 50,000 in 1978, but the total number of unemployed persons assigned to ABM projects was about 150,000![5] Impressive as the increases of ABM since 1972 may be, the average number of unemployed placed in public work creation measures in 1978 would still only make up 0.21% of the total dependent labor force.

[5]This figure should probably be revised downwards for recent times because the average duration in office and clerical work, and especially in social services, is higher than in other ABM activitites, and the percentage of these activitites increased noticeably. Breuer and Hellmich (1979, p. 169) found that 84% of women (a sample of 182) were assigned for longer than 7 months.

Table 3

Adjusted Gross Employment and Unemployment Impact
of General Work Creation Measures (ABM) in Germany

	1974	1975	1976	1977	1978
(1) Take-up (average number of persons in ABM)	3,000	16,000	29,000	38,000	50,000
Unemployed assigned by local employment agencies	9,000	48,000	87,000	114,000	150,000
(a) Subsidies share of total projects costs	50%	40%	40%	50%	60%
(2) Gross employment impact	8,000	41,000	75,000	72,000	90,000
Adjusted (by a) gross employment impact	4,000	16,500	30,000	36,000	54,000
(3) Gross unemployment impact	6,000	30,000	58,000	61,000	77,000
Adjusted (by a) gross unemployment impact	3,500	13,500	28,500	35,000	53,000

Source: Spitznagel, 1979, pp. 200–203; own calculations.

In addition to the unemployed persons placed directly in ABM, immediate employment effects can be calculated in terms of the number of persons employed by firms executing these projects as permanent personnel, whose jobs are "secured" by activity assisted by ABM money. This effect depends of course on the type of project, and is higher in construction measures than in office and clerical work. On average this effect was calculated to be 15% of the gross employment effect (in 1974), with a tendency to decrease for the change of the project mix (12% in 1978). Indirect impacts as a result of multiplier effects also depend on the project mix, decreasing, for example, when the projects become more labor intensive as in office or social service activities. These indirect effects have been calculated as 47% in 1974, and as 31% in 1978.

The gross employment impact of ABM is therefore the sum of (1) the average number of persons assigned to the projects, (2) the number of jobs secured for permanent personnel working for contracting firms, and (3) the jobs created or maintained as a result of various secondary or indirect effects. This gross impact amounted in 1974 to 8,000, and increased in 1978 to 90,000. These figures, however, have to be adjusted because they are related to the total costs of the projects. In reality it has to be assumed that the sponsors would have assigned their own contribution of ABM projects to other projects. It has been estimated that this own contribution is quite substantial at around 40 to 60%, the highest of course where non-labor costs are involved, especially in construction work. Thus we have at least to adjust the gross employment impact by the opportunity costs (see Table 3). This adjustment is still not taking into account productivity differentials between ABM activities and alternative activities which might be substantial as Haveman (1978, pp. 257ff), for example, argued in his cost-benefit study of the Dutch Social Employment Program.

On the basis of the gross employment impact it is possible to estimate the impact on unemployment. It is figured that if these work creation measures had not been undertaken, a number of persons equal to the total jobs created or maintained would have been out of work. Of this total, it is assumed (from experience) that roughly two-thirds would have appeared on the rolls of the registered unemployed, and that the remaining third would have left the labor market and joined the ranks of the so-called "hidden unemployed." The impact of ABM grew from 6,000 in 1974 to 77,000 in 1978. Assuming again that the ABM sponsors' own contributions had been realized as (alternative) demand, and leaving aside potential productivity differentials, these figures would have to be adjusted to 3,500 in 1974 and 53,000 in 1978 respectively.

The above estimates of the employment effect are still based on the assumption that there are no substitutions or windfalls; thus they still present gross estimates and could be regarded as upper limits of the global employment impact. Up to now there has been no study available which tries to calculate the net impact on employment. But even if we take these upper limits of the adjusted employment effects, the impact of ABM on the overall labor market situation is very modest: At most, unemployment is being reduced by one quarter percentage point. By the sheer size of the program the inflationary impact could certainly be neglected. On the other hand, the likelihood that this type of selective employment policy could be further increased to a substantial amount is, for different reasons, very small.

The Distributional Effect of ABM

Even if the quantitative employment impact is obviously modest and partly doubtful,[6] a labor market instrument such as General Work Creation (ABM) might be successful in qualitative terms. One qualitative criterion is the distributional impact of ABM. The following results refer mainly to an excellent evaluation by Eugen Spitznagel (1979) and partly to my own calculations (Schmid 1980b).

[6]As I mentioned already, there are at present no studies available that estimate ABM's size of windfalls or substitution. A clue for at least some substitution is the increasing resistance of trade unions against ABM, especially in local governments where observations could be made that at the same time ABM was increased regular public jobs were decreased; another clue is the suspicion of the legislator who recently tightened the criteria of work "in addition" in the Labor Promotion Law, obviously to prevent large substitution effects.

It can be generally said that ABM projects in the tertiary sector are more easily influenced than others by distributional criteria: The direct employment effect is here much higher than, for example, in the construction industry where the indirect employment effect amounts to 68% of the total employment effect. Because the project mix of ABM moved during the last years toward relatively more "tertiary activities," an improvement of the distributional impact should be expected. This, however, can only partly be confirmed by observation.

The Labor Promotion Law mentions explicitly long-term and older unemployed as target groups for ABM; it refers implicitly to all unemployed who are hard to place with respect to the prevailing labor market situation, which means especially women seeking part-time jobs and persons with health restrictions. Long-term unemployed, however, are clearly underrepresented among the participants of ABM, and older unemployed whom one would expect to be overrepresented, are nowadays slightly underrepresented; by tightening the age criterion to 55 and above, the underrepresentation is becoming even greater. The proportion of women in ABM is also much below the proportion in unemployment, except in office and clerical work and in social services, but nevertheless is improving. Thus ABM was not suitable for opening up new employment prospects for women. Unemployed with health restrictions are also underrepresented. On the other hand, it was discovered that there were relatively more persons with cumulative "handicaps" (e.g., long-term unemployed plus health restrictions) in ABM than in the unemployment stock.

The percentage of young people in ABM corresponds to their respective percentage in unemployment. This observation, however, has to be qualified: The number of young ABM participants who are unskilled or early school leavers is above average, and most of them are in the relief type projects of agriculture, gardening, landscaping and forestry which certainly do not promote their qualification or their long-term employment prospects. Unskilled unemployed are generally overrepresented in ABM. It is more than questionable whether ABM activities, as they are presently organized, contribute to the labor market needs of these target groups. This holds true especially for young people whose ABM experience might be a further link in the chain of self-reinforcing failures.

Work Content and Job Prospects of ABM Measures

A small survey of women in General Work Creation Measures (Breuer/Hellmich, 1979) revealed an interesting ambivalence in the attitudes of participants toward ABM. On the one hand there was generally a high level of satisfaction with the measure. Special emphasis was given to the possibilities for social contacts and for self-assurance, which certainly reflects the short-term improvement in relation to the unemployment situation; to have work seems still to play a high role in one's self-esteem. On the other hand, the high level of uncertainty of future job prospects as well as the often boring or dirty nature of the jobs in ABM projects gave rise to a strongly negative attitude toward ABM. The explanation of this ambivalence can be found in the objective features of work content and job prospects of ABM measures. Within the framework of this study I can only mention the most important results regarding these qualitative aspects.

Connected with most of the present ABM projects is the danger of dequalification for the participants instead of an upward mobility in occupational terms. Spitznagel (1979) found that 15% of the ABM-participants were clearly occupied below their qualification level, and that only 2.4% were shifted upwards. The study of women in ABM (Breuer/Hellmich, 1979, p. 171) found, for instance, that 76.9% of the women in simple office or clerical work were professionally skilled, but much of the work in social services is unskilled, simple, dirty work such as helping with cooking, cleaning or washing. Of considerable importance is the finding that there is a strong correlation between the duration of ABM participation and the quality of the job.

The level of skills required in ABM jobs is also connected with the final integration into the regular labor force: The higher the qualification required in an ABM job, the higher the probability that the ABM participants are taken on in a regular job (p. 141ff)! Being taken on in a permanent job with the same employer, as well as the chance to find a regular job on the external market, depend also on the length of unemployment before ABM: The chances for long-term unemployed are considerably lower than the chances for short-term unemployed (Spitznagel, 1979, p. 213). The integration success immediately after the ABM measure was 30% in total. Fifteen percent of ABM participants have been taken on permanently by the same employer, with the integration success of men considerably higher than that of women; 53% of ABM participants were again unemployed; 5% were taken on again in an ABM project.[7] The best results were achieved in road building, construction, local utilities, and in social services. Potential substitution and/or displacement effects were not estimated. In principle both can occur: An employer hires an ABM person to do an originally regular job, and then takes him/her on in permanent employment, thus displacing another person who otherwise would have got the job.

---

[7]A survey some time after the ABM measure brought slightly improved results showed that 42% were now in regular work, 23% were unemployed, but 19% were again in ABM-measures (Spitznagel, 1979, p. 213). Breuer/Hellmich (1979) observed a taking-over rate of 22%; however, a considerable decrease of the expected taking-over to about 14%. The best results were observed in tax administration, with the chances of men better than those of women. But here again, potential substitution or displacement effects were not estimated!

The worst results in terms of integration were observed in coastal protection, landscaping, agriculture and forestry. Fifty percent of ABM participants in coastal protection and landscaping were already in ABM measures before, and it is to be assumed that a certain group of people, especially older ones, are regularly "employed" in ABM measures. Beside older people, those hardest hit by the vicious circle of "unemployment/non-employment-ABM-unemployment" are women. Spitznagel discovered this "ABM career" especially prevalent among young women: 13% of women in ABM stepped immediately after school or university attendance or after training into ABM jobs, and 17% of women were already in ABM measures.

A thoroughly positive feature of ABM for almost all participants is the financial aspect. Related to their previous unemployment status most people are financially better off during their ABM job. Their wages are related to standard wages, that is, to the wages resulting from collective bargaining between unions and employers.[8] Still more important for the majority of ABM participants seems to be the fact that they are entitled to receive unemployment benefits if unemployed after the ABM measure; this entitlement is of special importance for people (above all women) who received no benefits at all before their ABM job. The entitlement, however, is dependent on the time spent in the ABM job, which, as a rule of thumb, is about half of the time spent in ABM.

The ABM Dilemma

It is interesting to see that the financial aspect just mentioned is the real backbone of the labor administration's predominant philosophy with respect to ABM: Because ABM is financed (as most labor market policy in Germany) by the unemployment insurance fund, that is, by a common pool of employers and employees, every unemployed person should potentially be able to receive this "collective good" of ABM. Thus, in view of the alternatives—(a) to select carefully the ABM projects in terms of high output value and long-term employment prospects, and to keep people in ABM as long as necessary in order to improve their skills and thereby their chances of permanent integration, or (b) to launch ABM projects as much as possible and to rotate participants as much as possible in order to distribute the money to a wider range of unemployed, at least to most of the hard-to-place people—the labor administration will choose the second.

But it is exactly this philosophy which creates a dilemma: The more the labor administration seems to behave according to the "interests" of the

---

[8]The financial situation of ABM people is, however, not as good as that of comparable permanent employees because they cannot, for example, participate in fringe benefits bargained in collective agreements.

common pool, the less effective an instrument General Work Creation
(ABM) becomes. We have seen that the effectiveness of ABM both in quantitative and in qualitative terms was modest, partly doubtful, and in some
parts clearly negative. The global employment impact is modest because of
financial restrictions to further increase the scope of ABM measures, because
of the increasing danger of substitution effects, and furthermore because of
the increasing danger of generating a self-reinforcing ABM population. With
respect to global employment impact, ABM tends to be self-defeating in the
long run: To prevent windfalls or substitution, and to reach as many unemployed as possible, it creates only temporary work and rotates the participants; the short-term employment impact is to a great deal reduced in the
long run either because people become unemployed again, because they start
participating again in ABM measures, or because they enter into the "silent
labor reserve."

The distributional goal, to provide work mainly for the hard-to-place,
was also only partly met. Only people with cumulative risks were found to be
overrepresented in ABM projects; long-term unemployed and women are
clearly underrepresented. The explanation for this is apparent partly on the
demand side, partly on the supply side. Although the employment agencies
have the right to assign the unemployed to the projects, ABM sponsors are
creaming as much as possible, that is, selecting the best from the unemployment stock. Sponsors often withdraw their offers if the labor administration
is not able to provide skilled unemployed, or sponsors may internalize the
unemployment structure by not developing any more demanding projects.
The taking-on of women, for example, could be improved by further extending ABM projects in the field of social services. But most of social services,
especially those with professional skill requirements, are permanent tasks,
and either the labor administration is not allowed to sponsor such projects, or
else such projects are not realized because ABM participants are only temporarily assigned (at present 6 month as a rule, and one year as an exception),
and because the future financing of the project is uncertain. Thus it is under-
standable that the most common objection raised by sponsors against ABM is
the short duration of assignment.[9]

The explanation for the poor performance of ABM with respect to job
content and long-term employment prospects lies in the same direction.
Temporary jobs which fulfill both criteria of ABM ("work in addition", and
"work in the public interest") tend to be unskilled, boring, dead-end jobs,
and their long-term employment prospects are modest or even non-existent,
as in cases where self-enforcing ABM careers are induced.

[9]See, for instance, Breuer/Hellmich, 1979, pp. 120; Scharpf/Gensior/Fiedler, 1979, pp.
174.

Some Considerations Toward an Integrative Employment Strategy for Hard-to-Place People

The Necessary Integration of Supply and Demand Oriented Measures

Public employment programs in the conventional form just described seem to be effective in a modest way mainly as short-term instruments in addition to other anti-cyclical measures. In a situation of short-term lack of global demand, the financial advantage for ABM participants compared to the alternative of unemployment might even correspond with a financial advantage for the exchequer, which saves unemployment benefits and gains additional taxes via increased income and consumption.[10] Empirical evidence as well as theoretical considerations also have shown that conventional employer wage subsidies are not satisfactory in dealing with long-term structural problems either, especially with problems of hard-to-place people.[11] The basic rationale of pure employer wage subsidies seems to be wrong in the assumption that the reduction of wage costs induces employers to increase employment or that the wage subsidy compensates for the risk connected with the hiring of "problem groups."

The main shortage, however, on the supply side is qualifications; this holds true especially for the hard-to-place or so-called problem groups. Professional skills are also bottlenecks from the demand point of view which is part of the explanation for Germany's quasi-full employment situation, that is, the coexistence of considerable unemployment at full employment or even overemployment, thus creating inflationary bottlenecks for global expansionary strategies. The main bottlenecks on the demand side are, according to most empirical studies or surveys (Nerb, 1978, pp. 72ff), not wage costs but low expectations of employers with respect to long-term demand. Traditional global policies to assure this long-term demand are limited for different reasons, among which the most important are certainly the inflationary pressure *and* the limits of further public deficit spending. If these assumptions are correct, an employment strategy concentrating on bottlenecks

[10]For the development of this argument, see, for example, Mukherjee (1976), Koller (1979); the same might be true for employer wage subsidies in the sense of the argument developed by Kaldor (1936) and Rehn (1976).

[11]For a thorough discussion of Public Job Creation or Employer Wage Subsidy from an American point of view see the contributions in Palmer (1978)—especially the synoptic view by Garfinkel/Palmer, and Haveman/Christainsen (1978). For an overview about the most important employer wage subsidy programs in the U.S., Britain and Sweden, see Calame (1980). For an excellent evaluation of a wage subsidy program in France which was apparently more successful, see Colin/Espinasse (1979); this program, however, was targeted to school leavers, and included explicit training elements.

seems to be promising because it puts short money to the shortest factor, thus hopefully inducing a self-supporting chain-reaction. Selective employment policies become in such situations a precondition for successful global policies.

Obviously, neither conventional public employment programs nor employer wage subsidies, as I have described, deal with these labor market shortages. We need, however, an integrative employment strategy which deals in a combined way with both types—demand and supply—of shortage. The bottleneck of employment policy seems to be just this combination or integration, the main elements of which are the following:

a) a stabilization of long-term demand by selective normative regulation, by supporting immediately productive services, and by improving the social infrastructure,
b) the elimination of skill shortages by selective employer subsidies for investment in human capital (productive job maintenance), by creating training and counseling facilities especially oriented to problem groups, and by supporting flexible working time and partnership in families.

To realize this integrative employment strategy, two further conditions have to be met:

c) an institutionalized connection between labor market policy and other sectoral policies, such as social and economic policy,
d) an improvement of the conflict potential of "marginal workers" (better interest representation).

The following paragraphs briefly explain these elements.

The Stabilization of Long-term Demand

If the market does not induce sufficient demand expectations, policy can at least support such a demand in selected areas of high political relevance and of high consensus. This can be done by normative guidance or regulation, by extending social services and by supporting private services with an immediate productive character.

Future demand can be created when public regulations assure that specific standards are to be met. Such standards are already known, for instance security and hygienic standards. One can imagine more of such "normative pre-guidance" (Scharpf, 1980, pp. 14ff) in areas such as energy saving, environmental protection, obligatory facilities for handicapped, traffic regulation, and noise protection.

Experience hints at considerable latent demand in social services, such as protected work places for handicapped, care of old people, care of addicts and ex-addicts, care of convicts and ex-convicts, care of young foreigners in learning the native language and institutions; this list could be extended. One positive experience with the General Work Creation scheme was that local communities and public interest organizations used the subsidies to give evidence of the long-term demand for social services not met before. There was, however, low use in realizing such latent demand because there was no institutionalized way of guaranteeing the long-term financing of successful projects. The German government, however, recently launched a special program (the so-called 500 million program), which pays 100% of the wage costs in social service projects for 2 years *if the sponsors can guarantee that the jobs afterwards become regular jobs.*[12] This program seems to be the right step towards a simultaneously demand and supply oriented employment program.

Another, more indirect, way of supporting long-term demand is by giving support to the development of private services such as counseling in matters of law, technology transfer, energy saving, alternative or "soft" energy technologies, and house modernization; this list too can be extended. The advantage of this type of productive services is that they will be economically self-sustaining in the long run and can be paid by fees if publicly organized.

The Elimination of Skill Shortages

"With the age of software the age of personnel investments has started."[13] This or comparable statements can now often be heard or read. Another common topic is the thesis of "structural under-investment in human capital," represented for instance by the theory of property rights which says that firms are systematically under-investing because they cannot assure the return on human capital investment. Everybody is able to move after the training to the potential competitor (if any exist!), thus creating a typical so-called prisoner's dilemma.[14] A business administration thesis strengthens this argument by saying that personnel investment is not as creditable as capital investment. Whereas for capital investment employers can always find external money for pre-financing, they have to finance personnel investment themselves in advance.[15] Profitable, thriving firms can do it, but less profitable and weak firms cannot.

---

[12]Nordrhein-Westfalia is providing subsidies for an additional third year. The 500 million program runs from Aug. 1979 to Aug. 1980, and supports only 23 local employment agencies out of 142, all of them having an unemployment rate of 6% or more. Four research institutes are presently involved in an accompanying evaluation.

[13]*Wirtschaftswoche* No. 22, 30.5.1980.

[14]See, e.g., Fitzroy/Müller, 1977.

[15]Scharpf, 1980, p. 13; Dierkes/Freud, 1975, p. 315–335.

If these assumptions are correct, a preventive subsidy of human capital investment in specific cases or job protection and preservation by extensive training seems to be more promising than efforts at re-integrating already unemployed persons with wage subsidies. It is known that the motivation of learning, further training and retraining is much higher if people's jobs are secured and if the training is done as much as possible in connection with the concrete job situation. Such preventive training measures can stop the huge monthly inflow into unemployment which is, as we know from detailed studies, about three times higher than the unemployment stock.[16] The more the subsidy affects an existing skill bottleneck, the higher the induced additional demand for labor which might then also affect people at the end of the labor queue.

Germany recently launched two programs which seem to be successful steps towards eliminating shortages of qualified workers. One is the subsidization of research personnel in small and medium sized firms;[17] the other is the subsidization of in-plant training in cases where firms are obviously concerned with processes of restructuring and/or reorganization in regions with above average unemployment.[18] Systematically combining longer periods of short-time work with in-plant training could also be considered.[19]

Even if the already mentioned policies are successful, labor market policy will still be confronted with a considerable number of hard-to-place people who need, according to my analysis, not so much wage compensation as intensive counseling, medical care, and training in order to improve their "competitive ability," and in addition their self-confidence and self-esteem. Because the needs of these people are very different, the establishment of multifunctional training centers at the local labour market is necessary. These training centers may have different forms in institutional terms: purely publicly organized, or institutional networks between public and private training facilities, or purely private, using for example idle training capacities of large firms. Important as a first step for hard-to-place people above and beyond financial incentives is the provision of substantial help in the form of personnel services, training places and technical assistance.[20]

[16]For detailed studies in structure and dynamics of unemployment in Germany, see Egle (1979), Freiburghaus (1978), Schmid (1980a).

[17]The program was introduced in 1978 and pays 40% of the gross wages of research personnel (after a specific amount 25%) and up to a specific ceiling; only small and medium sized firms are entitled to get the subsidy (up to 1000 employees or up to 150 Mill. DM sales). The adoption of the program has exceeded expectations for it.

[18]The program pays 90% of wages for in-plant retraining and further training, 80% of wages for "other training." Firms are entitled only when they are faced with processes of restructuring and reorganization, and when they otherwise would not have launched the training courses.

[19]For a thorough discussion of this possibility, see Schmid/Semlinger (1980).

[20]For more details, see Schmid/Semlinger (1980).

The last point I mentioned as precondition for an integrated demand and supply policy is one which needs more and special attention: A flexible working time policy is necessary for women and men as well. As a matter of fact, women will, in the long run, no longer play the role of a "peripheral labor force." If this assumption is correct, the regular 8 hour full-time jobs occupied by men might be the real bottleneck which will be the main target of future selective policies.

Desiderata of Institutional Reforms and Respective Research

It should be very clear that policy programs alone will not solve all the problems raised in this paper. For the integrative strategies proposed here to be effective, they need obviously much more institutional backing than the traditional one-dimensional measures. Here is a vast and open research field; we know at the moment more or less in which direction the research should go, but not what the results will be.

Another desideratum is the matter of employment *politics*, that is, policy formation, interest representation and political power. It might well come out that neither a strong normative regulation (for instance, quota rules for every kind of problem group or minority), nor a massive incentive program, nor an extension of collective goods really solve the problems of hard-to-place people. In any case, there seems to be a need for an improved institutional representation of their interests, that is, for the development of "negotiation systems" or, put in more traditional terms, of more co-determination or participation. One example in the right direction seems to be the Swedish institution of "adjustment groups" which some years ago were established in all larger firms. These adjustment groups are composed of members of trade unions, local employment agencies and firms. They regularly take care of all the interests of handicapped, disabled and old people, and they have the right to develop initiatives. A thorough study on the functioning of this new institution has still not been carried out.

References

Breuer, W. and A. Hellmich (1979), *Frauen in Arbeitsbeschaffungsmaßnahmen. Eine empirische Untersuchung der Arbeitsbeschaffungsmaßnahmen für Frauen in sieben Arbeitsamtsbezirken Nordrhein-Westfalens*. Köln: MAGS-Arbeit und Beruf 25.

Calame, A. (1980), *Wage Subsidy Programmes: Experiences in Great Britain, Sweden and the USA.* Publication Series of the International Institute of Management of the Science Center Berlin, IIM/80-1.

Colin, J. F. and J. M. Espinasse (1979), "Les Subventions à L'Emploi. Un Essai D'Analyse," *Travail et Emploi* 1: 37–49.

Dierkes, M. and K. P. Freud (1975), "Personalaufwandsplanung als Bestandteil der Personalplanung - US-amerikanische Erfahrungen, Ansätze, Methoden," in H. Schmidt/H. Hagenbruck/W. Sämann (Hrsg.), *Handbuch der Personal planung*. Frankfurt-New York: 315–335.

Egle, F. (1979), *Ansätze für eine systematische Beobachtung und Analyse der Arbeitslosigkeit*. Nürnberg: BeitrAB36 des Instituts für Arbeitsmarkt- und Berufsforschung der Bundesanstalt für Arbeit.

Fitzroy, F. and D. Müller (1977), "Contract and the Economics of Organization". *Discussion Paper Series of the International Institute of Management of the Science Center Berlin*, IIM/dp77-25.

Freiburghaus, D. (1978), *Dynamik der Arbeitslosigkeit. Umschlagsprozeß und Dauerverteilung der Arbeitslosigkeit in der Bundesrepublik 1966 –1977*. Meisenheim am Glan: Verlag Anton Hain.

Garfinkel, I. and J. L. Palmer (1978), "Issues, Evidence, and Implications," in J. L. Palmer (ed.), *Creating Jobs: Public Employment Programs and Wage Subsidies*. Washington: The Brookings Institution.

Hanf, K. (1978), "Work Creation in the Federal Republic of Germany: A Well-Aimed Drop in the Bucket". *Discussion Paper Series of the International Institute of Management of the Science Center Berlin*, IIM/dp78-98.

Haveman, R. H. (1978), "The Dutch Social Employment Program," in J. L. Palmer (ed.), *Creating Jobs: Public Employment Programs and Wage Subsidies*. Washington: The Brookings Institution.

Haveman, R. H. and G. B. Christainsen (1978), *Public Employment and Wage Subsidies in Western Europe and the US.: What We're Doing and What We Know*. European Labor Market Policies. A Special Report of the National Commission for Manpower Policy, Special Report No. 27. Washington.

Johannesson, J. and G. Schmid (1979), *The Development of Labor Market Policy in Sweden and in Germany: Competing or Convergent Models to Combat Unemployment?* Publication Series of the International Institute of Management of the Science Center Berlin, IIM/79-6.

Johannesson, J. and G. Schmid (1980), "The Development of Labor Market Policy in Sweden and in Germany: Competing or Convergent Models to Combat Unemployment?" *European Journal of Political Research*. 8: 387–406.

Kaldor, M. (1936), "Wage Subsidies as a Remedy for Unemployment," *The Journal of Political Economy* 44 (6): 721–42.

Koller, M. (1979), "Die Kosten der Erwerbslosigkeit," *Mitteilungen aus der Arbeitsmarkt- und Berufsforschung* 4: 186–191.

Mukherjee, S. (ed.), (1976), *Unemployment Costs*. London: Political and Economic Planning, Broadsheet No. 561.

Nerb, G. (1978), "Beschäftigungspolitische Verhaltensweisen von Unternehmern. Ergebnisse von Ifo-Umfragen," *Ifo-Schnelldienst* 18/19: 72–78.

Palmer, J. L. (ed.) (1978), *Creating Jobs: Public Employment Programs and Wage Subsidies*. Washington: The Brookings Institution.

Rehn, G. (1976), "Recent Trends in Western Economies: Needs and Methods for Further Development of Manpower Policy," in E. Ginzberg (ed.), *Re-Examining European Manpower Policies*. Washington: National Commission for Manpower Policy.

Scharpf, F. W. (1980), Beschäftigungsorientierte Strukturpolitik. *Discussion Paper Series of the International Institute of Management of the Science Center Berlin*, IIM/dp80-42.

Scharpf, F. W., S. Gensior, and J. Fiedler (eds.) (1979), *Arbeitsmarktpolitik für Akademiker? Vorschläge und Einwände*. Meisenheim am Glan: Verlag Anton Hain.

Schmid, G. (1980a), *Strukturierte Arbeitslosigkeit und Arbeitsmarktpolitik. Empirische und theoretische Analysen zur Verteilungsdynamik der Arbeitslosigkeit und zur Arbeitsmarktpolitik in der Bundesrepublik Deutschland*. Königstein/Ts.: Athenäum Verlag.

Schmid, G. (1980b), "Public Finance Measures to Generate Employment for Hard-to-Place People: Employer Wage Subsidies or Public Employment Programs?" *Discussion Paper of the International Institute of Management of the Science Center Berlin*, IIM/dp80-51.

Schmid, G. and K. Semlinger (1980), *Instrumente gezielter Arbeitsmarktpolitik: Kurzarbeit, Einarbeitungszuschüsse und Eingliederungsbeihilfen. Durchführung, Wirksamkeit und Reformvorschläge*. Königstein/Ts.: Anton Hain.

Schmid, G. and H. Wilke (1980), "Quantitative Wirkungsanalyse von Arbeitsmarktprogrammen am Beispiel der Eingliederungsbeihilfen für schwervermittelbare Arbeitslose: Ein Anwendungsfall und seine methodischen Probleme." *Discussion Paper of the International Institute of Management of the Science Center Berlin*, IIM/dp80-31.

Spitznagel, E. (1979), "Arbeitsmarktwirkungen, Beschäftigungsstrukturen und Zielgruppenorientierung von Allgemeinen Ma βnahmen zur Arbeitsbeschaffung (ABM)," *Mitteilungen aus der Arbeitsmarkt- und Berufsforschung* 4: 198–216.

Résumé

L'article offre une analyse détaillée de deux types de subventions pratiquées en République Fédérale d'Allemagne: aux salaires versés par les employeurs et de programmes d'emploi public, destinées à l'intégration des handicapés dans le marché du travail. L'accent est mis sur leurs effets sur l'emploi et la répartition. L'étude arrive à un jugement assez négatif sur les subventions visant seulement les salaires pour un temps limité, aussi bien dans le secteur public que privé. Ce ne sont pas les coûts de la main d'oeuvre, mais le manque de qualification, pris dans un sens large, qui gêne le recrutement des handicapés. L'article propose, en conclusion, les perspectives d'une stratégie intégrée en faveur de l'emploi qui combine une politique sélective de la mise au travail des handicapés avec des mesures en faveur de l'offre de telle sorte que les insuffisances réelles du marché du travail, et particulièrement le manque de qualification soient traitées.

The Distributional Impact of Targeted Public Employment Programs

Sheldon Danziger
George Jakubson*

The Evolution of Targeted Public Employment as an Antipoverty Policy

The War on Poverty was declared by President Johnson in January 1964. The strategy proposed included a broad range of policy instruments, but did not include either a public jobs program for the poor or an increase in cash assistance (except for the aged and disabled), although these were advocated by several policymakers at the time. In the years following the declaration of the War on Poverty, a number of employment programs were established or expanded. Although diverse in their goals and the groups which they served, they shared a common focus—the enhancement of individual skills through classroom or on-the-job education and training. Program graduates were given job search assistance and then launched into the labor market to compete for employment positions. There was little concern with the public provision of postprogram jobs because unemployment rates in the late 1960s had fallen to historically low levels.

Despite the subsequent proliferation of programs, total expenditures on employment and training have represented less than 5 percent of government funds directed toward the poor for the entire post War on Poverty period.

While a guaranteed jobs program continued to be viewed as unnecessary, a guaranteed income in the form of a negative income tax gained in popularity and was endorsed by a Presidential Commission in 1969. However, it was never adopted. But the income maintenance system did rapidly expand—both in terms of new programs and increased benefit levels in exist-

*The authors acknowledge the support of funds granted to the Institute for Research on Poverty by the Department of Health and Human Services pursuant to the Economic Opportunity Act of 1964. John Bishop, Peter Gottschalk, Robert Haveman, Stanley Masters, John Martin, Robert Plotnick, and Eugene Smolensky provided helpful comments on an earlier draft. The authors' analysis of the Supported Work Program owes much to many discussions with and the work of Peter Kemper.

Public Finance and Public Employment. Proceedings of the 36th Congress of the International Institute of Public Finance. Jerusalem, 1980.

ing programs. As greater transfer benefits became available to greater numbers of poor people, the work disincentives and the high budgetary costs of the transfer system were called into question. The public viewed increasing transfer recipiency as evidence that large numbers were choosing dependency and avoiding work.[1]

A concern for both the antipoverty outcome and the process by which poverty was reduced resulted in a renewed search for an antipoverty strategy that could increase the work effort of the poor. Because income maintenance policy could not both increase work effort and reduce the number of people receiving welfare, renewed attention was focused on employment and training policies. The labor supply orientation of the early employment and training programs had been called into question by the high unemployment rates—particularly those of youth, women, and minorities—of the 1970s. Concern shifted from merely augmenting the skills of the disadvantaged to increasing the number of employment opportunities. The first public service employment (PSE) program since the Great Depression was enacted in 1971, primarily as a countercyclical device. PSE slots were increased by the Comprehensive Employment and Training Act of 1979 and have become the largest component of the employment and training budget. Amendments to this act in 1976 targeted a greater percentage of the PSE jobs on the disadvantaged, particularly the long term unemployed and welfare recipients.[2]

The negative income tax developments in income maintenance policy and the PSE jobs emphasis in employment and training policy were integrated in 1977 by President Carter's proposal to reform welfare, the Program for Better Jobs and Income (PBJI). PBJI proposed a universal negative income tax with one income guarantee for those not expected to work, and a lower income guarantee for those expected to work. This latter group would have also been eligible for a targeted PSE job. PBJI represents the first

---

[1]The negative income tax experiments suggested that work discentives were relatively small for male heads of household, and somewhat larger for female heads of household and wives. Nonetheless, a call for cutbacks in income maintenance programs appears regularly in the popular press and in numerous academic articles. For a review of the efficiency effects of the transfer system, see Danziger, Haveman, and Plotnick (1980).

[2]PSE is not concerned solely with reducing structural unemployment and poverty, or overcoming the work disincentives of transfer programs. For a discussion of its other functions—satisfying needs not met by the private sector or regular public employment, reducing the severity of the business cycle, improving the social or psychological well-being of the worker and his/her family—see Palmer (1978, 1980).

Although this paper analyzes only the direct provision of public jobs, there are other types of targeted public employment programs—earnings or wage subsidies which are paid to disadvantaged workers, or tax credits to employers who hire them. Both of these kinds of policies are currently in effect in the U.S. (e.g., the Earned Income Tax Credit, the Targeted Jobs Tax Credit). For a discussion of a broad range of direct job creation measures, see Haveman (1980).

attempt in the U.S. to guarantee jobs to the poor, and thus to remove the onus of poverty and unemployment from the individual.[3]

Although PBJI was not enacted, a demonstration project was begun in 1975 to provide jobs to disadvantaged workers. It offers an opportunity for examining the antipoverty potential of a program that links existing income maintenance programs with a guaranteed job strategy.

The Supported Work Demonstration Project[4]

Supported Work is a targeted public employment program in which persons with severe labor market disadvantages were employed in special settings for about one year. The program is designed to provide participants with work skills and attitudes that would increase their post-program employment and earnings. It also attempts to produce useful social output during the program. Participants work in small groups with others with similar disadvantages under close and supportive supervision. Some of the placements were operated by the local Supported Work agency whereas others were contracted to private firms or government agencies. Demands for punctuality, attendance, and productivity were initially low, and slowly increased until normal labor market standards were reached. Wage rates began at low levels, and gradually increased as the participants advanced through the program. Participants were required to leave Supported Work after a specified period (usually 12 months) whether or not they had found another job. Job placement efforts were provided, and in some instances a worker moved from a Supported Work job to a regular job in the same firm or agency.

There were four groups of disadvantaged participants and four control groups in the Supported Work Demonstration—former drug addicts, former law offenders, unemployed youth, and long term welfare recipients who were female heads of household. Because of our concern with analyzing the integration of income maintenance and employment policy, we focus here only on the welfare group. All of the other participants had only limited access to existing income maintenance programs.[5]

To be eligible for Supported Work, a woman had to have limited employment experience (unemployed at time of program entrance, no more

---

[3]For a discussion of recent developments in the U.S., see Orr and Skidmore (1980). Analysis of the Program for Better Jobs and Income can be found in Danziger, Haveman, and Smolensky (1977), and Danziger and Plotnick (1979).

[4]This section draws from several analyses of the Supported Work program. See, Kemper and Moss (1978), Masters and Maynard (1980), and Kemper, Long, and Thornton (1979).

[5]We should also point out that the program seems to have been most effective for the women receiving welfare.

than 10 hours per week of employment in each of the last 4 weeks, and no regular job in the last 6 months), no child under the age of 6 years, and significant welfare experience (currently a recipient, and on welfare for 30 of the past 36 months). Participation in Supported Work was voluntary.

Several aspects of the demonstration allow us to simulate the effects of a national program that combines an income maintenance with a targeted public employment strategy. First, detailed data on program costs and benefits, including the value of output produced by the participants, are available. Second, detailed background and longitudinal data gathered on the randomly-chosen Supported Work participants and on those randomly assigned to the control group who had full access to existing welfare programs allow us to analyze the impact of the addition of a targeted public employment program to existing welfare programs. We used data gathered when the women were Supported Work participants to evaluate economic outcomes (employment, transfer recipiency, poverty, etc.) that would result from the implementation of a targeted public employment program which provided continuous access to a job—that is, a program that did not require participants to leave a targeted job after a specified period. Similarly, we used post-program data to evaluate economic outcomes that would exist if the program were transitional and provided access only for a one-year period. The data on controls enable us to gauge the effects of the existing welfare system.

Methodology

We chose a nationally representative sample from the March 1975 Current Population Survey (CPS) that closely approximated the population of welfare recipients who were eligible for the Supported Work demonstration. Using the Supported Work data, we estimated a set of regressions for experimentals and a separate set for controls. We then applied the regression coefficients from each of these samples to the characteristics of the women in the CPS, and imputed values to each woman in the CPS which predict her income and work effort in two situations—if she had access to (1) a Supported Work job, or (2) the current welfare system that was available to the controls.[6] A maximization procedure in which each woman chooses the situation

[6]These regressions and a technical Appendix are available from the authors by request. We used estimates for the economic variables for both the targeted public employment program and the existing income maintenance system. We did not use the actual economic variables in the CPS or compare actual and imputed values, however. There may be some unobserved characteristic, such as work ability, that caused a woman's actual earnings to exceed the value predicted by our equation using the data on the control sample. When we predict her earnings in the jobs program, our equation will not account for this unobserved factor. This means that if we compare a predicted value with an actual value the difference between the two would be

which yields maximum income was simulated from which we derived the aggregate costs, benefits, and distributional effects that would result if a Supported Work type program were to be implemented on a national scale.

We began with a sample of nonwhite female heads of household from the CPS. We restricted the sample to nonwhites since only 5 percent of the actual Supported Work participants were white. We further restricted the sample to women who seemed to satisfy the Supported Work eligibility criteria—i.e., women who were between the ages of 25 and 54, who had children between the ages of 6 and 18, and who lived in a household currently receiving welfare income.[7] This yields an eligible (weighted) sample of 459,037 nonwhite female household heads, which represents 25 percent of the 1,785,369 nonwhite female household heads in 1975, and 44 percent of those receiving welfare.

Regression Model and Antipoverty Effects

We used data gathered during the 9th month of the Supported Work demonstration to proxy a world in which any eligible woman could choose to work at a targeted public job. At this point in the demonstration, a member of the experimental group could claim a job. These data are used to simulate a state in which the women have continuous access to a targeted job. We used the data gathered during the 27th month of the demonstration to proxy the situation of a woman who had been eligible for a transitional job, but was not currently eligible. These data represent a state where the women have had only a one-time access to a job, and reveal the longer-run results of such transitional access.

For each time period (months 1–9 and months 19–27) and for each group of women (experimentals and controls) we estimated reduced form regressions for earnings, monthly hours of work, and other income (primarily income from government transfers). The explanatory variables in each of the regressions are personal characteristics that are available in both the Supported Work and CPS data.

---

distorted. For our purposes, it is more important to accurately predict differences between two situations than to predict well the level in any situation. Using two predicted values more accurately preserves the likely differences between them than using a mixture of actual and predicted values.

[7]A greater percentage of our initial sample was classified as Supported Work eligible than would have been so classified by the program. The discrepancy arises because the CPS has data only on current welfare recipiency, so many women listed as receiving AFDC would not have received it for 30 of the past 36 months. A similar data problem led us to ignore the unemployment criteria. Thus, our CPS sample is probably not as disadvantaged as the Supported Work sample.

Because many in the control sample were not working in either time period, and because many experimentals were not working after they had left Supported Work, we estimated many of the regressions as Tobits. The remaining regressions where the dependent variable rarely was zero were estimated using ordinary least squares.[8] For computational convenience, the two-step Tobit estimation suggested by Heckman (1980) was used. In the first step we estimated the probability that a woman will have positive earnings (or other income) as a function of her personal characteristics. A probit estimator was used for this first stage and the sample includes all women. In the second step we estimated, using ordinary least squares, the amount of these earnings (or other income) for only those women with positive earnings (or positive other income). The independent variables included all the personal characteristics from the first step, plus a variable λ, which is a function of the probability that the woman has positive earnings (or positive other income).[9]

---

[8]The percentage of experimentals and controls with no earnings or hours or other income and the estimation procedure are as follows:

	9 Month Experimentals	9 Month Controls	27 Month Experimentals	27 Month Controls
No Earnings or Hours	3% (OLS)	64% (TOBIT)	52% (TOBIT)	60% (TOBIT)
No Other Income	4 (OLS)	1 (OLS)	20 (TOBIT)	9 (TOBIT)

[9]Consider a latent variable, $\tilde{y}$, which, conditional on X, is normally distributed around a regression line:

$$\tilde{y} = \beta X + \epsilon, \text{ where } \epsilon \sim N(o, \sigma^2).$$

Now $\tilde{y}$ is observed only if it is positive; when it is negative, the observed variable, y, takes on the value of zero:

$$y = \begin{matrix} 0, \tilde{y} < 0 \\ \tilde{y}, \tilde{y} > 0 \end{matrix}$$

For example, let $\tilde{y}$ be desired hours of work in the labor market, and y be actual hours. Under competitive conditions, actual and desired hours are equal when desired hours are nonnegative. However, when desired hours are negative, the individual is at the corner solution of zero hours of work.

Our estimation technique is as follows. Let D equal a dummy variable which takes on the value of 1 if a positive value of the dependent variable y is observed:

$$D = \begin{matrix} 0, y = 0 \\ 1, y > 0. \end{matrix}$$

Then $E(y \mid x) = EE(y \mid x, D)$

$$= \Pr(D = 1 \mid x) \, E\,(y \mid x, D = 1) + \Pr(D = 0 \mid x) \, E\,(y \mid x, D = 0)$$

$$= \Pr(D = 1 \mid x) \, E\,(y \mid x, D = 1)$$

$$= \Pr\left(\frac{\epsilon}{\sigma} > \frac{-\beta x}{\sigma}\right) E\left(y \mid x, \frac{\epsilon}{\sigma} > \frac{-\beta x}{\sigma}\right)$$

The estimated coefficients from the Supported Work experimentals were applied to the appropriate characteristics of the women in the CPS sample. This yields an estimate of what earnings, hours and other income would have been if women had continuous access to a public employment program, and then if they had transitional access. The coefficients from the controls were used to produce estimates of the economic outcomes of the existing income maintenance programs.

Table 1 shows the mean value of the imputations for the CPS sample. Each woman has an imputation for each entry in the table. For example, contrast the first two columns. Column 1 shows that if all women had continuous access to a targeted public job, their mean annual income would be $6251, and they would work 134 hours per month. The jobs program increases work effort, earned income, and total income, and reduces other (transfer) income. If the women had not been in the program (column 2) they would have had a total income of only $3981, worked only 22 hours per month, and relied more heavily on income maintenance transfers (other income).

Columns 3 and 4 show that if the women had access to a targeted job for only a transitional period, the mean difference in economic well-being would significantly narrow in the long run (by 27 months). For those in a transitional rather than a continuous program, earnings and hours decline while other income increases; total income drops to $5100. The mean predicted differentials between those in the transitional program and those in the existing income maintenance system are only $460 annual income, and 19 hours.[10]

$$= \left[\Phi \left(\frac{\beta x}{\sigma} \right) \right] [\beta x + \sigma \lambda]$$

where $\quad \lambda = \phi \left(\frac{\beta x}{\sigma} \right) \Big/ \Phi \left(\frac{\beta x}{\sigma} \right)$

ϕ = density of a standard normal variable

Φ = distribution function for a standard normal variable.

The Heckman (1980) procedure estimates $Pr(D = 1)$ using probit analysis. The results of the probit analysis are then used to construct an estimate of λ, which becomes an explanatory variable in an OLS regression of y on x and $\hat{\lambda}$ for that part of the sample for which $D = 1$. This procedure yields consistent estimates of β.

Our imputation procedure follows directly from the estimation

$$\hat{\lambda} = [\hat{p}(y > 0)] [\beta x + \hat{\sigma} \hat{\lambda}],$$

where $\hat{p}$ is the estimated probability and $\hat{\beta}, \hat{\sigma}$ are the estimated coefficients, and $\hat{\lambda}$ is the estimate of λ derived from the probit step.

[10]We have ignored the possibility that the nature of the program induced behavioral changes. Participants in a temporary program like Supported Work may have acted differently during the experiment than they would have if the program were continuous. For example, the experimentals may have increased their in-program work effort and reduced future work effort in response to the program.

Table 1

Imputed Mean Values[a]

Dependent Variable	Continuous Access to Job[c]		Transitional Access to Job[d]	
	Targeted Public Employment Program	Existing Income Maintenance Only	Targeted Public Employment Program	Existing Income Maintenance Only
Earnings[b]	$4525	$ 785	$2744	$1570
Other (Transfer)[b] Income	1726	3196	2356	3070
Total Income[b]	6251	3981	5100	4640
Hours Worked	134	22	64	45

Source: Computations by authors in which regressions were estimated from Supported Work data tapes and then applied to the characteristics of eligible women drawn from the 1975 Current Population Survey data tape.

[a] The sample, when weighted, represents 459,037 nonwhite female heads of household from the CPS who we predict would be eligible for a Supported Work program.

[b] All imputed values are expressed in 1977 dollars. Earnings and income data are in annual terms; hours are monthly.

[c] Based on 9 month data.

[d] Based on 27 month data.

Table 2 presents the results of our simulation of the program's effects on the women's demand for targeted public jobs and on measured poverty.[11] Column 1, for the continuous access case, shows that 80.3 percent of the women who met our simulated Supported Work eligibility requirements would be poor if they merely had access to the current income maintenance system, whereas only 34.5 percent would be poor if they had access to the jobs program. If the women were free to choose the situation yielding the maximum income, all 459,037 would choose the job. Column 2 shows that the antipoverty effect of a transitional program is substantially lower. If there were no targeted employment program, 64.3 percent of the eligibles would be poor, whereas if there were a transitional jobs program, 56.3 percent would be poor. However, if the women could choose the situation which maximizes their income, 45.8 percent would be poor, and 295,120 women would choose a targeted job. This represents a substantial increase in the potential demand for public employment, since only about 600,000 slots were available for all persons in 1978.

The maximization procedure used in our simulation probably produced an upper-bound estimate of the effect of a jobs program on poverty and on the demand for targeted jobs because we did not value foregone leisure or fully account for all the costs and benefits of employment. A woman who

[11]We use the official U.S. government measure of poverty which varies by family size. In 1978 the poverty line for a family of four was $6628, about 35 percent of the median family income.

Table 2

Simulation Results: The Demand for Targeted Public Jobs
and the Incidence of Poverty

	Access to Targeted Job	
	Continuous[a]	*Transitional*[b]
1. Current income maintenance system only:		
Incidence of poverty[c]	80.3%	64.3%
2. Addition of targeted employment program:		
Incidence of poverty	34.5	56.3
3. Maximization:		
Incidence of poverty if women choose situation with		
highest income	34.5	45.8
Percentage of women choosing job	100.0	64.3
Number of jobs demanded	459,037	295,120

Source: Computations by authors in which regressions were estimated from Supported Work data tapes and then applied to the characteristics of eligible women drawn from the 1975 Current Population Survey data tape.

[a] Based on 9 month data.

[b] Based on 27 month data.

[c] The incidence of poverty is defined as the percentage of women in the group whose yearly income falls below the official government poverty lines.

finds her total income to be $1 higher with a job than with the current system chooses the job regardless of her change in leisure. Similarly, we neglected any costs associated with work (e.g., payroll taxes, child care costs, transportation expenses). The only neglected benefits from work are the social and psychological esteem she or her family may derive from her working and reduced welfare dependency, or the value of the employment experience in future periods.

This upper-bound bias is reinforced by the fact that participation in Supported Work was voluntary. Thus, if the experimentals were more highly motivated than average, their gains from the program might be higher than those that would result from a national program. If this were the case, then the gains we attributed to the women in the CPS sample will be overstated. It should be noted that even though the increased earnings from the targeted public employment program result in reduced income maintenance payments (other income), dependence on income transfers remains high. Also, the most optimistic scenario in Table 2 shows that 34.5 percent of the sample remains poor (the rate for the entire U.S. population in 1975 was about 11 percent). Thus, for the very disadvantaged, targeted public employment should be viewed as a complement to and not a substitute for income maintenance transfers.

If the wage rates of the targeted jobs had been higher, the incidence of poverty would have been lower. There are several reasons why a program for the disadvantaged might pay low wages. First, the lower the wage, the lower the probability that persons who are able to find regular jobs will be attracted to a subsidized jobs program. Second, given a fixed program budget, the lower wage means more participants can be enrolled. Third, even the low wage probably exceeds the marginal productivity of these workers.

We have shown that a transitional program has the potential for reducing poverty among eligible female welfare recipients by about 30 percent, whereas a continuous program could cut poverty by about 60 percent. However, there would be a demand for an additional 150,000 jobs under a continuous program rather than a transitional one (see the last line in Table 2). After we estimate the additional costs of these jobs in the next section, we can contrast two equal cost alternatives: the addition of the jobs program with an equivalent expansion of the current transfer system.

Benefit-Cost Analysis and Efficiency Effects

Up to this point, we have analyzed a targeted public employment program from the standpoint of participants. We have examined their increased employment and income and reduced poverty, but we have not considered the program's efficiency effects. The benefit-cost data gathered during the demonstration values the benefits attributable to the program, compares them to the costs, and allows us to examine the efficiency impact. The program's "net present value," the difference between benefits and costs, is available on a per participant basis. By examining the transfers and program benefits received by participants and the transfer and program costs borne by the taxpayers, we can see what implications the taxpayers' preference for public employment over income maintenance programs might have upon the public budget. The benefit-cost analysis compares the Supported Work experimentals to the controls, and thus compares the addition of a targeted public employment program to the set of existing income maintenance programs.

The benefit-cost results reported here are based on Peter Kemper, David Long, and Craig Thorton's analysis (1979), but have been modified to fit our extrapolation to the CPS data and a national program.[12] The targeted

[12]The Kemper-Long-Thornton (KLT) benefit-cost analysis is quite thorough. Detailed data is presented on project input, overhead, and central administrative costs. Participant labor costs and fringes are the costs to the taxpayers. These costs, reduced by the foregone earnings of participants (measured by the earnings of the control sample), represent the net benefit to participants. Benefits are estimated from experimental-control differences and include in-program output, post-program output, tax liabilities of participants, transfer recipiency, and the use of alternative education and employment programs. The most difficult benefit to estimate is the value of in-program output that serves as an offset to the project costs. The approach taken by KLT is to use the price an outside supplier in the regular labor market would charge for the output, *not* the input costs of the program.

Table 3

Simulation Results:
Poverty and Work Effort with Program Budget Costs Held Constant,
Continuous Access to a Targeted Job

	Current Income Maintenance System	*Continuous Access to Targeted Jobs or Current Income Maintenance System*	*Augmented Income Maintenance System*
1. Extra budget costs applied	0	$1899 million	$1899 million
2. Extra budget costs applied, as a percentage of existing costs for female headed families	0	50.6%	50.6%
3. Incidence of poverty, targeted sample[a]	80.3%	34.5%	51.7%
4. Incidence of poverty, all female headed families[b]	55.2%	43.4%	39.8%
5. Index of work effort, targeted sample[a]	100	576	79
6. Index of work effort, all female headed families[b]	100	124	97

[a] Targeted sample contains 459,037 nonwhite female heads of household receiving welfare and meeting eligibility criteria for targeted job.

[b] There are 1,785,369 nonwhite female headed families.

public employment program had relatively small social costs—$1907 per participant per year for a continuous access program, and $683 for a transitional one. These costs are smaller than those found for other jobs programs because the women produced valuable outputs while on the job and reduced their reliance on existing income transfers. The same program would have had much greater social costs for participants not already receiving income transfers.[13] The net benefits to participants were $2229 and $1716 for the two types of program.

The budgetary costs to nonparticipants were $4136 per job for the continuous case and $2399 for the transitional case. If the program were to be implemented on a national scale, and the demand for jobs were as shown in Table 2, then the aggregate budgetary costs of the program would be $1899 million for a continuous program and $708 million for a transitional one.[14]

[13]The benefit-cost estimates were derived at a point at which all of the program costs had been incurred, and do not include any future benefits that might have resulted beyond the 27th month. If the increased earnings and reduced transfer dependency were to continue into the future, the net costs to society and to the taxpayer could become net benefits. KLT's estimates of these future effects yield positive net present values.

[14]We disregarded the difficulties inherent in establishing a national jobs program of this size and type. For a discussion of some of the problems, see Danziger, Haveman, and Smolensky (1977).

Table 4

Simulation Results:
Poverty and Work Effort with Program Budget Costs Held Constant,
Transitional Access to a Targeted Job

	Current Income Maintenance System	Transitional Access to Targeted Jobs or Current Income Maintenance System	Augmented Income Maintenance System
1. Extra budget costs applied	0	$708 million	$708 million
2. Extra budget costs as a percentage of existing costs for female headed families	0	19.2%	19.2%
3. Incidence of poverty, targeted sample[a]	64.3%	45.8%	56.3%
4. Incidence of poverty, all female headed families[b]	51.1%	46.3%	46.0%
5. Index of work effort, targeted sample[a]	100	174	96
6. Index of work effort, all female headed families[b]	100	107	99

[a] Targeted sample contains 459,037 nonwhite female heads of household receiving welfare and meeting eligibility criteria for targeted job.
[b] There are 1,785,369 nonwhite female headed families.

We used these estimates to simulate a proportionate expansion of the existing transfer system, and produce comparisons between the current system and the targeted jobs program that hold budget costs constant. These simulation results are shown in Table 3 and 4.

Comparison of Equal Budget Cost Alternatives: Targeted Public Jobs and Augmented Income Maintenance System

Lines 1 and 2 of Table 3 show that the budgetary costs of $1899 million represent a 50.6 percent increase in current income maintenance costs for the 1,785,369 nonwhite female household heads. Whereas the jobs program targets all $1899 million on 459,037 of these women (our estimate of eligibles), an expansion of the current system would benefit all current welfare recipients and make additional women eligible. We simulated a proportional expansion of existing income guarantees by increasing each current recipient's welfare benefit by 50.6 percent. Because increased transfers lead to reduced earnings, we reduced our estimates of their earnings using the income elasticities from the Seattle-Denver Income Maintenance Experiments.[15]

[15]Keeley et al. (1978) report an estimate of the income effect on hours to be .1011. We assumed that changes in hours and earnings were equal in proportional terms. Our simulation increased incomes but did not change program tax rates, so there is no substitution effect.

The results on the poverty effect for the targeted sample for all of the nonwhite female headed families show that access to a job means a larger reduction in poverty than the augmented income maintenance system for the targeted sample—the incidence falls from 80.3 percent to 34.5 percent or 51.7 percent. However, for the entire sample the reduction due to the augmenting of the current system is greater—the incidence falls from 55.2 percent to 43.4 percent or 39.8 percent.

Although the differences in poverty due to the additional $1899 are similar, the differences in work effort are not. The jobs program leads to increased work effort, while expanding the current system reduces work effort. Work effort under the current system for the targeted sample (line 5) and for all female heads (line 6) is indexed at 100. The jobs program leads to over five times as much work effort as the current system for the targeted sample, a 24 percent increase for all nonwhite female heads. Expansion of the current system reduces work effort by 21 percent for the targeted sample and by 3 percent for the entire sample.

The results in Table 4 for the transitional program are similar. The additional expenditures, $708 million, or 19.2 percent of current costs, have smaller impacts than those of the continuous program. Again, the anti-poverty impacts are similar—the jobs program increases and the augmented current system decreases work effort.[16]

Conclusion

We have analyzed data from the Supported Work demonstration, and estimated the distributional and efficiency effects of a targeted public employment program of national scale for female welfare recipients.[17] We found

---

Our simulation is overly targeted, however. We raised welfare income, holding tax rates constant and therefore, raised the guarantee. But we ignored the fact that raising the guarantee raises the breakeven levels and results in a larger number of women eligible for welfare. The increased expenditures for the augmented income maintenance system would be more widely distributed than is shown here. Thus, the estimates shown in the last columns of Tables 3 and 4 should be viewed as upper bounds.

[16]Tables 3 and 4 do not report our maximization simulation for the comparison of the jobs program with the augmented income maintenance system. If the women chose the situation with the maximum income, then the demand for jobs would be lower than that shown in Table 2: 347,646 jobs from a continuous program and 198,211 from a transitional one.

[17]As we have suggested throughout the paper, the extrapolation from the Supported Work demonstration to a National Program should be viewed as illustrative. Besides the prediction errors always associated with regression models, selection bias would be present if the voluntary nature of participation in the demonstration were correlated with some observed characteristics. Also no experiment of limited duration will be able to anticipate behavioral changes that might be induced by a permanent program. All of these caveats relate to participant behavior. But our method also rests on some assumptions about the labor market. We assumed that whenever an experimental wanted to work post-program, her labor supply would be met by increased labor demand. This would not be the case if labor demand were less than perfectly elastic and the woman either could not find work or displaced others.

that the reduction in poverty and the increase in work effort were much larger when continuous rather than transitional access to a job was provided. The benefit-cost analysis, however, reveals a reverse pattern. Although the net present value to society of both types of programs is negative, the social and budgetary costs of the continuous program are higher.

We began by referring to the American preference for aiding the poor through employment rather than income maintenance programs. Increased expenditures on targeted employment could both increase work effort and reduce poverty. Equivalent increased expenditures on the existing income maintenance system would reduce poverty by about as much, but would also reduce work effort. The choice between an increase in transfers and the implementation of a targeted jobs program must be made on the basis of value judgments. Our own view is that a targeted jobs program would permit a reorientation of antipoverty policy towards the major goal of the War on Poverty—the reduction of poverty through earned incomes.

References

Danziger, S., Haveman, R., and Plotnick, R. 1980. "Retrenchment or Reorientation: Options for Income Support Policy." *Public Policy* 28, Fall, pp. 473–490.

Danziger, S., Haveman, R., and Smolensky, E. 1977. *The Program for Better Jobs and Income: A Guide and a Critique.* Washington, D.C.: Joint Economic Committee of the U.S. Congress.

Danziger, S., and Plotnick, R. 1979. "Can Welfare Reform Eliminate Poverty?" *Social Services Review* 53, June, pp. 244–260.

Haveman, R. 1980. "Direct Job Creation." In E. Ginzberg (Ed.), *Employing the Unemployed: An Assessment of Federal Programs.* New York: Basic Books.

Heckman, J. 1980. "Sample Selection Bias as a Specification Error." In J. P. Smith (Ed.), *Female Labor Supply.* Princeton: Princeton University Press.

Keeley, M., Robins, P., Speigleman, R., and West, R. 1978. "The Labor Supply Effects and Costs of Alternative Negative Income Tax Programs." *Journal of Human Resources* 13, Winter, pp. 3–36.

Kemper, P., Long, D., and Thornton, C. 1979. *The Supported Work Evaluation: Final Benefit Cost Analysis.* Princeton: Mathematica Policy Research.

Kemper, P., and Moss, P. 1978. "Economic Efficiency of Public Employment Programs." In J. Palmer (Ed.), *Creating Jobs.* Washington, D.C.: Brookings Institution.

Masters, S., and Maynard, R. 1980. *Supported Work: Impacts for the AFDC Target Group.* Princeton: Mathematica Policy Research.

Orr, L., and Skidmore, F. 1980. *The Evaluation of the Work Issue in Welfare Reform.* Paper presented at the Middlebury College Conference on Welfare Reform, Middlebury, Vermont.

Palmer, J. (Ed.). 1978. *Creating Jobs.* Washington, D.C.: Brookings Institution.

Palmer, J. 1980. "Jobs Versus Income Transfers." In E. Ginzberg (Ed.), *Employing the Unemployed: An Assessment of Federal Programs.* New York: Basic Books.

Résumé

Aux Etats-Unis, les gouvernants et le public marquent la préférence pour une stratégie contre la pauvreté qui accroît le revenu gagné par les défavorisés. Malgré cette préférence, ces quinze dernières années, la majeure partie de la réduction de la pauvreté est venue d'une augmentation des transferts des revenus publics et non pas d'une augmentation de l'emploi et des revenus. En conséquence, plusieurs initiatives récentes de politique économique ont souligné la création d'emploi dans les services publics au bénéfice des défavorisés.

Cet article étudie l'évolution de l'emploi et de la formation en tant que composante de la politique contre la pauvreté. Il analyse ensuite la possibilité d'intégrer les programmes d'emploi public finalisés à des programmes de maintien du revenu existant pour ceux d'entre les défavorisés qui sont capables de travailler.

Nos résultats empiriques sont basés sur un projet de démonstration récent—travail subventionné—où l'on a rassemblé des renseignements détaillés à la fois sur leurs effets, sur l'efficacité du travail et la répartition des revenus. Nous concluons qu'une augmentation des dépenses pour un emploi public finalisé atteindrait des objectifs anti-pauvreté identiques mais aurait des effets plus souhaitables sur l'effort de travail qu'une expansion équivalente de programmes de transferts courants. Il convient cependant de considérer ces programmes d'emploi plutôt comme un complément, que comme un substitut à des programmes destinés à maintenir le revenu existant.

8242
8135
8226
U.S.

Compensation in the Public Sector:
The Importance of Pensions

*Joseph F. Quinn**

The determination of appropriate pay in the public sector is difficult. Profit maximization offers guidance in the private sector, but governments do not maximize profits. Many governmental units in the United States have explicitly adopted a doctrine of comparability with the private sector as the basis for wage determination. The Federal Salary Reform Act of 1962, for example, requires that "federal pay rates be comparable with private enterprise pay rates for the same level of work" (Smith, 1977, p. 16). The comparisons are made on the basis of annual wage surveys conducted by the Bureau of Labor Statistics.[1] Most states and many local jurisdictions have adopted similar procedures.

These comparisons, however, are not simple to make because compensation is a multi-dimensional concept. Obvious components are wage and salary, and fringe benefits such as pension contributions, disability, life and health insurance, and paid vacations. Other dimensions, such as job stability and the working environment, are no less important but much more difficult to measure. The approach taken at the federal level has been to ignore all the components except wage and salary, and to try to match these basic pay levels with those in the private sector. Given the large aggregate importance of fringe benefits, it is clear that total compensation for similar levels of work can differ considerably by sector if only one of the components is equalized.

*The research was supported by funds granted to the Institute for Research on Poverty, University of Wisconsin, Madison, by the Department of Health and Human Services, and by funds from a Boston College, Mellon grant. The data were provided by the Social Security Administration. Programs to extract pension and Social Security information were developed by Richard V. Burkhauser, Irene Powell, and the author. I would like to thank the Conference discussants, Anita Pfaff, Ved Gandi, and Robert Leu, as well as Morley Gunderson and Jan Blakeslee, for their helpful and constructive comments.

[1]A thorough history of the comparability doctrine and a description of the surveys used can be found in Smith (1977).

Public Finance and Public Employment. Proceedings of the 36th Congress of the International Institute of Public Finance. Jerusalem, 1980.

What have been the consequences of this comparability doctrine, and of the many problems which exist in making it operational? How well has this approach worked in equalizing compensation in the two sectors? The many attempts to evaluate the final outcome have concentrated on the wage and salary component, the dimension along which comparisons are explicitly made, and by far the easiest to measure. Very few efforts have been made to compare other dimensions. This paper describes differences in the most important fringe component—pension benefits. In particular, I compare retirement benefits of workers in the private sector with those of federal, state, and local government employees. In general, the pension results confirm the conclusions drawn from salary comparisons—that public employees, on average, do seem to be paid more than their private sector counterparts, but that the extent (or existence) of the rent differs by level of government.

The first section of this paper briefly reviews the evidence on the wage and salary component. Section II presents some comparisons of various aspects of pensions—coverage, age of earliest eligibility, and the size of benefits, the latter measured both by the annual dollar flow and the wealth (or asset) equivalent of this income stream. Section III presents and discusses three major caveats concerning these simple benefit comparisons, and is followed by a summary and conclusion.

I. Wage Comparisons in the Public and Private Sectors

Two approaches have been used to compare pay levels in the public and private sectors. The first is to compare wages for particular job classifications, holding constant the nature of the task. Such studies (such as Fogel and Lewin, 1974, and Perloff, 1971) have found that public sector pay usually exceeds that in the private sector in the low and middle skill ranges, but may be inferior at the management and professional levels.

The major shortcoming of this research strategy is that it ignores the quality of the work force within a given occupation. Governments may be paying more, but hiring workers with higher productivity. Thus, the second approach in this literature specifically emphasizes the productive characteristics of the employees (education, training, experience, etc.), and utilizes microdata sources to test whether wage differentials exist after differences in human capital have been considered. It is equivalent *people*, not equivalent jobs, that are compared. An attempt is made to decompose overall wage differences into a component which can be attributed to employee characteristics and a component which cannot.[2] The latter, if positive, is interpreted as the rent associated with employment in the public sector.

---

[2]This methodology is described in more detail in Quinn (1979).

Extensive research of this type has been done by Sharon Smith (1977) and reviewed by Gunderson (1980). Smith concludes that wage rates are higher in federal employment than in the private sector, even after measurable human capital differences have been considered. The unexplained differential (the rent) is higher for women than for men, and higher for nonwhites than for whites. When the state and private sectors are compared, Smith finds wages about the same for men, and higher in public employment for women. At the local government level, men appear to earn slightly less and women slightly more than in the private sector.

Using a richer data set drawn from older workers in 1969, and an expanded functional form for the wage equations, I have made similar estimates with a sample of white men. I found a positive rent of about 20 percent in the federal sector, about 17 percent in the state sector, and a negative differential of about 6 percent in local employment.[3] Given the differences in the samples, the years and the wage equations, I consider the results to be very similar to Smith's for the federal and local sectors, but quite different for the state sample. I find evidence of positive rent there where she does not.

From these studies and others, a number of conclusions emerge. There is strong evidence that lower and middle level federal workers are paid more than their measurably equivalent private sector counterparts. At the local level, the evidence is also clear—wage rates do not appear excessively high, and in fact may be lower than the individuals could earn in the private sector. At the state level, the evidence is mixed, and the estimates range from no difference to substantial positive rent.

Why should these rents exist? The first hypothesis to be considered is that they do not, but that higher wages are merely offsetting deficiencies in other components of the compensation package.[4] I find no evidence that this is the case, particularly with respect to pensions, the most important fringe benefit.

II. Pensions Comparisons in the Public and Private Sectors

Pension plans are more difficult to compare than wages or earnings because there are so many of them and because they have so many diverse features. A recent Pension Task Force (1978, p. 326) identified 64 federal employee plans, and over 6600 state and local plans in 1975, and this is only a

---

[3]See Quinn (1979, p. 51). As will be explained below, the public sectors included in this analysis consist only of public administration, which accounts for between one-third and one-half of total government employment.

[4]Both Ronald Ehrenberg (1980) and Robert Smith (1980) have presented evidence that there does appear to be a tradeoff between salary and pension contributors *within* the public sector. In this paper, I find no evidence that this explains the wage differences *across* sectors.

small fraction of the number of private plans in existence. These plans differ in all dimensions—eligibility, benefit calculation rules, age of benefit receipt, vesting, portability, and inflation protection both before and after retirement.

Munnell and Connolly (1979) have compared public and private sector fringe benefits by "contrasting the dominant government practice with that prevailing in industry" (p. 30). In other words, they try to identify "typical" plans and to compare their features. They conclude that public sector pensions, on average, are superior (p. 38). Coverage is much more extensive—nearly all full-time public employees are covered, compared to only half of wage and salary personnel in the private sector. Retirement benefits are generally higher in the public sector, largely because of post-retirement cost-of-living adjustments. Finally, retirement ages are generally lower in government plans, which increases the lifetime value (or wealth equivalent) of these benefits.

In this research, a different approach is used. Rather than attempt to identify "typical" pension plans, I investigate an actual sample of individuals nearing retirement age. The data source contains detailed information on certain plan features, and these are compared by sector.

The sample is drawn from the Retirement History Study (RHS), a 10-year longitudinal study of the retirement process conducted by the Social Security Administration.[5] In 1969, a large sample of men and unmarried women aged 58 to 63 were interviewed, and then reinterviewed at 2-year intervals. At this time, data from four waves (1969 through 1975) are available for a sample of nearly 8700 respondents. Eliminating farmers and the self-employed, those with very serious health limitations, members of the Armed Services and those who worked without pay, I obtained a sample of approximately 6500 persons for this analysis.

There are two ways to identify the sector of employment in these data. The first is to use class of worker. All respondents in the RHS were asked whether they are employed in the private sector, the government sector, or are self-employed on their current job (or last job if not currently employed). The advantage of this classification is that it identifies all government workers; the disadvantage is that it does not disaggregate by level of government. Since there is strong evidence that compensation differs by level of government, this is a serious drawback. The level of government can be identified by the three-digit Census industry code, but only for those government employees in public administration. Other government workers, such as college professors, nurses, or electricians are located in their appropriate industry, and not designated as government employees. To maximize the

---

[5]For more detail on this data source, see Ireland et al. (1976).

Table 1

Pension Coverage, by Sector, 1969
Men and Women Aged 58–63

Sector (N*)	Covered	Not Covered
Private (5331)	43.7%	56.3%
Government (1169)	78.8	21.2
Federal pub. adm. (155)	92.3	7.7
Postal pub. adm. (61)	90.2	9.8
State pub. adm. (87)	87.2	12.8
Local pub. adm. (145)	69.6	30.4

*Sample size with good coverage data.

information to be gleaned, I have utilized both sources, and identified all respondents as private or government employees, and then disaggregated the government public administration subset by sector (federal, postal, state, or local). The sample sizes appear in Table 1.

In 1969, 20 percent of these respondents were not employed—17 percent were out of the labor force (presumably retired) and 3 percent were unemployed. To reduce selectivity bias (for example, those with high pension benefits are more likely to have retired), I have retained all the respondents in the analysis, and combined information on the current job for those employed and on the last job for those not.

Table 1 illustrates the striking differences in pension coverage by sector. Only 44 percent of the sample in the private sector were covered in 1969, compared to nearly 80 percent of those in government. In public administration, 84 percent were covered, ranging from 70 percent in the local government sector to 92 percent at the federal level. Some of this is due to differences in tenure distributions—years on the current (or last) job. Although the median values are almost identical for the private and government sectors (13.2 and 13.5 years), there is wide diversity within government (federal, 19.2 years; postal, 21 + years; state, 10.1 years; local, 13.2 years). This reflects the relatively recent growth in the state and local sectors.

Not only are government workers much more likely to be covered, but those who are can retire earlier. Table 2 presents distributions of the age of first pension eligibility (for full or reduced benefits) for those who are covered. In the private sector, only 31 percent are in plans which pay benefits before age 61, compared to 41 percent of those in government, and over half in federal, postal, or state public administration. Thirty percent of those in private employment must wait until at least age 65—a much higher proportion than the 12 and 15 percent in federal and postal work.

Table 2

Age of First Pension Eligibility, by Sector, 1969
Men and Women Aged 58–63

Sector (N*)	Age (Years)							Summary	
	≤50	51–55	56–60	61–62	63–64	65	66+	≤60	<65
Private (2094)	1.7%	10.6%	18.4%	37.2%	2.6%	26.8%	2.7%	30.7%	70.5%
Government (818)	3.1	14.2	23.8	27.6	4.4	21.6	5.1	41.1	73.1
Federal pub. adm. (125)	1.6	18.4	35.2	28.8	4.0	11.2	0.8	55.2	88.0
Postal pub. adm. (47)	2.1	17.0	44.7	17.0	4.3	10.6	4.2	63.8	85.1
State pub. adm. (57)	3.5	24.6	26.3	12.3	7.0	19.3	7.0	54.4	73.7
Local pub. adm. (90)	4.4	11.1	23.3	24.4	2.2	27.8	6.6	38.8	65.4

*Sample size with good eligibility data.

Table 3

Pension Benefit Level, by Sector, 1969
Men and Women Aged 58–63

Sector (N*)	Benefit Level (in thousands of dollars)										Median Benefit	
	0	<1	1-2	2-4	4-6	6-8	8-10	10-15	15-20	20+	All	With Ben > 0
Private (4863)	50.3%	11.8%	13.9%	15.1%	5.2%	2.4%	0.7%	0.4%	0.1%	0.1%	$ 0	$1939
Government (1054)	19.9	10.6	13.8	21.3	14.0	9.6	5.2	3.3	1.5	0.5	$2535	$3469
Federal pub. adm. (140)	7.1	1.4	8.6	20.7	20.0	17.1	12.1	9.3	2.9	0.7	$5220	$5575
Postal pub. adm. (54)	14.8	7.4	5.6	16.7	25.9	24.1	5.6	0.0	0.0	0.0	$4425	$4996
State pub. adm. (74)	18.9	5.4	12.2	21.6	9.5	20.3	5.4	1.4	2.7	2.8	$3250	$4284
Local pub. adm. (122)	22.1	13.1	18.9	16.4	13.1	8.2	3.3	3.3	0.0	1.6	$1783	$2848

*Sample size with good pension data.

233

Table 3 shows the size of benefits for which these respondents are eligible.[6] All those with good pension data, including those not covered, are included and median values are shown with and without the zero respondents. We have already seen that public sector employees (especially federal) are more likely to be covered, and generally able to retire at an earlier age. It also appears that they are eligible for larger benefits. Among those reporting positive benefits (actual or expected), the median value in the government sector is $3469, nearly 80 percent higher than the private sector median of $1939. By level of government, the differences are even more dramatic. The federal median ($5575) is nearly three times the private figure, the postal average ($4996) is two and one-half times, the state median ($4284) is twice as large, and the local sector average ($2848) is almost 50 percent higher. Of course, when the zero figures (most prominent in the private sector) are included the differences are even larger, and ratios cannot be calculated since the private sector median is $0.

The use of wealth or asset equivalent of an income stream (such as future pension benefits) is a very convenient method of combining the three pension features discussed thus far—coverage, age of eligibility, and pension amount. This pension wealth is simply the present discounted value, in 1969, of the pension stream for which the individual is eligible; in particular,

$$\text{WEALTH} = \sum_{j=0}^{n} (\text{BEN}_j)(\Pr(j + 1/j))(1 + r)^{-j},$$

where BEN_j is 0 until eligibility, and the constant pension benefit amount thereafter,

$\text{PR}(j + 1/j)$ is the probability of living through year $j + 1$ having lived through year j (from standard mortality tables),

n equals $100 - $ age in 1969[7], and

r is the discount rate (5 percent)[8].

---

[6]Pension benefit amounts are derived from three sources in the Retirement History Study. The first source is retrospective sections of the questionnaires in which the respondents who have retired since the last questionnaire are asked about their last jobs. This should be very accurate information. If the individuals do not retire during the four waves of data we have, we turn to sections on expected retirement benefits. If good data have still not been obtained, we turn to actual benefit receipts for those who have been retired for at least 2 years. The last caveat is required since income data cover a calendar year, and we do not know during how much of that year the particular income source was received. For example, $3000 in pension income could reflect an annual flow of $3000, $6000, or $36,000, depending on whether the benefit had been coming for the whole year, half the year or only a month. The caveat increases the probability that a full-year amount is being reported.

[7]I arbitrarily assume everyone is dead by age 100.

[8]In 1969, the average rate of inflation over the previous 5 years was 3 percent. I allowed for a 2 percent real rate of return, and therefore used a 5 percent discount. The choice of any particular number, of course, is arbitrary.

Table 4

Pension Wealth,[a] by Sector, 1969
Men and Women Aged 58–63 (percentage distribution)

Sector (N*)	Pension Wealth (in thousands of dollars)											Median Wealth	
	0	<10	10–20	20–30	30–40	40–50	50–60	60–70	70–80	80–100	100+	All	With Wealth[b] > 0
Private (4644)	52.6%	14.5%	13.3%	8.7%	5.0%	2.6%	1.4%	0.8%	0.4%	0.4%	0.5%	$ 0	$16,917
Government (934)	22.5	15.7	13.2	10.9	10.1	6.1	5.0	4.6	3.4	4.0	4.5	$18,939	$29,037
Federal pub. adm. (117)	8.5	3.5	9.4	12.0	15.4	5.1	9.4	7.7	8.5	11.1	9.4	$42,353	$50,372
Postal pub. adm. (51)	15.7	5.9	5.9	11.8	9.8	15.7	13.7	11.8	9.8	0.0	0.0	$40,573	$45,573
State pub. adm. (64)	21.9	7.8	12.5	10.9	7.8	4.7	7.8	6.3	9.4	3.1	7.8	$27,156	$40,106
Local pub. adm. (109)	24.8	19.2	17.4	8.3	7.3	3.7	7.3	4.6	0.9	2.8	3.7	$13,448	$21,205

[a] Discount rate = 5% for all sectors.

*Sample size with good pension wealth data. Respondents eligible for multiple pensions have been excluded.

Table 5

Differences in Mean Pension Benefit and Wealth Levels
between Private Sector and Various Government Sectors,[a]
for Those Respondents with Pensions

	Benefit Level		Wealth Level[b]	
Sector	Absolute	Percentage	Absolute	Percentage
Private[c]	—	—	—	—
Government	+$1,949	+80%	+$14,595	+78%
Federal pub. adm.	+$3,687	+199%	+$29,263	+200%
Postal pub. adm.	+$2,013	+107%	+$21,643	+136%
State pub. adm.	+$3,024	+153%	+$24,220	+165%
Local pub. adm.	+$1,600	+55%	+$9,037	+47%

[a] From regressions which adjust for final wage rate and years of seniority.
[b] Discount rate = 5% for all sectors.
[c] Reference category.

Two individuals eligible for the same annual benefit will have different
wealth values if the years of eligibility are different. The sooner one is eligible
(the fewer the number of zeros) the higher the asset value.

Pension wealth distributions are shown in Table 4, along with medians,
with and without the zeros.[9] The wealth values confirm that pensions are
much more generous in the public sector. With the exception of the government aggregate and the local sector, the ratios (relative to the private median)
are higher than those derived from Table 3, reflecting the earlier ages of
eligibility. The local exception may be explained by the age distribution—
this subset has the highest average age, and therefore slightly fewer years of
benefits to sum up.

Benefit calculation formulas vary considerably over plans, but the two
most important factors are years of service and final wage rate or earnings
level. To remove differences in these factors from the comparison, I ran
regressions of benefit and wealth levels (for those with positive amounts) on
years of tenure and final wage rate, and a series of sectoral dummy variables.
The dependent variables were entered in linear and logarithmic form, yield-

[9]Unlike the benefit amounts, which were specific to the individual's current (or last) job, the
wealth figures include all pensions for which the individual is or will be eligible. To eliminate the
possibility of attributing more than one pension amount to a single job, all respondents eligible
for multiple pensions have been excluded from Table 4. The sample sizes are therefore smaller
than in Table 3. Note that while we lose only 5 percent of the private sector workers, we lose 11
percent of the government employees (16 percent of the federal, 6 percent of the postal, 14
percent of the state, and 11 percent of the local). Multiple pensions are more common in the
public sector.

ing absolute and relative differentials associated with each sector.[10] The results, for both benefit levels and wealth, after seniority and final wage rate have been considered, are found in Table 5.

Clearly there are substantial differences which are not explained by these factors. Federal pension benefit and wealth levels are 200 percent higher than in the private sector, the state figures are over 150 percent higher, and the local values are about 50 percent higher. And these figures ignore the differences in coverage. There is no evidence here that the higher wage rates paid in the public sector (at the federal level at least) are compensating for inferior features of this fringe benefit. On the contrary, public sector pensions appear to be substantially more generous than those in the private sector.

III. Three Major Caveats

There are three major caveats which can be applied to the simple analysis thus far, and which may change the relative size of the benefits by sector.

1. Many government pensions plans require contributions from the employees. For example, most federal plans include an employee contribution of 7 percent of pay. For state and local plans, the typical rates are 6 and 5 percent, respectively (Pension Task Force Report, 1978, p. 138). Although this sometimes occurs in the private sector as well, it is far less common. Since I am interested in compensation by the employer and not savings behavior by the individual, use of the entire benefit overstates the level of compensation by the amount of the employee contribution. Recent estimates are that employees provide 16 percent of the total contributions to the federal plans, 35 percent to state and local systems, and less than 8 percent in the private sector (p. 135). In the analysis that follows, these percentages are deleted from the wealth figures to derive a more accurate estimate of this component of compensation.[11] Since the employee contributions are higher in the public sector, this will tend to reduce the differences noted above, especially at the state and local levels.

---

[10]In the semi-log form, the percentage difference associated with being in a particular group is $e^{\beta-1}$, where β is the estimated coefficient for that group. This will approximately equal β for values of β near 0.

[11]I am avoiding the extremely difficult question of incidence here—who is really making contributions. If earnings are lower than they would have been by the amount of the employer contribution, then the employee is actually making the entire contribution, regardless of who is signing the checks. The same problems arise with respect to Social Security. In this paper, I am assuming that contributions reflect the true incidence.

2. Nearly all private employees, 76 percent of local employees, and 85 percent of state employees are covered by Social Security (p. 59). In contrast, postal workers and members of the Federal Civil Service are not. Since employers are responsible for half of the Social Security contribution, this should be included as part of retirement benefit compensation. I have calculated the total wealth value of each individual's current and future Social Security benefits, and added half of this to the adjusted pension wealth for private, state and local sector workers.[12] The effect of this addition will be to lower substantially the relative magnitude of the federal and postal employer contributions, since these are the two sectors excluded from the Social Security system.

3. The final caveat concerns inflation protection. Workers in the public sector are much more likely to have their benefits protected against inflation *after* retirement. Nearly all (98 percent) federal employees enjoy automatic cost-of-living adjustments without limit (p. 109). Although less than 5 percent of state and local employees enjoy such complete protection, 90 percent are in plans which make cost-of-living adjustments automatically, but with a ceiling (often 3 percent), or on an ad hoc basis. In contrast, only 6 percent of private plans include automatic cost-of-living adjustments (Munnell and Connolly, 1979). In an era of chronic inflation, this can be an extremely important feature of a pension plan.

Although the degree of inflation protection is not reflected in the initial benefit amount, it can be in the wealth equivalent. One of the components of the discount rate (one of the reasons that a dollar today is preferred to a dollar in the future) is inflation. A benefit stream which is constant in *real* terms should be discounted at a lower rate than one which is constant in *nominal* terms, and therefore eroded by inflation. The higher the discount rate used, obviously, the lower the asset value of any given income stream.

In Tables 6 and 7, I utilize three scenarios to illustrate the impact of these three factors—employee contributions, Social Security coverage, and inflation protection. In the first, inflation protection is ignored (the same

---

[12]The Retirement History Study includes the complete Social Security earnings record for each respondent. With these historical data, I am able to calculate the precise benefit each person would receive when eligible. I have included in this stream the spouse's benefit when the respondent is married, and the probability of survivor's benefits if she outlives him. The wealth value is then calculated by taking the present discounted value of this stream, with zeros prior to eligibility.

Since this Social Security wealth is derived from the respondent's entire work history, attribution of the entire amount to the current job will overstate this employer's contribution. I reduce the magnitude of this problem by restricting the sample here to only those private, state, and local sector employees with more than 20 years of seniority on the job. For federal and postal workers, this restriction is not necessary, since they are not in the Social Security system.

This procedure will still tend to overstate the employer's contribution, since all cohorts of Social Security recipients thus far have received more than an actuarially fair return on their contributions. See Burkhauser and Warlick (forthcoming).

Table 6

Median Retirement Wealth Attributable to Employer Contributions,[a] 1969 by Sector, Men and Women Aged 58–63, for Various Discount Rates

	Scenario I		Scenario II		Scenario III	
	Sector	r	Sector	r	Sector	r
	Private,	*5%*	*Private,*	*5%*	*Private*	*10%*
	Fed, Postal,	*5%*	*Fed, Postal,*	*2%*	*Fed, Postal,*	*2%*
	State, Local	*5%*	*State, Local*	*2%*	*State, Local*	*5%*
Sector (N*)	*Median*	*% over Private*	*Median*	*% over Private*	*Median*	*% over Private*
Private(1615)	$31,355	—	$31,355	—	$27,466	—
Government						
Federal pub. adm. (117)	$37,153	+18%	$47,153	+50%	$47,153	+72%
Postal pub. adm. (51)	$33,469	+7%	$44,153	+41%	$44,153	+61%
State pub. adm. (19)	$49,177	+57%	$62,476	+99%	$49,177	+79%
Local pub. adm. (35)	$36,109	+15%	$43,007	+37%	$36,109	+31%
[State & Local (54)]	($41,765)	(+33%)	($50,000)	(+59%)	($41,765)	(+52%)

[a] For private sector, .92 (Pension Wealth) + .50 (SS Wealth); for federal and postal sectors, .84 (Pension Wealth); for state and local sectors, .65 (Pension Wealth) + .50 (SS Wealth).

*Sample size with good data, and with over 20 years tenure if private, state or local (see note 12).

discount rate—5 percent—is used for all sectors), but the other two issues are treated. Half of the employees' Social Security wealth is included, and employee contributions to their own pensions are excluded. Scenarios II and III acknowledge all three issues, and utilize discount rates which reflect the degree of inflation protection. Scenario II is a low-inflation scenario, in which the common 3 percent cap on state and local cost-of-living adjustments is not binding. A 2 percent discount rate (a reasonable real return on investments) is used for all government workers, and a 5 percent rate (which includes 3 percent inflation erosion) is applied in the private sector. This is a reasonable scenario for the late 1960s. The final scenario is more appropriate for the high inflation decade of the 1970s. Federal and postal workers, with complete inflation protection, use a 2 percent rate; state and local employees, with partial protection, use a 5 percent rate; and individuals in the public sector, with almost no protection, discount future benefits at 10 percent.

Table 6 presents median wealth values, by sector. In scenario I, much of the public sector advantage has disappeared, indicating that the contribution issues are important. The federal median employer contribution is only 18 percent higher than the private sector figure, and the postal advantage has almost disappeared. The state programs now appear to be the most generous, because of their Social Security coverage. The local sector advantage remains

Table 7

Differences in Wealth from Total Employer Retirement Contributions,[a] for Those Respondents with Pensions, for Various Discount Rates

	Scenario I		Scenario II		Scenario III	
	Sector	r	Sector	r	Sector	r
	Private,	5%	Private,	5%	Private,	10%
	Fed, Postal,	5%	Fed, Postal,	2%	Fed, Postal,	2%
	State, Local	5%	State, Local	2%	State, Local	5%
Sector	Absolute	Percentage	Absolute	Percentage	Absolute	Percentage
Private[b]	—	—	—	—	—	—
Government						
Federal pub. adm.	+$14,913	+43%	+$23,070	+62%	+$26,417	+72%
Postal pub. adm.	+$ 6,629	+20%	+$17,140	+46%	+$20,695	+57%
State pub. adm.	+$20,468	+68%	+$31,195	+88%	+$24,842	+80%
Local pub. adm.	+$ 3,393	+18%	+$ 8,947	+34%	+$ 7,828	+30%

[a] For private sector, .92 (Pension Wealth) + .50 (SS Wealth); for federal and postal sectors, .84 (Pension Wealth); for state and local sectors, .65 (Pension Wealth) + .50 (SS Wealth). From regressions which adjust for final wage rate and years of seniority.

[b] Reference category.

small but positive. Scenarios II and III illustrate the tremendous importance of cost-of-living protection, especially with high inflation. The federal advantage jumps to 50 (II) or 72 (III) percent, and the state's, in Scenario II, to nearly 100 percent. When all three caveats are considered, local benefits appear to be about a third more generous than those in the private sector.

Table 7 shows regression results which illustrate absolute and percentage differences after seniority and the final wage have been considered. In no case are government pensions inferior to those in the private sector, but the size of the advantage depends greatly on the scenario. Even when the inflation features are ignored, both federal and state pensions dominate those in the private sector. The state is the most generous because of the Social Security coverage, with an average assert value over $20,000 higher than private, and $5,500 higher than federal. When cost-of-living features are considered, all four government sectors dominate the private. In the low inflation scenario, when state and local adjustment caps are unimportant, the state programs remain the most generous. During high inflation, the unlimited adjustments at the federal level assume greater importance, and approximately offset the lack of Social Security coverage. In the last scenario, probably the most relevant for today (although the data are from 1969), federal and state retirement benefits appear to be 70 to 80 percent higher than in the private sector, while local government personnel enjoy an advantage of about a third.

IV. Summary and Conclusions

Retirement contributions are the largest component of fringe benefits, comprising about 40 percent of total fringe expenditure (Munnell and Connolly, 1979, p. 30). This research indicates that retirement packages are considerably more attractive in the public sector than they are in private employment. Public employees, at the federal, state, and local levels, are much more likely to be covered by a pension plan, and generally able to collect benefits at an earlier age. And those who do collect are eligible for higher amounts. This last comparison is complicated by the fact that federal employees are excluded from the Social Security system and because public employees are more likely to be in contributory plans. When adjustments for these factors are made, the superiority of the public plans is maintained, but is diminished considerably.

One of the most important advantages of public sector pension benefits is their inflation protection after retirement. At the federal level, the protection is complete, since there are no limits on the size of the automatic cost-of-living adjustments. At the state and local levels, the protection is often only partial because of adjustment ceilings which are less than the rate of inflation. In the private sector, on the other hand, there is almost no automatic protection. This factor is conveniently treated by varying the discount rates used in calculating the asset equivalents of future pension benefit streams. When this dimension is also included in the analysis, I conclude that relative to the private sector, pension benefits are 60 to 80 percent higher in federal and state employment, and about 30 percent higher in the local government sector.

When this evidence is combined with that on the most important component of compensation, wages and salaries, I conclude that there is positive rent associated with federal and state employment. Individuals in these sectors are paid more than their measurably equivalent private sector counterparts. At the local level, the evidence is mixed. Wages appear slightly lower, but pension coverage and benefits are superior.

What little evidence does exist on other components of compensation does nothing to dispel this notion. Munnell and Connolly (1979, pp. 39–43) claim that public employee disability and survivors' benefits are more generous than those in the private sector. Job stability also appears to be higher in the public sector. Fogel and Lewin (1974) report that employee turnover rates are much lower in state, local, and federal employment than in private manufacturing. Hall (1972) using 1966 turnover data, estimates that the probability of a government sector male becoming unemployed is less than half the probability of a private wage and salary employee. The common wisdom is that incompetent employees are much more difficult to dismiss under government civil service regulation than in the private sector.

Total compensation for measurably equivalent workers seems to be higher in the public than in the private sector. I have described elsewhere some hypotheses on why this may have occurred (Quinn, 1979). They concern the incentives facing legislators (or the Executive) who determine pay schedules, the incentives facing managers in charge of promotions, and the importance of non-productive characteristics in the hiring process. Many of these incentives are difficult to change. They may be inherent to nonprofit organizations, especially ones with ability to tax, and they have a long tradition. Some immediate improvements could be made, however, if a basic tenet of the comparability doctrine were changed. Comparisons should be made on the basis of overall compensation, not merely the wage and salary component. This research has indicated that retirement benefits are very different by sector, and probably compound an inequality which already exists in basic pay, at the lower and middle levels at least. Such an expansion of the comparison base has been recommended by both the President's Panel on Federal Compensation (Rockefeller, 1975, p. 25) and by President Carter (see Munnell and Connolly, 1979, p. 27), and should be given serious consideration.

References

Burkhauser, Richard V. and Jennifer L. Warlick. "Disentangling the Annuity from the Redistributive Aspects of Social Security," *Review of Income and Wealth*, (forthcoming).

Ehrenberg, Ronald G. "Retirement System Characteristics and Compensating Wage Differentials in the Public Sector," *Industrial and Labor Relations Review*, *33* (July 1980): 470–483.

Fogel, Walter and David Lewin. "Wage Determination in the Public Sector," *Industrial and Labor Relations Review*, 27 (April 1974): 410–431.

Gunderson, Morley. "Public Sector Compensation in Canada and the U.S.," *Industrial Relations*, *19* (Fall 1980): 257–271.

Hall, Robert. "Turnover in the Labor Force," *Brookings Papers on Economic Activity*, 3(1972): 709–756.

Irelan, Lola M. "Retirement History Study: Introduction," in *Almost 65: Baseline Data from the Retirement History Study* (Research Report No. 49). Social Security Administration, Office of Research and Statistics, 1976.

Munnell, Alicia H. and Ann M. Connolly. "Comparability of Public and Private Compensation: The Issues of Fringe Benefits," *New England Economic Review* (July/August 1979): 27–45.

Pension Task Force Report on Public Employee Retirement Systems. Committee on Education and Labor, House of Representatives, 95th Congress, 2nd Session (March 15, 1978).

Perloff, Stephen H. "Comparing Municipal Salaries with Industry and Federal Pay," *Monthly Labor Review*, *92* (October 1971): 10–13.

Quinn, Joseph F. "Wage Differentials Among Older Workers in the Public and Private Sectors," *Journal of Human Resources*, *14* (Winter, 1979). 41–62.

Rockefeller, Nelson A. (Chairman). *Staff Report of the President's Panel on Federal Compensation*. Washington: U.S. Government Printing Office, 1975.

Smith, Robert S. *Pensions, Underfunding and Salaries in the Public Sector*. Paper presented at NBER Conference on the Economics of Compensation, Cambridge, Mass. (November 21–22, 1980).

Smith, Sharon P. *Equal Pay in the Public Sector: Fact or Fantasy?* Princeton, N.J.: Industrial Relations Section, Princeton University, 1977.

Résumé

Une recherche antérieure a suggéré que les taux de salaire sont plus élevés dans l'emploi du secteur public fédéral (et peut-être au niveau des états aussi) que dans le secteur privé. Cela semble vrai, même si l'on considère les différences mesurables du capital humain. Cet article étend l'analyse aux retraites, compléments de salaire les plus notables, sur la base d'un important échantillon d'hommes approchant l'âge de la retraite.

Cette étude montre que les conditions de la retraite sont bien plus attrayantes dans le secteur public, qu'elles ne le sont dans l'emploi privé. Les fonctionnaires, au niveau fédéral, des états et local sont bien plus susceptibles d'être couverts par un plan de pension et peuvent, en général, toucher les allocations à un âge moindre. Ceux qui touchent, ont droit à des sommes plus élevées. Cette dernière comparaison se complique du fait que les employés fédéraux sont exclus du système de Sécurité sociale et que les fonctionnaires sont davantage susceptibles de figurer dans des plans contributifs. Après ajustements de ces facteurs, la supériorité des plans publics demeure, mais considérablement diminuée.

L'un des avantages les plus importants, des allocations de retraite du secteur public, tient à leur protection contre l'inflation après la mise à la retraite. Au niveau fédéral, la protection est complète puisqu'il n'y a pas de limites au nombre des ajustements automatiques au coût de la vie. Au niveau des états et au niveau local, la protection n'est souvent que partielle, à cause de plafonds d'ajustement qui sont moins élevés que le taux d'inflation. Dans le secteur privé, d'autre part, la protection automatique est pratiquement inexistante. On étudie ce facteur, de façon commode en faisant varier les taux d'escompte utilisés pour calculer les équivalents en actifs des futurs montants des retraites. Une fois cette dimension incluse aussi dans l'analyse, on arrive à la conclusion que par rapport au secteur privé, les allocations de retraite sont de 60 à 80 pour cent plus élevées dans l'emploi fédéral et des états, et environ de 30 pour cent plus élevées dans le secteur local public.

Quand on combine ce résultat avec celui de la composante la plus importante de la compensation salaire horaire et salaire mensuel, on arrive à la conclusion qu'une rente positive est associée à l'emploi fédéral et à l'emploi par les états. Les personnes sont payées davantage dans ces secteurs que leurs homologues du secteur privé. Au niveau local, le résultat est mélangé. Les salaires sont légèrement inférieurs mais la couverture des retraites et les allocations sont supérieures.

The Effect of Public Sector Wage Policy on Income Distribution and Labor Allocation

Eytan Sheshinski

Introduction

Government intervention in the process of wage determination takes a variety of forms. Discussions of this question refer most commonly to statutory regulation of wages (which is primarily concerned with establishing minimum rates and the protection of low-paid workers), arbitration procedures, and intervention in collective bargaining. The recent growth of the public sector relative to the private sector in Western economies has shifted the focus of this discussion to the direct and indirect effects of wage policies in the public sector on the overall labor market conditions and on income distribution. By direct effects I mean the level of pay by the government in different occupations. Indirect effects refer to the "secondary" effects, generated through changes in the occupational structure, as induced by wage policies in the public sector.

In this paper I focus on the effects of government's wage policy *within* the public sector on the distribution of income in the private sector as well as the overall income distribution. By means of a very simple model originally suggested by Tinbergen (1951) and followed by Roy (1951) and Houthakker (1974), I study the effects of the public sector's wage schedule on the distribution of the labor force between sectors and on the distribution of income.

Let us first look at some facts concerning income differentials between the private and public sectors in some Western economies. Smith (1977) has studied pay differences between these sectors for the U.S. economy. While no systematic difference was found for the *average* pay across different comparable occupations, there seems to be a clear negative correlation between the wage ratio (public/private) and the level of income. From her findings one can compute the relative averages shown in Table 1.

Public Finance and Public Employment. Proceedings of the 36th Congress of the International Institute of Public Finance. Jerusalem, 1980.

Table 1

Relative Average Earnings of Men in Occupational Groups
in the United States 1958–1970

Group	Percentage of Average for All Groups, Both Sectors	
	Private Sector	Public Sector
Higher Professional	298	180
Lower Professional	124	154
Administrators and Managers	271	160
Clerks	100	110
Foremen	149	130
Skilled Manual	117	100
Semiskilled Manual	85	89
Unskilled Manual	79	85

Source: From Smith (1977).

It is quite clear from the table that the spread of wages is much smaller in the public sector than in the private sector. The obvious question is whether the public sector is getting individuals of lower ability *within* each occupation. If so, then there is presumably an additional effect, namely, if individuals with high ability within the high-paying occupations tend to work in the private sector and similarly for low-ability individuals in the low-paying occupations, then the income distribution in the private sector tends to be less egalitarian the more egalitarian is the wage policy in the public sector. Some evidence for that tendency in the Israeli economy can be deduced from the studies of Hanoch (1963) and Levy (1975).

We shall now turn to a simple model of the choice of work among sectors showing the dependence of income distribution within and between sectors on the public sector's wage policy.

The assumptions of the model are no doubt too simple to provide a realistic description. Nevertheless, they will be shown to have fairly realistic implications for the distribution of income and the labor force allocation.

A Basic Model of Labor Force Distribution

Each individual is assumed to maximize his earnings by choosing among occupations according to his aptitude for each occupation. We focus on the choice between public sector and private sector employment. Let the individual's aptitudes be summarized by the pair (a_1, a_2) where a_1 is his marginal product in the public sector and a_2 is his marginal product in the private sector. For simplicity, these productivities are assumed to be independent of the labor force allocation between the sectors. The individual's working time is assumed to be fixed at unity. The time devoted to the ith occupation is x_i, $0 \leq x_i \leq 1$. The wages paid by each sector, w_i, are assumed to depend on his aptitude: $w_i = w_i(a_i)$. It is thus assumed that the individual's aptitude can be identified.

The individual is supposed to be indifferent between occupations and hence to allocate his working time so as to maximize his income. Thus,

$$\text{Max}_{x_1, x_2} [w_1 x_1 + w_2 X_2] \tag{1}$$

subject to

$$x_1 + x_2 = 1. \tag{2}$$

The maximum is reached by working all the time in the sector for which his wage is greatest. Normally there is only one such occupation. If there is more than one, then the allocation of time is indeterminate.

This simple micro-model lends itself readily to aggregation over individuals, provided suitable continuity assumptions are made. For this purpose we shall assume that the pair (a_1, a_2) varies randomly over the population with a continuous density function $f(a_1, a_2)$. The distribution function, $F(a_1, a_2)$, is then also continuous. To eliminate the indeterminacy mentioned above, only density functions and wage schedules $w_i(a_i)$ where ties (i.e., $w_1 = w_2$) have a zero probability will be considered. Otherwise, no restrictions are imposed on the joint density function. In particular, aptitudes may or may not be independent of each other.

The (cumulative) distribution function for incomes in sector i will be called $G_i(z)$, and the corresponding density $g_i(z)$. The overall distribution function is $G(z) = G_1(z) + G_2(z)$, and the density is $g(z) = g_1(z) + g_2(z)$.

If w_i are strictly monotone-increasing functions of a_i, then the basic implication of the model for the distribution of income is

$$G(z) = F[w_1^{-1}(z), w_2^{-1}(z)] \tag{3}$$

where $z = w_1(a_1) = w_2(a_2)$ and w_i^{-1} are the corresponding inverse functions.

The distribution of income in any occupation can be derived similarly. For example,

$$G_1(z) = \int_0^z \int_0^{z_1} f[w_1^{-1}(z_1), w_2^{-1}(z_2)] \frac{1}{\Delta} dz_1 dz_2 \tag{4}$$

where $\quad \Delta = w_1'[w_1^{-1}(z_1)]w_2'[w_2^{-1}(z_2)], \ w_i' = \dfrac{dw_i(a_i)}{da_i}.$

We shall assume throughout that the private sector pays individuals their marginal product, i.e.,

$$w_2(a_2) = a_2. \tag{5}$$

The focus of the analysis is the impact of the wage policy in the public sector on income distribution, labor force allocation, and output levels. To simplify, we shall confine the analysis to linear wage schedules and use a bivariate exponential distribution selected for computational convenience rather than realism. Then, let

$$w_1 = \alpha + \beta a_1 \tag{6}$$

where α, β ($\beta > 0$) are constants. The density function of aptitudes is assumed to be exponential:[1]

$$f(a_1, a_2) = \hat{\theta}_1 \hat{\theta}_2 \overline{e}^{\,\hat{\theta}_1 a_1 - \hat{\theta}_2 a_2} \tag{7}$$

where $\hat{\theta}_1$, $\hat{\theta}_2$ ($\hat{\theta}_1 > 0$, $\hat{\theta}_2 > 0$) are constants. By (4)–(7),

$$G_1(z) = \theta_1 \theta_2 \, e^{\theta_1 \alpha} \int_\alpha^z \int_0^{w_1} e^{-\theta_1 w_1 - \theta_1 w_2} dw_1 dw_2 \tag{8}$$

$$= \frac{\theta_1}{\theta_1 + \theta_2} [e^{-\theta_2 \alpha} e^{-(\theta_1 + \theta_2)(z-\alpha)} - 1] - e^{-\theta_1 (z-\alpha)} + 1$$

where $\theta_1 = (\hat{\theta}_1 / \beta)$, $\theta_2 = \hat{\theta}_2$. Similarly,

$$G_2(z) = \theta_1 \theta_2 e^{\theta_1 \alpha} \int_\alpha^z \int_\alpha^{w_2} e^{-\theta_1 w_1 - \theta_2 w_2} dw_1 dw_2 \tag{9}$$

$$= \frac{\theta_2}{\theta_1 + \theta_2} [e^{-\theta_2 \alpha} e^{-(\theta_1 + \theta_2)(z-\alpha)} - 1] - e^{-\theta_2 z} + e^{-\theta_2 \alpha}.$$

Adding up, we find

$$G(z) = e^{-\theta_2 \alpha} e^{-(\theta_1 + \theta_2)(z-\alpha)} - e^{-\theta_1 (z-\alpha)} - e^{-\theta_2 z} + 1 \tag{10}$$

$$= [1 - e^{-\theta_1 (z-\alpha)}][1 - e^{-\theta_2 z}].$$

The income density within the public sector is given by

$$g_1(z) = \theta_1 e^{-\theta_1 (z-\alpha)} [e - e^{-\theta_2 z}], \tag{11}$$

---

[1]This distribution is the product of two univariate exponentials and therefore does not allow for dependence. Bivariate exponentials with dependence have been introduced by Marshall and Olkin (1967), but they violate the assumption that the probability of ties is zero.

and in the private sector,

$$g_2(z) = \theta_2 e^{-\theta_2 z}[1 - e^{-\theta_1(z-\alpha)}]. \tag{12}$$

Hence, the overall income density is

$$g(z) = \theta_1 e^{-\theta_1(z-\alpha)} + \theta_2 e^{-\theta_2 z} - (\theta_1 + \theta_2)e^{-\theta_2\alpha}e^{-(\theta_1 + \theta_2)(z-\alpha)}. \tag{13}$$

Notice that although the density function of abilities is J-shaped for each sector, the density of income in each looks much more like the income distributions encountered in reality. See Figure 1 and Lydall (1968).

Suppose now that the government undertakes a progressive wage policy, i.e., $\alpha > 0$, $\beta < 1$. It is immediately seen from (8)–(12) that the effect of such a policy on the income distribution *within* each sector and on the overall income distribution is ambiguous. Such comparisons depend, of course, on the constraints imposed on α and β as well as on the parameters $\hat{\theta}_1$ and $\hat{\theta}_2$. This point will be clarified shortly.

In order to calculate directly inequality measures, one is also interested in the cumulative income distribution function for each sector. Let

$$I_1(z) = \int_\alpha^z zg_1(z)dz = \alpha + \frac{1}{\theta_1} - e^{-\theta_1(z-\alpha)}\left(z + \frac{1}{\theta_1}\right) \tag{14}$$

$$- \frac{\theta_1}{\theta_1 + \theta_2} e^{-\theta_2\alpha}\left[\alpha + \frac{1}{\theta_1 + \theta_2} - e^{-(\theta_1 + \theta_2)(z-\alpha)}\right.$$

$$\left. \left(z + \frac{1}{\theta_1 + \theta_2}\right)\right].$$

$$I_2(z) = \int_\alpha^z zg_2(z)dz = e^{-\theta_2\alpha}\left(\alpha + \frac{1}{\theta_2}\right) - e^{-\theta_2 z}\left(z + \frac{1}{\theta_2}\right) \tag{15}$$

$$- \frac{\theta_2}{\theta_1 + \theta_2} e^{\theta_2\alpha}\left[e^{-(\theta_1 + \theta_2)\alpha}\left(\alpha + \frac{1}{\theta_1 + \theta_2}\right)\right.$$

$$\left. - e^{-(\theta_1+\theta_2)z}\left(z + \frac{1}{\theta_1 + \theta_2}\right)\right].$$

Denote by $I_i = \lim_{z \to \infty} I_i(z)$, the total income in sector i. By (14) and (15)

$$I_1 = \alpha + \frac{1}{\theta_1} - \frac{\theta_1}{\theta_1 + \theta_2} e^{-\theta_2\alpha}\left(\alpha + \frac{1}{\theta_1 + \theta_2}\right) \tag{16}$$

and

$$I_2 = e^{-\theta_2\alpha}\left[\frac{\theta_1}{\theta_1 + \theta_2}\alpha + \frac{1}{\theta_2} - \frac{\theta_2}{(\theta_1 + \theta_2)^2}\right]. \tag{17}$$

The Lorenz curve is the derived relation between $I_i(z)/I_i$ and $G_i(z)/G_i(\infty)$.

The effect of a given "wage policy," (α, β), on outputs in each sector, Y_1, is calculated as follows. In the private sector incomes are equal to marginal products. Hence $Y_2 = I_2$. In the public sector, the relation between output, a_1, and income is given by (6). Hence, private total output is

$$Y_1 = \int_\alpha^\infty \left(\frac{z - \alpha}{\beta} \right) g_1(z)dz \tag{18}$$

$$= \frac{1}{\beta} \left[\frac{1}{\theta_1} - \frac{\theta_1}{(\theta_1 + \theta_2)^2} e^{-\theta_2 \alpha} \right]$$

Aggregate output, Y, is

$$Y = Y_1 + Y_2 = \frac{1}{\beta \theta_1} + e^{-\theta_2 \alpha} \left[\frac{\theta_1}{\theta_1 + \theta_2} \alpha + \frac{1}{\theta_2} \right. \tag{19}$$

$$\left. - \frac{\theta_2}{(\theta_1 + \theta_2)^2} - \frac{\theta_2}{\beta(\theta_1 + \theta_2)^2} \right].$$

One can readily calculate that $\alpha = 0$, $\beta = 1$ is a global maximum of Y.[2]

Some Numerical Examples

For numerical illustration, we shall take arbitrary values, $\hat{\theta}_1 = .02$ and $\hat{\theta}_2 = .01$. These values imply that the distribution of abilities is more equal with respect to public sector employment relative to private sector employment. This corresponds to observed facts about skill and educational levels distributions in the two sectors. As already noted, although the density function of abilities is J-shaped for each sector, the density of income in each looks like the income distributions encountered in reality (Figure 1).[3] The comparison between wage policies can be made under alternative assumptions about the restrictions imposed on the parameters (α, β). We have carried out the calculations under the assumption that the size of employment in the private sector (and hence in the public sector) is constant.

When $\alpha = 0$, $\beta = 1$, we have from (9), using the chosen values for θ_1 and $\hat{\theta}_2$,

$$\lim_{z \to \infty} G_2(z) = \frac{\hat{\theta}_1}{\hat{\theta}_1 + \hat{\theta}_2} = \frac{2}{3}. \tag{20}$$

---

[2]Simply calculate that at $\alpha = 0$, $\beta = 1$, $\dfrac{\partial Y}{\partial \alpha} = \dfrac{\partial Y}{\partial \beta} = 0$, and the second-order conditions

$\dfrac{\partial^2 Y}{\partial \alpha^2} < 0$, $\dfrac{\partial^2 Y}{\partial \beta^2} < 0$, $\dfrac{\partial^2 Y}{\partial \alpha^2} \dfrac{\partial^2 Y}{\partial \beta^2} - \left(\dfrac{\partial^2 Y}{\partial \alpha \partial \beta} \right)^2 > 0$, hold.

[3]For clarity, the vertical axis in Figure 1 is blown up to a factor of one hundred.

Figure 1. Bivariate Exponential Income Distributions for Alternative Wage Policies in the Public Sector.

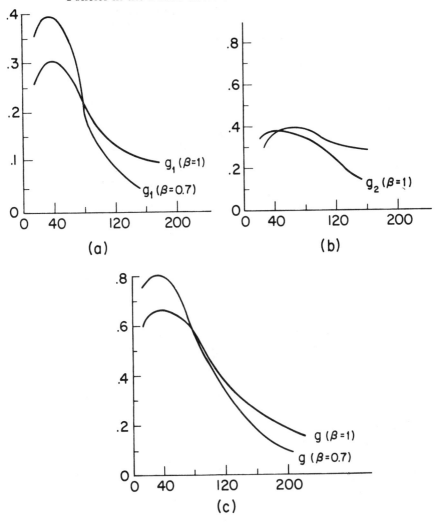

In general, for any (α, β), $\lim_{z \to \infty} G_2(z) = \dfrac{\theta_1}{\theta_1 + \theta_2} e^{-\theta_2 \alpha}$. We therefore restrict the parameters (α, β) by the relation

$$\frac{\theta_1}{\theta_1 + \theta_2} e^{-\theta_2 \alpha} = \frac{2}{3} \tag{21}$$

which implies that two-thirds of the labor force is employed in the private sector.

Table 2

Income Densities within Each Sector
and the Overall Income Density[a]

z	$\beta = 1$			$\beta = 0.7$		
	g_1	g_2	g	g_1	g_2	g
20	0.243	0.270	0.513	0.395	0.194	0.589
40	0.296	0.369	0.665	0.406	0.381	0.787
60	0.272	0.383	0.655	0.314	0.415	0.729
80	0.222	0.358	0.581	0.216	0.387	0.604
100	0.171	0.318	0.489	0.141	0.339	0.479
120	0.127	0.273	0.401	0.081	0.288	0.375
140	0.092	0.231	0.323	0.053	0.240	0.294
160	0.065	0.193	0.259	0.032	0.199	0.231
180	0.045	0.160	0.206	0.019	0.164	0.183
200	0.032	0.132	0.164	0.011	0.135	0.146

[a] With 1/3 of the labor force in the public sector.

From Table 2 and Figure 1 one observes the remarkable effect of changes in β on income distribution within each sector and on the economy as a whole. Imposition of a progressive wage schedule, with $\beta = 0.7$ ($\alpha = 10.5$), reduces significantly, by a factor of three, the upper tail of the income density in the public sector, and increases, though less dramatically, the inequality in the private sector. In Figure 2 we have drawn the Lorenz curves for the two sectors. In both sectors, the curves pertaining to the $\beta = 1$ and $\beta = 0.7$ cases intersect, which implies that an evaluation of alternative policies depends on the social welfare function one adopts. It is interesting that overall inequality as measured by the Gini coefficient increases (from 0.31 to 0.32) as β decreases from 1 to 0.7.

The effects of wage policies in the public sector on the size of real outputs are presented in Table 3. As β decreases from unity to 0.5, the output of the public sector decreases by about 18 percent while the output of the private sector increases by about 3.5 percent. Total output decreases moderately by 1 percent.

The above results clearly depend on the constraint that the allocation of the labor force between the sectors must remain constant. An alternative constraint would be to fix the level of output in one of the sectors, or the ratio between the outputs of the two sectors. The results pertaining to these alternative assumptions are as expected. When the size of the output of the public sector is fixed, then a progressive ($\beta > 1$) wage policy in the public sector has a remarkable *negative* effect on the output of the private sector, reflecting the increased proportion of the labor force allocated to the public sector, as needed to maintain its output. In all cases, total output decreases,

Figure 2. Bivariate Exponential Income Distributions for Alternative Wage
Policies in the Public Sector.

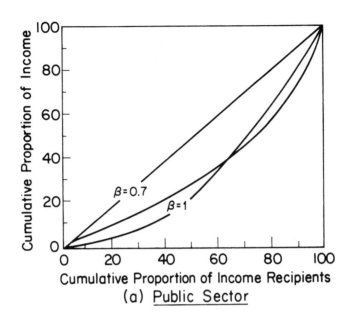

(a) Public Sector

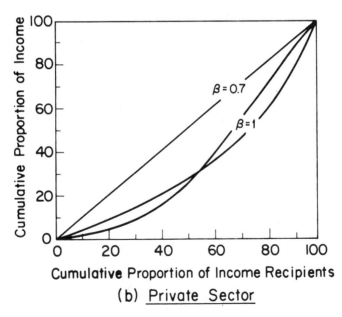

(b) Private Sector

Table 3

Outputs in the Public and Private
Sectors and Total Output

β	Y_1	Y_2	Y
1.0	27.8	88.9	116.7
0.9	27.0	89.6	116.6
0.8	26.2	90.3	116.5
0.7	25.3	91.0	116.3
0.6	24.4	91.6	115.9
0.5	23.3	92.1	115.5

in some cases very significantly (depending on type of constraint imposed); income inequality decreases in the public sector and increases in the private sector, while the overall effect on income distribution is ambiguous.

Welfare Analysis

The next step in the analysis is to find the socially optimum wage policy, i.e., a wage policy that maximizes, say, a utilitarian social welfare function, W,

$$\max_{\alpha,\beta} W = \int_0^\infty u(z)g(z)dz. \tag{22}$$

The constraints of the problems are, however, not obvious. The government may choose wage schedules which satisfy the constraint that the value of the public sector's output is equal to the total incomes of those employed in this sector (assuming that the government's output is sold),

$$\int_0^\infty zg(z) = \int_0^\infty \left(\frac{z-\alpha}{\beta} \right) g(z)dz$$

or

$$\alpha = (1 - \beta) I_1/G_1 \tag{23}$$

where

$$G_1 = \lim_{z \to \infty} G_1(z)$$

If the government has available tax/subsidy instruments, then the analysis becomes more complicated since the optimum wage policy will depend on the nature of these instruments (e.g., income taxation) and the issue of the *optimum mix of wage and tax policies* arises. These are issues which I shall not attempt to analyze in this paper.

Reservations and Possible Generalizations

We have examined the effects of wage policies in the public sector on the sectoral distribution of the labor force and on incomes. While the underlying model has been extremely simple, it seems to yield quite realistic conclusions. The assumptions, however, are too simple to provide a framework for certain important issues, three of which I would like to raise.

First, one expects a positive correlation between individual aptitudes in different occupations. We have assumed in our examples that aptitudes are distributed independently. It would be interesting to study the effects of wage policies for varying degrees of correlation between aptitudes.

Second, the underlying production functions have been overly simplified. In particular, marginal products, a_1 and a_2, are independent of the allocation of the labor force. More generally, one should explore the *interaction* of employment in the public sector on marginal productivity in the private sector, and vice versa. More specifically, suppose that total output, Y, is a function of two types of employment: public, L_1, and private, L_2: Y = $F(L_1, L_2)$. Now, suppose

$$L_i = \int_0^\infty a_i X_i(a_i) da_i$$

where $X_i(a_i)$ is the number of laborers in sector i with aptitude a_i. The function $X_i(a_i)$ is determined by individual maximization, as in the basic model. Competition in the private sector implies that $w_1(a_1) = a_1 F_1(L_1, L_2)$, while $w_2 = w_2(a_2)$ is a choice function. Clearly, in analyzing this model, terms such as $F_{12} = \partial^2 Y / \partial L_1 \partial L_2$, i.e., complementarity or substitution between public and private employment, will be crucial.

Finally, it has been assumed throughout that the government (planner), as well as private employers, can identify the true aptitude of each individual. This is a rather extreme assumption, particularly as it concerns the public sector. One could, however, modify the model to include imperfect information. Houthakker (1974), for example, has postulated that the *probability* an individual with aptitudes (a_1, a_2) works in sector i (p_i) is given by

$$p_i = \frac{e^{ka_1}}{e^{ka_1} + e^{ka_2}} \cdot$$

Clearly, when k = 0 all sectors have an equal probability of being chosen, while k → ∞ is the case analyzed above.

References

Hanoch, G. (1963). *Income Differentials in Israel*. The Falk Institute, Jerusalem, Israel.
Houthakker, H. (1974). "The Size Distribution of Labour Incomes Derived from the Distribution of Aptitudes." In Sellekaerts, W., ed., *Econometrics and Economic Theory*. London: Macmillan.
Levy, H. (1975). *Lifetime Income Patterns in Different Occupations in Israel*. Bank of Israel, Jerusalem, Israel.
Lydall, H. F. (1968). *The Structure of Earnings*. Oxford: Clarendon Press.
Roy, A. D. (1951). "Some Thoughts on the Distribution of Earnings." *Oxford Economic Papers*, New Ser., *3*, 135–146.
Smith, S. P. (1977). *Equal Pay in the Public Sector: Fact or Fantasy*. Princeton, N.J.: Industrial Relations Section, Princeton University, Research Report Series No. 122.
Tinbergen, J. (1951). "Some Remarks on the Distribution of Labour Incomes." *International Economic Papers*, 195–207.

Résumé

L'intervention du gouvernement dans le processus de détermination des salaires a de nombreux effets directs et indirects. La politique des salaires dans le secteur public par exemple, affecte la distribution du travail entre les secteurs publics et privés et altère la répartition du revenu dans le secteur privé, tout comme la répartition globale des revenus. On utilise un modèle simple du choix du travail entre les secteurs pour démontrer la dépendance de la répartition du revenu à l'intérieur, et entre les secteurs, sur la politique des salaires du gouvernement. Les effets des politiques progressives des salaires du secteur public sur la réduction des inégalités dans le secteur public, leurs accroissements dans le secteur privé et la réduction de la production globale sont illustrés par ce modèle. On pourrait l'étendre pour analyser d'autres problèmes importants, comprenant l'interdépendance des fonctions de production privée et publique et l'incertitude quant à la capacité des employeurs à apprécier les aptitudes des ouvriers.

Productivity Measurement in the Public Sector: The Case of Police Services

Edward Scicluna
David K. Foot
Richard M. Bird*

Productivity measurement and performance in the public sector has recently received renewed attention as a result of the rise of the "new conservatism." Both the size of the public sector in most countries and the relatively low level of economic knowledge about its activities make this problem important. In Canada, for example, about one-quarter of all economic activity now originates in the so-called "noncommercial" industries, most of which fall within the public sector: the federal, provincial and local governments, hospitals, educational institutions, and other nonprofit organizations. Yet surprisingly little is known about these activities. Until recently, for example, adequate and consistent time series data on public sector employment and wages were hard to find.[1] Moreover, because the output of "noncommercial services" is estimated in the national accounts as equal to the value of the inputs used to produce them, meaningful discussion of the comparative productivity of the private and public sectors is impossible because productivity changes in the public sector are, by definition, zero.

This paper is concerned with the possibility of improving the measurement of public sector productivity. The first section of the paper reviews briefly some conceptual issues bearing on this subject as well as some previous attempts to measure public sector productivity, and outlines an alternative conceptual approach that overcomes some of the problems inherent in previous work. The second section presents the results of applying this approach to municipal police services in Ontario, Canada, and suggests the potential usefulness of carrying out similar studies in other areas of public sector activity.

*Thanks to International Institute of Public Finance Congress participants and to Robert Haveman for comments on an earlier version of this paper.
[1] For a thorough review of this question, see Bird, Bucovetsky, and Foot (1979).

Public Finance and Public Employment. Proceedings of the 36th Congress of the International Institute of Public Finance. Jerusalem, 1980.

I. Measuring Productivity in the Public Sector

Concern with performance measurement in Canadian federal govern-ment departments has developed mainly in the last decade. In the late 1960s the Treasury Board—the central agency concerned with managing expenditure—began developing and implementing the Planning, Programm-ing and Budgeting System (PPBS) and Management by Objectives (MBO) programmes. By 1970, however, while some limited advances had been made in the specification of objectives for government programmes as well as in the classification of the major activities making up each programme, the Trea-sury Board decided that the PPBS as originally conceived was not really operational.[2] The Operational Performance Measurement System (OPMS) was therefore introduced to provide a more workable systematic approach to the evaluation of government programmes through monitoring changes in "efficiency" and "effectiveness," usually rather narrowly defined in terms of simple physical measurements. By 1976, OPMS coverage extended to 166,000 government employees in 23 federal departments and agencies, rep-resenting 39 percent of total authorized man-years (including the armed forces).[3]

Modest efforts to measure productivity in the federal government sector along similar lines had been begun earlier by Statistics Canada (Garston, 1973). These early studies, despite their defects, indicated clearly that the increase in labour productivity in the government sector was as a rule *not* zero (as is assumed in the national accounts), although there was a good deal of variation from year to year and from function to function. They also suggested that the rate of productivity growth was less than the rate of growth in the average compensation in the public sector—in other words, that unit labour costs were rising.

Another early study of the Canadian public hospital sector similarly measured a set of final outputs delivered by hospitals to doctors and to patients, where final outputs were defined as those that would be sold if hospital activity were carried out in the commercial sector. These measures indicated once again that an assumption of constant productivity change, let alone zero productivity (as assumed in the national accounts), was clearly inappropriate, since from 1961 to 1970 hospital productivity varied consider-ably (Bones and Allen, 1973). Moreover, although the unit cost of hospital services went up more than twice as fast as the implicit GNP deflator during this period, this study suggested that the rate of increase of labour pro-ductivity in the hospital sector was far from zero. Not surprisingly, it was

---

[2]For an effective critique, see Hartle (1978). Hartle also summarized the earlier experience in a 1972 article.

[3]Andras (1976) suggested that OPMS could be extended to two-thirds of federal govern-ment operations.

highest in the most capital-intensive sectors (laboratories, operating rooms) where significant technological innovations had been introduced.[4]

Problems in Productivity Analysis

None of the studies cited above had much to say about the *reasons* for the observed results. To understand what such figures mean, one must consider more carefully just what we are trying to do when we measure productivity in the public sector. The general form of a productivity index is the comparison of an output-input ratio at a particular point in time and space with a corresponding ratio at another point. Since both outputs and inputs are measured in real terms the changes in the respective ratios are sometimes referred to as changes in physical productivity. (Only when input prices are constant is a productivity increase reflected in cost reduction.) Productivity is thus a measure of the efficiency with which physical inputs are transformed into physical outputs. How this measure behaves over functions and over time—and what significance is to be attached to this behaviour—thus depends upon what inputs are compared with what outputs and upon how inputs and outputs are measured.

Single-factor productivity indexes, such as the familiar labour productivity index used in the studies cited earlier, do *not*, for example, measure how hard or how well public employees work. The behaviour of workers is of course not irrelevant, but their measured "productivity" is likely to depend more upon the amount and type of capital with which they work than on their "effort": recall, for example, the earlier reference to the higher measured productivity in the more capital-intensive activities in public hospitals. Single-factor indexes are thus gravely deficient in ignoring the contribution to output of other factors of production. What is really required to measure productivity satisfactorily is a total input (factor) measure such as net or gross total factor productivity.[5] Unfortunately, little progress has yet been made towards constructing such measures in the public sector, largely owing to our inability to obtain data that accurately measure the output and (to a lesser extent) the input variables entering into the production relationship.

The main measurement problems encountered in this task are identification and aggregation (which includes the quality control problem). For many

---

[4]Similar work on government productivity has been carried out in the United States. A recent U.S. survey, for example, which covered 61 percent of federal civilian employment, found the average annual rate of increase from 1967 to 1973 in the productivity of the U.S. federal government to be 1.6 percent (1.9 percent increase in output, less 0.3 percent increase in man-years), with substantial variations both over time and by function (the changes in productivity for different functions ranged from −2.4 percent to +5.8 percent) (Ardolini and Hohenstein, 1974).

[5]See, for example, Denny and May (1978).

organizations it is difficult to identify and measure a physical unit of output. For example, what is the output of a bank: the number of accounts serviced, the number of transactions, etc.? This problem is most acute in the service industries where the output is a service which can have many dimensions, some of which may be virtually nonquantifiable yet constitute an important part of the output (e.g., the "atmosphere" of a restaurant). Moreover, few organizations produce a single output: Joint production is the norm, not the exception, and the statistical analysis associated with the practical implementation of productivity measurement is greatly complicated by the existence of joint products.

Such problems, while not unique to public sector organizations, are likely to be most acute there. In some public sector cases, direct measures for service are possible (e.g., letters delivered, volume or weight of garbage collected), but in others proxy measures must be used (e.g., number of benefit cheques issued, number of police arrests), and in still others there appears to be no obvious output measure (e.g., national defense, consumer protection).[6] In all these cases, the construction of quality-adjusted output measures over time is difficult (e.g., garbage collection is moved from the backdoor to the curb).

Multiple outputs are also the norm in the public sector. For example, police are engaged in the prevention, enforcement, and solution of various crimes and offenses as well as in considerable administrative work (attending court, etc.). Similarly, almost any government programme has multiple objectives, which may often involve important trade-offs. For example, improving the efficiency with which benefit cheques are issued by a welfare programme may have the dual objectives of rapid response time and minimum error. Decreasing the former may increase the latter, and vice versa.

The aggregation problem arises because of nonhomogeneity—it is highly unlikely that each of the physical units of input and output is identical. Person-hours of labour, for example, surely are not the same across individuals because different people have different inherent characteristics (some work well under pressure, some do not) and different acquired characteristics (different amounts and types of education). The problem of aggregating capital of different vintages has received even more attention in the literature, without, however, any apparent satisfactory practical resolution. Even materials aggregation may be difficult: for example, although energy units may be directly comparable (using kilowatt-hours), tons of steel may not be (since there are many different types). Aggregation of public sector

---

[6]It should be noted, however, that some such activities may be characterized in terms of the nonoccurrence of undesired events (wars, accidents, crime); for some stimulating suggestions on how to approach this problem, see Shoup (1969, chapter 5).

output units presents more serious problems—for example, an arrest for property crime is equivalent to how many arrests for violent crimes?

Accounting for quality changes is in essence an aggregation problem. To be able to assess changes in productivity for a single output it is necessary to compare measures over time. The output being measured must be identical intertemporally: Is a 1979 university degree as good as a 1970 one? Productivity gains may be reflected in improvement in output quality, but these will only be reflected in productivity measures if the output measure employed is quality-adjusted. The change in output can thus be defined as an aggregate of appropriately-weighted indexes of quantity and quality characteristics, as developed in section II of this paper.[7]

An Alternative Approach

The search for better output proxies for public sector activities has naturally been carried out within the constraints of available descriptive statistics. Such indicators as crime rates, death rates, and educational test scores are readily identified with certain government programmes and have therefore often been used in the PPBS approach to government budgeting. To use such indicators as output proxies in productivity analysis, however, is a short but dangerous step. Estimating the number of crimes prevented by two different programmes, assuming all other things being equal, may be justified in programme evaluation, but the results over time associated with a given programme as a rule also reflect changes in the environment.

A more promising approach to the output measurement problem is that taken by Bradford, Malt and Oates (BMO) (1969), who emphasize the distinction between "outputs" and "consequences." They call the former D-output and the latter C-output. Let the following be a series of means-end relationships (or production and utility functions): $D = f(I)$; $C = g(D,E)$; $U = u(C,Z)$, where I represents a matrix of inputs, D a matrix of "direct outputs," E a matrix of environmental factors (age structure of the population, etc.), and f, g, and u represent functional forms. Utility (U) is a function of consequences C (crime prevention, etc.) and a matrix Z which represents the level of provision of other public goods and the quantities of private goods consumed by the individual.

This simple framework emphasizes the unreliability of using consequences as output proxies in a changing environment. The probability of

---

[7]In the absence of equilibrium market prices, weighting could either be in terms of consumers' marginal utility or producers' marginal cost. The model in the next section of this paper uses the latter set of weights as aggregators.

being hurt in the street, for example, is as much affected by " 'the propensity to riot' in the community and the driving habits of local residents," as by the "output" produced by the police force as such (BMO, p. 187). For changes in "consequences" to reflect changes in "output proper," environmental factors must be constant.

Having distinguished these two concepts of output, BMO then suggest that for police services, where inputs (I) are presumed to involve people, cars, and communications systems, "the resulting vector D of direct outputs might include as components the number of city blocks provided with a specified degree of surveillance (by patrolmen on foot or automobile patrols), the number of blocks provided with readily available police-officer reserves, the number of intersections provided with traffic control, and so on" (p. 186). Unfortunately, useful as it is, this approach, too, glosses over the subtle differences between "operational (or direct) output" or "activities" (what BMO call D-output) and "output proper". In the case of police services, "output proper" is the prevention of crime, accidents, etc. attributable to police activity. Identifying activities with real output (output proper) is as confusing as identifying output with consequences. Conceptually, the three levels should be kept separate.

In the case of police services, for example, the BMO paradigm may be extended by adding "output proper" (D') as follows: $D = f(I)$; $D' = g(D,Q)$; $C = h(D',E)$; $U = u(C,Z)$, where, as before, I is a matrix of inputs (men, cars, communications services), D is a matrix of "direct outputs" or activity measures (crime and accident rates), Q is a matrix of quality characteristics (arrest rates, property recovery rate, performance), C,U,E and Z are defined as before, and f,g,h, and u are functional forms. D' is then a measure of "output" (e.g., crime prevention due solely to police activity). The output of a public sector service may thus be defined on the one hand as that outcome or consequence (emanating from an activity) which is adjusted by the *exclusion* of environmental factors, and on the other hand as that activity or workload which is adjusted by the *inclusion* of quality (or efficiency) measures.[8] If "quality" (Q) is unchanged, then D' becomes equivalent to D, and if the environment (E) is also unchanged, both become equivalent to C.

In this framework, BMO's "direct output" (D) becomes a measure of intermediate output. Using this measure as a proxy for final output assumes that efficiency changes in the second stage of the service production function—the relation between D and D'—are, by definition, nil. If such

[8]In the service sector activity is best described in terms of workload: population being served, number of students, number of patients (over a period of time), or, in the case of police, crimes reported. Note that D' can be expressed as $D' = h^{-1}(C,E)$, where h^{-1} is an inverse function of h. Output (D') can actually be estimated in two equivalent ways: (a) as a quality-adjusted activity $D' = g(D,Q)$ or (b) as an environmentally-adjusted consequence $D' = h^{-1}(C,E)$. The former approach is followed here.

changes in efficiency due to quality changes exist but are excluded from the calculation, the final productivity measure is only partial.[9]

Since D' output as such is not directly observable, the best proxy may then be defined as a weighted aggregate of workload (activity) and quality characteristics.[10] To measure output in this sense one therefore needs to (a) identify these characteristics, (b) measure them, and (c) aggregate them (the weighting problem). The next section illustrates the application of these general concepts and principles to the particular case of police services.

It may be worthwhile to emphasize first, however, that in principle there is no conceptual difference between measuring public and private sector output. In both cases, it is not easy to measure the ultimate benefit to the citizen of government activity. Private productivity measures do not, for example, measure the ultimate benefit of private activity to citizens. (For instance, no attempt is made to evaluate the output of margarine in terms of the resulting decline in heart disease.) Both public and private sector productivity measures instead measure the direct output of some chain of activities combining inputs.

In the case of the private sector this output is then sold in the market, so that there is a market valuation of the output—which is often taken (on the basis of a set of very strong assumptions) to measure the contribution to "welfare" of that output and hence of that combination of inputs. In reality, however, measures of output in the private sector are simply that—measures of output, not of utility or welfare. They are measured when they pass from the production to the distribution sphere, that is, when they enter the market.

In the public sector of the economy, there is also a boundary, precisely analogous to that crossed in the private sector, except that it is not pecuniary in nature (Bones, 1976). The problems of measuring productivity in the noncommercial sector are thus not qualitatively different from those in the commercial sector. The only difference is the practical one that arises because as a rule the products of the public sector are not sold in the market, thus making it necessary to measure outputs in terms of total unit costs rather than by market prices.[11] The real problem in measuring public sector productivity is to identify a meaningful unit of output. What has been suggested above is that the "activities" approach (of measuring "intermediate outputs"), when "quality-adjusted", provides an acceptable proxy in many cases. This is the procedure followed in the application presented in the next section.

---

[9]Since quality changes may be positive or negative, the direction of bias is unknown.

[10]That is, the functional form g must be approximated.

[11]In the case of some private sector outputs, too, the same procedure is used, on the assumption that there is not too great a divergence, or a relatively constant one, between unit costs and market prices.

II. Measuring Police Output and Productivity

It was noted above that resistance to higher taxes is increasingly being reflected in the actions and concerns of public officials, who have started to take a closer look at expenditure budgets. Police services in the province of Ontario, Canada, are no exception to this rule. The Ontario Police Commission (Ministry of the Solicitor General, 1979) reported recently, for example, that "the activity chart of the Advisory Services Branch indicates that 1978 was a year highlighted with investigations and adequacy surveys of Municipal Police Forces... demonstrating the growing concern with financial constraints at the municipal level" (p. 5). Since 1975 this branch has been providing comparative budget and resource information packages to Chiefs of Police and concerned agencies of the provincial government, including such performance cost data as the ratio of police personnel to municipal population, lost time (vacations, sickness), and average hourly wages and salaries.

Instead of operating on the basis of history and tradition, police managers are thus now expected to account for differences in such measures between their police force and other forces of comparable size. Since differences in such measures as police man-hours per capita may be accounted for by differences in the volume of police work or in the efficiency of the service, however, the exercise of comparing such data still begs the more important questions. What is required is an estimate of the police manpower and equipment complement that could be expected to cope at the same level of effectiveness with the volume of police work facing a given municipal police force, taking environmental differences into account. Only then can any unexplained deviations between actual and predicted police inputs be interpreted as a measure of efficiency (or inefficiency).

One way to arrive at such a measure is through the production function approach.[12] Phrases such as "total factor productivity change" or "change in productive efficiency" are labels which describe the observed shifts in the production function being estimated.[13]

---

[12]This discussion, and all empirical results in this paper, are taken from Scicluna (1979), which should be consulted for more detailed explanation of the necessarily very compressed discussion here.

[13]Productivity is defined as a ratio of output to input. In the single output-multiple input case, total factor productivity can be defined as a ratio of output to an aggregated index of inputs, and productivity changes (measured as a percentage), can be measured by the difference between output change and an aggregation of input changes. To see this, denote output by Y, inputs by $X_j (j = 1 \ldots k)$ and productivity by P so that the single output production function can be written in implicit form as $F(Y, X_1 \ldots X_k, P) = 0$. If this is separable into its three components (output, inputs, and productivity), it can be written as $Y - PF'(X_1 \ldots X_k) = 0$. Total factor productivity is then defined as the ratio $P = Y/F'(X_1 \ldots X_k)$. If F' is linear homogeneous and represents the least-cost input combination, then P is equivalent to Hicks-neutral technical change and $\frac{\dot{P}}{P} = \frac{\dot{Y}}{Y} - \sum_{j=1}^{k} S_j \frac{\dot{X}_j}{X_j}$, where S_j is the share of input j in total cost. Productivity change is therefore a difference between an output change and an aggregate of input changes.

The production process of police services is conceived as separable in two stages—thus permitting a two-stage maximization (and consequently a two-stage estimation) procedure. In the first stage the police "manager" maximizes an aggregated *input* index, consisting of police officers (L), civilian employees (N), and patrol cars and communications equipment (K), subject to a budget constraint and exogenous factor prices. The two cost-shares equations resulting from the first order conditions can then be jointly estimated to yield consistent and asymptotically efficient parameter estimates of the input aggregator function.[14] In the second stage the police "manager" maximizes an aggregated *output* index of five "quality" variables (the arrest rate for each type of offense or crime) and six workload variables (types of crimes and offenses), subject to an input index with weights given by the parameter estimates of the first-stage maximization. The workload of reported crime and offense rates is determined by the demographic-social structure of the area (the environment). In order to complete the model, a set of offense-generating functions is required, primarily to account for the simultaneous relationship between the offense rate and the arrest rate. This aspect is not developed in the present paper, however.[15]

The functional specification used to estimate the police output and input aggregator functions is a second order logarithmic approximation of a generalized CES production function with constant though unrestricted (Allen's) partial elasticities of substitution.[16] Besides estimating the required productivity measures, this general functional form estimates the output

---

In the present analysis the production function is extended to a multiple output-multiple input case, which can be written in implicit form as $F(Y_1 \ldots Y_n, X_1 \ldots X_k, P) = 0$. Analogously, by imposing separability as a maintained hypothesis, the production function can be rewritten so that productivity can be expressed as a ratio of an output *aggregate* to an input aggregate, and changes in productivity can be expressed as the difference between changes in the output aggregate and the input aggregate.

[14]The two cost-shares equations are derived from two MRS equations, which in turn are derived from three marginal product equations (the first order conditions).

[15]In addition to the production function effects of offense rates on arrest rates, there is of course the deterrent effect of arrest rates on offense rates, as adequately described in economic models of crime, see Becker (1978).

[16]This specification is based on the work of Uzawa (1962) and Kmenta (1967). Referring back to note 13, the assumption of monotonicity permits the normalization on one output variable so that $f(Y_1 \ldots Y_n, X_1 \ldots X_k, P) = Y_1 + \tilde{f}(Y_2 \ldots Y_n, X_1 \ldots K_k, P) = 0$. Under the additive separability assumptions this can be written as $Y_1 = -\tilde{f}(Y_2 \ldots Y_n, X_1 \ldots X_k, P) = -\tilde{f}$ $[f_1(Y_2 \ldots Y_n) + f_2(X_1 \ldots X_k)]$ or $Y_1 \; \tilde{f}_2(X_1 \ldots X_k) = -\tilde{f}_1(Y_2 \ldots Y_n)$, where $\tilde{f}_2 = \tilde{f}f_2$, etc. This last equation is the one estimated here, with the maintained hypothesis for *logarithmic* separability (i.e., all variables are measured in logs) and f_1 and $\tilde{f}_2$ specified as second order approximations of a generalized CES function. The function $\tilde{f}_1$ includes six workload (or D) variables measured by crime rates and five quality (or Q) variables measured by arrest rates, that is, $\tilde{f}_1(Y_2 \ldots Y_n) \equiv D' = g(D, Q)$. This is the output aggregator function. The function $\tilde{f}_2$ includes three input variables (L, N and K), that is, $\tilde{f}_2(X_1 \ldots X_k) = \tilde{f}_2 \equiv D$. This is the input aggregator function. The actual equation estimated is of the form

$-\ln Y_1 + \alpha_k \ln K + \alpha_L \ln L + \alpha_N \ln N + \gamma_{KL} (\ln K - \ln L)^2 + \gamma_{KN} (\ln k - \ln N)^2$
$+ \gamma_{LN} (\ln L - \ln N)^2 = \beta_0 + \beta_2 \ln Y_2 + \ldots + \beta_{11} \ln Y_{11} + \theta_{23} (\ln Y_2 - \ln Y_3)^2 +$
$+ \ldots \theta_{10,11} (\ln Y_{10} - \ln Y_{11})^2.$

elasticity of each input, the input elasticity of each output, and the underlying returns to scale.[17] This general form also permits testing hypotheses regarding the structure of technology—in particular, whether or not to reject the Cobb-Douglas and CES specifications as appropriate restrictive functional forms.

A sample of 99 municipal police forces in Ontario in 1978 provides the data base for the estimation of the model. Police budget and resources information gathered by the Ontario Police Commission was kindly made available to us. Respondents with incomplete information and nonrespondents representing an additional 29 police forces (mostly one-person forces) were excluded from the sample. Crime and offense rates and arrest rates were also gathered by the Ontario Police Commission. These data, normally published by Statistics Canada in a more aggregate form, were unpublished at the time of the study. The conviction rates for crimes and offenses were calculated from data in the Court Statistics Annual Report of the Ontario Ministry of the Attorney General for 1977/78.[18]

The Input Aggregator Function

The structural coefficients of the input aggregator function defined over three inputs (police officers, civilian employees, and transportation/communications services) were estimated by the "Factor Shares Method," using an iterative minimum distance estimator.[19] Table A-1 in the Appendix presents the parameter estimates of the input aggregator function obtained by imposing a generalized CES, a CES, and a Cobb-Douglas specification. The two most widely used production functions—the CES and Cobb-Douglas—are both rejected as being inappropriate specifications for this application. A second important result derived from the observed concavity of the function is that in the short run (with constant budgets) police "managers" appear to minimize costs by substituting police personnel for civilian employees in response to relative price changes. A final observation based on Table A-1 is that police services are in fact highly labour intensive.

The Output Aggregator Function

The output aggregator function contains eleven output components, six workload variables (violent crimes, property crimes, other crimes, parking

[17]The estimated production function can thus answer such policy questions as, what percentage increase in police manpower is required to obtain a one percent increase in the arrest rate of property crime?
[18]The appropriate demographic variables for the offense-generating functions (not reported here) were gathered from the Statistics Canada 1976 Census.
[19]See note 14.

violations, FPM offenses, and traffic accidents) and five "quality" variables (the arrest rate for each workload component excluding parking violations). This equation is estimated by both OLS and 2SLS.[20]

The hypothesis of functional separability was tested for each type of regression (OLS and 2SLS, weighted and unweighted).[21] The equation was first estimated in unrestricted form conditional only upon the maintained hypothesis of symmetry between the second order parameters.[22] The second regression was designed to test the separability between the workload variables (offense rates) and the quality variables (arrest rates). The third and fourth hypotheses tested were Cobb-Douglas separability and linear homogeneity respectively. The relevant likelihood ratio tests indicate that all the separability hypotheses are rejected.[23] Most economic studies of crime and police have tended to use an aggregated index of crime in their police production function.[24] As the results of the separability restriction imposed on the multiproduct production function clearly show in the case of our sample, such aggregation is unjustified.

Due to the number of parameters present in the totally unrestricted regression equation (66), the equation is too cumbersome for meaningful analysis of its parameter estimates. Moreover, the high degree of multicollinearity present—especially when instrumental variables are used—makes the structural parameter estimates sensitive to slight changes in the structural form. Tables A-2 and A-3 in the Appendix therefore reproduce the regression estimates of the parameters of the output aggregator function using weighted and unweighted OLS and 2SLS estimators on a Cobb-Douglas form with constant returns to scale.[25] These regression estimates have been selected for presentation here for the following reasons: (1) multicollinearity has been tested and found to be least harmful in these equations; (2) the t-test statistics strongly reject the null hypothesis of zero input elasticities for most of the variables; (3) the normalization of the input elasticities in this presentation makes comparisons easy.

---

[20]In the latter case all the right-hand variables, namely, the crime and offense rates and arrest rates, are substituted by their instruments. The exogenous variables in the input aggregator function and the supply of offenses functions (not reported here) are used to obtain these instruments.

[21]There are various forms and degrees of separability. Our additive separability restrictions require that the Allen partial elasticities of substitution between any two outputs be identical (as in the C.E.S. function). A stronger separability restriction requires these parameters to be equal to unity (as in the Cobb-Douglas case).

Because the hypothesis of heteroscedasticity could not be rejected in some of the equations, each equation was reestimated using an appropriate weighting factor for each variable.

[22]The symmetry restrictions are obtained from the symmetric Hessian matrix of the twice differentiable production function. This restriction implies that the parameters of the relevant cross partial derivations must be equal.

[23]Each test except the first was made conditional on the nonrejection of the previous test.

[24]See, for example, Ehrlich (1973); Blumstein, Cohen, and Nagin (1978).

[25]The output estimates were normalized on the violent crime rate (see note 16).

Table 1

Aggregated Input Elasticities for Crime Rates, Noncrime Rates,
Crime and Offense Rates and Crime and Offense Arrest Rates
Derived by OLS and 2SLS

	OLS		2SLS	
	Unweighted	Weighted	Unweighted	Weighted
(a) Crime Rates	0.72	0.93	0.52	0.61
(b) Noncrime Rates	0.28	0.07	0.48	0.39
	1.00	1.00	1.00	1.00
(c) Crime and Offense Rates	0.44	0.50	0.52	0.61
(d) Arrest Rates	0.56	0.50	0.48	0.39
	1.00	1.00	1.00	1.00

Sources: row (a) is sum of rows (3) to (4) and (8) to (10) in Tables A-2 and A-3; row (b) is sum of rows (5) to (7) and (11) to (12); row (c) is sum of rows (2) to (7); row (d) is sum of rows (8) to (12).

The results, as summarized in Table 1, suggest that a high proportion of police resources are devoted to dealing with increases in measured crime activity. Estimates of this proportion range from 52 percent to 93 percent, depending on the specification used.[26] On the other hand, if the arrest rate were to be held constant, a one percent increase in all crimes and offenses rates would require on average an increase of around one-half of one percent increase in police resources. (This estimate of course reflects the maintained constant returns to scale hypothesis in these estimates; with increasing returns to scale, the demand on police resources should be less.) Finally, doubling the arrest rate for all crimes and offenses while keeping the level of crime constant would necessitate an increase of around 50 percent in police resources.

The constant returns to scale hypothesis was next tested on the weighted and unweighted OLS and 2SLS regressions. Linear homogeneity in output variables imposes one additional restriction on the Cobb-Douglas form. The value of the test statistic exceeds the critical value, which means the constant returns hypothesis is rejected for this sample.[27]

The returns-to-scale parameter for the output aggregator function is equal to the inverse of the sum of the first order parameters of the Kmenta-Uzawa translog equation used in this analysis.[28] In the OLS regressions,

[26]These figures reflect the effects of both the increased workload (crimes) and changes in quality (crime rates). The precise derivation is shown in Table 1.

[27]For 2SLS regressions the test statistic was based on the sum of squared residuals: The results were the same as for OLS.

[28]Note that the output aggregator regression contains one input index as dependent on a number of output variables. If the sum of the first order parameters is less than unity, then increasing returns to scale are indicated.

where multicollinearity between the first and second order variables was not observed to be high, increasing returns to scale, with a value ranging from 1.67 to 1.85, were estimated. (The only exception was the unweighted OLS regression with the Cobb-Douglas restriction imposed, where the returns-to-scale-parameter rose to 3.19.) In the 2SLS regression, however, the returns-to-scale parameter was quite unstable, varying between a low of 0.72 and a high of 2.4. The high values were consistently reported by the un-weighted regressions and the low values by the weighted regressions.

Since the OLS regressions had the better fit, a value of 1.7 suggesting substantial increasing returns to scale for police operations can be considered a representative estimate for the sample. Increasing returns to scale of this magnitude suggest a strong case for the amalgamation of police forces into larger regional forces—a policy which has been pursued actively in Ontario in recent years. To see whether this policy is sound, however, the efficiency of such regionalized forces also needs to be considered, a problem which returns to productivity measurement.

Productivity Measures

Productivity may be defined as the ratio between an input aggregator function and an output aggregator function.[29] The *fitted* values of the dependent variable of the output aggregator function represent the "expected" output index for each police force based on the appropriately weighted sum of workload and quality variables. The *actual* values are the weighted sum of factor inputs predicted by the input aggregator function. Unexplained differences between the actual and predicted values of the dependent variable of the output aggregator function will be (by definition of the OLS assumptions) randomly distributed with mean zero. Police forces with a higher complement of resources than that predicted by the model (positive residuals) are thus defined as *less efficient* than those with a smaller complement than predicted (negative residuals).[30]

The ordering of police forces using these measures can only give approximations to a cross-sectional productivity index since residuals may also result from measurement errors and misspecification of the model. Notwithstanding such problems, however, these rankings should be more meaningful than the partial measures of efficiency now used, such as police officers per capita or the aggregate crime rate.

As would be expected from the earlier discussion, the use of different regression equations may affect the ordering of police forces. Such changes in

[29]See notes 13 and 16.

[30]In this application all variables are measured in logs so the difference of logs is of course equivalent to the ratio of variables. Hence this difference reduces to the measure of total factor productivity in this application.

rank orderings were tested using rank correlation methods. The correlation coefficient between OLS and 2SLS weighted and unweighted regressions remained surprisingly high. The lowest value of 0.316 was observed between the OLS weighted Cobb-Douglas with constant returns regression and the OLS weighted partly restricted regression (with separability between crime rates and arrest rates). Because of constraints on computer capacity the totally unrestricted regression could not be used in this exercise. The second-best partly restricted regression was used instead.

When the regionalized forces and larger city forces were ordered in two separate groups, the city police forces showed higher productivity than the regionalized police forces. The mean residual of the former is -0.01 and the latter -0.0006.[31] Both groups, however, show higher productivity measures than the provincial average. To compare the ordering produced by this model and that derived using the police/population index as a measure of efficiency, Spearman's correlation coefficient was estimated and found to be insignificantly different from zero. Hence it appears that the "efficiency" measures currently in use, such as the police/population index, are very imperfect substitutes for the more justifiable quality-adjusted measures presented in this paper.

III. Conclusion

This brief review of the subject of productivity measurement in the public sector and the condensed presentation of an alternative approach to the subject yields four main conclusions. First, the BMO approach to productivity measurement in the noncommercial sector should be extended to distinguish between operational output and output proper. Second, it is apparent that the single factor productivity measures that have so far received most attention in this field are inherently incomplete and unsatisfactory in their neglect of the contribution of capital to productivity. To avoid this problem, economists have generally attempted total factor productivity estimations, often with prior restrictions on the functional forms. A third conclusion from the present analysis, however, is that restrictions imposed on functional forms and hence on aggregate productivity measures should be carefully considered and tested before being invoked. Finally, the approach suggested above of using residuals for productivity rankings appears worthy of further investigation. In the particular case of municipal police forces in Ontario, the ranking resulting from this approach is very different from that resulting from the simplistic "efficiency" measures now commonly used.

---

[31]Recall that negative residuals imply a smaller complement than that predicted by the model.

Appendix

Table A-1

Input Aggregator Parameter Estimates[a]

| Parameters[c] | Maintained Hypotheses[b] | | |
	Generalized C.E.S.	C.E.S.	Cobb-Douglas
α_K	0.158	0.120	0.088
	(13.204)	(18.524)	(19,761)
α_L	0.727	0.763	0.829
	(47.495)	(66.440)	(151.870)
α_N	0.115	0.117	0.083
	(—)	(—)	(—)
γ_{KL}	0.019	0.007	—
	(6.162)	(—)	
γ_{KN}	0.006	0.004	—
	(2.429)	(—)	
γ_{LN}	0.011	0.007	—
	(3.464)	(6.233)	
Substitution Parameters (ρ_{IJ})			
ρ_{KL}	0.878	−0.410	0.000
ρ_{KN}	0.541	−0.410	0.000
ρ_{LN}	−0.669	−0.410	0.000

[a] Obtained using an iterative minimum distance estimation procedure; t statistics in parentheses.

[b] The conditional maintained hypotheses are the normalization ($\alpha_K + \alpha_L + \alpha_N = 1$), equality, and symmetry restrictions.

[c] K = transportation and communication services, L = police officers, N = civilian employees.

Table A-2

OLS Cobb-Douglas Output Aggregator Parameter Estimates

	Unweighted OLS	Weighted OLS
(1) Intercept	−4.604	−4.501
	(24.225)*	(25.804)**
Activity Variables (D)		
(2) Violent Crime Rate	0.075	0.147
	(—)	(—)
(3) Property Crime Rate	0.117	0.294
	(1.905)*	(5.754)*
(4) Other Crime Rate	0.141	−0.056
	(2.412)*	(0.996)
(5) Federal, Provincial & Municipal (FPM) Offenses Rate	0.054	0.030
	(1.591)**	(0.866)
(6) Traffic Accidents Rate	0.044	0.022
	(0.929)	(0.517)
(7) Parking Violations	0.011	0.059
	(0.816)	(5.221)
Quality Variables (Q)		
(8) Violent Crime Arrest Rate	0.179	3.303
	(3.125)*	(5.046)*
(9) Property Crime Arrest Rate	0.141	0.062
	(2.392)*	(0.974)
(10) Other Crime Arrest Rate	0.063	0.180
	(1.200)	(3.737)*
(11) FPM Offenses Arrest Rate	0.211	−0.078
	(2.921)*	(1.351)**
(12) Traffic Accident Arrest Rate	−0.030	0.037
	(0.883)	(1.276)
R^2	0.904	0.927

*Significant at 5 percent level (critical value 1.645).
**Significant at 10 percent level (critical value 1.282).

Table A-3

2SLS Cobb-Douglas Output Aggregator Parameter Estimates

	Unweighted 2SLS	Weighted 2SLS
(1) Intercept	−4.154	−4.146
	(6.313)*	(13.199)*
Activity Variables (D)		
(2) Violent Crime Rate	−0.158	0.235
	(—)	(—)
(3) Property Crime Rate	0.001	0.254
	(0.006)	(2.785)*
(4) Other Crime Rate	0.330	−0.183
	(1.222)	(1.341)**
(5) Federal, Provincial & Municipal (FPM) Offenses Rate	0.015	0.168
	(0.122)	(2.128)*
(6) Traffic Accidents Rate	0.328	0.094
	(1.769)*	(0.740)
(7) Parking Violations	−0.001	0.041
	(0.020)	(2.045)*
Quality Variables (Q)		
(8) Violent Crime Arrest Rate	−0.057	0.424
	(0.268)	(3.802)*
(9) Property Crime Arrest Rate	0.202	−0.258
	(0.928)	(1.689)*
(10) Other Crime Arrest Rate	0.444	0.391
	(2.037)*	(4.003)*
(11) FPM Offenses Arrest Rate	−0.087	−0.167
	(0.347)	(1.556)**
(12) Traffic Accident Arrest Rate	−0.017	0.031
	(0.119)	(0.515)
Sum of squared residuals	.300	.148
Standard error of estimate	.606	.409

*Significant at 5 percent level (critical value 1.645).
**Significant at 10 percent level (critical value 1.282).

References

Andras, R. 1976. *Performance Measurement in the Public Service of Canada.* Mimeograph. Ottawa: Treasury Board.

Ardolini, C., and Hohenstein, J. 1974. "Measuring Productivity in the Federal Government." *Monthly Labor Review,* November, pp. 13–20.

Becker, G. S. 1978. "Crime and Punishment: An Economic Approach." *Journal of Political Economy,* 76 (March–April): 169–217.

Bird, R. M., Bucovetsky, M. W., and Foot, D. K. 1979. *The Growth of Public Employment in Canada.* Toronto: Butterworth, Institute for Research on Public Policy.

Blumstein, A., Cohen, J., and Nagin, D. 1978. *Deterrence and Incapacitation.* Washington, D.C.: National Academy of Sciences.

Bones, H. P. 1976. *Notes on Some Methodological and Empirical Problems in the Measurement of Non-Commercial Output.* Mimeograph. Ottawa: Statistics Canada.

Bones, H. P., and Allen, L. C. 1973. *The Outputs of the Hospital Industry: A Proposal for Their Identification and Measurement.* Mimeograph. Ottawa: Statistics Canada.

274   E. SCICLUNA, D. K. FOOT, AND R. M. BIRD

Bradford, D. F., Malt, R. A., and Oates, W. E. 1969. "The Rising Cost of Local Public Services." *National Tax Journal*, 22: 185–202.
Denny, M., and May, J. D. 1978. *Testing Productivity Models*. Working paper no. 7805. University of Toronto, Institute for Policy Analysis.
Ehrlich, I. 1973. Participation in Illegitimate Activities: A Theoretical and Empirical Investigation. *Journal of Political Economy*, 81 (May/June): 521–565.
Garston, G. J. 1973. "Productivity Measurement in the Canadian Non-Commercial Industries." In U.S. Department of Labor, Bureau of Statistics, *North American Conference on Labor Statistics*. Washington, D.C.: U.S. Department of Labor.
Hartle, D. G. 1972. "Canadian Experience with New Budgetary Methods." *Public Finance*, 27(2): 239–246.
Hartle, D. G. 1978. *The Expenditure Budget Process in the Government of Canada*. Toronto: Canadian Tax Foundation.
Kmenta, J. 1967. "On Estimation of the CES Production Function." *International Economic Review*, 8:180–189.
Ontario, Ministry of the Solicitor General. 1979. *Annual Report 1978*. Toronto.
Scicluna, E. 1979. *The Measurement of Output and Productivity in the Public Sector: Police Services*. Mimeograph. University of Toronto.
Shoup, C. S. 1969. *Public Finance*. Chicago: Aldine.
Uzawa, H. 1962. "Production Functions with Constant Elasticities of Substitution." *Review of Economic Studies*, 29: 291–299.

Résumé

Les problèmes conceptuels et empiriques concernant la mesure de la productivité dans le secteur public sont examinés et on propose une méthode d'analyse différente (basée sur les Travaux de Bradford, Malt et Oates). Cette méthode est ensuite appliquée pour mesurer la production et la productivité des forces de police municipale dans l'Ontario, au Canada. Les résultats mettent en lumière les effets des changements qui interviennent dans le taux des crimes et des arrestations en fonction des ressources de la police, d'une organisation policière fonctionnelle, et de l'efficacité et productivité relatives des différentes forces de police municipale.

8250, 8226
9/30
9330
6358
West Germany

Determinants of Public Productivity

Horst Hanusch*

Introduction

At present the economies of Western nations face a dilemma. On the one hand they have to spend more and more resources to ensure provision of raw materials and energy. On the other hand they are involved in a form of economic development characterized by rapid growth of the service sector, especially of the nonmarket part of the economy. Governments consume an increasing share of the GNP and employ a growing part of the national labor force.

Since all efforts to reduce government expenditures in the past have had little success, for several reasons, a growing number of economists are stressing the *production side* of the public economy. They propose to study the process of government production more thoroughly than has been done before and to develop the necessary means for improving public sector efficiency. Especially in the United States, substantial efforts have been made in the last decade to measure and to improve productivity in the public sector.[1]

*I wish to thank Lothar Semper for fruitful discussions, Andreas Obersteller and Markus Sailer for able research assistance, and especially Peter Meyer, who did most of the computation.
[1]Studies of the U.S. federal government have been made (see below) by Bowden, Vogely, and Lytton; the Bureau of the Budget; the General Accounting Office; the Office of Management and Budget; and the Civil Service Commission. At present local governments are the focus of productivity research in the United States. I mention only the studies by Ridley and Simon; Bradford, Malt and Oates; Ross and Burkhead; and Spann. The reason for the shift in interest lies primarily in the growing economic and political importance of local governments.

See W. Bowden, "Technological Changes and Employment in the United States Postal Service," *Monthly Labor Review*, 35 (1932); W. A. Vogely, *A Case Study in the Measurement of Government Output* (Santa Monica, 1958); H. D. Lytton, "Recent Productivity Trends in the Federal Government: An Exploratory Study," *Review of Economics and Statistics*, 41 (1959), pp. 341–359; Executive Office of the President, Bureau of the Budget, *Measuring Productivity of Federal Government Organizations* (Washington, D.C., 1964); C. E. Ridley and H. A. Simon, *Measuring Municipal Activities* (Chicago, 1938); D. F. Bradford, R. A. Malt, and W. E. Oates, "The Rising Cost of Local Public Services: Some Evidence and Reflections," *National Tax Journal*, 22 (1969), pp. 185–202; J. P. Ross and J. Burkhead, *Productivity in the Local Government Sector* (Lexington, 1974); R. M. Spann, "Rates of Productivity Change and the Growth of State and Local Government Expenditures," in T. E. Borcherding, ed., *Budgets and Bureaucrats: The Sources of Government Growth* (Durham, N.C., 1977), pp. 100–129.

Public Finance and Public Employment. Proceedings of the 36th Congress of the International Institute of Public Finance. Jerusalem, 1980.
Copyright © 1982 by Wayne State University Press, Detroit, Michigan, 48202.

In the German Federal Republic (West Germany), studies concerning public productivity are far below the level already reached in the United States. There exists only a small number of special studies dealing with local services such as waste disposal and hospital care.[2]

As one of the first, this study computes the productivity of three local service sectors in West Germany: hospital care, local mass transport, and public theaters. The empirical investigations concentrate upon possible determinants of productivity in the public sector production process. The study does not compare productivity in different communities or local productivity development over time. It is part of a larger research program at the University of Augsburg concerning the productivity of the local public sector in Germany. The program has just started; the empirical results given in this paper are the first to be obtained.

Productivity Measurement in the Public Sector

By general definition, productivity is a concept to compare output and input in real terms for a certain process of production at a particular point in time. It can be conceived in a partial and in a global version. The first version limits itself only to *one* factor as an input variable, the second version includes *all* input factors of a production process.

There is no doubt about the formal concept of productivity in economic science and in political practice. This holds true for production processes in the market economy as well as in the public sector. With regard to the production of governmental services, however, many economists are uncertain about how to give the basic concept of productivity an economic content. Two dimensions of the problem are discussed in the literature: (1) the definition and measurement of public output, and (2) the quantification of resources utilized in the public production process.

Measurement of Governmental Output

Questions concerning the measurement of public output are among the most important and difficult to be addressed in public finance. For many years the economic and political sciences have endeavored to find acceptable solutions.

[2]See for example W. W. Pommerehne, "Private versus öffentliche Müllabfuhr: Ein theoretischer und empirischer Vergleich," *Finanzarchiv*, 35 (1977), pp. 272–294; G. Stefani, "Die Produktivität der öffentlichen Unternehmen," *Annalen der Gemeinwirtschaft*, 42 (1973), pp. 127–185; J. Siebig, "Konzeption und beispielhafte empirische Anwendung eines Wirtschaftlichkeitsindikators für das Krankenhaus," *Zeitschrift für Wirtschafts- und Sozialwissenschaften*, 99 (1979), pp. 273–297.

Difficulties in measuring public output depend mainly on two factors: (1) the characteristics of public activities and, as a result, (2) the wide range within which public output can be defined and measured.

With respect to (1), modern governments perform in a wide variety of fields of economic and political activity. From a functional point of view their activities can be characterized as the intent to achieve certain goals within different kinds of politics. For instance, (a) with regard to "Ordnungspolitik," government provides the legal and the organizational framework without which a well-ordered social and economic life could not exist; (b) with regard to economic and fiscal policy, government intervenes in market processes in an effort to achieve goals such as economic stability, growth, distributive justice, and allocative efficiency; (c) with regard to the politics of satisfying the needs of citizens, government provides specific public goods like defense, health, mass transport, education, etc. Among all these activities there are interdependencies and certain structural relations.

With respect to (2), the theory of program budgeting and social indicator research have shown that it is in fact impossible to define the output of a specific activity by a single indicator. Public outputs are rather parts of a complex system consisting of basic elements and higher-ranked program categories. Thus, every output can be analyzed as a phenomenon of a lower or higher conceptual level. A rising level of abstraction in defining governmental services enlarges the spectrum of supply activities and simultaneously diminishes the possibility of characterizing public output by concrete and operational indicators.

Much of the confusion in the discussion of public services is related to these characteristics. In addition, in the literature on public productivity, there exist various ideas on how to *quantify* the output of different public services. Generally two positions are discussed, as follows.

One group of authors[3] suggests that public output must be seen in a comprehensive way. In this view, the input of resources in public sector production has two purposes: first, the production of specific services at a low output level; second, the achievement of definite and final goals on a higher output level. In the first case emphasis is on the *efficiency* dimension of public output; in the second case the *effectiveness* component is considered. Both are interrelated and have to be measured with different kinds of indi-

[3]See for example N. E. Terleckyj, "Recent Trends in Output and Input of the Federal Government," *Proceedings of the Business and Economic Sector, American Statistical Association, 1964,* p. 76; C. R. Wise and E. M. McGregor, Jr., "Government Productivity and Program Evaluation Issues," *Public Productivity Review,* 1 (1975/76), p. 6; H. P. Hatry, "The Status of Productivity Measurement in the Public Sector," *Public Administration Review,* 38 (1978), p. 28; W. L. Balk, *Improving Government Productivity: Some Policy Perspectives* (Beverly Hills, 1975), p. 12; M. M. O'Rourke, "Productivity in the Federal Government: An Overview," *Public Productivity Reveiw,* 3 (1978), p. 4; Committee for Economic Development, *Improving Productivity in State and Local Government* (New York, 1976), p. 14.

cators. In the literature, effectiveness is also discussed as "final output,"[4] "C-output,"[5] "outcome,"[6] "impact,"[7] or "consequences."[8] These terms also include the *quality* aspect of public output. This aspect must be taken into account, in addition to the "output proper" concept considered in a pure efficiency framework.

A second group of economists[9] suggests that productivity measurement in the public sector should be concerned with the efficiency aspect only. It should be based exclusively on physical output indicators. This view is based on the judgment that empirical research is confronted with a lack of data which makes it difficult to find appropriate indicators for the quality of public services. Furthermore, in theoretical analyses it is hard to find output indicators which can include in one term both the efficiency and the effectiveness component.

Our empirical study will be confined to quantitative analysis and neglect quality aspects. We proceed in this manner mainly because of lack of data. German local statistics provide no information about differences in the quality of public services. On the whole, however, there will be no great differences in output quality between single communities in Germany, primarily because of a well-functioning revenue-sharing system. The quality problem may thus be neglected in a study reflecting productivity determinants for different communities in a certain year. It would be a more serious question in an analysis concerning the temporal development of local productivity.

Measurement of Input

On the input side of the public production process, there are no fundamental differences between private and public production. In both sectors, factors like labor, capital, energy, material, technology, and organizational skills are used. The public sector, however, is often supposed to produce with a high level of labor intensity.

The integration of all input factors into a term of total productivity leads to a serious theoretical problem: the aggregation of different dimensioned

---

[4]R. W. Bahl and J. Burkhead, "Productivity and the Measurement of Public Output," in C. Levine, "Managing Human Resources, A Challenge to Urban Governments," *Urban Affairs Annual Review*, 13 (1977), p. 261.

[5]Bradford, Malt, and Oates, "Rising Cost of Local Public Services," p. 186.

[6]F. Levy, A. J. Meltsner, and A. Wildavsky, *Urban Outcomes* (Berkeley, 1974), p. 1.

[7]E. Ostrom, "Exclusion, Choice and Divisibility: Factors Affecting the Measurement of Urban Agency Output and Impact," *Social Science Quarterly*, 54 (1974), p. 691.

[8]J. P. Ross and J. Burkhead, *Productivity*, p. 47.

[9]See for example W. S. Shallman and W. E. Beasley, "Productivity Measurement in the Federal Government," *Atlanta Economic Review*, 24 (1974), p. 48; O. L. Ervin, "A Conceptual Niche for Municipal Productivity," *Public Productivity Review*, 3, No. 2 (1978), p. 17; Ross and Burkhead, *Productivity*, p. 11.

inputs.[10] The problem exists even if one tries to combine the two most important factors, labor and capital, into a comprehensive input indicator. With respect to capital, productivity research is confronted with the shortcomings of the cameralistic accounting system. Until now, public finance was not able to establish a capital account in the public sector, to apply methods of depreciation and costing. Therefore no valid data on capital input in government production are available for empirical research. As a consequence most empirical studies limit themselves to the concept of partial productivity. This limitation is taken into account here by restricting the computations to labor productivity ratios.

Research on Determinants in the Public Sector

The research on what determines productivity in the public sector is in its infancy. Two directions of interest can be distinguished. On the one hand are efforts to discover the functional relationships between factor inputs and public service outputs. Within simple models, the influence of input variations on output quantities is derived and often presented in the form of a Cobb-Douglas production function.[11]

On the other hand, existing output-input relations are computed for specific public activities of certain communities and factors are specified which may influence these relations. Two approaches can be found in the literature. The first approach is primarily related to the *theory of organization*,[12] and looks at such variables as automation, technological improvement, management incentive and information systems, organization of departments, and work analysis. These studies, however, do not go beyond theoretical analysis. This is not surprising because of the difficulties encountered when formulating operational indicators and quantifying them empirically. For this study, data for organizational variables which can be measured on cardinal scales were also unavailable.

The second approach centers on socioeconomic variables.[13] Despite all of the shortcomings in statistical data, a few studies have succeeded in con-

---

[10]J. W. Kendrick, "Public Capital Expenditures and Budgeting for Productivity Analysis," in M. Holzer, ed., *Productivity in Public Organizations* (Port Washington, 1976), pp. 196–204; F. Forte, "Controlling the Productivity of Bureaucratic Behaviour," in H. Hanusch, ed., *Anatomy of Government Deficiencies* (Detroit, 1982; forthcoming).

[11]See for instance M. S. Feldstein, *Economic Analysis for Health Service Efficiency: Econometric Studies of the British National Health Service* (Amsterdam, 1967), p. 32; D. Verry and B. Davies, *University Costs and Outputs* (Amsterdam, 1976), p. 198.

[12]See for example Joint Federal Productivity Project, "Factors That Have Caused Productivity Change," in Holzer, ed., *Productivity in Public Organizations*, pp. 309–315; M. J. Gannon and F. T. Paine, "Factors Affecting Productivity in the Public Service: A Managerial Viewpoint," *Public Productivity Review*, 1 (1975/76), pp. 44–50; Siegfried, "Public Sector Productivity," p. 30.

[13]See for example D. Z. Czamanski, *The Cost of Preventive Services* (Lexington, 1975), p. 54.

fronting theoretical speculations with empirical computation. An instructive example for this kind of investigation is the study by R. M. Spann.[14] He examines such governmental activities as police and fire protection, financial administration, general expenditures, highways, and public welfare, considering the following determinants as exogenous variables in a multiple regression analysis: per capita bureau employment, the growth rate of population, population per square mile, local government expenditures per capita, and percentage change in employee's wages.

The approach taken here is also based on socioeconomic determinants, extended by technological variables. In this way, a determinant is defined as a factor influencing either the input or the output of the local production process or both simultaneously. The sample of variables is chosen in a manner to cover a wide range of factors. Clearly, however, this approach cannot include all relevant determinants, and the selection is strongly restricted by the available statistics. In consequence, it is possible that the significance of the applied variables may be over- or underestimated. However, as long as the theory of public economics is not able to offer any model containing the whole range of determinants and their interrelationships in connection with local activities, one must resort to ad hoc econometric estimations. The determinants used in this analysis can be divided into four groups: technological determinants, determinants concerning the structure of the population, fiscal determinants, and political determinants.

Empirical Estimates

The econometric investigation covers three fields of local services: the public hospital care system, local mass transport, and public theaters. The required data are taken from the *Statistisches Jahrbuch deutscher Gemeinden*, the statistics of the *Verband öffentlicher Verkehrsbetriebe*, and the *Theaterstatistik*. On the basis of these statistical materials, a multiple regression analysis using cross-section data is conducted for the years 1974 and 1978 and communities with more than 50,000 inhabitants. In the analysis, it is assumed that the services examined in the communities under consideration are homogeneous. More detailed information is to be found in the discussions of the empirical results.

In an economic model, productivity (P) of a public service is specified as a function of chosen determinants (D1, . . . , Dn):

$$P = f(D1, \ldots , Dn).$$

---

[14]Spann, "Rates of Productivity Change."

Apart from identifying the relevant determinants, the specification of the functional relationship is a central problem of empirical analysis. A priori, no specific functional dependence can be assumed. Therefore, I have tested the following four functional forms:

$$P = d_0 + d_1 \cdot D_i; (1, \ldots, n) \tag{1}$$

$$P = d_0 + d_1 \cdot D_i + d_2 D_i^2; \tag{2}$$

$$P = d_0 + d_1 \cdot D_i + d_2 D_i^2 + d_3 D_i^3; \text{ and} \tag{3}$$

$$P = d_0 \cdot D_i^{d_1} \tag{4}$$

The empirical tests for all productivity measures and all determinants using the nonlinear equations 2–4 show no superior results compared with the linear approach of equation 1. Therefore all the computations of my study are based on the functional relationship given in equation 1. In order to derive the effect on productivity for all selected determinants, this simple approach is extended to a multiple regression analysis.[15]

The Hospital Care System

The final aim of the hospital care system can be formulated as the maintenance of an optimal health standard for the population. Unfortunately, this objective cannot be quantified solely by an economic output measure. Therefore, in economic studies the output of hospitals is usually reduced to lower-level but operational indicators like "number of patients treated" and "days of attendance."[16] This study uses these output measures. They are brought into relation with different measures of labor input in order to define productivity.

In the productivity terms P1 to P3, output is defined as "number of patients treated," and in P4 to P6 as "days of confinement." Both measures of output are brought into relation with the following indicators of input: "total staff," "administrative staff," and "physicians and nursing staff." (See Table

[15]A multiple approach of the form $P = \alpha_0 \cdot D_1^{\alpha 1} \ldots D_n^{\alpha n}$ does not lead to basically different results.

[16]See for example H. P. Hatry and D. M. Fisk, *Improving Productivity and Productivity Measurement in Local Government* (Washington, D.C., 1971), p. xvi; W. L. Dowling, *Hospital Production: A Linear Programming Model* (Lexington, 1976); Feldstein, *Economic Analysis;* M. Timmermann and J. Siebig, "Möglichkeiten und Grenzen der Wirtschaftlichkeitsmessung im Krankenhaus: Kritische Analyse ausgewählter Effizienzindikatoren," *Betriebswirtschaftliche Forschung und Praxis*, 32 (1980), pp. 125–137.

Table 1

Multiple Regression for Hospital Care System (West German Cities over 50,000)

	P1	P2	P3	P4		P5		P6
	1974	1974	1974	1974	1978	1974	1978	1974
D1	0.82**	2.23**	1.43**	1.39**	1.53**	3.83**	4.49**	2.43**
D2		20.94**	-7.44**			33.29**	25.94**	-11.92**
D3								
D4	18.67**	52.81**	30.28**	28.61**	39.77**	77.67**	110.39**	48.60**
D5	-0.99**	-2.56**	-1.94**					
D6								
D7								
D8								
D9								
D10	-0.38*	-0.98*	-0.78*	-0.83**		-2.20**		-1.70*
D11	0.30*	0.88*	0.74*			1.06*		0.98*
D12					-2.10*		-6.67*	-0.01*
Constant	11.76	-29.76	49.40	-1.67	18.76	95.83	-123.25	36.52
R^2	0.719	0.813	0.706	0.675	0.584	0.727	0.657	0.708
F-test	23.05	39.16	21.61	18.72	13.56	23.91	18.55	21.79
Number of Cases	121	121	121	121	129	121	129	121

Source: Calculations with data from Statistisches Jahrbuch Deutscher Gemeinden.
Table Notes:
*Statistically significant at the 0.1 level.
**Statistically significant at the 0.01 level.
For values lacking the hypothesis a = 0 cannot be rejected.
The regressions are statistically significant at the 0.01 level.
For 1978 the Durbin-Watson test excludes the uncorrelated residuals by pairs only for the productivity measures P4 and P5.

Symbols:

P1 = number of patients treated/total staff.
P2 = number of patients treated/administrative staff.
P3 = number of patients treated/physicians and nursing staff.
P4 = days of confinement/(total staff · 100).
P5 = days of confinement/(administrative staff · 100)
P6 = days of confinement/(physicians and nursing staff · 100).
D1 = number of beds per physician.
D2 = number of the total administrative staff per employee.
D3 = average bed capacity of a hospital.
D4 = average bed capacity utilized.
D5 = average length to stay.
D6 = resident population of community.
D7 = density of population.
D8 = foreigners per total population.
D9 = resident population per private partitioners (nonhospital).
D10 = birth rate.
D11 = death rate.
D12 = division of power between CDU (Christlich Demokratische Union) and SPD (Sozialdemokratische Partei Deutschlands), measured by the ratio SPD-members of municipal council/CDU-members of municipal council.

283

1.) The determinants include five technological determinants (D1 to D5), six determinants concerning the population structure (D6 to D11), and a political determinant (D12).

In order to take account of the homogeneity problem, the data include neither private nor university hospitals; the analysis uses only data from community hospitals which do not have specialized medical departments.

The empirical results in Table 1 show that the intensity and direction of a determinant's influence on productivity strictly depend on the measure of productivity used. All of the technological determinants have a significant effect on the productivity of hospitals. The number of beds per physician (D1) is positively correlated with all productivity measures. This determinant seems to be a dominant factor for the productivity in the whole hospital care system.

The determinant D2 has a positive influence on P2 and P5, a negative influence on P3 and P6, and does not influence P1 and P4. The negative influence of D2 on P3 and P6 may be explained as follows: If nursing staff is not to be encumbered with administrative affairs, more administrative staff is required and the productivity indices P3 and P6 increase. The lack of effect of D2 on the productivity of the total staff (P1 and P4) indicates that there may exist offsetting effects between the productivity of the physicians and nursing staff on the one side and of the administrative staff on the other side. As a consequence, variations of the relation "total staff/administrative staff" do not affect the productivity of the total staff. There is no impact of the hospital capacity (D3) on productivity.

Economies of scale cannot be observed in the hospital sector. The capacity of beds (D4) is positively correlated with all productivity measures. This direction of influence was expected because this determinant itself can be interpreted as a sort of productivity index.

The average length of stay (D5) is negatively correlated with the productivity measures P1, P2, P3. An interpretation for this result may be the fact that a growing average length of stay pushes down the number of patients, if the number of beds is constant. The number of days of confinement as an output measure is, of course, not affected by D5.

With regard to the population structure determinants, neither D6 nor D7 nor D8 appear to influence productivity in any way. The same holds true for determinant D9, the provision of ambulatory health care.

The birth rate (D10) as well as the death rate (D11), which are taken as proxies for the age scale of the population, show the expected influence on productivity only for the year 1974.

Fiscal determinants could not be constructed and tested because of lack of data. The political determinant D12 affects productivity in 1978 negatively.

Table 2

Multiple Regression for Local Mass Transport (West German Cities over 50,000)

	P1		P2		P3	
	1974	*1978*	*1974*	*1978*	*1974*	*1978*
Df	212.03*	204.17*	74.64**	48.88**	−56.15**	−40.74**

Source: Calculations with data from Verband öffentlicher Verkehrs-betriebe.
Notes:
  *Statistically significant at the 0.1 level.
  **Statistically significant at the 0.01 level.
  The other determinants indicated no statistically significant impact on productivity.
  The regressions are statistically significant at the 0.01 level.
Symbols:
  Df = revenues of local mass transport per passenger.
  P1 = passenger-kilometers/employees.
  P2 = seat-kilometers/employees.
  P3 = number of passengers transported/employees.

Local Mass Transport

The data used for the local mass transport do not include transport services provided by city underground railway systems—the Deutsche Bundespost and the Deutsche Bundesbahn. These were excluded to satisfy the condition of data homogeneity.

Three productivity measures are computed: passenger-kilometers/employees (P1), seat-kilometers (including standing room available)/employees (P2), and the number of passengers transported/employees (P3).[17]

The following technological determinants are employed: length of tramway transit lines/length of bus transit lines (D1); number of tram seats (including standing room available)/number of bus seats, including standing room available (D2); length of total transit lines (D3).

The population structure and the political determinants used are identical with those applied in the hospital care system, except for D3. In addition,

[17]In empirical productivity analysis, the output of mass transport system is usually indicated by "number of passengers transported" or the "kilometers (miles) performed." See for example A. R. Tomazinis, *Productivity, Efficiency, and Quality in Urban Transportation Systems* (Lexington, 1975), pp. 164-167; Stefani, "Produktivität der öffentlichen Unternehmen," pp. 163-170; H. P. Hatry et al., *How Effective Are Your Community Services?* (Washington, D.C., 1977) p. 242.

a population structure determinant, "population in urban and suburban area/population in urban area," and a fiscal determinant, "revenues of local mass transport per passenger" (D_t), are introduced for the local mass transport.

For both years only the fiscal determinant shows a significant effect on all productivity measures. The results are given in Table 2.

Public Theaters

The empirical investigations use data for those theaters housing performing arts activities—opera, ballet, musical (operetta), plays, performances for young people, and concerts. In Germany, no fundamental differences exist among theaters. The nature and the structure of the offered performances are relatively homogeneous for the theaters investigated. The output of the theaters is quantified by "number of performances,"[18] and this variable is confronted with three input indicators: "total staff," "artists," and "nonartists."

The population structure determinants and the political determinant used in the econometric computations are the same as those used in the local transport system with the exception of "population in urban and suburban area/population in urban area." The technological and fiscal determinants are modified as shown in Table 3. It lists only the significant results. Determinants D2 and D6 affect productivity negatively. Perhaps the size of a theater and relatively high revenues per spectator ease the economic situation of theaters in Germany and therefore reduce their productivity. The average utilization of capacity (D4), on the other side, has a positive influence on productivity, whereas the direction of influence of D9 varies with the chosen productivity measure.

The productivity index P2 decreases with an increasing share of premières. The reason for this result can be seen in the fact that first performances require more artistic staff than ordinary ones. Regarding P1 and P3, positive, negative, and no influences are observed. To explain these results, further disaggregations of data would be necessary.

Conclusion

Productivity studies for the public sector become more and more relevant in economic theory and political practice. They are a necessary and

[18]See for example C. D. Throsby and G. A. Withers, *The Economics of Performing Arts* (Melbourne, 1979), p. 11.

Table 3

Multiple Regression for Theaters (West German Cities over 30,000)

	P1		P2		P3	
	1974	*1978*	*1974*	*1978*	*1974*	*1978*
D2		−0.0009**	−0.003**	−0.002*	−0.0006*	−0.002*
D4		0.48**	1.59*	1.38*	0.36*	0.96**
D6	−97.33**	−81.86*	−333.11**	−314.93*	−181.22**	−158.55*
D9	−0.18**	−0.22**	0.69**	0.58*	−0.21**	−0.36**

Source: Calculations with data from Theaterstatistik.
Notes:
*Statistically significant at the 0.1 level.
**Statistically significant at the 0.01 level.
For values lacking the hypothesis a = 0 cannot be rejected.
The other determinants indicated no statistically significant impact on productivity.
The regressions are statistically significant at the 0.01 level except the regression for P2 in 1978 is only statistically significant at the 0.05 level.
Symbols:
P1 = number of performances/staff.
P2 = number of performances/artists.
P3 = number of performances/nonartists.
D1 = number of seats/resident population.
D2 = number of seats.
D3 = percentage of premières.
D4 = average utilization of capacity.
D5 = number of total staff per nonartist.
D6 = revenues/number of spectators.
D7 = revenues/operating subsidies.
D8 = percentage of operating revenues.
D9 = total personnel budget/personnel budget for artists.

informative instrument for all efforts trying to analyze and to increase the efficiency of public activities. In the future, however, a number of methodological and empirical problems have to be solved in order to reach a high level of scientific significance. This study is no more than a preliminary attempt. It has to be improved and extended by further and more comprehensive analyses.

Résumé

Cet article est consacré à un sujet dont l'importance est croissante dans la théorie et la pratique économique : la mesure de la productivité dans la prestation de services publics. D'un point de vue théorique, les principaux problèmes que les études de productivité doivent résoudre sont la définition des intrants et des extrants et la détermination des facteurs qui influencent la productivité.

La partie empirique de l'article est consacrée à différents domaines d'activités publiques en Allemagne de l'Ouest. On calcule les effets de plusieurs déterminants selon des mesures variées de productivité dans 3 secteurs : soins hospitaliers, transports locaux en commun et théâtre. Les résultats empiriques varient en fonction des indicateurs de productivité, les déterminants et les années considérées.

C'est une étude préliminaire qui doit être améliorée et développée par une analyse ultérieure plus complète.

3712
0250
3221
8250
U.S.

Models of Excessive Government Spending: Do the Facts Support the Theories?

Edward M. Gramlich*

Recent rhetoric in the United States, both in political debates and professional journals, suggests a growing fear that government spending is getting out of control. Total government spending as a fraction of GNP has risen for long periods of time now, and simple extrapolation of this trend leads to a prediction that tax rates and expenditure shares could eventually approach unity. Long before that happens, high marginal tax rates could reduce work effort and limit economic growth. In response to these fears, citizens in many states, most notably California and most recently Massachusetts, have passed tax limitation amendments to their constitutions.

These fears stand in contrast to two prevailing positive theories of governmental behavior used extensively in the public finance literature: the median voter theory of Hotelling (1929), Bowen (1943), and Downs (1957), and the mobility theory of Tiebout (1956). According to the first theory, government spending can never become excessive because political competition for votes will insure that spending is exactly what the median voter wishes it to be. According to the second, even if this does not happen, or even for nonmedian voters, the competition of other jurisdictions in providing decent-sized public sectors will keep all public sectors from getting out of line. With these two checks, how can government spending ever get too big or out of control?

Essentially three types of theories have been used to resolve the apparent inconsistency:

a) Productivity disparity theories. Productivity advances for government servants are presumed to be smaller than those for private sector workers. If so, the relative cost of government services will rise over time, as first

*This paper borrows extensively from previous work that I have done with Paul Courant and Daniel Rubinfeld. I would like to thank both for their stimulating collaboration, for allowing me to borrow from their work here, and for their comments on an earlier draft. I am also indebted to the Department of Housing and Urban Development and the National Science Foundation for their research grants.

Public Finance and Public Employment. Proceedings of the 36th Congress of the International Institute of Public Finance. Jerusalem, 1980.

modelled by Baumol (1967), and this could lead to a steadily growing share of output devoted to the public sector.[1] It is important to note that unlike the other theories, this productivity disparity theory does not involve any political market failures; it is a theory of government growth but not of microeconomic inefficiency in the determination of the size of government and tax rates.

b) Real expenditure theories. Patterned after the bureaucratic growth theories of Niskanen (1971), these models posit that for one reason or another bureaucrats have a taste for higher levels of government employment than do private sector voters. As people get hired into the public sector, they find their utility functions altered, and this can raise the demand for public spending by the median voter.[2] A variation on this theme is the agenda control mechanism of Romer-Rosenthal (1978); once government employees are brought into existence, they can control voter choices and force the private sector to vote for yet higher government employment levels.

c) Relative wage theories. Government bureaucrats are in the enviable position of being suppliers who vote on the demand side. Because of that, the fact that they are often unionized and organized, and because they have more to gain from higher public wages than private employees have to lose, they may be able to form coalitions to elect sympathetic candidates who will raise public sector wages above competitive levels and increase the size of government.[3]

Apart from the general observation that government spending is now large and getting larger in the United States, remarkably little empirical evidence has been produced to support any of these hypotheses. In this paper I try to see if the hypotheses can be verified. I use evidence of various sorts—macrostatistics on government spending in the U.S., a 1978 survey of Michigan tax limitation voters,[4] and cross-sectional wage surveys—to see whether some of the main predictions of each theory can be substantiated and how instrumental each theory might have been in shaping the growth of government in the United States. As a caveat, I should say at the outset that the paper follows others in describing government growth by the size of the government budget, ignoring the new trend toward public regulation of the

---

[1]It could also lead to a steadily falling share, and indeed this seemed to worry Baumol more. An amendment to this model is provided by Bush-Mackay (1977), who show that with Cobb-Douglas utility functions and an endogenous capital market the share of government employment and output values in the respective overall totals will be constant.

[2]Other papers in this tradition are Bush-Denzau (1977), Borcherding-Bush-Spann (1977), and Orzechowski (1977). In this volume, Pommerehne-Schneider test some related hypotheses with Swiss data.

[3]This possibility was mentioned by Tullock (1974), Buchanan (1977), and Reder (1975). Courant, Gramlich, and Rubinfeld (1979) have modelled the process, reaching less horrifying conclusions. The paper by Quinn in this volume deals with a related issue.

[4]See Courant, Gramlich, Rubinfeld (1980) for a more extensive report on the results of this survey.

private sector. It is a good deal harder to define government's presence in this nonbudgetary area, though perhaps it will soon become important to conduct some parallel analyses.

The paper begins with a summary of the facts of governmental growth in the United States—exactly what type of spending has grown, by how much, and whether this growth is explainable by orthodox econometric estimates of relevant behavioral parameters. Then I follow this macroanalysis with a review of the evidence in favor of or against each of the three classes of theories of governmental spending growth or size.

How Rapid and Explainable Has the Growth of Government Been?

It is of course impossible to know if the growth in, or level of, government spending is excessive without knowing whether spending levels correspond to voter tastes. Those in turn are impossible to divine conclusively, but two approaches for doing so have been used. The first is to reason that in a democracy the actions of government will reflect the tastes of the median voter, and then to estimate these tastes from a "revealed preference" perspective. The obvious weakness is that there is no way to prove or disprove the underlying median voter assumption. The second approach is to use survey methods and ask people whether they think government is too large, small, or what. From these data actual spending outcomes can be directly compared to the tastes of the median (or any other) voter. The weakness of this approach is that it is inevitably hypothetical—respondents do not have to act on the basis of their answers.[5]

I will deal with survey data later on in the paper, but for now let me focus on the first method. As one illustration of it, Borcherding (1977) has shown that the growth of government spending in the twentieth century in the U.S. has far exceeded what would be predicted from behavioral estimation of price and income elasticities from cross-section data. This comparison is tenuous for many reasons: there are differences between cross-section and time series estimates of parameters; any check based on growth rates assumes that the government was at the optimal size at the start of the period; tastes for public spending might have changed over the twentieth century; in many cases the parameters from, say, local education equations must be used to predict desired growth in national defense spending, a very dubious extrapolation. However, Borcherding's method does illustrate some interesting facts

---

[5]Some economists have come up with interesting experimental ways of inducing survey respondents to reveal preferences. See, for example, Bohm (1972). At present these results refer only to small programs and not overall spending levels, and there are many types of spending where it would be difficult to use the methods. We should however, keep posted for future advances in these techniques.

about the recent growth of government in the United States, so I pursue it briefly.

The method can be set out as follows: One first posits a utility function for the median (ith) voter of the form

$$U_i = u_i(C_i, X_i), \tag{1}$$

where U_i stands for the median voter's utility, C_i for his private consumption, and X_i for the utility benefits perceived from a level of government spending. These benefits are in turn related to government spending by a crowding equation first used by Borcherding-Deacon (1972) and Bergstrom-Goodman (1973):

$$X_i = E/N^{a_1}, \tag{2}$$

where E is the level of government spending and N is community population. The parameter a_1 is zero for pure Samuelsonian public goods, where added consumers do not reduce the benefits of public spending perceived by the ith voter, and one at the other extreme where benefits are reduced proportionately. It is sometimes alleged that finding $a_1 = 1$ implies that "public" services are like private goods and should be located in the private sector, but that assertion does not follow at all. The public good problem (good for which $a_1 = 0$) represents only one of the many rationales for supplying goods through the public sector, and it is possible to think of several services where a_1 is close to one and where there could be strong reasons for public sector provision. Examples that spring to mind are education, redistributive transfers, and innoculations. Knowing that a_1 is close to one may be a necessary condition for having a service supplied privately, but it is not a sufficient condition.

The median voter then maximizes utility in the usual way, subject to the constraint that he must pay some proportional share of the cost of publicly provided goods. Since tax payments are roughly proportional to income, the "tax price" can be set equal to

$$P_i = W_g Y_i/Y, \tag{3}$$

where P_i is the tax price of public spending for the ith voter, or the cost to the voter of a dollar of public spending, W_g is the real wage for public employees (assumed to be proportional to the gross cost of public services), Y_i is the ith voter's pretax income, and Y is community income.

Solving all of this and using the commonly accepted logarithmic demand approximation yields

$$E/N = c_0 Y_i^{c_1}(W_g Y_i/Y)^{c_2} N^{a_1(1+c_2)-1}, \tag{4}$$

with c_1 and c_2 referring to the income and price elasticities respectively. This is the public spending equation usually estimated by empirical researchers, sometimes with other variables representing spending "needs" included. Such an expression has been estimated with time series and cross-section data alike, for various governmental aggregates and functional categories, and the results appear to be quite robust. The results from a sample of eleven recent studies are shown in Table 1. There it can be seen that mean estimates are c_1 = .65 (the income elasticity), c_2 = −.51 (the relative price elasticity), and a_1 = .97 (the crowding parameter). These parameters will be used in the calculations below.

The determination of whether government spending levels are excessive then focuses on growth rates. Assuming that government spending was at its optimal level at the start of some time interval, has its growth exceeded that predicted by differencing equation (4)? Assume that median income grows at the same rate as per capita income

$$\mathrm{dln}\ Y_i = \mathrm{dln}\ Y - \mathrm{dln}\ N, \qquad (5)$$

and substitute into (4) to obtain

$$\mathrm{dln}\ E = c_1\mathrm{dln}\ Y + c_2\ \mathrm{dln}\ W_g + [a_1(1+c_2) - c_2 - c_1]\ \mathrm{dln}\ N. \qquad (6)$$

Expression (6) uses observed percentage changes in overall GNP (Y), the real wage of public employees (W_g), and overall population (N) to determine

Table 1

Estimates of Public Expenditure Demand Parameters

Study	TS or CS[a]	Date	Type	c_1	c_2	a_1
Ashenfelter-Ehrenberg (1975)	PCS	58–69	SL Employment	.78	−.72	n.c.
Barlow (1970)	CS	60	Mich. Sch. Dist.	.64	−.34	n.c.
Bergstrom-Goodman (1973)	CS	60	Mich. Cities	.88	−.41	.98
Borcherding-Deacon (1972)	CS	62	SL Agg.	.83	−.76	.92
Feldstein (1975)	CS	70	Mass. Sch. Dist.	.48	−1.00	n.c.
Gramlich (1978)	TS	54–77	SL Agg.	.70	−.36	n.c.
Gramlich-Rubinfeld (1982)	CS	77	Mich. Counties	.40	−.06	1.01
Inman (1978)	CS	68–69	N.Y. Sch. Dist.	.72	n.c.	n.c.
Johnson-Tomola (1977)	TS	66–75	SL Emp.	.62	−.56	n.c.
Lovell (1978)	CS	70	Conn. Sch. Dist.	.32	−.83	n.c.
Ohls-Wales (1972)	CS	68	SL Agg.	.74	−.11	n.c.
Mean				.65	−.51	.97
St. Dev.				.17	.29	.02

[a] TS means a time series analysis, CS a cross-section analysis, and PCS a pooled cross-section analysis.

Table 2

Explained and Unexplained Components of the Growth of Government Spending and GNP (all variables in real terms, in annual rates of growth)

			Exhaustive Expenditures				
Decades	(1) Overall dln E	(2) Federal dln E	(3) Federal Nondef. dln E	(4) SL dln E	(5) Overall Nondef. dln E	(6) Predicted by Eqn (6)[a]	Addendum: (7) dln Y
1929–1939	.043	.118	.099	.017	.037	−.003	.001
1939–1949	.043	.076	.000	.016	.012	.032	.043
1949–1959	.057	.063	−.018	.051	.037	.019	.038
1959–1969	.041	.028	.066	.054	.055	.017	.040
1969–1979	.007	−.020	.026	.027	.026	.018	.027
Current Share of GNP	.201	.070	.024	.131	.155	—	

		Nonexhaustive Expenditures		
Decades	(1) Overall dln T	(2) Federal dln T	(3) Federal Non SS dln T	(4) Predicted by Eqn (6)[b]
1929–1939	.113	.109	.109	.003
1939–1949	.101	.129	.126	.033
1949–1959	.022	.022	−.013	.031
1959–1969	.069	.060	.143	.031
1969–1979	.064	.066	.060	.021
Current Share of GNP	.119	.110	.053	—

[a] Using $c_1 = .65$, $c_2 = -.51$, and $a_1 = .97$.
[b] Using $c_1 = .65$, $c_2 = 0$, and $a_1 = 1.0$.

predicted changes in real government spending. Strictly, (6) is only true for exhaustive expenditures that claim resources (public employees); the corresponding expression for transfer payments (T) would set, $a_1 = 1$ and $c_2 = 0$.

Table 2 gives calculations similar to Borcherding's for the last five decades, the period of rapid growth in public expenditures in the United States. The top panel of the table shows the results for exhaustive expenditures, where the government is directly purchasing the productive services of the economy. Comparing the actual numbers in column 1 with those predicted by equation (6) in column 6, we see that overall exhaustive spending increases have exceeded predictions by a fairly sizable margin in the four decades between 1929 and 1969, exactly the point made by Borcherding. But interestingly, in the most recent decade total exhaustive spending fell short of that predicted by equation (6) by .011—spending would have been predicted to rise by 1.8 percent per year and in fact only rose by 0.7 percent per year. A plausible reason for the difference is that federal government spending was inflated by the Vietnam War in 1969, so columns 3, 4, and 5 repeat the comparison just for nondefense spending. Taking overall nondefense exhaustive spending in column 5, we see that the seventies residual is now positive (2.6 percent per annum as against a predicted growth of 1.8 percent), but by a much smaller amount than has historically been the case. Also it should be noted that this 2.6 percent growth rate of government spending over the decade is below the growth rate for GNP, given as an addendum in column 7. Government exhaustive spending may be too large relative to GNP (or for that matter too small), but the share of government spending in total output seems to have stopped growing and is now increasing at rates that more or less correspond to the behavioral parameters estimated from cross-section data.

But there is a continuing source of growth in government budgets: the nonexhaustive expenditures that are shown on the bottom panel of Table 2. These nonexhaustive expenditures are transfer payments for interest on the public debt, mainly at the federal level.[6] They might not raise the same fears of government uncontrollability because the private sector recipients still retain command over the economy's resources, but of course many of them do represent involuntary transfers from taxpayers to beneficiaries. It is just as possible to imagine either real spending or relative wage type theories of government growth and private sector exploitation through transfer payments as it is for exhaustive expenditures.

Whatever philosophical judgments are made about the qualitative nature of transfer payments, these payments have persistently risen much more rapidly than exhaustive expenditures, and now total almost 12 percent of GNP. Even in the recent slowdown decade, all types of transfers have risen much more rapidly than GNP and also than the prediction of equation (6). Part of the very recent growth in this item was due to the over-indexation of both social security benefits and federal retirement pensions for inflation, two technical flaws in the relevant legislation that have now been corrected. Presumably those corrections will narrow the growth disparities, but of course that remains to be seen.

Productivity Disparity Theories

The recent evidence on governmental growth is therefore mixed—some categories of spending are growing more rapidly than GNP and some are not;

---

[6]Note in the bottom column that the current share of GNP of all transfer payments is .119, and that of federal transfers is .110. Hence state and local transfers are less than one percent of GNP. One common mistake in calculations of this sort is to add total federal expenditures to total state and local expenditures, hence double-counting grants from the federal to state and local governments. Here I avoid that problem by defining nonexhaustive expenditures net of grants.

some are growing more rapidly than would be predicted on the basis of cross-sectionally estimated parameters and some are not. The next question is whether this excess growth, if indeed it exists, can be explained from any sort of model of the political or economic processes. I now turn to the three types of models mentioned at the outset.

The first treatment of the problem of government growth can be found in the productivity disparity model of Baumol (1967). He postulated that the relative price of public goods would rise over time because of the innate lack of productivity growth in the public sector. If nominal wages rose at the same rate in the public and private sectors, the gross price of a unit of output would be constant in the private sector and rise at the rate of private sector productivity in the public sector. Depending on various elasticities, the share of output and employment devoted to the public sector could rise, fall, or stay the same. Though it has since become fashionable to worry about a rising share of public output, Baumol in fact was more worried about a falling share.

There have been many developments, both theoretical and factual, that have changed the results of Baumol's model in surprising ways. At a theoretical level, the price Baumol should have been worried about was the tax price faced by the median voter (P_{xi}) for a unit of utility services flowing from government expenditures. In percentage form, this is just a reexpression of equations (2), (3) and (5):

$$dln\ P_{xi} = dlnW_g - (1-a_1)\ dln\ N. \qquad (7)$$

Even if wages rose at the same rate in both the public and private sectors and if there were no productivity growth in the public sector (Baumol's assumptions), the tax price faced by the median voter would fall by virtue of the growth of population (as was pointed out by Bush-Mackay, 1977). But offsetting this latter fact is the crowding problem: If the utility created by one unit of public factor services is also diminished by population growth according to the crowding parameter a_1, movements in the tax price of a unit of utility would more closely approximate the original Baumol gross factor price.

In constructing these growth models, both Baumol and Bush-Mackay used rather restrictive assumptions on the form of the demand function. Baumol examined the case where real output shares were maintained, and found that an increasing share of the labor force would be hired into the nonprogressive government sector to maintain these shares. Bush-Mackay assumed that the median voter had a Cobb-Douglas utility function with unitary income and price elasticities, and found that value output shares were constant, as was the proportion of the labor force hired by the public sector, but that the real share devoted to the public sector declined. When elasticities are nonunitary, however, the expression giving the growth in real public spending is just that given in equation (6), a function of the growth of overall real income, real gross factor prices, and community population. Since in the straightforward Baumol model there is no public sector productivity, the rate of growth of public employment will equal dln E—that is, also the right side of equation (6). The shares of real output and employment devoted to the public sector will then be rising or falling depending on parameters c_1 (the income elasticity of public goods), c_2 (the relative price elasticity), and a_1 (the crowding parameter).

To see whether actual estimated parameters give a rising or a falling share, we would simply plug the estimates from Table 1 into equation (6), just as was already done in Table 2. The results there indicate a predicted Baumol growth rate for public spending and employment of .018 for the 1949–1979 period. Comparison rates of population increase are .013 and of overall real GNP increase are .035. These findings then fall somewhere between the predictions of Baumol and of Bush-Mackay: The real share of output devoted to government spending would be expected to decline slightly (as predicted by the Bush-Mackay model but not the simple Baumol model), but the share of the labor force hired by government would be expected to rise slightly (as predicted by the simple Baumol model but not the Bush-Mackay model).

But before fretting unduly about these supposed empirical predictions, it is well to ask a more basic question about the assumptions of the Baumol model. The model starts from the premise that because of disparities in productivity growth rates, the relative price of factor services (or the real wage of public employees) will be rising over time. At least in recent years, this assumption is a difficult one to validate.

Regarding productivity in the public sector first, it is intrinsically difficult to measure public sector productivity, but there have been several attempts. The Civil Service Commisson (1972) first tried to measure productivity change for 17 executive agencies covering 56 percent of federal civilian employment: surprisingly, they found an annual average rate of productivity change over the 1967–1972 period of 1.2 percent. Recently the same office, renamed as the Office of Personnel Management (1980), updated this study to 50 agencies covering 65 percent of federal civilian employees: They found an average rate of productivity change of 1.4 percent from 1967–1978, and of 1.7 percent for 1978–1979. There are serious and well-known difficulties in making these estimates, but for what it is worth, they suggest that there are positive rates of productivity change at the federal level.

Things are more ambiguous for local governments. Bradford-Malt-Oates (1969) found that costs per pupil day in U.S. public schools rose at a 6.7 percent annual rate over the 1947–1967 period, 4.4 percent more rapidly than prices in general (as measured by the GNP deflator). This implies that productivity growth was −4.4 percent *unless* either the quality of schooling increased or it became more difficult to teach children, two propositions that cannot be proven directly one way or the other. Spann (1977) conducted a series of investigations that have similar ambiguities—for many services it can be shown that public employees have risen relative to the clientele, but there is no way of knowing whether quality or needs have changed also. In fact, his one area where needs and quality of services appear to be best held constant, highways, shows local public sector productivity increases of 3.5 percent for the mid-sixties. Whether any of these numbers can be believed or extrapolated is at best an open question, but the common view that there is little productivity change in the public sector is at least open to question.

On the other side, in recent years the U.S. private sector has suffered a widely-noted and much analyzed slowdown in productivity growth. Between 1948–1965 (choosing years of prosperity to avoid cyclical distortions), private nonfarm productivity advanced at an annual rate of 2.8 percent, at a rate of 2.0 percent between 1965–1973, and at a rate of 1.1 percent since that time. There are many competing explanations for this drop in productivity—the addition of less productive workers to the work force (hurting overall average productivity), environmental restrictions, rising relative prices for natural resource products, the drop in the share of output devoted to capital formation, and so forth. But careful attempts to explain the slowdown still leave most of the post 1965 slowdown totally unexplained.[7] Whatever is causing the change, if it keeps on there will be no productivity disparity to activate the Baumol model in the first place.

The upshot of all this is that at least for recent years the Baumol productivity disparity explanation has not accounted for much growth in real government spending. Even if productivity disparities were present, under realistic empirical estimates of relevant elasticities they have caused only a miniscule increase in the share of the labor force devoted to the public sector, and a drop in the share of real output (see Table 2). But in the past decade, the productivity disparities have not even existed. Private sector productivity has risen at a rate that appears, at best, to be no higher than in the public sector, and real public sector wages (input prices) have been essentially constant. As long as these trends continue, there is nothing to activate the Baumol model, and little reason to fear that it will lead to progressively larger shares of output devoted to the public sector and progressively higher tax rates.

Real Expenditure Theories of Excess Government Spending

Baumol's model is a model of government growth but not inefficiency. Government spending could require a large share of national output, but there is no reason why this share would not be optimal, in the sense that marginal

[7]See Norsworthy-Harper-Kunze (1979) and Christainsen-Haveman (1981) for current analyses of the problem.

benefits and competitive costs of public spending are equated at the margin. We now consider two theories that imply distortions in this competitive outcome.

There are many variants of the real expenditure theories of excessive government spending—problems in agenda setting, interest groups and log-rolling, bureaucratic inertia, and so forth. Without meaning to downplay these theories, I want to focus here on taste differences: specifically the fact that government bureaucrats may want more public spending than do private sector voters, and that this leads to excessive levels of government spending. The most widely known argument along these lines is that of Niskanen (1971), who argues that since bureaucrats cannot compete for any surplus generated by their agency, they will compete to have large agencies with many employees to supervise. A complementary motive that also implies economic inefficiency is that those already working in the public sector may have a job security motive for wishing to enlarge it, they may get higher wage levels for supervising more workers, or indeed marginal private sector work-ers may hope to enlarge the public sector so that they too can get a spoils system job. But not all such taste differences imply that higher public sector demands for public goods are illegitimate. For one thing, public employees might work in the public sector because of their innate interest in public goods; for another, they might have better information than private voters about the true value of public services.

If these excessive government spending theories are analyzed in the content of the median voter theory, as if the taste of the median voter repre-sents the optimal level of public spending, taste differences between public and private employees can raise public spending when two conditions are fulfilled: the tastes of public workers *change* when workers are hired into the public sector, and they change from below-median to above-median by the hiring of a public worker. These conditions are impossible to prove or dis-prove, and as a pragmatic shortcut, the condition usually invoked to establish the theories is that public bureaucrats have more political power per capita than private sector voters. If they did not, it would be hard to imagine how the differing tastes could greatly change overall voting outcomes. Gov-ernmental employees at all levels still comprise only about one-fifth of the labor force in the United States, and in any particular vote the interests of public workers for one level (say the federal government) are not necessarily allied with those at another (local government). Hence to make these real expenditure arguments convincing, it must be alleged that because of their better organization and higher vote participation rates, public sector votes are disproportionately weighted.

Even at this more pragmatic level, there are important philosophical problems with the argument. For one thing, just as different tastes could be intrinsic and legitimate, so could different turnout rates. Public employees may simply turnout at higher rates because they care more. For another, there is the swing voter problem. Whatever the numerical strength of various voting blocs, if one group can maneuver itself into a position where its members comprise the swing vote, it has enormous power. But such maneuverings are hard to deal with analytically because the strategic situation changes from election to election. Hence the efforts of economists to analyze voting power have focused on more tractable, if perhaps less interesting, questions.

As one approach, Borcherding-Bush-Spann (1977) have dealt with the proportional representation election model (each voter is as powerful as every other) and have calculated a bureaucrat's power index that accounts for turnout differentials between public and private sector citizens. Under this power index, if public workers turnout more regularly than private voters, they get disproportionate voting power. But this disproportionate power only matters if public sector voters have different preferences than private sector voters: Otherwise the outcome of the vote would be no different than if only private voters were voting. Hence the Borcherding-Bush-Spann power index must be supplemented by a term that adjusts for the potentially different and more uniform tastes of public sector voters.

This adjustment can be made in the following simplified proportional voting model. Let g be the share of the labor force composed of public employees at the relevant level, P_g the probability that bureaucrats will vote for a piece of legislation or a political candidate, P_p the same probability for private voters, and V_g and V_p the voting participation rates of bureaucrats and nonbureaucrats respectively. A measure will pass or a candidate will be elected if

$$gP_gV_g + (1 - g)P_pV_p \geq .5 (gV_g + (1 - g) V_p). \tag{8}$$

Manipulating this expression yields

$$P_p + \frac{(P_g - P_p)(gV_g)}{gV_g + (1 - g)V_p} \geq .5, \tag{9}$$

If $P_g = P_p$, bureaucrats may have more power than private voters because of higher turnout or whatever, but that power will not matter. The outcome of the vote will be the private sector only outcome, P_p, regardless of the participation rates of government bureaucrats (V_g). But if $P_g \neq P_p$, the differential power does matter, the more so the higher the share of bureaucrats in the total vote (gV_g relative to the denominator). The so-called voting power index of Borcherding-Bush-Spann is just that share, or $gV_g/(gV_g + (1-g) V_p)$. Equation (9) has broadened it by including differential voter tastes.

Bureaucrats can change an outcome from what it would be if only private sector voters were voting whenever $(P_g-P_p) (gV_g)$ is nonzero. The conventional wisdom is that bureaucrats exert disproportionate power both because their turnout rates (V_g) are high and because their tastes are different ($P_g \neq P_p$). In fact, this conventional wisdom is based on incredibly sparse empirical estimates. Most economists writing on the subject cite a study done of Austin, Texas, voters in a 1933 municipal election, which found $V_g = .87$, $V_p = .53$, and did not even measure P_g and P_p.[8] These estimates of V_g and V_p are plausible, but it could still be viewed as stretching things to base so much theory on an obscure 47-year-old journal article.

Some more recent data can be taken from a study of Michigan voters in the tax limitation vote of 1978. This survey was a random sample of 2000 Michigan households taken right after a tax limitation referendum. It polled residents on whether and how they voted, as well as on a series of attitudinal, income and tax price variables. The results are shown in Table 3. Column 2 shows voter participation rates (V_p or V_g) and column 3 vote probabilities (P_p or P_g). The context was a vote on the Headlee Amendment, a proposal to limit own state government revenue to a fixed share (9.4 percent) of state personal income. The proposal passed by 52 percent overall, and by 56 percent in this sample,[9] with overall sample vote participation rates of 62 percent. Note that participation rates are about 10 points higher for "Pure Public" voters, much smaller than the Austin participation disparities in 1933. On the other hand, voter tastes are now quite different. The share of public sector voters voting for the Headlee limitation amendment averages about 20 percentage points below that of the private sector voters. Evaluating expression (9) with the "Not Working" voters allocated to the private sector and the "Pure" and "Mixed Public" to the public sector yields:[10]

$$P_p = .606, \quad V_p = .609, \quad P_g = .440, \quad V_g = .678,$$

so that expression (9) can be written as

$$.606 - .046 > .5. \tag{10}$$

If public employees had no vote at all, or voted for the amendment with a probability P_p, the amendment would have passed with a .606 share of the vote. As it was, it passed with a .56 share of the vote. The presence of public employees with higher turnout rates and different vote probabilities lowered the overall passage rate by 4.6 percentage points—not enough to defeat this

[8]See Martin (1933) for a look at the famous work.

[9]This disparity implies that there was some selective recall, a not uncommon finding in surveys of voting behavior. Evaluating the voting power of bureaucrats is still possible if correct recall rates are no different between the public and private voters.

[10]Allocating all the pure and mixed public voters to the public sector in all likelihood imparts an upward bias to the bureaucrats voting power index. Some of the mixed public/private voter households may earn a much larger share of their income in the private sector, and others may be participants in competitive labor markets and not earn any actual or potential rents.

Table 3

Tastes and Participation Rates of Public and Private Employee Respondents,
from a Random Sample of Michigan Households, 1978

Type	(1) Number	(2) Vote Participation Rate (%)	(3) Vote for Tax Limit Amendment (%)
All Respondents	2001	62.4	56.3
Private Sector	1163	58.5	61.4
Not Working	322	69.5	57.8
Pure Public[a]	292	68.7	40.2
Mixed[b]	224	66.5	48.9
Federal Govt.[c]	48	52.6	67.8
State Govt.[c]	46	60.4	35.5
State Univ.[c]	24	60.1	47.7
Local Govt.[c]	60	86.0	46.1
School Dist.[c]	104	76.6	41.2

[a] Respondent is single and works in the public sector, is in household where the only working spouse works in the public sector, or is in a household where both spouses work in the public sector.

[b] Both spouses are working, one in the public sector and one in the private sector.

[c] The location of the public sector job for the respondent. Respondents who are spouses of public sector workers are not included, implying that the sum of the items under this footnote adds to less than the sum of the Pure Public and Mixed Public categories.

particular tax limitation amendment, but enough to make the vote a good deal closer. Calculations based on the work of Neufeld (1977) indicate that "biases" of this size would swing about 10 percent of the school millage election results in the state of Michigan, raising overall education spending by perhaps about one percent. Hence while there is now a plausible and empirically verifiable ballot-box explanation for excessive levels of government spending, the impact is not large and some very strong assumptions are needed to make the case.[11]

Relative Wage Theories

The other means by which government spending can rise to inefficient levels is by plain old monopoly power on the part of public sector labor groups. Public servants are in the unique and enviable position of being sellers who vote on the demand side. One need not be overly cynical to conjure up visions of public unions for mayoral candidates who promise

[11]The Pommerehne-Schneider paper in this volume tests excessive expenditure theories with actual expenditure data and finds, at least for Switzerland, slightly larger differences between representative and direct democracies.

implicitly to raise public wages if elected, which in turn attracts other workers into the public sector and strengthens the voting coalition. The role of the private sector in such a view is simply to pay higher and higher tax rates to finance the increasingly bloated level of public wages.

When one tries to model the process, as Courant-Gramlich-Rubinfeld (1979) did, the conclusions turn out to be somewhat more restrictive. Taking the worst possible case, assume that the public employees of a local government have complete control over their wage level and can set it in a monopolistic manner. The median voter, whether in the public or private sector, is then allowed to choose a level of government employment (E), and private employees are given the additional ability to leave the community if the tax price of public services is driven to excessive levels by these monopolistic public servants. In this case the solution for levels of W_g and E turns out to depend on a simultaneous solution of two equations, one essentially like (4) that gives the public employment level given W_g, and another that gives optimal (from a public employee's standpoint) wages for a given level of E.

The latter expression can be derived simply by assuming public employees have conventional utility functions

$$U_g = U_g(C_g, E), \tag{11}$$

where the g subscript now refers to all members of the public sector, taken for simplicity to have homogeneous tastes and to be admitted to the public sector only if the voting process creates more public sector jobs. To find the maximum, or optimal, level of W_g for each E, the E argument in (11) can be held fixed, and the optimization exercise involves simply maximizing the private consumption of public employees with respect to W_g. The only trick is that since Y equals the wage bill of the public plus the private sector, it can in principle rise or fall with W_g—it will rise if the higher public sector wage income is not offset by lower private sector wage income, or fall if the higher public sector wage income and tax rates inspire emigration or reductions in labor supply. Solving the optimization exercise yields

$$W_g = Y/E(2-\eta), \tag{12}$$

where $\eta = \dfrac{dY}{dW_g}\dfrac{W_g}{Y} \leq 1$, as the expression for the real wage level desired by public employees. The important news in (12) is that public wages and employment levels are inversely correlated. As E increases, higher public wages entail higher income tax rates even for public employees, reducing their after-tax income even though before-tax income is increased. Also, we note that the lower η is and the more mobile the private sector, the lower W_g. When $\eta = 0$, the optimal wage is set so that government spending is just half of total output; when $\eta = -1$, government spending is one-third, and so forth.

Finding that employment and wage levels are inversely correlated implies that there are severe limits on government employee wage exploitation of the private sector. In the first place, when voting on E, public employees will be torn between choosing an E that maximizes their utility as consumers of public output and one that provides optimal levels of rent. For another, there is now a difficult tradeoff for public employees. They can vote to expand the public sector to give themselves more political power (raising g in equation 9), but this very action *reduces* the optimal wage level. Or they can try to keep the public sector small and optimal wages high, but this action reduces the probability they will have enough voting power to raise public wages above competitive levels in the first place.[12]

Does the evidence support this view of the public sector wage determination process? There have been many attempts to explain government wage rates, but most have not tried to distinguish wage differentials according to whether private voters do or do not have a credible exit threat. But it is perhaps possible to glean at least some information from empirical work on public sector wage differentials.

A first question is whether public sector workers in fact get any noncompetitive rents. The answer depends on the study you look at, but there is a good deal of evidence of positive rents. Results from three human type studies are listed in Table 4. They indicate that not only are rent levels generally positive, but also that rents are highest for the federal government, whose jurisdiction is hardest to emigrate. These results are then greatly strengthened by a later analysis by Quinn (in this volume): He shows that other terms of the wage bargain such as pension arrangements, disability, tenure, and job interest are also seen to be more favorable for public than private employees.

Even more convincing supporting evidence comes from the work of Inman (1980) and Ehrenberg-Goldstein (1975). Inman showed that the presence of competitive suburbs with income levels comparable to those in a central city—implicitly, negative values of η—does appear to hold down wages for policemen and firemen by a large and statistically significant amount. Ehrenberg-Goldstein have reinforced the same conclusion from a different standpoint. They show that the union organization of suburban employees raises central city public wages (by reducing the credibility of private employees' exit threat), while the organization of central city em-

---

[12]The tradeoff might not be as stark as it seems and was given in the original paper if $a_1 \neq 0$. The original paper assumed that $a_1 = 0$, and thus desired E would be the same even if high W_g levels forced some private voters to emigrate. If they do, and if $a_1 \neq 0$, desired E will be reduced by the lower demographic demand (equation 2), leading to more rent exploitation possibilities and higher W_g levels.

Table 4

Percentage Differentials between Public and Private
Pay Levels, Controlling for Human Capital Variables

	(1) Smith (1980)		(3) Quinn (1979)	(4) Mitchell (1979)
	Males	*Females*	*Males*	*Both Sexes*
Federal Government	11	21	20	2
State Government	−6	3	17	−16
Local Government	10	0	−6	−2

ployees raises suburban public wages. Both the existence of public sector
rents, and their negative correlation with the private employees' exit threat
then tend to support also the wage monopoly rationale for some degree of
excess government spending.

Summary and Implications

This analysis of the size and controllability of government budgets thus
contains some mixed signals. On the other hand, it does not appear that the
growth of government is *uncontrolled* or *uncontrollable*. In earlier decades
government grew at rates that exceeded those predicted on the basis of cross-
section elasticity estimates, but at least in the seventies that has not been true
for exhaustive expenditures, and not as true for transfer payments. Certain
institutional adjustments to limit future growth in both transfer payments
and state and local expenditures promise to cut actual government growth
rates even more, and stabilize if not reduce the share of total output devoted
to government.

On a theoretical level, Baumol's productivity-disparity model which
could give a rising share of output devoted to government, does not accurately describe the world for at least two reasons. For one, the income elasticity of demand for public spending is low, implying that even if it is more
costly to produce public sector output, not as much of that (as a share of
GNP) will be demanded as the economy grows. For another, the model is
activated by productivity change disparities between the private sector and
government. But productivity change in the private sector has been falling
off, and apparently there may be some positive productivity growth in the
public sector. Hence the relative cost of government output in fact has not
been rising for the past decade and there is nothing to activate the unbalanced
growth model.

But simply saying that government spending is not uncontrollable does not say that government spending is at its efficient level where all marginal benefits of public output equal marginal costs, and where all factor wages are at competitive levels. There are essentially two reasons for suspecting that government spending may be above this microefficiency ideal in the United States, and both reasons do come with some confirming evidence. For one thing, public employees, by virtue of their higher turnout rates and different taste for public spending, might cause electoral outcomes that differ from those desired by the private sector's median voter, and could be responsible for a slight enlargement of the size of the public sector. For another, the interaction between this voting power and the labor organization of public employees implies that these employees are able to gain noncompetitive rents, apparently more so the lower the fear of exit of private taxpayers. Under most reasonable assumptions these rent levels will be limited by private sector resistance to high tax rates, but they nevertheless can exist and appear to in many empirical studies.

References

Ashenfelter, O. C. and R. G. Ehrenberg, "The Demand for Labor in the Public Sector," in D. S. Hamermesh, ed., *Labor in the Public and Nonprofit Sectors*, Princeton, N.J., Princeton University Press, 1975.

Barlow, R., "Efficiency Aspects of Local School Expenditures," *Journal of Political Economy*, vol. 78, Sept. 1970, pp. 1028–1040.

Baumol, W. J., "Macroeconomics of Unbalanced Growth: The Anatomy of Urban Crisis," *American Economic Review*, vol. 57, June 1967, pp. 415–426.

Bergstrom, T. C. and R. P. Goodman, "Private Demand for Public Goods," *American Economic Review*, vol. 63, June 1973, pp. 280–296.

Bohm, P., "Estimating Demand for Public Goods: An Experiment," *European Economic Review*, vol. 3, 2:1972, pp. 111–130.

Borcherding, T. E., "The Sources of Growth of Public Expenditures in the United States, 1902–1970," in T. E. Borcherding, ed., *Budgets and Bureaucrats*, Durham, N.C., Duke University Press, 1977.

Borcherding, T. E., W. C. Bush, and R. M. Spann, "The Effects on Public Spending of the Divisibility of Public Outputs in Consumption, Bureaucratic Power, and the Size of the Tax Sharing Group," in T. E. Borcherding, ed., *Budgets and Bureaucrats*, Durham, N.C., Duke University Press, 1977.

Borcherding, T. E. and R. T. Deacon, "The Demand for the Services of Nonfederal Governments," *American Economic Review*, vol. 62, Dec. 1972, pp. 891–901.

Bowen, H., "The Interpretation of Voting in the Allocation of Economic Resources," *Quarterly Journal of Economics*, vol. 58, Nov. 1943, pp. 27–48.

Bradford, D. F., R. A. Malt, and W. E. Oates, "The Rising Cost of Local Public Services: Some Evidence and Reflections," *National Tax Journal*, vol. 32, June 1969, pp. 185–202.

Buchanan, J. M., "Why Does Government Grow?," in T. E. Borcherding, ed., *Budgets and Bureaucrats*, Durham, N.C., Duke University Press, 1977.

Bush, W. C. and A. T. Denzau, "The Voting Behavior of Bureaucrats and Public Sector Growth," in T. E. Borcherding, ed., *Budgets and Bureaucrats*, Durham, N.C., Duke University Press, 1977.

Bush, W. C. and R. J. Mackay, "Private versus Public Sector Growth: A Collective Choice Approach," in T. E. Borcherding, ed., *Budgets and Bureaucrats*, Durham, N.C., Duke University Press, 1977.

Christainsen, G. B. and R. H. Haveman, "Public Regulations and the Slowdown in Productivity Growth," *American Economic Review*, vol. 71, May 1981.

Courant, P. N., E. M. Gramlich, and D. L. Rubinfeld, "Public Employee Market Power and the Level of Government Spending," *American Economic Review*, vol. 69, Dec. 1979, pp. 806–817.

Courant, P. N., E. M. Gramlich, and D. L. Rubinfeld, "Why People Vote for Tax Limitation: The Michigan Case," *National Tax Journal*, vol. 33, March 1980, pp. 1–20.

Downs, A., *An Economic Theory of Democracy*, New York, Harper, 1957.

Ehrenberg, R. G. and G. S. Goldstein, "A Model of Public Sector Wage Determination," *Journal of Urban Economics*, vol. 2, July 1975, pp. 223–245.

Feldstein, M. S., "Wealth Neutrality and Local Choice in Public Education," *American Economic Review*, vol. 65, March 1975, pp. 75–89.

Gramlich, E. M., "State and Local Budgets the Day After It Rained: Why Is the Surplus So High?" *Brookings Papers on Economic Activity*, 1, 1978, pp. 191–216.

Gramlich, E. M. and D. L. Rubinfeld, "Micro Estimates of Public Spending Demand Functions and Tests on the Tiebout and Median Voter Hypotheses," *Journal of Political Economy*, 1980.

Hotelling, H., "Stability in Competition," *Economic Journal*, vol. 34, March 1929, pp. 41–57.

Inman, R. P., "Testing Political Economy's 'As If' Proposition: Is the Median Voter Really Decisive?" *Public Choice*, vol. 33, 4:1978, pp. 45–66.

Inman, R. P., "Pensions, Wages, and Employment in the Local Public Sector," *COUPE Papers on Public Economics*, No. 4., 1980.

Johnson, G. E. and J. D. Tomola, "The Fiscal Substitution Effect of Alternative Approaches to Public Service Employment Policy," *Journal of Human Resources*, vol. 12, Winter 1977, pp. 3–26.

Lovell, M. C., "Spending for Education: The Exercise of Public Choice," *The Review of Economics and Statistics*, vol. 60, Nov. 1978, pp. 496–503.

Martin, R. C., "The Municipal Electorate: A Case Study," *Southwestern Social Science Quarterly*, Dec. 1933.

Mitchell, D. J. B., "The Impact of Collective Bargaining on Compensation in the Public Sector," in B. Aaron, J. R. Grodin, and J. L. Stern, eds., *Public Sector Bargaining*, Madison, WI, Industrial Relations Research Institute, 1979.

Neufeld, J., "Tax Rate Referenda and the Property Taypayers' Revolt," *National Tax Journal*, vol. 30, Dec. 1977, pp. 441–456.

Niskanen, W. A., *Bureaucracy and Representative Government*, Chicago, IL, Aldine-Atherton, 1971.

Norsworthy, J. R., M. J. Harper, and K. Kunze, "The Slowdown in Productivity Growth: Analysis of Some Contributing Factors," *Brookings Papers on Economic Activity*, 2, 1979, pp. 387–422.

Ohls, J. C. and T. J. Wales, "Supply and Demand for State and Local Services," *Review of Economics and Statistics*, vol. 54, Nov. 1972, pp. 424–430.

Orzechowski, W., "Economic Models of Bureaucracy: Survey, Extensions, and Evidence," in T. E. Borcherding, ed., *Budgets and Bureaucrats*, Durham, N.C., Duke University Press, 1977.

Quinn, J. F., "Wage Differentials Among Older Workers in the Public and Private Sectors," *Journal of Human Resources*, vol. 14, Winter 1979, pp. 41–62.

Reder, M. W., "The Theory of Employment and Wages in the Public Sector," in D. Hamermesh, ed., *Labor in the Public and Nonprofit Sectors*, Princeton, N.J., Princeton University Press, 1975.

Romer, T. and H. Rosenthal, "Political Resource Allocation, Controlled Agendas, and the Status Quo," *Public Choice*, vol. 33, 4: 1978, pp. 27–44.

Smith, S., *Public-Private Wage Differentials in Metropolitan Areas*. Mimeograph, 1980.

Spann, R. M., "Rates of Productivity Change and the Growth of State and Local Government Expenditures," in T. E. Borcherding, ed., *Budgets and Bureaucrats*, Durham, N.C., Duke University Press, 1977.

Tiebout, C., "A Pure Theory of Local Expenditures," *Journal of Political Economy*, vol. 64, Oct. 1956, pp. 416–424.

Tullock, G. R., "Dynamic Hypothesis of Bureaucracy," *Public Choice*, vol. 19, Fall 1974, pp. 127–132.

U.S. Civil Service Commission, *Measuring and Enhancing Productivity in the Federal Sector*, Joint Economic Committee Print, Washington, D.C., 1972.

U.S. Office of Personnel Management, *Measuring Federal Productivity*, Washington, D.C., U.S. Government Printing Office, 1980.

Résumé

Cet article considère certaines critiques selon lesquelles la dépense publique, aux Etats-Unis, est soit trop importante, soit devient incontrôlable. Si l'on considère la croissance, notre analyse suggère que des mesures variées des dépenses publiques globales montrent actuellement une hausse comme le laisseraient supposer des estimations standards des élasticités des revenus et des prix, bien que dans les décennies précédentes la croissance ait été plus rapide. Les dépenses de transferts croissent toujours plus rapidement que ne le laisseraient supposer les calculs d'élasticité, mais cet excès même de croissance semble fonction de facteurs institutionnels récemment corrigés. Ces mêmes calculs montrent que les prédictions de Baumol, qui prévoyait que la part de la dépense publique dans la production globale serait régulièrement croissante ou décroissante, ne semblent pas se confirmer. En ce qui concerne leurs niveaux, cet article passe en revue les théories qui suggèrent que les fonctionnaires votent soit pour des niveaux plus élevés de dépenses publiques, soit s'emploient à obtenir des salaires plus élevés que ceux du marché. Bien qu'il y ait quelque vérité dans chacune de ces critiques, aucun des deux phénomènes ne semble grandement modifier les niveaux de la dépense publique globale. Les taux plus élevés de participation au vote des fonctionnaires et leurs tendances à voter sur les questions de limitations d'impôts montrent que la présence des fonctionnaires peut tout au plus changer les résultats électoraux de quelques points en pourcentage. Pour les salaires publics, cet article montre qu'il y a une limite naturelle à l'exploitation salariale, établie à la fois par l'identité de balance budgétaire interne et à la fois par la menace de mobilité externe des employés du secteur privé. Des estimations empiriques montrent en fait de faibles rentes du secteur public, en particulier dans les secteurs où la menace de mobilité est la plus faible.

3210
3240
0250
8250
Switzerland

Unbalanced Growth Between Public and Private Sectors: An Empirical Examination

Werner W. Pommerehne
Friedrich Schneider*

Felix qui possit rerum
cognoscere causas
(Inspired by Virgil, *Georgica*, 2, 490)

I. Introduction

Public expenditures have in the last few decades increased absolutely as well as relative to the GNP in many countries, including Switzerland.[1] There are many approaches to explaining this phenomenon,[2] including some which look for the causes in the following factors:

— Lagging productivity in the public sector as compared to the private, resulting from technological differences between the two
— Increased demand for services provided by the government
— Pressure on the supply side generated by interest groups (including the public bureaucracy), and by representative governments only weakly controlled by the voters/taxpayers

We examine these factors for explaining "unbalanced" growth between the public and private sectors, taking the Swiss local level for our empirical examination.

*Helpful comments on an earlier draft of this paper were made by Peter Zweifel. The final version has benefited from comments from our discussants Han Emanuel, Edward M. Gramlich, and Horst Hanusch, and from the floor, especially from Robert W. Bacon, Jørgen Lotz, and Richard A. Musgrave. Financial support from the Swiss National Science Foundation (NF-1821-078) to Friedrich Schneider is gratefully acknowledged, as is the aid of Sandra Stuber in editing the paper for English.

[1]We do not want to tax the reader here with figures. A detailed analysis of this development is given for six major industrial countries, including Switzerland, in Pommerehne (1977). Further evidence for various countries since the 1950s is contained in Nutter (1978).

[2]See, for example, the studies by Amacher, Tollison and Willet (1975) and Tarschys (1975).

Public Finance and Public Employment. Proceedings of the 36th Congress of the International Institute of Public Finance. Jerusalem, 1980.

Part II examines the technological aspect, that is, the hypothesis of lagging productivity. In Part III, demand aspects are also taken into consideration, and an indirect test for lagging productivity is presented based on a sample of 48 Swiss municipalities that function as *direct* democracies. The results show that here the actual growth in local government exhaustive expenditures from 1965 to 1975 can be well explained by lagging productivity and increased demand for public services. However, not all places have direct control of government and the bureaucracy by the voters/taxpayers. Thus Part IV examines a group of 62 Swiss municipalities which are *representative* democracies to see whether they allow the government and public bureaucracy more leeway than they have under direct democracy, and, if so, whether this results in representative democracies having an even more marked degree of unbalanced growth between the public and private sectors. The results suggest that there is some evidence for this kind of supply side side pressure. In Part V we discuss some possible objections to our analysis and draw some conclusions.

II. Lagging Productivity in the Local Public Sector: The Technological View

Baumol's Model of Unbalanced Growth

The central assumption of the by now classic Baumol model (1967) is that economic activities can be grouped into (1) technologically progressive activities, where innovations and capital accumulation effect an exponential rise in output per manhour (the manufacturing sector being the prototype), and (2) nonprogressive activities, which permit few and only sporadic increases in productivity (prototypical here are the personal service sector and the local public sector in particular). An important aspect of nonprogressive activities is that only as an exception can techniques be introduced that allow mass production. An example may be borrowed from the performing arts: As Alan Peacock (1969, p. 325) so neatly put it, "Removing Judge Brack from the cast of *Hedda Gabler* would certainly reduce labour input to Ibsen's masterpiece, but it would also destroy the product. Nor could one increase the productivity of the cast by performing the play at twice the speed."[3] Another example is the personal attention which teachers must give students because of the individuality of their problems. A second and related aspect, also

[3]The performing arts are perhaps the best example for the lagging productivity hypothesis and are the local public service sector that has been studied the most from this perspective. See, for example, Baumol and Bowen (1966, Chap. 8), Baumol and Oates (1972), Throsby and Withers (1979, Chap. 4), Leroy (1980, Chap. 3), and Withers (1980).

clearly shown by these examples, is the high labor intensity as compared to the progressive, private sector. This holds for a lot of local public services such as the court system, police and fire protection, and health care. The differences between technologically progressive and nonprogressive activities should not be overstressed of course, and there are many activities that fall somewhere in between. But we can genuinely distinguish between a sector with a low, and one with a high growth rate for labor productivity.

For our purposes in analyzing local public sector growth, the Baumol hypothesis can be developed as follows. The output of the nonprogressive, public sector (X_1) is produced solely by labor (L_1) functioning at a constant level of productivity. In the progressive private sector, on the other hand, labor productivity grows exponentially at rate r, which also produces an exponential growth in the output of this sector (X_2).[4] Thus

$$X_{1t} = a_1 \cdot L_{1t}, \tag{1}$$

$$X_{2t} = (a_2 \cdot e^{rt}) \cdot L_{2t}, \tag{2}$$

with L_2 the labor force in the private sector, t the time index, and a_1, a_2 some constant terms. From these equations we derive the ratio of government output to total output

$$\frac{X_{1t}}{X_{1t} + X_{2t}} = \frac{a_1 \cdot L_{1t}}{a_1 \cdot L_{1t} + (a_2 \cdot e^{rt}) \cdot L_{2t}} \tag{3}$$

The wage rates in both sectors are assumed to be equal, and follow the development of labor productivity in the private sector:

$$w_t = w_0 \cdot e^{rt}, \tag{4}$$

where w_0 is a constant. This assumption is plausible under the long-term perspective adopted here because in the long run there is some mobility in all labor markets.[5]

The cost per unit of output in the public sector follows from equation (4):

$$c_{1t} = \frac{(w_0 \cdot e^{rt}) \cdot L_{1t}}{a_1 \cdot L_{1t}} = w_0 \cdot e^{rt}/a_1, \tag{5}$$

---

[4] The rate of labor productivity for the nonprogressive sector $(r_1 > 0$, but $r_2 > r_1)$ may also be positive. To simplify our analysis, and without any loss of generality of the result, we assume that r_1 is equal to zero.

[5] Recent statistical evidence that the wage rate in the public sector in Switzerland follows that in the private sector is given by Kleinewefers (1978).

312   W. W. POMMEREHNE AND F. SCHNEIDER

whereas in the private sector we have

$$c_{2t} = \frac{(w_0 \cdot e^{rt}) \cdot L_{2t}}{(a_2 \cdot e^{rt}) L_{2t}} = w_0/a_2.$$ (6)

Hence the unit cost of output in the public sector (c_{1t}) will steadily increase with the rate of productivity in the private sector, while that in the private sector will remain constant.

Several properties of the system can be derived from these equations, especially if we suppose—to a large extent in accordance with reality—that the total labor force is constant.[6] First, if time (t) increases, the ratio of government output to total output (equation 3) can only be maintained if labor is transferred from the private to the public sector, resulting in a steady decline in labor in the private sector. Secondly, if labor is transferred from the private to the public sector, government exhaustive expenditure will increase faster than private sector expenditure because the same money wage rate is paid in both sectors (equation 4), but the public sector suffers from lagging productivity. To put it another way: If government exhaustive expenditure increases at the same rate as private sector expenditure, public sector output as a share of total output must steadily decrease over time as compared to private sector output.

Measuring Local Public Sector Productivity: The Quest for the Holy Grail

Measuring the increase in public sector labor productivity is indeed a quest for the Holy Grail. If direct productivity measures are full of pitfalls even in the private sector, they are much more problematic here. Problems arise because public services cannot be standardized as they are consumed *uno actu* with their production. Thus it is difficult to define and measure output, and there is a general lack of knowledge about how to adequately specify the production function. Due to the diversity of municipal services this is particularly true for the local public sector.[7]

The few empirical studies done so far on local public sector productivity can be divided into two groups: (1) Those which assume a relationship between the inputs and direct output (analogous to measurement of private

[6]The total labor force in our overall sample of 110 Swiss municipalities was 1.341 million in 1965, and 1.298 million in 1975; that is, it decreased at an average annual rate of only 0.15 percent.

[7]For a discussion of the various difficulties in measuring productivity in the local public sector, see Urban Institute (1974); Ross and Burkhead (1974); series of contributions, especially those of Hatry (1972, 1978) and Burkhead and Hennigan (1978) to two "Symposia on Productivity in Government" of the *Public Administration Review;* and a number of papers, especially those of Gannon and Paine (1975/76) and Ervin (1978/79) in the *Public Productivity Review.*

sector productivity); (2) those which take the effects as the unit of analysis, that is, output as measured in terms of benefits that are more widely defined. Despite the great differences in the concepts of productivity used, both types of studies have come to the same general conclusion, that the labor productivity growth rate is much lower in the local public sector than in the private. This is so even when it is compared to that of the private service sector, the area within the private sector that shows the smallest increase in productivity.[8] Productivity growth in the local government sector often seems to come close to zero or to be even negative.[9] John Ross and Jesse Burkhead (1974, Chap. 6), for instance, in their close analysis of local public education, welfare, police and fire protection in five major U.S. cities, state that little or no evidence of a productivity increase can be found. This conclusion is also arrived at by various recent studies done on a variety of local public services.[10] All of the authors recognize that the quality of local public services has improved, and that in some cases major technological advances have been made, but they contend that the increase in output has not been commensurate with the accompanying increase in costs. The major reason for rising costs in these service areas is, they believe, lagging productivity.

When local public sector productivity lags behind the growth rate of productivity in the private sector, does this mean that local public spending must necessarily increase over time—or that local exhaustive expenditure must increase faster than total GNP? Purely technological considerations do not answer these questions. For this an analysis of the demand for local government services is necessary, which also allows indirect testing of the lagging productivity hypothesis.

III. The Demand for Local Public Services

The Extended Model

As several authors have pointed out,[11] the development of public exhaustive expenditure, absolutely and as a share of GNP, depends on the

[8]This last is shown for the United States by Fuchs (1968), and by Gollop and Jorgenson (1977). Fuchs has found similar differences in the productivity growth of various private sectors in Western European countries.

[9]Edward Gramlich in his article in this volume quotes several studies from the Civil Service Commission (itself a government institution) showing a positive rate of productivity increase in the *federal* sector of the United States. However, this does not allow us to conclude that the same result holds for the local level.

[10]See Bradford, Malt, and Oates (1969); Bones and Allen (1973); Feldstein and Taylor (1977). The older studies are ably reviewed by Spann (1977a).

[11]Compare Lynch and Redman (1968), Bradford (1969), Keren (1972), Jackson and Ulph (1973), Bush and Mackay (1977).

demand expressed for it by the consumers/taxpayers. This demand in turn depends on the relative prices of the output units, and on the consumers/taxpayers' income. A positive rate of productivity growth in the private sector generates an income effect in addition to a relative price-substitution effect (which usually dampens the demand for public sector services), and it is possible that a rise in income will lead to a net increase in the demand.

In line with previous attempts to empirically estimate price and income elasticities of the demand for publicly provided services with the help of the median voter model,[12] we shall begin with a constant elasticity of demand function:

$$X_1^{IN} = c \cdot (p \cdot t)^{\alpha} \cdot Y^{\beta}, \tag{7}$$

where X_1^{IN} is the consumable *quantity* of the local public service, p its price, t the share of municipal tax receipts that the median voter's local tax constitutes, Y the median voter/taxpayer's real income, α, β the price and income elasticities of the median voter's demand, and c a constant.

Besides these determinants of the median voter's demand for local government services, we must also consider the fact that the government sector's output may have no pure public good characteristics. We have thus introduced a crowding equation first used by Borcherding and Deacon (1972):

$$X_1^{IN} = X_1 \cdot N^{-\theta}, \tag{8}$$

where X_1 is the physical quantity, and N the number of consumers of public services that coincides with the group of voters/taxpayers. The crowding parameter θ indicates whether the service under consideration has pure public good ($\theta = 0$) or pure private good ($\theta = 1$) characteristics. An additional factor influencing demand is population per capita of labor force, used to try to reflect the variation in demand arising from differences in household size. Introducing these additional factors into equation (7) and rearranging the demand function leads to

$$X_1 = c \cdot p^{\alpha} \cdot t^{\alpha} \cdot Y^{\beta} \cdot N^{\gamma} \cdot (B/N)^{\delta}, \tag{9}$$

where $\gamma = \theta(1 + \alpha)$, (B/N) is the ratio of total population to total labor force, and δ the elasticity of demand for local public sector output related to household size. The theoretically expected signs are negative for price elasticity α and positive for income elasticity β, and for the elasticities of demand related to labor force and household size, γ and δ.

---

[12]See Bergstrom and Goodman (1973) and, applying this approach to Swiss municipalities, Pommerehne (1978).

Local government exhaustive expenditure equals the quantity of local public sector output demanded times the price of the local service

$$X_1 \cdot p = E = c \cdot p^{(\alpha+1)} \cdot t^\alpha \cdot Y^\beta \cdot N^\gamma \cdot (B/N)^\delta, \tag{10}$$

where E is government exhaustive expenditure. This equation can be used to empirically examine the hypothesis that the local public sector is nonprogressive, that is, that it functions at a constant level of productivity over time.

Empirical Examination of the Model's Predictive Ability

As the extended Baumol approach predicts specific growth rates for government exhaustive expenditure, the estimated coefficients of equation (10) can be used to make forecasts which are then compared to the actually observed data. If productivity in the local public sector is indeed stagnant, and if the demand for local public goods is adequately captured by the median voter model, then the level of exhaustive expenditure predicted must come very close to the actual one.

The model also lets us predict the relative growth rates of specific exhaustive expenditure items. If we ignore cross-price elasticities of demand among the various local government services and assume that the relative price for all spending categories increases at the same rate, we can predict that government exhaustive expenditure *ceteris paribus* will most rapidly increase over time for those services for which the income elasticity of demand is the highest, and the price elasticity of demand the lowest (in absolute terms). Conversely, it will increase least rapidly for those having the lowest income elasticity and highest price elasticity of demand. From this we can expect a close positive relationship between the rank orders of the predicted and actual growth rates.

The model's predictive ability is tested with data from 48 Swiss municipalities having direct democracy for the period 1965–1975. The median voter approach is suitable for direct democracies in Switzerland as only a small number of signatures is needed to have an issue brought before the local assembly, which is open to all voters/taxpayers who wish to participate. Decisions may be taken in the assembly, but in most cases their final approval is subject to confirmation or rejection by the whole electorate in an obligatory referendum held afterwards. As all of these municipalities also have the institution of optional referendum, we can expect the government and public bureaucracy to have only a small amount of leeway for deviating from the wishes of the voters/taxpayers.

As our data base allows us only to explain and forecast the spending levels of the years 1965 and 1975, a cross-section analysis is done. For our forecast purposes equation (10) is rewritten in per capita of labor force terms in order to avoid problems of heteroskedasticity in estimation, which gives us estimation equation

$$\ln(E/N)_{ij} = \ln c^*_{ij} + \alpha \ln t_i + \beta \ln Y_i + (\gamma - 1) \ln N_i \\ + \delta \ln (B/N)_i + e_{ij}, \tag{11}$$

where the subscript $i = 1,2\ldots$ m refers to the municipalities, $j = 1,2,\ldots$ n refers to the various local government services, e_{ij} is the random term capturing all other influences, and $\ln c^*_{ij}$ equals $\ln c_{ij} + (\alpha + 1) \ln p_{ij}$. As it is assumed that p_{ij} is constant over units and municipalities, the term $(\alpha + 1) \ln p_{ij}$ can be added to the intercept $\ln c_{ij}$. The right-hand side parameters of equation (11) have been estimated by OLS techniques for the base year 1965, and are used to forecast the level of real government exhaustive expenditure in 1975.[13] The average annual growth rate over the whole period can now be calculated and compared with the actual annual growth of real government exhaustive expenditure per capita. Real exhaustive expenditure per capita (E/N) is defined as the average municipal exhaustive expenditure for 1965/66 and 1975/76, each figure divided by the total labor force and deflated by the government sector price index (assuming a zero growth rate of labor productivity; average values of expenditure are taken in order to reduce the occurrence of outliers due to, for example, bulky investments). This price index corresponds to the private sector price index, less the rate of increase in productivity in the private sector.[14] Real income of the median voter is defined as the income of the voter/taxpayer holding the median income position after federal and state government taxes are deducted, deflated by the private sector price index.

The OLS estimation of equation (11) for 1965 has the result[15]

$$\ln (E/N)_{\text{Aggregate}} = - 4.86 \ln c^* - 0.77^* \ln t + 1.07^{**} \ln Y \\ (-5.19) (6.36)$$

$$ -0.71^{**} \ln N + 0.08 \ln (B/N) \\ (-3.71) (0.40)$$

---

[13]It should be noted that this procedure is only applicable when there is a static labor force and/or when the output of the public sector is purely private. In our case we can observe increases as well as decreases in the labor force in the municipalities; however, as was computed from the coefficients, the calculated degree of publicness θ does not significantly differ from 1.

[14]This price index is used, as our model is, in terms of relative prices (p_2/p_1) rather than absolute prices (an alternative procedure would be to let the private sector output the numéraire commodity and set $p_1 = 1$). As an approximation for the private sector price index the GDP deflator is used. The growth rate of productivity in the private sector for the period examined is calculated from GDP data for the municipalities, subtracting wages and salaries in the public sector and using the private sector labor force as the denominator.

[15]The figures in parentheses are the t-values; one asterisk indicates statistical significance at the 95 percent level, two asterisks at the 99 percent level of confidence; $\bar{R}^2$ is the coefficient of determination, adjusted for the degrees of freedom (d.f.).

Table 1

Actual and Predicted Average Level and Average Growth Rate
of Local Government Aggregate Real Exhaustive Expenditure,
48 Direct Democracies, 1965-1975

Actual Average Level of Expenditure 1975 (SFr. per capita)	Predicted Average Level of Expenditure 1975 (SFr. per capita)	Theil's Coefficient of Inequality[a]	Actual Average Annual Growth Rate 1965-1975 (%)	Predicted Average Annual Growth Rate 1965-1975 (%)
3304	3300	0.24	7.85	7.69

[a] A Theil coefficient of inequality greater than 1 indicates a forecast worse than a naive one (trend extrapolation); a coefficient close to 0 shows an accurate prediction.

$$\overline{R}^2 = 0.75; \text{d.f.} = 42; \text{residual variance} = 0.026.$$

The model's overall performance is very good; it explains 75 percent of the endogenous variable's variance, and all elasticities have the expected signs and are—with the exception of that for household size—highly statistically significant. Thus the voter/taxpayer's demand for publicly provided goods seems to be adequately captured.

Going back to our first hypothesis, the estimated coefficients are used to predict ex ante the levels of aggregate real exhaustive expenditure for each of the 48 direct democracies in 1975, and then to calculate their average annual growth rate over 1965-1975.[16] The results shown in Table 1 are highly favorable for the Baumol hypothesis of stagnant productivity in the local public sector. The predictions of the level and the calculated growth rate come very close to the actual values. As the low value of Theil's coefficient of inequality indicates, the result holds for a vast majority of the 48 municipalities.

Referring to the second hypothesis, the predicted levels and calculated growth rates for real exhaustive public expenditures, disaggregated by function, do indeed show a pattern between the predicted and actual growth rates (see Table 2).

When the actual growth of expenditure for an individual spending category is higher (or lower) than the actual increase in aggregate expenditure, the predictions made with the help of equation (11) show in all cases the same deviation from the predicted aggregate growth rate. This result is quite good, as can also be seen from the close positive relationship between the rank orders of the calculated and actual annual growth rates. The Spearman's rank

---

[16]For this and the following growth rate computations, the ex post predicted levels of exhaustive expenditure for the 48 direct democracies are used.

Table 2

Actual and Predicted Average Levels and Average Growth Rates of Local Government Real Exhaustive Expenditure by Function, 48 Direct Democracies, 1965–1975 [a]

Municipal Service Sector	Actual Average Expend. Level 1975 (SFr. per capita)	Predicted Average Expend. Level 1975 (SFr. per capita)	Theil's Coefficient of Inequality	Actual Average Annual Growth Rate 1965–1975 (%)	Predicted Average Annual Growth Rate 1965–1975 (%)	Intercept (ln c*)	Tax price (α)	Income (β)	Labor Force (γ)	Household Size (δ)	$\bar{R}^2$
							— OLS-Estimates for Real Exhaustive Expenditure by Function, 1965 [b] / Elasticities of Demand Relating to:				
Administration	322	317	0.32	5.00	4.80	−12.07	−0.72** (−3.04)	1.67** (6.24)	−1.06** (−3.49)	−0.36 (−1.06)	0.55
Law, police and fire protection	112	108	0.35	5.80	4.62	−3.47	−0.58* (−2.18)	0.53 (1.75)	−0.27 (−0.79)	0.68 (1.77)	0.36
Education	938	933	0.24	7.23	6.60	−3.95	−0.32 (−1.50)	0.73** (3.00)	−0.28 (−0.10)	0.78* (2.53)	0.49
Health, hospital	171	168	0.28	5.11	4.84	−18.33	−2.02** (−4.18)	2.00** (3.65)	−1.31** (−2.10)	−0.48 (−0.69)	0.47
Social assistance	319	306	0.22	7.71	7.66	−0.41	−0.80* (−2.52)	0.61 (1.68)	−0.25 (−0.61)	1.26** (2.75)	0.53
Municipal roads	320	318	0.26	4.54	4.10	−6.85	−0.77** (−2.80)	1.23** (3.95)	−0.96* (−2.69)	0.05 (0.12)	0.46
Environmental protection	1150	1046	0.29	11.62	9.00	−8.59	−1.19** (−4.08)	1.46** (4.44)	−1.33** (−3.55)	−0.34 (−0.82)	0.51

[a] Due to rounding errors the seven actual average levels of exhaustive expenditures do not sum up accurately to the actual average level in Table 1.

[b] The figures in parentheses are the t-values. One asterisk indicates statistical significance at the 95 percent level, two asterisks at the 99 percent level of confidence.

order correlation coefficient is 0.893. If we assume that the growth rate of productivity in the local public sector is zero and that the increase in demand for local public services is adequately captured, we would expect exactly this result. We will therefore use the forecast method as our reference approach for investigating the extent to which pressure on the supply side causes unbalanced growth in democracies having a lesser degree of direct control by the voters/taxpayers.

IV. The Supply Side of Local Public Services

The Institutional Framework

In contrast to the direct democracies, the 62 representative democracies seem to offer many more opportunities for deviating from the voters' preferences. Only some of them have the obligatory referendum,[17] and the institution of optional referendum is also rare. Voters can express their wishes in a binding manner at general elections, but these occur at only discontinuous intervals. Even then they are limited to voting for the party or candidate whose program best fits their preferences, rather than exercising direct control over the issues themselves. Except at election time the voters are unable to control the government, and they thus have only weak incentives for trying to do so. In view of this we can expect the government to pursue its own goals to a greater extent, and also to be more susceptible to pressure from economic interest groups and the public bureaucracy.

As several authors have argued,[18] under such conditions the interactions of those involved in local politics will tend to positively influence local public expenditure. An increase in local exhaustive expenditure may benefit the bureaucracy as well as specific interest groups. As is illustrated below, the bureaucracy may act to reap utility from a large public budget, which results in more of a public service being provided and in output of services growing faster than is demanded by the median voter/taxpayer. By doing this it is able to extract for itself a large part of the consumer surplus created by its services which otherwise could not be internalized because of the nonappropriability of its "profit." Another view is that public bureaucrats may have additional arguments in their utility function besides public sector output and the size of the budget, such as specific inputs (e.g., better equipment, a larger staff than otherwise). Appropriation of these inputs allows the bureaucracy to acquire

---

[17]Whether or not the government must hold a referendum usually depends on how much the project costs. Thus it is common in Swiss representative democracies for a big project to be cut up into pieces of such size that no referendum is required.

[18]A survey of the various studies is given in Pommerehne and Frey (1978).

parts of the consumer surplus by ways other than maximizing output, that is, it provides public sector services at a higher than minimal cost and reaps benefit from the slack. All these incentives work—*ceteris paribus*—towards a higher level of exhaustive expenditure in representative democracies than in direct ones. Moreover, the government in a representative democracy may use its greater financial leeway to take actions based on ideology or to help it secure reelection. It may restrict its additional spending towards the end of an election period; but what interests us here, under a long-term consideration, is that the overall trend which can be expected in local public spending will be upward. Thus our hypothesis concerning the influence of institutional differences is that *ceteris paribus* the level and rate of growth of public expenditures will be higher in representative democracies than in direct democracies.

Empirical Examination of Institutional Influences

Whether the level and rate of growth of government exhaustive expenditure *ceteris paribus* is higher in representative democracies can be measured in two ways: (1) by explicitly modelling the behavior of government and interest groups (including the public bureaucracy) when there is weak control by the voters/taxpayers; (2) by simulating how big the expenditure increase in representative democracies would be if there were the same strong control as in direct democracies.

We have chosen the second method because none of the models known to us adequately captures and isolates the direct influence of the behavior of government and the interest groups. We therefore used the estimated coefficients of the median voter model for the 48 direct democracies to simulate the levels and growth rates of the 62 representative democracies under *ceteris paribus* conditions.[19] For purposes of comparison we have also added the forecast results gained when the median voter model is applied to representative democracies in order to estimate the various elasticities of demand (though we are aware that the model is inappropriate in this institutional framework). The results of the simulations, the actual values and the predicted increases in government exhaustive expenditure are presented in Table 3.

The level and computed growth rate for aggregate expenditure is, as expected, far below the actual increase in the simulation results. The simulated growth rate, for instance, is 5.68 percent per annum, accounting for

---

[19]The following simulations have been done under *ceteris paribus* conditions; that is they capture the much smaller income increase that occurs in the representative democracies as compared to the direct democracies (see Appendix Table A-1).

Table 3

Simulated, Actual, and Predicted Average Levels and Average Growth Rates of Local Government Real Exhaustive Expenditure, Aggregate and by Function, for 62 Representative Democracies, 1965–1975[a]

Municipal Service Sector	Simulated Expenditures[b]		Actual Expenditures		Predicted Expenditures[c]		
	Simulated Average Expend. Level 1975 (SFr. per capita)	Simulated Average Annual Growth Rate 1965–1975 (%)	Actual Average Expend. Level 1975 SFr. per capita	Actual Average Annual Growth Rate 1965–1975 (%)	Predicted Average Expend. Level 1975 (SFr. per capita)	Theil's Coefficient of Inequality	Predicted Average Annual Growth Rate 1965–1975 (%)
Aggregate	2141	5.68	2954	8.05	2981	0.39	8.50
Administration	210	2.20	292	4.68	424	0.67	9.10
Law, police and fire protection	80	4.55	131	5.26	112	0.57	5.32
Education	526	2.08	784	5.45	854	0.71	7.55
Health, hospital	54	1.15	172	4.08	160	0.69	12.91
Social assistance	267	7.58	271	8.10	167	0.91	4.80
Municipal roads	259	3.10	322	4.00	578	0.78	10.52
Environmental protection	715	8.06	982	10.55	650	0.27	6.72

[a] Due to rounding errors the seven actual average levels of exhaustive expenditures do not sum up accurately to the aggregate.

[b] The growth rates of the 62 representative democracies are simulated by using the estimated coefficients of the median voter model for the 48 direct democracies. The levels of expenditure for the different municipal service sectors are then calculated for the years 1965 and 1975, and from these the growth rates.

[c] The predicted growth rates are calculated by applying the median voter model to the 62 representative democracies. The model is estimated for the 62 representative democracies for 1965 and the estimated coefficients are then used to predict the levels of expenditure for the municipal services for 1965 and 1975. The growth rates are then calculated from the predicted levels.

only 70.6 percent of the observed increase in aggregate expenditure (8.05 percent per annum). All of the individual spending categories are likewise underestimated. These results indicate that *ceteris paribus* there was a greater increase in public spending in representative democracies than in direct ones, due to the weaker control of government. There was also a greater divergency between the simulated and actual ranking orders of the growth rates for the various service categories than was predicted for municipalities having direct democracy (the Spearman's rank order correlation coefficient is 0.633).

The amount of the additional effect that the weaker control of government and bureaucracy had on expenditure growth can be calculated. When we correct the forecast for representative democracies (70.6 percent of actual expenditure increase) by the same amount as is *not* explained for direct democracies (2.9 percent, computed from Table 1), then about 72 percent of the actual expenditure growth rate for representative democracies is captured. Thus roughly 28 percent of the actual increase may be due to pressure on the supply side.

It is possible to question the adequacy of our procedure. It may be that, contrary to our hypothesis, representative democracies do *not* offer greater leeway for deviating from the median voter's wishes, and that the median voter model is still applicable. If we were to apply it and then forecast expenditure growth, the rates so predicted might come closer to the actual ones than those resulting when the coefficients for the direct democracies are used. As the right side of Table 3 shows, the growth rate of the aggregate does indeed come somewhat closer (there is an overprediction of almost 6 percent), but there is no consistent relationship among the predicted and actual growth rates of the expenditures by category. Indeed, the Spearman's rank order correlation coefficient is −0.809, indicating a strong negative relationship between the predicted and actual rank orders. Moreover, if the median voter model is applied for democracies with weak voter/taxpayer control of the government and bureaucracy, it must be remembered that the estimated coefficients will be biased and will not reflect the median voter demand—precisely because of the institutional framework.[20]

---

[20]This becomes clear when the OLS estimate for the aggregate exhaustive expenditure is considered:

$$\ln (E/N) = -1.58 \ln c^* -0.42^{**} \ln t + 0.49^* \ln Y$$
$$(-2.31) \qquad (2.06)$$
$$-0.35^* \ln N + 0.08 \ln (B/N)$$
$$(-2.17) \qquad (0.63)$$
$$\bar{R}^2 = 0.30; \text{ d.f. } = 57; \text{ residual variance} = 0.034.$$

Comparison with the estimate for direct democracies shows that the coefficients for the income and price elasticity variables are now much less statistically significant and much smaller in absolute size. Only 30 percent of the variance of the endogenous variable is statistically explained; and comparison of the residual variances of the error term with the $\hat{F}$-test indicates a significantly inferior result (at the 95 percent confidence level) as compared with that for direct democracies.

V. Discussion and Conclusions

It is obvious that there are reasons besides those discussed here which could also explain the increase in government exhaustive expenditures in representative democracies, so that our conclusions about the influence of supply side pressure on public expenditure growth may be overdrawn. Let us agree that other forces are also at work, and that the influence of institutional differences on unbalanced growth may thus be relatively weaker. Let us also forget the precise figure of 28 percent additional exhaustive expenditure due to the assumed pressure of the government and interest groups in our representative democracy sample.

It can be argued, for instance, that a part of the *ceteris paribus* greater expenditure increase in these democracies relates to changes in the environment. One example would be growing population and increasing urbanization, both of which lead to more frequent and more intensive interactions among people, with the consequence that the cost of providing a *given* amount of public service increases. However, it would still have to be explained why such a relationship should hold in the case of representative democracies, and not for direct democracies. One could argue that representative democracies usually have a larger population and encompass a greater urbanized area than do direct democracies. This is true for Switzerland. But if we drop the eight municipalities having more than 100,000 inhabitants each from the sample of representative democracies, those remaining are similar in size to the direct democracies but there is still no major change in our forecast results—and no major improvement in forecast precision.[21] There are many other arguments and objections which are per se quite correct (e.g., the possibly unequal rise in input prices of the various public services among municipalities, or the nonneglectability of cross-price elasticities); but it would still have to be shown why they should hold more for representative democracies than for direct ones.[22] As predictive ability is one of the best ways to test the validity of an approach, it would have to be shown that a modified approach which takes account of these influences would have equally good or even superior predictive ability than our model does.

Our discussion so far has only dealt with the additional influence that institutional differences may have on public spending. Going back to the beginning of the paper, we can ask ourselves what does lagging productivity really mean? It may mean that there is already slack in the provision of public

[21] This also holds when additional variables are included in our estimation equations, such as population density, degree of agglomeration, and other environmental variables which may account for an increase in the cost per unit.

[22] Table A-1 shows for both samples the means of the actual values of levels and growth rates for all dependent and independent variables, as well as their standard deviations. The variance is also analyzed for the dependent variables (correcting with co-factors, using the same independent variables as in the regressions); the computed F-statistics show that there is no statistically significant difference between the samples.

services—even in direct democracies. As Peacock and Wiseman (1979, p. 12) have put it,

> [w]e are not obliged to believe, *pace* Baumol and others that the cause of unbalanced growth lies in the inherently greater labor intensity in the public sector compared with the private sector. We know of no evidence to suggest that the *technical* barriers opposing in the public sector are higher than in the private sector. We suspect that the institutional barriers are greater.

This would mean that, besides the differential impact of the institutional influences, there is some additional supply side pressure in *both* types of democracies.

Appendix

Table A-1

Means and Standard Deviations of the Dependent and Independent Variables, and $\hat{F}$-Statistics of the One-Way Analysis of Variance[a]

	48 Direct Democracies			62 Representative Democracies			$\hat{F}$-test	
	Levels (SFr.)		Growth Rates[c] (%)	Levels (SFr.)		Growth Rates (%)		
							Level (SFr.)	Level (SFr.)
Variable[b]	1965	1975	1965–1975	1965	1975	1965–1975	1965	1975
Aggregate exhaustive expenditure	1680 (1115)	3304 (2503)	7.85	1533 (59)	2960 (1516)	8.05	2.06 (42;2)	2.03 (42;2)
Administration	205 (163)	322 (257)	5.00	197 (157)	292 (271)	4.68	0.87 (42;2)	0.94 (42;2)
Law, police and fire protection	59 (45)	112 (97)	5.80	76 (45)	131 (88)	5.26	1.12 (42;2)	1.24 (42;2)
Education	484 (269)	938 (556)	7.23	461 (332)	784 (640)	5.45	0.35 (42;2)	1.74 (42;4)
Health, hospital	93 (129)	171 (265)	5.11	98 (152)	172 (272)	4.08	0.39 (42;2)	0.14 (42;4)
Social assistance	167 (151)	319 (252)	7.71	123 (83)	271 (326)	8.10	1.34 (42;2)	0.94 (42;2)
Municipal roads	240 (223)	320 (240)	4.54	229 (175)	322 (322)	4.00	0.78 (42;2)	0.31 (42;2)
Environmental protection	432 (626)	1150 (853)	11.62	349 (171)	982 (582)	10.55	1.87 (42;2)	1.56 (42;2)
Tax price[d]	6.24 (2.91)	10.61 (5.60)	4.75	5.29 (4.38)	7.87 (5.57)	3.70		
Median income[d]	8.193 (2.298)	21.902 (2.855)	9.30	8.013 (1.599)	20.339 (1.898)	8.85		
Labor force[d]	5.624 (3.828)	5.656 (3.737)	0.05	19.445 (40.544)	18.655 (38.403)	−0.40		
Household size[d]	2.012 (1.014)	2.146 (1.100)	0.06	1.766 (1.524)	1.810 (1.422)	0.30		

[a] The standard deviations are given in the parentheses below the means of the levels, the parentheses below the $\hat{F}$-statistics show the degrees of freedom.

[b] All real exhaustive expenditure data are per capita values.

[c] The means of the growth rates are calculated averaging the *individual* growth rates of the 48 and 62 democracies.

[d] Co-factor for the one-way analysis of variance of the expenditure variables.

References

Amacher, Ryan C., Robert D. Tollisson, and Thomas D. Willet, "Budget Size in Democracy: A Review of the Arguments," *Public Finance Quarterly*, 3 (July 1975), pp. 99-121.

Baumol, William J., "The Macroeconomics of Unbalanced Growth: The Anatomy of Urban Crisis," *American Economic Review*, 57 (June 1967), pp. 415-426.

_____, and William G. Bowen, *Performing Arts: The Economic Dilemma*. Cambridge, Mass.: MIT Press, 1966.

_____, and Wallace E. Oates, "The Cost Disease of the Personal Services and the Quality of Life," *Skandinaviska Enskilda Banken Quarterly Review*, 1 (No. 2, 1972), pp. 44-54.

Bergstrom, Theodore C., and Robert P. Goodman, "Private Demand for Public Goods," *American Economic Review*, 63 (June 1973), pp. 280-296.

Bones, Erman P., and L. G. Allen, *The Outputs of the Hospital Industry: A Proposal for Their Identification*. Mimeograph. Ottawa, University of Ontario, 1973.

Borcherding, Thomas E., and Robert T. Deacon, "The Demand for the Services of Non-Federal Governments," *American Economic Review*, 62 (Dec. 1972), pp. 891-901

Bradford, David F., "Balance on Unbalanced Growth," *Zeitschrift für Nationalökonomie*, 29 (No. 3-4, 1969), pp. 291-304.

_____, R. A. Malt, and Wallace E. Oates, "The Rising Cost of Local Public Services: Some Evidence and Reflections," *National Tax Journal*, 12 (June 1969), pp. 185-202.

Burkhead, Jesse and Patrick J. Hennigan, "Productivity Analysis: A Search for Definition and Order," *Public Administration Review*, 38 (Jan./Feb. 1978), pp. 34-40.

Bush, Winston C., and Robert J. Mackay, "Private versus Public Sector Growth." In Thomas E. Borcherding, ed., *Budgets and Bureaucrats: The Sources of Government Growth*. Durham, N.C.: Duke University Press, 1977, pp. 188-210.

Ervin, Osbin L., "A Conceptual Niche for Municipal Productivity," *Public Productivity Review*, 3 (No. 2, 1978/79), pp. 15-24.

Feldstein, Martin, and Amy Taylor, *The Rapid Rise of Hospital Cost*. Mimeograph. Cambridge, Mass., Harvard University, 1977.

Fuchs, Victor, *The Service Economy*. New York: Columbia University Press, 1968.

Gannon, Martin J., and Frank T. Paine, "Factors Affecting Productivity in the Public Service: A Managerial Viewpoint," *Public Productivity Review*, 1 (No. 2, 1975/76), pp. 44-48.

Gollop, Frank M., and Dale W. Jorgenson, *U.S. Productivity Growth by Industries, 1947-1973*. Mimeograph. Cambridge, Mass., Harvard University, 1977.

Hatry, Harry P., "The Status of Productivity Measurement in the Public Sector," *Public Administration Review*, 38 (Jan./Feb. 1978), pp. 28-33.

_____, "Issues in Productivity Measurement for Local Governments," *Public Administration Review*, 32 (Nov./Dec. 1972), pp. 776-784.

Jackson, Peter M., and D. T. Ulph, *The Relative Price of Public Sector and Private Sector Goods*. Mimeograph. Stirling, University of Stirling, 1973.

Keren, Michael J., "Macroeconomics of Unbalanced Growth: Comment," *American Economic Review*, 62 (March 1972), p. 149.

Kleinewefers, Henner, "Die Personalbestände im öffentlichen Dienst der Schweiz 1950 bis 1975" (The Number Employed in the Public Sector in Switzerland, 1950 to 1975), *Schweizerische Zeitschrift für Volkswirtschaft und Statistik*, 114 (Sept. 1978), pp. 421-446.

Leroy, Dominique, *Economie des arts du spectacle vivant* (Economics of the Performing Arts). Paris: Economica, 1980.

Lynch, Lawrence, K., and E. L. Redman, "Macroeconomics of Unbalanced Growth: Comment," *American Economic Review*, 58 (Sept. 1968), pp. 152-155.

Nutter, G. Warren, *Growth of Government in the West*. Washington, D.C.: American Enterprise Institute, 1978.

Peacock, Alan T., "Welfare Economics and Public Subsidies to the Arts," *Manchester School of Economic and Social Studies*, 37 (Dec. 1969), pp. 323-335.

_____, and Jack Wiseman, "Approaches to the Analysis of Government Expenditure Growth," *Public Finance Quarterly*, 7 (Jan. 1979), pp. 3-23.

Pommerehne, Werner W., "Quantitative Aspects of Federalism: A Study of Six Countries." In Wallace E. Oates, ed., *The Political Economy of Fiscal Federalism*. Lexington: Heath, 1977, pp. 275-355.

———, "Institutional Approaches to Public Expenditure: Empirical Evidence from Swiss Municipalities," *Journal of Public Economics*, 9 (April 1978), pp. 255-280.

———, and Bruno S. Frey, "Bureaucratic Behavior in Democracy: A Case Study," *Public Finance*, 33 (No. 1-2, 1978), pp. 98-112.

Ross, John P., and Jesse Burkhead, *Productivity in the Local Government Sector*. Lexington: Heath, 1974.

Spann, Robert M., "Rates of Productivity Change and the Growth of State and Local Government Expenditure." In Thomas E. Borcherding, ed., *Budgets and Bureaucrats: The Sources of Government Growth*. Durham, N.C.: Duke University Press, 1977a, pp. 100-129.

———, "The Macroeconomics of Unbalanced Growth and the Expanding Public Sector," *Journal of Public Economics*, 8 (Dec. 1977b), pp. 397-404.

A Symposium: Productivity in Government, *Public Administration Review*, 32 (Nov./Dec. 1972), pp. 739-850.

A Symposium: Productivity in Government, *Public Administration Review*, 38 (Jan./Feb. 1978), pp. 1-86.

Tarschys, Daniel, "The Growth of Public Expenditures: Nine Modes of Explanation," *Scandinavian Political Studies*, 10 (1975), pp. 9-31.

Throsby, C. David, and Glenn A. Withers, *The Economics of the Performing Arts*. Melbourne and London: Edward Arnold, 1979.

Urban Institute, ed., *Measuring the Effectiveness of Basic Municipal Services*. Washington, D.C.: Urban Institute, 1974.

Withers, Glenn A., "Unbalanced Growth and the Demand for Performing Arts: An Econometric Analysis," *Economic Inquiry*, 46 (Jan. 1980), pp. 735-742.

Résumé

Cet article analyse trois facteurs pour expliquer une croissance non équilibrée entre le secteur public et le secteur privé:

1. une productivité retardataire dans le secteur public comparée à celle du secteur privé
2. une demande en hausse pour les services publics
3. une pression du côté de l'offre, de la part de l'Etat et des groupes d'intérêts (y compris la bureaucratie publique), concernant des dépenses publiques.

L'examen empirique a été mené avec des municipalités suisses, ayant une démocratie directe ou représentative, sous la forme d'une prévision des niveaux et d'un calcul des taux de croissance moyenne annuelle des activités publiques locales pour la période 1965-75. Les résultats attendus laissent penser que l'augmentation des dépenses exhaustives des démocraties directes peut être fort bien prévue si l'on tient compte de l'augmentation de la demande et si l'on suppose un taux de croissance zéro de la productivité dans le secteur public. Dans le cas de démocraties représentatives, toutefois, une part beaucoup plus petite de la croissance des dépenses réelles peut être prévue, quand on suppose que s'exerce le même fort contrôle des électeurs/contribuables que celui qui existe dans les démocraties directes. Une analyse plus poussée des résultats laisse penser que l'on devrait considérer les influences qui s'exercent du côté de l'offre avec plus d'attention qu'on ne le fait habituellement.

327–340

9330
8210
8242

The Macro-economics of Worksharing: A Simple Simulation Approach

W. Siddré
E. de Regt*

1. Introduction

We investigate the macro-economic implications of a reduction in the length of the working-week, emphasizing the opportunity cost of this kind of worksharing. For this purpose a macro-economic model, not empirically tested, describing a small open economy was constructed. Non-linearities prevent us from deriving the reduced-form equations of the simultaneous model, therefore we had to use a numerical simulation approach.

Why do we want to study the repercussions of worksharing policies? Since the second half of the seventies, a high unemployment rate has persisted in the Netherlands. Attempts to cure this unemployment by means of fiscal, monetary and other policies do not appear to have been very successful. Therefore, keeping declining economic growth in mind, the labour unions and other observers of the economic scene argue in favor of worksharing (a redistribution of the available labour demand among total labour supply).

Secondly, even if "all three objectives (full employment, price level stability and efficient division of output) can be achieved by an appropriate mix of tax, expenditure and monetary policies" (Musgrave, this volume), and in our models it is possible to achieve these targets (certainly the first objective), there remains a case for evaluating alternative policies. In his article in this volume, Musgrave pleads for public employment when unemployment is "selective." The authors feel, however, that even in such a situation an

*The authors gratefully acknowledge the suggestions and comments received during the Congress of the International Institute of Public Finance, Jerusalem 1980. We especially thank A. van Bakhoven, R. Boelaert, I. Byatt and H. van Miltenburg for their comments during the Congress. Moreover we want to thank J. Paelinck, A. van Schaik, J. Theeuwes, H. Tjan and D. Wolfson for their stimulating remarks. During the revision of the paper, we very much appreciated the editorial suggestions of Robert H. Haveman. All remaining obscurities remain ours.

Public Finance and Public Employment. Proceedings of the 36th Congress of the International Institute of Public Finance. Jerusalem, 1980.

economist should try to compare the effectiveness of alternative policies. One of the other policies to be compared with public employment might be worksharing. Within our framework of analysis, however, we cannot evaluate the cost-effectiveness of targeted public employment programs, designed to reduce pockets of unemployment. Our model has a macro-economic character.[1]

Besides public employment—here defined as governmental demand for labour—and worksharing schemes, other policy alternatives, such as a wage policy, a policy designed to reduce bottlenecks in the labour market and some tax policies, can simultaneously be evaluated within our macro-economic framework.

In section 2 we present a heuristic description of the model. In section 3 a short description of the simulation approach used is given, and some simulation results, such as public expenditures, public employment and tax policies, are presented. Section 4 analyzes different schemes of shorter hours, and section 5 offers our evaluation.[2]

2. Model Characteristics

Introductory Remarks

We present here a sketch of a macro-economic model of a small open economy—in this case, the Dutch economy—and attempt to capture some of its important features with 18 behavioral equations.[3] Several restrictive assumptions, however, reduce the richness of the economy described. The most important simplifications are (1) a one-commodity and one-type-of-labour economy, (2) the absence of a monetary sector, (3) flexibility of commodity prices, (4) wages only dependent on price movements, and (5) a fully flexible exchange rate. By means of these assumptions we integrated demand- and supply-economics in a systematic fashion. Therefore, using a comparative static analysis, various policies, including shorter hours (see section 4), can be analyzed within the same framework.

In a sense the model has classical features: flexible prices guarantee an equilibrium of quantities supplied and demanded in the domestic commod-

---

[1]In another type of model shorter hours could be designed for special age, professional or regional groups. The effectiveness of worksharing could then be compared with targeted public employment.

[2]In Siddré and de Regt (1981) the model and the simulation results presented below are more thoroughly analyzed. This discussion paper is available on request.

[3]In the formal presentation of the model, we add roughly 40 definitional equations to these behavioral equations. This formal presentation can be found in our discussion paper.

ity market. However, wage movements do not necessarily equate supply and demand in the labour market. Imperfections within that market determine an employment level below notional demand and supply. A flexible exchange rate eliminates surpluses or deficits on the current account of the balance of payments. The opportunity cost of policy alternatives cannot occur in the guise of a balance of payments disequilibrium.

Domestic Production

The supply of commodities in the private sector of the economy is derived from static profit maximization subject to an aggregate production function as a technical constraint. The production function is a CES-function with constant returns to scale, with both capital and labour as inputs expressed in working-hours. We abstract from technical progress. A production function with substitution between inputs may *a priori* be more favorable to worksharing than one with fixed coefficients. The latter possibility means that a reduction in working-time per labourer implies a proportional reduction of production. With substitution possibilities a loss of capacity can, at least partly, be offset.

In each period, the available capital stock is a predetermined variable depending on technical obsolescence and lagged gross investment. The capital stock is continuously fully utilized, whereas labour is not fully employed.

Profit maximization subject to a given price of domestic production and a given capital stock yields a labour demand equation with capital-hours, real wage costs and an index of labour hours as arguments. Because of imperfections of the labour market, the actual level of employment in the private sector is less than notional demand. Although capital is fully utilized, the actual level of production is smaller than the potential level, which can be obtained by substitution of the notional labour demand in the production function.

Labour Market

Unemployment and vacancies occur simultaneously because of imperfections in the labour market.[4] Two sources of unemployment can be distinguished in our model. Our employment function introduces frictional unemployment because the actual level of employment (in man-years) is always smaller than the exogenous labour supply on the one hand and the notional demand for labour on the other hand.

---

[4]Underlying reasons for these imperfections are imperfect (and not costless) information, search behavior and aggregation, see, for example, Hansen (1970) and Holt (1970).

There is, however, another source of unemployment, to be called structural unemployment. With fully utilized capital goods, labour supply can exceed labour demand. Because of our assumption of flexible commodity prices, we do want to emphasize that our model has no room for a Keynesian-type of unemployment. Private firms are not rationed in the market of final goods.

The total demand for labour in man-years in the economy can easily be obtained by adding the public demand to the private demand. By assuming the same vacancy rate in the public and private sector of the economy, total employment can be allocated to these two sectors. An increase in the exogenous public sector demand for labour reduces the employment in the private sector, but on balance the total level of employment increases: We incorporate a sort of crowding-out effect in the labour market.

We distinguish two types of wage rates. In the private sector wages are solely determined by the price-index of the consumption price. This aspect of wage formation, called a wage-price escalator, is nowadays—at least in the Netherlands—a highly disputed matter. The public sector wages are linked through a wage-trend policy to those in the private sector. A fixed ratio, not necessarily equal to one, exists between both wage rates.

Private Expenditures

Consumer expenditures depend on disposable transfers and disposable wage income; the marginal propensities to consume are allowed to differ. The fraction of total consumption spent on domestically produced goods is an increasing function of the price of imported commodities, expressed in guilders, and a decreasing function of domestically produced goods.

Gross investment demand equals realized investment and depends only on disposable profits. The same allocation scheme as with consumption between imported and domestically produced goods applies to investment. Exports depend on the competitiveness of the economy, as measured by the price of exports vis à vis the foreign price level.

Public Sector

The government, or public sector, exerts an exogenously fixed demand for domestically produced commodities. These expenditures are not of a capital nature. In the public sector itself no commodities are produced. At the same time, the government exerts an exogenous demand for labour. Finally, unemployment benefits are paid; these transfers per capita equal a constant fraction of the average wage.

Total public sector expenditures are financed by taxes: Employees pay payroll-taxes, enterprises profit-taxes and households income-taxes. Because the tax rates are exogenously fixed, public sector tax income does not necessarily equal its expenditures.

Final Remarks

In the above paragraphs we considered several blocks of equations, describing respectively the supply side, the labour market and the demand side. Obviously the model contains several links between these blocks of equations. First, however, we want to stress again the employment equation. This type of modelling of the labour market enables us to compare within the same model the effects of reducing labour market frictions and the effects of worksharing with more traditional types of fiscal policy.

Emphasizing the links between the various blocks of equations, we sketch a few important interdependencies. The notional demand for labour, after confrontation with labour supply, determines the actual level of employment. Employment determines actual production, while this production volume, together with nominal final demand, may induce price movements. This latter variable can influence wages and real wages which have feedback effects on notional labour demand. Moreover possible movements of prices also have effects on capital formation, which again may influence the desired level of labour demand.

Although a few lags are specified mainly for computational reasons, the model is highly simultaneous.[5] In our comparative static and numerical analysis the lag specification does not influence our final results.

3. Simulation Method and Some Preliminary Results

In this section we illustrate the working of the model in a very traditional way by means of some variations in exogenous variables. The repercussions of shorter hours are analyzed in section 4.

The Simulation Method

The model described in the previous section is, for various reasons, a non-linear model. We recall here the CES-production function, the

---

[5]In Siddré and de Regt (1981) we pay attention to the lags specified and to some computational aspects.

unemployment-vacancy relation and the set of equations describing the unemployment-benefit schemes. These non-linearities force us to use a numerical, simulation approach in which we define an equilibrium solution as a model solution which is reproduced period after period, if no further exogenous changes occur. A model-period does not necessarily correspond with a time unit like a quarter or a year.

The exogenous shocks are applied to the system in an initial equilibrium situation.[6] The simulation program stops when a new equilibrium solution occurs; after that we calculate the relative changes between the new and initial equilibrium solution.[7] The number of model-periods required to complete this exercise varies between 20 and 90. Some additional computations showed that in most simulations 75% of the changes from the initial equilibrium situation to the new equilibrium took place within the first 15 model-periods.

Basic Simulation Results

We present two tables with our basic simulation results.[8] In Table 1 we present the results of exogenous changes in public sector expenditures, in tax rates, in the unemployment-benefit ratio, and in the wage-trend policy. In Table 2 we represent some results of changes in exogenous variables relating to the labour market. In both tables variants with and without wage-price indexation are demonstrated.

More public sector expenditures (see columns 1 and 9 of Table 1) lead to more production and reduce unemployment (the initial level being 6.7%) and the real disposable wage income while a public sector deficit arises. Such a deficit has no further repercussions in the model. However, we constructed a second model in which, through flexible tax rates, no public sector surplus or deficit can occur. We call this second version the balanced-budget model, whereas the model of section 2 is called the unbalanced-budget model.[9] If in the balanced-budget model a public sector deficit tends to occur, the payroll tax rate and the tax rates on wage income and on unemployment-benefit income will rise.

---

[6]For a discussion of the initial equilibrium situation see Siddré and de Regt (1981).

[7]We have not attempted to provide formal proof that such a new equilibrium solution necessarily exists. However, during our simulations a new equilibrium was always reached. We stopped the iterations when the absolute change of all lagged occuring variables was less than 5.10^{-5}.

[8]We only present tables with the results of 10% exogenous shocks in one direction. Although the model is non-linear, variants in the other direction have an opposite sign and roughly the same absolute values.

[9]In this paper we do not present tables with simulation results of the balanced-budget model.

Table 1

Exogenous Changes of Policy Variables in the Unbalanced-Budget Model

Exogenous Shock / Endogenous Variables	No Wage-Price Indexation								With 75% Wage-Price Indexation							
	gf (1)	τ_1 (2)	τ_2 (3)	τ_3 (4)	τ_1,τ_2,τ_3 (5)	τ_4 (6)	μ (7)	ν (8)	gf (9)	τ_1 (10)	τ_2 (11)	τ_3 (12)	τ_1,τ_2,τ_3 (13)	τ_4 (14)	μ (15)	ν (16)
Percentage Changes																
1. Production volume in private sector	2	1	1	0	2	5	−0	−2	1	2	0	0	2	9	0	0
2. Price national product	1	−1	1	0	−0	−5	−0	−1	4	−6	6	+0	−0	−20	−1	−8
3. Employment in private sector (man-years)	2	1	1	0	2	2	−0	−2	2	2	1	0	2	5	−0	−1
4. Capital intensity	−1	0	−1	0	−1	7	+0	1	−1	1	−2	0	−1	11	+0	3
5. Labour productivity (working-hours)	−0	0	−0	0	−0	3	0	+0	−0	+0	−1	0	−0	4	+0	1
6. Average real disposable wage income	−1	1	2	0	2	4	+0	−2	−1	1	1	0	2	5	+0	−1
7. Labour cost per unit output in private sector	+0	−1	+0	0	−1	−2	0	−0	−3	−6	5	+0	−1	−18	−1	−7
Level Variables (%)																
8. Unemployment rate	5.2	6.0	5.7	6.6	5.1	5.0	6.8	8.1	5.5	5.6	6.2	6.7	5.1	3.5	6.8	7.4
9. Share of government budget surplus	−0.2	0.0	−0.2	0.0	−0.3	−0.3	0.0	0.4	−0.4	0.4	−0.6	0.0	−0.3	1.1	0.1	1.0

Columns

(1) and (9): volume of government expenditures, gf, + 10%.
(2) and (10): payroll tax rate, τ_1, − 10%.
(3) and (11): wage-income tax rate, τ_2, − 10%.
(4) and (12): unemployment-benefit income tax rate, τ_3, − 10%.
(5) and (13): payroll, wage-income, and unemployment-benefit income tax rates, τ_1,τ_2, and τ_3, − 10%.
(6) and (14): tax rate on profits, τ_4, − 10%.
(7) and (15): unemployment-benefit ratio, μ, changes from 0.80 to 0.75.
(8) and (16): wage-trend policy, ν, changes from 1.14 to 1.00.

Table 2

Exogenous Labour Market Changes in the Unbalanced-Budget Model

Exogenous Shock Endogenous Variables	No Wage-Price Indexation				With 75% Wage-Price Indexation			
	ℓhg^d (1)	ℓ^s (2)	uimp (3)	wau (4)	ℓhg^d (5)	ℓ^s (6)	uimp (7)	wau (8)
	Percentage Changes							
1. Production volume in private sector	+0	4	0	−2	0	1	0	−10
2. Price national product	+0	2	0	12	1	24	−0	91
3. Employment in private sector (man-years)	0	6	0	−1	0	4	0	−6
4. Capital intensity	+0	−3	−0	−2	0	−7	−0	−10
5. Labour productivity (working-hours)	+0	−1	0	−1	0	−3	0	−4
6. Average real disposable wage income	0	−4	0	−1	−0	−5	0	−5
7. Labour cost per unit output in private sector	−0	1	0	11	1	21	0	84
	Level Variables (%)							
8. Unemployment rate	4.4	11.3	6.6	7.6	4.5	12.7	6.6	10.9
9. Share of government budget surplus	−0.1	−0.6	0.0	−0.8	−0.2	−1.9	0.0	−3.8

Columns

(1) and (5): labour demand public sector (working-hours), ℓhg^d, + 10%.
(2) and (6): labour supply (man-years), ℓ^s, + 10%.
(3) and (7): imperfection rate of the labour market, uimp, − 10%.
(4) and (8): wage push in the first period, wau, + 10%.

Columns (5) and (13) of Table 1 show the effects of such a simultaneous change of tax rates in the unbalanced-budget model. If we lower these three tax rates, the production volume in the private sector rises and so does the real disposable wage income. Prices hardly change, labour cost per unit of output falls, and a public sector deficit appears. Our figures in columns (5) and (13) can be obtained approximately by summation of the separate changes of the tax rates mentioned in columns (2) to (4) and (10) to (12), where obvious signs occur. The endogenously determined higher tax rates due to increased public sector expenditures in the balanced-budget model ultimately result in a lower production volume and higher unemployment rate if a wage-price indexation is assumed.

In the unbalanced-budget model changes in the tax rate on profits (columns 6 and 14) have a very significant influence on the production volume; unemployment and prices decline and real disposable wage income increases. Although we do not want to emphasize the absolute levels of the changes of the variables, we do want to stress the fact that whenever profits are made reducing the taxes on profits is relatively effective compared to other policy changes. The same applies in the balanced-budget model.

Lowering the unemployment-benefit ratio (columns 7 and 15) has a very small effect in both models. Abolition of the wage-trend policy (columns 8 and 16) in the unbalanced-budget model leads to lower production volume and lower prices. In the balanced-budget model, however, the opposite effects occur.

In Table 2 we present some effects of changes in exogenous labour market variables. More labour demand in the public sector (columns 1 and 5) lowers unemployment in both models. A rising labour supply (columns 2 and 6) leads to more employment in the private sector in the unbalanced-budget model, whereas employment declines in the balanced-budget model. Real disposable wage income declines in both models.

Changes in the parameter representing labour market imperfections (columns 3 and 7) have very small effects, whereas, as one might expect, an exogenous positive change in the autonomous component of the nominal wages (columns 4 and 8) has very powerful effects. The volume of production and real disposable wage income decrease and prices strongly rise. Once more we repeat an observation made earlier: These changes have to be compared with the changes induced by changes in the other policy variables.

4. Effects of Worksharing

Outline of the Model

To introduce shorter hours into the model we use two variables representing a time-index of labour and capital hours. Reducing the time-index of labour hours can be interpreted as shorter working-hours per day or fewer working-days per week. *Mutatis mutandis* the same applies to capital hours. For reasons of simplicity we do not consider overtime work. It must, however, be emphasized that a "reduction in the basic working week is likely to result in some 'leakage' into higher overtime" (Allen, 1980, p. 2). To the extent that additional overtime takes place, our model overestimates the effects of worksharing.

We must be aware of the fact that both labour and capital hours are closely linked to each other. When there is no shift-work, the time-indices of labour and capital hours are equal. More generally, a proportional reduction of labour and capital hours does not alter the relative amount of shift-work. If capital hours, however, are modified less than proportionally, additional rotation schemes have to be introduced. Although we do not consider the cost of introducing such changes in practice, we realize that this cost may be high.

We treat two types of shorter hours, both implying permanently reduced working-hours by 10%. The assumptions with respect to the capital hours are (1) a corresponding, proportional 10% reduction, and (2) a 10% increase in capital hours through additional rotation schemes. These assumptions determine the short run effects on average and marginal productivities per manhour: they remain constant in case 1 but rise in case 2.[10] However, the average and marginal productivities per man decline in the short run.[11]

In both alternative policies, we make two different assumptions with respect to the wage rates in our model-period. First, these wage rates remain constant, except for induced changes due to wage-price indexation clauses. In this variant, the wages per hour initially rise. In the second variant the wage rates per hour initially remain constant and wage rates per model-period decline by 10%. Through the wage-trend policy, public sector employees experience the same proportional reduction; moreover, unemployment-benefits are subject to the same proportional reduction. Note that the initial wage reduction of 10% is not necessarily sufficient to reduce expenditure claims in such a way that no aggregate excess demand, and therefore no inflation, results.[12]

A few final remarks. An important assumption underlying our analysis is that worksharing policies are only adopted in the open economy considered. If shorter hour policies are adopted internationally the decline in competitiveness would be reduced, affecting our simulation results. We already mentioned that labour supply is exogenously fixed. It is, however, likely that worksharing policies will influence participation rates and that labour supply may rise. This may reduce the favorable effects on unemployment. Finally, our simulations do not take into account the adjustment-cost of the production process within the private sector. We also ignore cost of recruitment and cost of lay-offs of labour.

Simulation Results

One might argue that the initial equilibrium solution is quite sensitive to the choice of parameter values. However, this does not necessarily imply that

---

[10]Short run effects are defined as the immediate effects consequent upon shorter hours within the set of equations describing the production possibilities, *ceteris paribus*.

[11]In Siddré and de Regt (1981) we formally derive some short run effects of shorter hours within the production structure.

[12]In principle, it is possible to compute the necessary amount of initial wage reduction so that no inflation occurs. Another possibility is to adjust, in combination with wage reduction, autonomous expenditures in such a way that initially no price changes occur.

Table 3

Worksharing Policies in the Unbalanced-Budget Model

Endogenous Variables	*10% Shorter Labour and Capital Hours*				*10% Shorter Labour Hours, and 10% Longer Capital Hours*			
	No Wage-Price Indexation		*With Wage-Price Indexation*		*No Wage-Price Indexation*		*With Wage-Price Indexation*	
Exogenous Shock	*(1)*	*(2)*	*(3)*	*(4)*	*(5)*	*(6)*	*(7)*	*(8)*
	Percentage Changes							
1. Production volume in private sector	−12	−9	−21	−12	−3	−1	−5	9
2. Price national product	20	6	145	23	3	−9	17	−38
3. Employment in private sector (man-years)	2	3	−4	1	3	5	2	9
4. Capital intensity	−8	−5	−18	−8	12	16	9	34
5. Labour productivity (working-hours)	−3	−2	−8	−3	4	6	3	11
6. Average real disposable wage income	−13	−13	−18	−14	−2	−1	−3	1
7. Labour cost per unit output in private sector	15	2	126	18	6	−5	20	−36
	Level Variables (%)							
8. Unemployment rate	3.2	2.5	7.2	3.4	2.3	1.6	3.0	0.6
9. Share of government budget surplus	−0.5	0.4	−4.4	−0.7	0.0	0.9	−0.8	4.5

Columns
(1), (3), (5) and (7): No initial wage adjustment per period.
(2), (4), (6) and (8): 10% downward initial wage adjustment per period.

our simulation results themselves (in relative changes) are strongly dependent on these parameter values. To analyze this second type of dependence, we did some sensitivity analyses.[13]

Starting from the initial equilibrium solution, we modified the value of one parameter and computed the new equilibrium situation (equilibrium 2). From this equilibrium we introduced a worksharing scheme and computed the new equilibrium situation (equilibrium 3). Next we computed the relative changes between situations 2 and 3. This procedure was repeated with various parameter values and for all parameters. The resulting relative changes do not contradict the simulation results presented in this paper.

Table 3 shows that in the unbalanced-budget model worksharing policies are likely to reduce unemployment. One should remember that our

[13]The results of various sensitivity analyses are presented in Siddré and de Regt (1981).

initial level of unemployment equals 6.7%. Only in column (3), where shorter working-hours are combined with shorter capital hours and where weekly nominal wages are not adjusted apart from wage-price indexation clauses, does unemployment rise. Generally the rise in total employment occurs both in the private and public sectors. From Table 3 it is obvious, however, that private employment does not proportionally rise with shorter working-hours.

Now consider the case of shorter working and capital hours (columns 1 to 4). Introduction of worksharing has the following long run effects:[14] a lower production volume of the private sector, higher prices, a declining capital intensity, a lower labour productivity per working-hour, and a declining real disposable wage income and higher labour cost per unit of private sector output. Moreover, the public sector budget tends to become negative, except when worksharing is accompanied by an initial wage adjustment without wage-price indexation.

When shorter working-hours are combined with longer capital hours the results point the same way. When capital hours rise, the capital intensity and labour productivity per working-hour obviously rise; when a downward initial wage adjustment is assumed, prices and labour cost tend to fall. With a symmetrically working wage-price indexation plan, declining wages and prices initiate a production growth in column (8).

As regards the unbalanced-budget we draw the following conclusion. The introduction of shorter hours has a positive influence on both public and private sector employment. There are, however, important opportunity costs. If wages per hour do not change in the initial period or if capital hours per machine are increased, this opportunity cost tends to fall. The same conclusions apply to the balanced-budget model; the effects are only somewhat more pronounced and opportunity cost is generally higher. Only in those cases in Table 3 where an important public sector surplus occurs do the balanced-budget model results appear to be more favorable than in the unbalanced-budget model.

5. Summary and Evaluation

In this paper we analyzed by means of a numerical simulation approach a theoretical macro-economic model incorporating the possibility of structural unemployment. Structural unemployment consists of frictional unemployment due to an implicit unemployment-vacancy relationship and of unemployment due to a shortage of production capacity.

[14]The long run situation is defined as the new equilibrium situation when all multiplier processes are worked out.

Using some alternative specifications, we compared the effects of various policy measures within a comparative static framework. The model is not intended to stress the absolute effects on the endogenous variables of these policies, but by means of our model some conclusions can be derived with respect to the relative efficiency of these policies.

We focused our attention on more traditional instruments of economic policy, such as public employment, public expenditures, a wage policy and tax policies. Moreover we discussed a policy of shorter working-hours. The traditional instruments such as a cut in the wage rate or in the tax rates have relatively powerful effects: private sector production rises while prices and unemployment fall. Additional public sector employment or expenditures on commodities can also reduce unemployment, but the effects on production volume and prices are small. These effects can even show an opposite sign if the resulting public sector deficit leads to higher tax rates. These policy instruments are therefore to be handled with care.

Obviously, it is possible to reduce structural unemployment by means of shorter labour hours. One should, however, be aware of the opportunity cost involved. This cost appears, among other things, in the guise of lower production volumes, higher commodity prices, and lower disposable incomes. The opportunity cost can be reduced if real wages per hour do not tend to rise, or if capital hours are increased. Lengthening the capital hours vis à vis working-hours seems to be a fascinating social invention which we only discuss in a restricted macro-economic framework. We had to neglect the cost of adjustments.

It seems important to note that short run effects of worksharing can drastically differ from long run effects; this stresses the importance of an integral supply and demand orientated macro-approach, and may clarify the difference between our results and those of Drèze and Modigliani (1979), who do not consider the demand side of the economy. In our model, the confrontation of aggregate supply and demand results in price movements, which in turn influence supply and demand.

References

Allen, R. (1980), *The Economic Effects of a Shorter Working Week*. Treasury working paper, no. 14.

Drèze, J. H. and F. Modigliani (1979), *The Trade-off between Real Wages and Employment in an Open Economy*. Discussion paper 7949. Center for Operations Research & Econometrics, Université Catholique de Louvain.

Hansen, B. (1970), "Excess Demand, Unemployment, Vacancies and Wages," *Quarterly Journal of Economics*, 84, pp. 1–23.

Holt, C. C. (1970), "How Can the Phillips' Curve be Moved to Reduce Both Inflation and Unemployment." In Phelps, E. S., ed. *Micro-economic Foundations of Employment and Inflation Theory*. MacMillan, London, pp. 224–256.

Siddré, W. and E. R. de Regt (1981), *Worksharing and Alternative Macro-economic Policies to Reduce Unemployment*. Discussion Paper. Institute for Economic Research, Erasmus University, Rotterdam.

Résumé

Plusieurs politiques économiques ayant pour but de réduire le chômage structural sont analysées dans le même cadre théorique. Notre modèle est d'une nature macroéconomique. Nous considérons les problèmes sous l'aspect de l'offre et de la demande. Parmi les politiques quelques unes sont d'un type traditionel, par example la politique des salaires, la politique fiscale et l'emploi public. D'autres sont moins traditionnelles, telles que la politique pour éviter les "bottlenecks" dans le marché de la main d'oeuvre et les politiques pour partager une certaine quantité de travail.

Cet article met l'accent sur l'importance d'une réduction du temps de travail. Ce dernier peut être un instrument de la politique économique. Les coûts d'opportunité d'une telle politique semblent être élevés. Une réduction du temps de travail combiné avec des heures-capital plus longues pourrait cependant être une possibilité interessante.